Cases in Hospitality Marketing and Management

Second Edition

ROBERT C. LEWIS, Ph. D.

University of Guelph
Ontario, Canada
and
Professor Emeritus
University of Massachusetts/Amherst

John Wiley & Sons, Inc.

New York/Chichester/Weinheim/Brisbane/Singapore/Toronto

Library of Congress Cataloging in Publication Data:

Lewis, Robert C.
    Cases in hospitality marketing and management / Robert C. Lewis.–
    –2nd ed.
        p.   cm.
    Includes bibliographical reference (p.   ).
    ISBN 0-471-16732-0 (pbk. : alk. paper)
        1. Hospitality industry—United States—Management—Case studies.
    2. Hospitality industry—United States—Marketing—Case studies. I. Title.
    TX911.3.M27L49   1997
    647.94′068′8—dc21   96-37343

Printed in the United States of America

10 9 8 7 6 5 4 3 2

To Peg, for her never-ending patience (maybe tolerance?), support, encouragement, and guidance.

Contents

Preface

The use of case studies as a pedagogical tool is becoming increasingly prevalent in hospitality programs. In the past hospitality cases just weren't readily available and current. The first edition of this book was written specifically to alleviate that problem. I have found the case study method to be such a powerful learning tool, with tremendous acceptance by students at all levels, that I sometimes wonder how I ever taught without it.

The major thrust of the cases in this book is on hospitality marketing and management. If you accept the premise, as I contend, that every act of hospitality management is also an act of marketing because it impacts the customer, then this text is a marketing and management tool that can be used in a number of different courses. First, each case clearly deals with management situations from more than one different perspective. Second, these cases contain basic information that relates to many facets of hospitality management. For example, in various cases can be found elements of food and beverage costs, financial statements, organizations, human resources, ownership relations, franchise agreements, architecture and design concepts, and a multitude of other factors that continuously revolve around us in this eclectic industry and are basic considerations in strategic decisions.

Similarly, although the book is divided into five major topic headings, these headings are anything but mutually exclusive. Every case has elements found in the other sections, be they quality, marketing environment, segmentation, positioning, all parts of the marketing mix, or whatever—these elements simply cannot be separated from one another. The categorizations thus are somewhat arbitrary and the user may want to rearrange them. See the matrix of case applications (Exhibit P.1).

A number of the cases have international settings. Some North American students find this off-putting. It should not be. We live today in a

Exhibit P.1
Matrix of Case Applications

Application	Case Number															
	1	2	3	4	5	6	7	8	9	10	11	12	13	14	15	16
Course Level																
Introductory	X	X		X	X	X	X		X	X	X	X	X	X	X	
Intermediate	X	X	X	X	X	X	X		X	X	X	X	X	X	X	X
Advanced	X	X	X	X	X	X	X	X	X	X	X	X	X	X	X	X
Graduate	X		X	X	X			X	X		X	X	X	X	X	X
Executive	X		X	X	X			X	X				X		X	X
Industry Sector																
Hotel	X		X			X		X		X	X	X		X	X	
Restaurant		X		X	X		X		X							
Resort/golf/tourism						X						X	X		X	X
Location																
North America	X			X	X		X	X	X	X	X		X	X		
Europe/South America		X	X			X						X			X	X
Primary Issues																
Corporate level	X	X		X	X	X		X							X	X
Missions	X	X		X		X	X								X	X

	1	2	3	4	5	6	7	8	9	10	11	12	13	14	15	16	17
Macro environment			X	X		X						X				X	X
Distinctive competence	X	X		X	X	X	X		X		X					X	X
Competition			X	X	X	X			X		X			X	X	X	X
Functional level	X	X	X	X		X	X		X	X	X	X	X			X	X
Consumer behavior	X	X		X	X				X	X		X			X	X	X
Business level		X	X	X	X	X	X	X	X	X	X		X	X			X
Implementation	X	X	X	X	X	X		X	X	X			X	X	X		X
Growth				X	X	X											X
Entrepreneurial		X		X	X	X	X		X				X	X	X		X
Positioning			X	X	X		X	X	X	X	X			X	X		X
International			X			X		X				X				X	X
Franchising								X							X		
Industry environment			X	X	X			X			X	X			X	X	X
Turnaround			X	X		X	X		X						X		
Pricing			X					X	X	X	X	X	X				X
Quality	X	X			X			X	X						X	X	X
Segmentation			X	X	X	X	X	X	X	X	X	X	X		X	X	X
Financial analysis				X				X		X	X	X	X	X			
Small business				X	X	X		X				X	X				
Human resources	X	X															X
Research analysis				X				X	X		X						
Communications						X	X	X	X	X	X						X
Product/service	X	X		X	X	X	X	X	X	X			X	X	X	X	X
Distribution								X				X		X	X	X	X

global environment. International exposure is a major theme in most business schools, and it behooves us all to understand international environments, especially in hospitality, where so many companies now operate on a global basis.

HANDLING CASE TEACHING

The cases in this book are of varying levels of difficulty. All can be used at more than one academic level as shown in the matrix in Exhibit P. 1. Again, the categorizations are somewhat arbitrary. In fact, each case has been classroom tested at various levels. Some obviously fit better than others, but since each instructor has her or his own way of teaching, this fit is really a question of self-determination. For example, Case 3, the São Paulo Hotel, works well as a fairly complex case at advanced levels. At lower levels, however, it also works well as a discussion case to introduce students to some international environments and the ways they impinge on decisions. In general, I have found that a majority of the cases can be used in one semester at any one level.

Most of the cases are problem oriented; that is, they are couched in terms of a decision still to be made for an unknown future. A few cases, however, present decisions that have already been made and describe what happened. These can be used as discussion cases or, if using a problem orientation, to determine (1) what was done right and wrong; (2) in hindsight, what could have been done had someone had the foresight to apply marketing and management tools; or (3) even what could be done now.

Case 4, Victoria Station Restaurants, for example, is a historical, chronological, rich case from the 1980s held over from the first edition. It contains considerable detail and a wealth of information on how a company made mistake after mistake, mostly tactical, due to an almost total lack of marketing acumen, and how it consequently failed in implementation. Numerous companies are making the same mistakes today. *Discussion:* What mistakes were made? Why? How do you avoid making similar ones?

Case 1, Ritz-Carlton Hotel Company, contrarily, is a "success" case. *Discussion:* What did they do right? Could they have done better? How would you replicate this today?

Because of the possible varied uses of the cases, suggested discussion or problem questions are not included at the end of each case. Instead, the instructor is recommended to make this decision depending on how the case is being used or at what level. Another reason for this absence is that, not infrequently, I deliberately do not give direction in my courses, particularly at advanced levels, but let the students find their own direction. This is consistent with the philosophy that students need to learn to think as they would have to do in the real world, rather than led down the primrose path. Students who have had cases in other classes with suggested questions repeatedly tell me that they tend to "search" the case for the answers so as to be prepared for class, but rarely get into enough depth to explore the nuances of the case. This can be very problematic in decision making—here or in the real world. The Introduction explains this issue further. Having said that, I should add that this method can be problematic in short time-period classes, when, for example, you have to cover an entire case in 50 minutes. In those situations, directed questions may be the only answer. These are included in the Instructor's Manual.

Case studies can be used as the sole basis on which a course is developed. Except at the advanced or executive level, however, this method can be a less-than-satisfactory process. One can get quite good at case handling and problem solving without ever understanding why one makes the decision one does. The result may be that the next time one encounters a similar problem, when things are different, the same decision doesn't work. Therefore, I always assign some reading, be it from a text or an article, along with cases in order to test some foundation or principle. Except in executive seminars, I almost always use a textbook and build the cases around the chapters. The order of cases in this book generally follows the order of most marketing texts.

Especially in marketing decisions, there may be more than one solution to any problem; moreover, the "right" solution is really never known until after the fact. Many students have a problem with this. They have long since learned that two and two must add up to four. In marketing, however, two and two may add up to almost any number, and it is important to understand this conceptualization process at a higher level of abstraction than that to which many of us are accustomed. Students still ask, "What would *you* do?" or, "What happened?" I try to answer both questions, assuming I know what happened, but am very careful to explain that neither my opinion, nor what the company did, nor why maybe it did or did not work, is necessarily the only or best solution.

The emphasis is really on how you get to the solution. Have you utilized all the available information? Have you appropriately analyzed it? Have you interpreted it correctly? And so forth. Two students may well have done this but arrived at different solutions. Credit should be given for the process and the ability to think and conceptualize. My own teaching style, I should note, is to have very interactive classes; that is, students respond to each other, not to me. I act as facilitator. This requires a longer class period, but the benefits are rewarding. Again, this process is explained in more detail in the Introduction.

ACKNOWLEDGMENTS

Many people have worked on these cases, as well as on many other cases that were left out of the book in order to keep it an acceptable length and to maintain a proper balance. Many cases in this edition come from others who have been kind enough to allow their cases to be reprinted here and to whom I am grateful. Some cases have been held over from the first edition because users said they and their students particularly liked them. These cases have been updated for this edition. In some cases, the original research and writing was done by graduate students. Their help has been monumental and is hereby acknowledged; this includes those (such as graduate students, executives, and undergraduates) who served as guinea pigs in the classroom and made valuable comments. Authors and contributors to each case are given on the first page of the case. I am indebted to them all. All cases have been edited and in some cases updated by me, and I stand responsible for those parts.

I am grateful to those industry people who were, and are, willing to share information and experiences so that others may learn from them. I am also especially grateful to Bryan E. Andrews, M.M.S. of Camosun

College, British Columbia, who gave a tremendous effort in helping me edit, write, and put together the Instructor's Manual.

Current cases are what we all like. In fact, however, there is probably at least a two-year minimum period between the writing of a case and the time it shows up in a published book. All cases aren't written at the same time, so for some there is an even greater time lag. My effort has been to try, when possible, to update, at least with a comment, each case just before it goes to the publisher—at least nine months before it is published. Last-minute notes are also made in the Instructor's Manual. Nonetheless, I believe that the cases in this book are virtually timeless. The same situations are still occurring, and there is much to be learned from them. Case 4, Victoria Station Restaurants, is a good example. In cases where dates are essential to the case because of certain events, I have left them in; where they are not essential, I have taken them out.

It is important to note that these cases were prepared as a basis for class analysis and discussion rather than to illustrate effective or ineffective handling of an administrative or managerial situation.

Note: If you have a case you are interested in having included in the next edition, please let me know.

Robert C. Lewis, Ph.D.
Puslinch, Ontario
June 1997

ABOUT THE AUTHOR

Robert Lewis was professor of marketing and strategy in hospitality and graduate coordinator at the University of Guelph, Ontario, from which he is now retired. He previously spent 10 years in the same position in the hospitality program at the University of Massachusetts where he is now professor emeritus. Dr. Lewis has also served as the Darden Eminent Scholar Chair in Hospitality Management at the University of Central Florida. Prior to academe, he spent 25 years in the hospitality industry in management and consulting before completing his Ph.D. in 1980.

Dr. Lewis is the senior author of *Marketing Leadership in Hospitality,* Second Edition, published by Van Nostrand Reinhold. He has also published over 80 articles in hospitality and other journals, including 25 in the *Cornell Quarterly,* and has written or supervised over 100 case studies. He has taught and conducted executive seminars and done consulting on three continents.

Introduction

The Case Method

Probably the primary reason for using case studies in business courses is their verisimilitude, their approximation of reality. Although cases do not give us all the information we would like to have, or possibly all that we could have in the real world—where we still never have all that we would like to have—they come as close as possible to that situation in an academic setting. Similarly, as in the real world, we have in cases more information than we need, or at least more than is relevant to the present situation. We must then separate the wheat from the chaff, the relevant from the irrelevant. We must define the problem(s); understand the causes, symptoms, ramifications, consequences, and repercussions; organize the facts and analyze and synthesize them; formulate, evaluate, and verify possible solutions; and choose and defend a particular solution or application.

Thus, what the case process really does is to bring theory, concepts, and facts into the realm of application and implementation. You may, for example, understand perfectly well the concepts of marketing planning, Porter's Five Forces model, environmental impacts, competitive advantage, superior quality, customer responsiveness, strategic marketing, marketing research, globalization, or implementation, but these will mean little to you until you actually apply them. In the case method of learning you get a chance to do this. A case study chronicles the events that managers have had to deal with and charts the manager's response or the manager's dilemma. Each case is different because each organization and each situation is different, but you will learn to appreciate and analyze the problems faced by many different hospitality companies and to understand how managers have tried to deal with them.

Two things are inherent in using cases in education. One is that you have to *think!* By that is meant that doing case studies is not an exercise in memorization. Like the real world, there is no place to look up answers and there is no one right answer. Instead, you have to *read between the lines,* assimilate and synthesize various pieces of information, apply concepts and theories, and project all this into a realistic situation. This takes a lot of thinking!

And it takes *time!* You can't read a case a few hours before class and expect to offer good analysis and solutions. Top executives can't do it, so why think that you can? Although good intuition is a great skill if you have it, it still has to be based on thorough analysis and synthesis of concepts applied to facts.

The second inherent factor in using case studies is *interaction.* While much can be learned from the information given in a case, and much can be learned from the cognitive process in analyzing the case, the ultimate test comes in being able to *articulate* and *explicate* this process. You may be the genius who has the secret to eternal life, but if you can't (1) articulate this secret, and (2) persuade someone to use it, then it will amount to naught. You may be asked to articulate and explicate your ideas in writing, and/or you may be asked to do it orally. Regardless, being able to articulate is an important part of the case method learning process.

The other part of interaction, which many of us too often forget, is *listening.* Sometimes we want to show how smart we are (or get points) by espousing our views without listening to those of others. Interaction is a two-way process. Listen and reply to others rather than ignore their points of view. Ask questions of them and of the instructor. It was Voltaire who said, "Judge a man not by his answers, but by his questions." Good executives listen and ask questions before making important decisions. Listening includes the ability to hear and comprehend disparate views that arise out of diversity, cross-functional integration, globalization, and other forces.

THE LEARNING CURVE

Now that you have reached a full-blown case course, you have gone through various stages of learning. You have learned to memorize "buzz words," definitions, and key facts, and you have learned to regurgitate this *knowledge* on multiple choice and true-and-false exams. Chances are you have also learned to *apply* this knowledge in written papers and exams to show that you *comprehend* it. In some cases you may even have been asked to *analyze* it. If you have had case studies in other courses, you may have been given a number of case issues to address.

Some or all of these skills and activities may also apply in the course that uses this book. It is time, however, to go to a higher level of learning. As cases are used in courses because of their verisimilitude to actual situations, then arriving at solutions for those cases should also approximate the verisimilitude of real-life decision making. You may not, right away, be the executive who makes final decisions. You may be one to six levels down but, nevertheless, be asked to provide a recommendation. Or you may be running your own business or your own department.

However it comes to you, at the top or the bottom of the organization, it will not come only with a few neat questions that you have to answer or with the information all neatly sorted out. Instead, you will have to decide what the real issues are, what the critical facts are, how they fit in this company, what the alternatives are, and what the recommended course of action is. You may even have to consider who will implement this decision, and how, since many decisions involve change that affects many people. And the best decision will fail if it is not properly implemented. Moreover, you might have to present this to your boss in only one or two pages or in a 10-minute presentation—and then defend it.

All this means going to a higher level of learning. Bosses don't have time to read through, or listen to, a barrage of garbage, especially if it is irrelevant or if they already know it. Instead, they want you to *synthesize* and *evaluate* your analysis, and be prepared to support it, so they can make a decision.

Although the cases in this book are far more complex, consider even a simple decision. Or is it so simple? The fast-food store across the street from yours has come out with a "Double Whammy, Slam Banger, Triple Treat" hamburger at $2.29 that is stealing your market. But your specialty is chicken. What should you do?

Consider just a few of the issues that might be involved in this decision: mission, the business you're in, short-term tactics versus long-term strategy, ethics, other competitors, bargaining power of buyers and suppliers, efficiency, quality, innovation, segmentation, price, service, customer responsiveness, barriers to imitation, sustainable competitive advantage, resources, capabilities, employees, diversification, cultures, organizational conflict, implementation, and control.

After you've *analyzed* all these factors, and more, based on *application* of your *knowledge* and *comprehension,* piece by piece, you need to boil it all down and bring it back together. This is called *synthesis.* After synthesis, you *evaluate.* That is, you make value judgments. Will it work? What is the upside? What is the downside? What if it doesn't work?

Exhibit I.1 shows what has become known as Bloom's hierarchy of learning. Study it carefully. You are now going to a higher, more complex, level of learning—a level that may well affect your future career progress, not to mention your progress in this course.

Synthesis

This stage of learning, new for many, requires a little additional explanation because it is not an easy task.

In analysis we learn to break a problem into its many parts such as the marketing, the financial, the organizational, and the environmental components. Many students—and managers—are good at this, but what they often don't do is put the pieces back together again. Too often the ability to analyze is valued over the ability to synthesize. Danny Miller notes it well:

> Analytical skills are fine for delving into problems, but they are inadequate for generating the insight needed for a workable solution. Analysis requires systematic probing, thoroughness and logic. Synthesis, on the other hand, calls for artful pattern recognition, receptiveness, and magical insight—traits much neglected in the Western world.

> If diagnosis is 80 percent analysis and 20 percent synthetic insight, the opposite is true for prescription, which aims to discover—or recover—a healthy configuration: one that reconciles the values, skills, strategies, and systems of the organization, the needs of its customers, and the challenges of its competitors. To complicate matters, few of these factors are entirely immune from organizational influence, yet few are entirely within managers' control. The trick is to find a focus, a center of gravity, that matches the most outstanding skill and capacities with the most pressing market needs. Managers must identify a theme or a vision for a configuration that is durable, defensible, and economically and politically feasible.[1]

[1] Danny Miller, *The Icarus Paradox: How Exceptional Companies Bring about Their Own Downfall* (New York: Harper Business, 1990), p. 208.

This is your job in this course! Mastering it will stand you in good stead throughout your entire career.

ANALYZING CASES

There are a number of ways to analyze cases. Which way is best depends a great deal on the type of case, the information in the case, what kind of decisions and/or applications are to be made, and finally, what works best for you. One test, however, is fairly unanimously agreed on: you need to read the case through first without taking notes, marking the case, or in any way trying to break it down. The idea, first, is to get the total picture.

The second time you read the case through, mark it or make notes on what is pertinent and relevant. Depending on the case, you will need to define the problem(s), gather the facts, analyze the information, do a SWOT analysis (strengths, weaknesses, opportunities, and threats), define alternatives, synthesize, arrive at solutions, and evaluate them. These steps are fairly standard for handling any problem-oriented case. Some cases in this book may be used more as discussion cases. Arriving at solutions as to what to do is not as critical as in other cases; in fact, these cases may lack enough information to find solutions, and part of your job may be to determine what information is needed and how to go about getting it, or what went wrong and why.

What follows is more specific for the cases in this text, essentially marketing and management cases. Suggested are two models found to be very useful in handling these cases. The first is the *marketing systems model,* shown in Exhibit I.2.

THE STRATEGIC MARKETING SYSTEMS MODEL

This model depicts as a system all the elements and factors that impact upon marketing processes and decisions. Although the model shows the process of decision making flowing from one stage to the next—as it does—there is essentially no marketing decision that does not also contain some vestige of every other element in this model. The point of the flow is that, as shown, one stage follows from the previous one at a lower level of abstraction. A problem often occurs when this flow does not logically

Exhibit I.1

Bloom et al.'s Taxonomy of Learning. [Adapted from B. S. Bloom, M. D. Engelhart, E. J. Furst, W. H. Hill, and D. R. Krathwohl, eds. *Handbook I: Cognitive Domain.* Vol. 1 of *Taxonomy of Educational Objectives: The Classification of Educational Goals.* (New York: Longmans, Green, 1956).]

Stage	Description
1. *Knowledge*	Is defined as the remembering of previously learned material. This involves the recall of a wide range of material, from specific facts to complete theories, but all that is required is the bringing to mind of the appropriate information. Knowledge represents the lowest level of learning outcomes in the cognitive domain.
2. *Comprehension*	Is defined as the ability to grasp the meaning of material. This may be shown by translating material from one form to another (words to numbers), by interpreting material (explaining or summarizing), and by estimating future trends (predicting consequences or effects). These learning outcomes go one step beyond the simple remembering of material.
3. *Application*	Refers to the ability to use learned material in new and concrete situations. This may include the application of such things as rules, methods, concepts, principles, laws, and theories. Learning outcomes in this area require a higher level of understanding than those under comprehension.
4. *Analysis*	Refers to the ability to break down material into its component parts so that its organizational structure may be understood. This may include the identification of the parts, inquiry into the relationship among the parts, and recognition of the organizational principles involved. Learning outcomes require an understanding of both the content and the structural form of the material.
5. *Synthesis*	Refers to the ability to put parts together to form a new whole. This may involve the production of a unique communication (classroom presentation), a plan of operations (research proposal), or a set of abstract relations (scheme for classifying information). Learning outcomes stress creative behaviors, with emphasis on the formulation of new patterns or structures.

Exhibit I.1 *(continued)*

Stage	Description
6. *Evaluation*	Is concerned with the ability to judge the value of material for a given purpose. The judgments are to be based on definite criteria. These may be internal criteria (organizational) or external criteria (relevance to the purpose), and the student may determine the criteria or be given them. Learning outcomes contain elements of all other categories, plus conscious value judgment based on clearly defined criteria.

occur. This usually leads to trouble, as you will discover. For example, a great decision at the functional level may be totally irrelevant if it is not consistent with the master strategy.

Although every case will contain every element of the model, and you should look for these elements, each case will concentrate more or less on one particular stage, as broken into sections in the table of contents. This does not mean, for example, that in a positioning-strategy case (see Exhibit I.2) you should ignore the communications mix. Rather, you should see how these elements fit together.

Thus, Exhibit I.2 can be used as a checklist. You have not really stated the case, and you cannot fully analyze it, until you have looked at each of the parts to see how they fit into the whole.

DEVELOPING MARKETING DECISIONS

The second recommended model, also a checklist, breaks down the parts, one by one, to get at the real issues and to see where they lead. You will find this analysis very useful in dissecting the cases.

First, the following checklist asks the questions to which you will need answers, either now or later.

1. *Why is there a problem?* The answer to this should be factual and measurable. This is usually what management sees as its problem; for example, occupancy is down, covers are off, we are losing market share,

Exhibit I.2

Strategic Marketing Systems Model

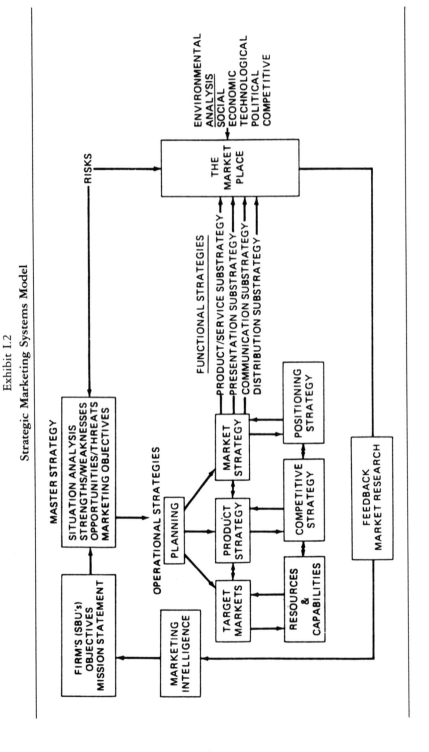

there is a chance to grow, the environment is changing, there is new competition, quality is down, etc. Note an important distinction: This is *why*, not *what*. The answer to this question—and this is important—is not the solution to the problem. It simply tells you why it exists, and you need to identify that first so that it can guide your direction in looking for a solution.

2. *What is the critical question(s)? What is the root problem?* At this stage you need to find the question that will lead to the answer after having done the analysis. To make this clear, we will work backwards in a simple example. Suppose the answer to the question "why is there a problem?" is: "We've been open six months and are only doing 40 covers a night." The root problem, jumping to a hypothetical solution, turns out to be that the market doesn't know we exist; that is, there is a lack of awareness. The critical question we would have asked is: "Why aren't more people coming here?"

Notice that this question could have had many answers; for example, the product is poor, it is perceived as overpriced, word of mouth is negative, we haven't targeted the right market, we're trying to do something we don't have the capabilities for doing, we lack distinctive competence, the positioning is wrong, the competition is undercutting us, and so forth. First, as you see, we have to ask the *right* question. Then we proceed with . . .

3. *What are the critical factors? What has to be changed?* Now we are into gathering the facts and sorting the wheat from the chaff. Here we have to examine the data. (Don't skip over those exhibits! They may contain important information!) We're really just gathering information at this stage, but we want it to be the right information, which is why we defined the critical question first. Once we have done this, but before we analyze it, we need to see if there are any . . .

4. *Conditions for solution* This is important because it helps to keep us from going astray. For example, in a case with a deteriorating hotel property, students will often define the solution as "renovation." Of course, if renovation means $50 million and the owner is not about to spend it, that "solution" isn't of much help. Conditions may be values or beliefs. Sometimes the conditions represent limitations that may be overcome, sometimes not. It is important to know what they are. The best solution is useless if it can't be implemented.

5. *Situation analysis*   This is where we look at all the elements of the systems model in Exhibit I.2 and do a SWOT analysis on each part. Strengths and weaknesses are internal to the company and need to be carefully explored. For example, a weakness might be location, which we can't change, or a product design, which we can change. Some weaknesses we have to live with and plan our strategy around accordingly. Others we try to turn into strengths. Even a so-called poor location can sometimes be turned into a strength.

Opportunities and threats are external to the company which sometimes has little, if any, control over them. We want to exploit opportunities and, again, try to turn the threats into opportunities. For example, a down economy is a threat, but there may be specific market groups that the company can take away from lower-rated competitors at a competitive price to ride out the storm.

If information is not available you may have to infer it from the best information you have and decide if it is worth going after additional information.

By addressing these issues and many more, and by deciding which ones are critical factors in the case, you have determined the "facts," or at least the facts as they can best be determined. You have done this using information in the case or information you inferred from the case. As far as you know, it is the best information you have.

Now you should look at the facts more closely. You need to ask: What assumptions can I make from this information? What further questions do I need to ask? What is missing, and is it worth the time and effort to get it? Is research needed? When you have answered these questions and done the additional work called for, you can then ask, "Okay, what tentative conclusions can I draw from this?" For example, you might have made the assumption that there is a one-time opportunity in the marketplace. Your conclusion, then, would be that you need to analyze this opportunity.

From the situation analysis, you should be able to identify not only problems and causes, but also the opportunities and what is required—and what is precluded—to take advantage of those opportunities.

Now is the time to start thinking about alternatives. If you think about them earlier in the process, you are likely to bias your analysis. For example, a case might say that the business did no advertising. You start thinking that a solution is to advertise. As you proceed through the analysis, you look for information to support that alternative, which may not be the right solution at all.

When cases are used as discussion cases, the only difference is that the solution may be somewhat elusive for lack of information. Your situation analysis, however, does not change. You are more likely to be looking for what worked or didn't work, and what could have been done differently.

FINALLY

After you have done all this work, you need to put it all in perspective. Whether you have been told to turn in the work or not, *organize it!* For many students, this may be the most important thing you will learn in a case course. If you cannot organize your thoughts in a way that others can follow, explicate your ideas succinctly, and articulate them clearly, you will not go far in business no matter how smart you are or what your grade point average is.

Check your work against your original questions. Why is there a problem? Does your solution address it? Have you answered the critical question(s)? If not, you may have the wrong answer—or the wrong question. Have you satisfied the conditions for solution? What are the risks? Are the resources available? What are the advantages and disadvantages—no solution is ever perfect or without some problem. This process, of course, is synthesis: you are putting the big pieces back together to make a cogent and succinct argument. Now evaluate it. What will happen if you implement this solution? What will happen if you don't? Who is going to implement it?

If you can answer these questions, you should be ready to present—in the classroom, on paper, or, in the real world, to your superiors—a cogent, clear, concise, succinct argument for your position, and hold your own in defending it against anyone. Holding your own doesn't mean not listening to other viewpoints, not considering new information or a new way to look at the information, or not accepting an alternative that may be better than yours. Considering these things is all part of the process of developing a solution. Sometimes it even helps to develop an antithesis, that is, an opposing viewpoint. There always is one. If you work in a group, playing devil's advocate is a good role for one of the members to take, in order to keep everyone on their toes.

What this means is: don't be shy, speak up, don't be afraid to argue and defend your position, and don't be afraid to compromise and accept someone else's position. Thinking clearly, using and analyzing the best information available, synthesizing and evaluating it, explicating, and articulating are what the real world is all about. What better place is there to learn these skills than here?

PERFORMANCE CRITERIA

In one form or another, written or oral, the following are some criteria on which you will be judged—perhaps for a grade in this course, perhaps for a promotion in your career. Heed them wisely.

1. Ability to make the required decision or judgment in a concrete situation.

2. Ability to think logically, clearly, and consistently; that is, conclusions should follow from assumptions, and reasoning should be consistent. What are the appropriate facts, assumptions, and realities?

3. Ability to present analysis and synthesis in a cogent and convincing manner.

4. Ability to apply common sense in a marketing and management context—the capacity to see the obvious and the relevant in analyzing consumer, competitive, industry, and market environmental factors and behavior; ability to apply the appropriate weight to fundamental issues and factors.

5. Ability to apply qualitative and quantitative analysis to problems and to break them down; that is, what do the facts and figures really mean?

6. Ability to transcend the concrete situation, to look at it from a broader perspective and higher level of abstraction, and then to synthesize it into a new configuration.

7. Ability to use available data to form a detailed and well-argued plan of action, and then to evaluate it.

8. Ability to think creatively—to go beyond the facts and figures and their more obvious conclusions, that is, to synthesize and evaluate.

The case that follows is really a discussion case, but it will get you started. You all know McDonald's, so it's familiar, but do you really know what makes the company successful in a marketing sense? Apply the marketing systems model in Exhibit I.2 to this case and see how it works. You should be able to find every element of the model in the case and ascertain how each led to McDonald's success, as well as to some problems.

PRACTICE CASE: McDONALD'S

In 1995, McDonald's celebrated its 40th anniversary. It has long been the largest food-service organization in the world, and its success story is unparalleled in the food-service industry. In 1993, McDonald's sold its 100 billionth hamburger. In 1984, the American Marketing Association awarded McDonald's its supreme accolade of "marketing company of the year." How did McDonald's get this way? The answer to that question demonstrates the concept of marketing.

Ray Kroc, McDonald's founder, probably never heard of the marketing concept. Yet Kroc and McDonald's are probably the best example we have in the hospitality industry of a successful marketer.

McConcept

Kroc found a particularly successful restaurant in San Bernadino, California, and approached the owners (the McDonald brothers) with the idea of franchising their concept of fast food (then an unknown term). When they finally reluctantly agreed, Kroc converted a product orientation into a marketing orientation that has since spelled out the reasons for McDonald's success.

Major demographic shifts were taking place on the American landscape in the 1950s and early 1960s. First, there was a massive movement of the middle-class population to the suburbs from cities. This population consisted of families, typically with 2.7 children, a wife and mother who stayed home, a casual lifestyle, and many trips to shopping centers and other suburban locations with the children in the back of a station wagon. There was also a perceptive increase in discretionary dollars for these families.

Kroc saw in these demographic movements a need for food-service establishments that provided uniformity and cleanliness, wherever and whenever a family might choose to eat, at affordable prices. Typically, in those days, one of a mother's most frustrating experiences was to enter a restaurant with children. Enduring the long wait for service was a harrowing experience, not to mention coping with the usual "greasy spoon" ambience and the unreliability of the product.

Recognizing these problems, Kroc developed the concept of QSC—quality, service, and cleanliness. Quality meant that the food was hot and tasted good. Rigid standards were established for the beef used for hamburgers, the potatoes used for french fries, and the recipe used for milkshakes. Service meant that it was quick and courteous and that orders were filled without hassle. Cleanliness meant that the surroundings were clean and neat, both inside and out. This included personnel, equipment, and product presentation. Perhaps Kroc's greatest coup in this respect was the large windows in the front of his stores, which revealed everything inside. Cleanliness not only existed; it was there for all to see. In 1955, this concept was totally unique.

Kroc initially identified his market as the large number of families across the United States who wanted budget-priced hamburgers produced fast in clean surroundings. Early advertising was targeted at this market, and McDonald's research revealed that over three-fourths of the company's sales were to families influenced by children. The early McDonald's sales pitch was aimed almost entirely at these children.

According to Kroc, McDonald's success was derived from finding something the market wanted, something that was basic and simple, and something that could be sold in volume and sold fast. "What could be more natural than meat and potatoes—that's what we sell at McDonald's," he said. McDonald's initial emphasis was on the customer and still is.

McProgress

Of course, menu expansion occurred. The market changed and McDonald's changed with it. There was the Big Mac in 1968 and the Quarter Pounder in 1972. There was the Filet-of-Fish sandwich, hot apple pie, McDonald Land cookies, Egg McMuffin, Chicken McNuggets, McD.L.T., in 1991 there was the McLean Deluxe burger for the calorie-conscious, and in 1996 there was the Arch Deluxe, "the burger with the grown-up taste." Innovative packaging was developed for takeout orders. Some of these innovations succeeded and some did not, but almost all new menu items originated with franchisees who got the ideas from their customers. The new ideas then went through extensive testing in McDonald's cooking labs, as well as in the field. It was McDonald's that changed America's habits when it rolled out "Breakfast at McDonald's."

In 1993, McDonald's struck still again. It initiated McChannel, which broadcasts "the latest on what's cookin' at McDonald's." Patrons tune in their car radios as they pull into the parking lots (signs give the FM frequency which can only be heard about 100 feet from the restaurant). The announcer begins by saying the station is intended "to make your visit even quicker and easier by telling you some specials before you order." These are quickly recited as McTheme music tinkles in the background.

McDonald's stuck with its original strategy and its continued reverence for the principles of Ray Kroc. Consistently, in good times and bad, McDonald's has been able to maintain, if not increase, market share against its rivals who "do or die" to catch the leader. More than that, McDonald's never took its eye off the customer. This strategy led to overseas expansion, although initially unprofitable, while other chains concentrated on saturating the domestic market.

In 1975, McDonald's inaugurated its "At McDonald's we do it all for you" campaign on the premise that McDonald's offers people more than just "quality, service, cleanliness." The campaign was designed to communicate that an experience at McDonald's is the sum total of the food, folks, and fun found there. That theme, although not put in those words, has continued and the emphasis remains on the experience the customer has at McDonald's, each and every time.

In addition to national programs, local operations participate frequently in community development and in local programs developed from local concerns such as safety, ecology, and nutrition. When communities suffer hardships, McDonald's is the first one there giving coffee to fire fighters, feeding victims, raising relief funds, and contributing to the cause. Ronald McDonald Houses, supported by local McDonald's restaurants, the medical community, and volunteer groups, serve as homes away from home for nearly 100,000 family members whose children are treated at nearby hospitals in the United States, Canada, and Australia.

A strong marketing research department conducts ongoing surveys to measure the company's strength with consumers and to provide direction for marketing strategy. In 1970, research found that most of McDonald's customers were young married couples with small children, children who led their parents to McDonald's. In the 1990s, these children, and those of the baby-boom generation that preceded them, have all been weaned on McDonald's and led their own children in that direction. From sponsoring

Saturday morning cartoons on television, McDonald's has moved on to sponsor the Olympics and major golf tournaments.

McFuture

McDonald's has always had plenty of competition. The stories of competitors that have come and gone, or hung on, would fill a few books. But for years they were largely copiers or imitators. On McDonald's 40th anniversary they were alternatives. Fast food—and not-so-fast food—has come a long way. What's a McDonald's to do?

Burger consumption has dropped, and the entire fast-food industry is slowing down. New rivals are dividing and conquering. Some are beating McDonald's on price and some even on speed. At a company that some say owes its success to a religion of standardization, McDonald's is rethinking all of the rules that Ray Kroc devised.

This means ambitious experiments in food and decor, and new formats from self-service to cafés to dinner menus to serving McDonald's fare on airplanes. It means experimentation with more than 150 menu items, from lasagna to corn on the cob to egg rolls, all of which threaten the much-copied operating system that produces the company's signature consistency and speed. And items such as pizza and chicken fajitas puts McDonald's up against well-entrenched competitors.

This is a far cry from Ray Kroc's "by-the-book" days. At a chain that once would give you anything you wanted as long as it was "two all-beef patties, special sauce, lettuce, cheese, pickles and onions on a sesame seed bun," there's a new message, according to Michael Quinlan, CEO: "Do whatever it takes to make a customer happy."

In another break with its principles of standardization, Quinlan has asked every restaurant to analyze its customers' expectations, and then customize their responses to the local market. TV commercials starring real crew members promise, "Whatever it takes, that's McDonald's today."

On its 50th anniversary in 2005, will McDonald's still "Do it all for you?"

Part I

The Concept of Marketing: Missions and Goals

Case One

Ritz-Carlton Hotel Company

Robert C. Lewis

Horst Schulze, President and Chief Operating Officer (COO) of Ritz-Carlton Hotel Company, was contemplating the fact that Ritz-Carlton had just been named the top hotel company in the United States for the second year in a row. "That's good," he thought, "but not good enough. *We're* not good enough and we have to get better."

Horst Schulze had come to Ritz-Carlton as Operations Vice President because it was a quality company. Now, as President and COO, he wanted to make it a company of even higher quality. He knew there were still plenty of customer complaints, and he knew the company was still losing customers. To Horst Schulze, one complaint was one too many, and one complaint could mean one customer lost, not to mention all the others to whom that dissatisfied customer might talk. Multiply that by a few dozen, he felt, and Ritz-Carlton could be losing thousands of customers a year.

Ritz-Carlton was making money at a time when some of its competitors in the luxury category were not. Its experienced management knew how to run hotels. Some of those hotels had the best product and the best restaurants in the business. "Great food, great product, great service, and great costs," thought Mr. Schulze, "but that's not good enough. We have to find a way to be even better. Real quality means zero defects and 100 percent customer retention. Those are the goals we have to shoot for."

This case was written by Robert C. Lewis, University of Guelph, Ontario. All rights reserved. It is largely drawn from a personal interview with James P. DiChiara, Vice President of Sales, and from a talk by Patrick Mene, Corporate Director of Quality, Ritz-Carlton Hotel Company. Quotations are paraphrased.

Horst Schulze knew that other upscale hotels were not going to stand by and let Ritz-Carlton walk away with their customers. These other hotels would be trying to steal Ritz-Carlton customers, especially those with complaints. And they would try to do it with product, service, and price—especially price. Ritz-Carlton couldn't afford to rest on its laurels; it had to go out and steal their customers, and keep them. "If we're 5 on a 10-point scale," he thought, "we're just lucky they're 4.9. And that means that some others are rating them number 1. Our goal has to be to be number 1 to everyone in our product class and to a few that aren't. And the way we do that is give each and every target customer what they want, when they want it, at a price they are willing to pay—and let them know about it. In other words, (1) we get them in the door, and (2) we give them a zero defect performance every time. That leads to 100 percent retention—no lost customers and plenty more coming when they hear about it."

RITZ-CARLTON HOTEL COMPANY

Ritz-Carlton Hotel Company was a management firm that developed and operated luxury hotels worldwide for outside owners and developers. As of 1994, it operated 30 hotels, 25 in the United States, two in Australia, and one each in Barcelona, Hong Kong, and Mexico. It had expansion plans in Seoul, Tokyo, Singapore, and Orlando, with hotels either under development or in the planning stage, and was actively seeking other international sites. Annual sales were about $500 million, but rates and occupancy varied by location.

The company was formed in 1983 when the Atlanta-based W.B. Johnson Properties purchased exclusive rights to the Ritz-Carlton trademark along with the Boston Ritz-Carlton Hotel. One Ritz-Carlton hotel, in Chicago, was operated by Four Seasons Hotels of Toronto under a previous arrangement. Four Seasons and Ritz-Carlton were considered the two top luxury hotel chains in North America but competed directly in only a few locations.

The Ritz-Carlton tradition originated in 1898 when a Swiss hotelier named César Ritz teamed up with renowned chef Auguste Escoffier to open the Ritz Hotel of Paris, thus initiating the concept of the deluxe European hotel. César Ritz established stringent standards that would become the foundation of any hotel bearing his name. He demanded that the food and beverage quality be second to none and that impeccable service be the crucial ingredient in creating his version of an ideal luxury hotel. The entry of a Ritz hotel into the United States came in 1927, when a Boston businessman bought the North American rights and opened the Ritz-Carlton Hotel in Boston. This hotel maintained high standards, but it had its ups and downs until W.B. Johnson Properties bought the hotel and the trademark rights.

RITZ-CARLTON AND THE BALDRIDGE AWARD

The Malcolm Baldridge National Quality Award was established by the U.S. Congress in 1987. This award recognized American companies that had achieved excellence through adherence to quality improvement programs. Named for the late Secretary of Commerce, the award was administered by the Commerce Department's National Institute of Standards and Technology. The goals of the award were to promote quality awareness, recognize quality achievement of U.S. companies, and publicize successful quality strategies. Two awards were to be granted yearly to companies in each of three categories: manufacturing, service, and small business. In the first four years of its existence, 12 firms won the award, but only one, Federal Express, was in the service sector.

History shows that Ritz-Carlton Hotel Company earned the Baldridge Award in 1992, but that is not where the story began. Six years earlier, Ritz-Carlton had become the standard of independent rating organizations as the only hotel company that consistently met their highest standards. This was not good enough for Horst Schulze. His approach to quality began long before the Baldridge Award was established and before Total Quality Management (TQM) became a common buzzword. It was during this effort that others suggested that he turn to the Baldridge criteria for guidance. Those criteria became a road map for quality improvement at Ritz-Carlton.

Ritz-Carlton Hotel Company did not adopt the Baldridge criteria in order to become more market-driven, but to become more competitive, not only in the hospitality business but also in the world of business in general. The offshoot of this decision, however, was that Ritz-Carlton did indeed go from being a product-driven company to a market-driven one.

PURSUIT OF QUALITY

Ritz-Carlton's history was one of reliance on the product and service provided to drive the company effort. According to Jim DiChiara, Vice President of Sales, "In the hotel industry, the '80s were a time to make a buck as fast as you could, to heck with quality, just put it out, sell it to a big investor, and move on." The people at Ritz-Carlton felt differently. DiChiara summed it up:

> The reality of life is that if you don't put the ingredients in the soup, you're not going to have a great soup. You ask people what they want in the soup, you make the soup, and then you ask them if they like the soup. It's pretty simple, but we tend to create our own boll weevils in business. We make it more difficult.

Jim DiChiara continued,

> Luxury hotels will become dinosaurs if service isn't better, and remarkably so, than that being provided by lower-level hotels. A room is a room is a room—a bed, a light, a carpet. We have to do something much better than that and let people know they can count on it. Luxury has become a rejected term. We need to focus on reliability. Successful companies don't just have great products; they do the best job in conveying values and what they have to offer to their markets.
>
> Take the room service delivery problem we had at the Buckhead Hotel. We tracked it and it all seemed to work as it should. The orders got taken quickly, the trays got put up quickly, and the room service waiter left promptly. But we couldn't figure out why it took so long to get to the room. In the old days we'd fire somebody for slow delivery, but that's not the answer anymore. Today, we have to find out why the system doesn't work.
>
> We'd never tracked these complaints. In fact, I'd go so far as to say we never knew we had a problem. That's what comes from being number one. That's a problem. That's a problem when someone is spending $300 a night. That's a problem when people see us as unbelievable because of the image we've created. We sent them all this collateral, we established dress codes—all those things that people saw as a little unbelievable.

Another thing was our advertising. It was catchy, sure, but was that what customers really wanted—English bone china, 18th-century oils, and conference rooms with fine antiques? We hadn't gone to our customers to find out what they really wanted—from a message standpoint what was really important to them in selecting a hotel. We needed to put a more rational spin on the way we did business—tie in the fact that we're reliable with the fact that we have some system of guaranteeing to customers that we will deliver on their expectations. We needed to give people a feel for what they will get when they come there. We were image-driven. When the market changes, it becomes a problem.

People talk about the beauty of our hotels. But, you know, I'll bet when they get back home they don't talk about the carpets and the chandeliers. I'll bet they talk about their experience. Because that's what they're really paying for—did we deliver on our commitment? If we're going to the great expense of putting these hotels together, are we making them user-friendly?

We wondered if we really knew our customers. How often did we go out and meet them? Were we treating different customers differently according to the things they want most? Maybe everyone doesn't want incredible personal service. Maybe we tied too much to the sales effort. Thus, the system dictates the outcome.

PRIORITIZING TQM

Jim continued,

So with Mr. Schulze's urging and strong backing, we began to look at the major issues in our business. First, what do customers want? We'd never asked them because we didn't want to disturb them. Second, how do we ensure that we deliver this to them? Third, how do we make the system work, for sure? Marketing does not stop at bringing the guest in—it is continuous. How they are treated is a marketing tool. Fourth, how do we communicate this to the market? Just tell them how great it is to be at a Ritz, as our ad agency says?

Another thing was our travel agents, wholesalers, and tour operators. Sometimes it seemed like we'd forgotten them. We were doing about 22 percent of our overall revenue through them. I wondered if we shouldn't be doing more—in fact, maybe we should be doing 50 percent. What drives their decisions? Do they share our philosophy?

These people spend 100 percent of their time on travel. There's lots of opportunity to solicit and book business from them and make them aware of the reliability of our product. That's what they really want to know. There are the big ones like American Express, IVI, and Maritz, but there are also 35,000 in small towns who, in total, can deliver a lot of customers. Were we serving them the way we should be? Were they focusing on price to drive the market or the product that we offer? Did they understand our policies? I knew one thing for sure—they don't like not getting commissions on business that they've booked, no matter what happens to it. And they don't like booking at one price and having the customer negotiate another.

Which gave us another thought. What about our reservation system? You know these games that people play. They call the hotel, they call the 800 number, they call the travel agent. For some hotels, not necessarily ours, they get different quotes from each call. This must get both confusing and frustrating, especially when they get to the hotel and find still different rates.

So we made third parties and rate consistency numbers five and six on our priority list. Meeting planners was number seven.

We'd get rave reviews from users after every meeting, but too often we only got one or two meetings out of a multiple set. We had a 42-step process to make sure these things went right. Maybe the system was breaking down with the meeting planners. Were sales and conference services working together? Maybe we were doing something wrong that didn't have anything to do with the product or service. When I attended a Meeting Planners International conference, one meeting planner told me he didn't even know we were in the meetings business. What do meeting planners want? How do we find out?

Related to that was the high turnover, 40 percent, that we had in sales and marketing personnel. We hired the best. We got them from Four Seasons, Hyatt, Marriott, Westin, Hilton, and so forth. You know those people; they're always moving around. So we made high turnover number eight.

Number nine was to look at those complaints. How do we handle them—for example, a late room-service breakfast? Of course we apologized. The GM would call them and repeat the apology. Then we'd send them a fruit basket—if it was really bad we gave away a room night.

I don't think a fruit basket would compensate me for being late to an 8:00 meeting because of room service, or missing breakfast all together. I think the days are over when we can pass on our inefficiencies to the customer. Not to mention the costs and confusion that we put into soothing a customer in a way that has no correlation with his or her problem. Our figures showed that it cost us about $250,000 a year *per hotel* in fruit baskets to handle these kinds of problems.

Finally, the luxury market is a thin market—and getting thinner everyday. We wanted to know how we could attract more of the top-end buyers just below that market—and I don't mean by cutting product, service, or prices. Let's call them the step-up buyers. How could we make ourselves attractive to a wider audience? Should we just chase after the luxury buyer? What about those who are bombarded by Hyatt, Hilton, Westin, Marriott, and so forth? They're conditioned to stay in those products. Maybe some of them don't know any better. How could we do a better job of reaching them? Could we define ourselves better? Attracting the step-up buyer became number 10 on our list.

THE NEW QUALITY VIEW

Patrick Mene, the Corporate Director of Quality for Ritz-Carlton, added his views of the Ritz-Carlton approach to quality and explained why Ritz-Carlton led its competitors.

Mene felt that people in the hotel industry believed it was location and price that determined success, while in luxury hotels the formula was adjusted slightly to become location and style. "They believe, too, that the design and aesthetics of the hotel are important. They will do a good job with flowers and the costuming of their staff, and their hotel will be stylish, comfortable, and clean." How was Ritz-Carlton different? Mene explained:

> Our hallmark is genuinely warm, friendly service. Our people are caring, relaxed, and yet refined. And they know that our customers expect to be waited on and do not want to have to wait for service. Year after

year we all have our customers polled to determine how satisfied they have been with the hotel staff who have served them. With 10 as the optimal score, Ritz-Carlton will receive an average score in the high nines, as opposed to the mid-sixes for our competitors.

Another story illustrates the Ritz-Carlton approach to service. You might see a maintenance worker in the hall working on a wall socket. And suddenly there is a guest with an empty ice bucket, looking uncertain about where to go. That maintenance worker will immediately insist on retrieving ice for that guest. Everyone is trained to break away to solve a problem and then snap back to his or her routine.

Of course, leadership and training assure that commitment to service. In the end, it is the combination of leadership and highly standardized systems that explains why we generated more revenue per available room than any other hotel chain.

Mene went on,

The way quality is achieved in most hotels is by brute force and great expense. The Ritz-Carlton way of thinking about process and systems is a dramatic contrast. At budget time, Ritz-Carlton sets dollar targets for prevention, inspection, and defect correction. I would guess our competitors are spending something like 5 percent on prevention, 35 percent on inspection, and 60 percent on defects.

Our research suggests that best practice changes the mix to 10 percent for prevention, 38 percent for inspection, and 52 percent for defects. But this year's targets for us look something like 17 percent for prevention, 28 percent for inspection, and 55 percent for defect correction.

The key thing is that our president believes that every dollar spent on prevention results in many less dollars spent on defect correction, and that he supports the measurement we do. Our competitors don't see this. They are guilty of reactionary management and have no data.

SUMMARY

"TQM is our game," said Jim DiChiara. He continued:

To us it means continuous improvement. It comes down to what can you do that the competition is not doing to give yourself a competitive advantage. TQM forces you to analyze your business process. How do you get from point A to point Z? You focus on the middle.

You know, when you get right down to it, maybe TQM should be called TQS, with the S standing for "sense." We've always done what we did intuitively—what we thought was important. We rushed to solutions to make decisions—we *fixed* the problem, not the cause. If we're not having the right impact on the customer, internally or externally, we're wasting our time. I think what we needed was some Total Quality Sense.

But let's not forget, as Mr. Schulze says, the founding reason for us to exist is to make money. We sell excellent service, but the purpose is to make money. You have to charge for the service, for the friendly employee. When we capture a guest, that guest is willing to pay more than at another hotel because they receive better value for the dollar. We want to accomplish simply the highest occupancy at the highest rate, the highest top line. We want consistent good business in slow times or good times and, consequently, a high return on investment. We clearly understand that we will not have investors if we don't deliver returns on investments.

Case Two

Hippopotamus Restaurants

Jacques Horovitz

What lies behind these restaurants whose emblem is a friendly hippopotamus with a broad smile and a mischievous glint in his eye? Hippopotamus represented a turnover of FF 600 million, a total work force of 958 people, and 17 restaurants (14 in Paris and 3 in the provinces), which served more than 4.5 million meals a year, which was over 12,000 customers per day. The name also evoked the story of a French company belonging to the son of a restaurateur, Christian Guignard, who decided to give up his study of medicine to launch into the restaurant business.

While staying in California, Guignard had had the opportunity to sample some excellent beef grilled over a wood fire in a steak house, the name of which he remembered: Hippopotamus. Back in Paris he persuaded his father to join him in opening a steak house on the avenue Franklin Roosevelt. This restaurant opened under the unusual name of Hippopotamus.

Beneath the eye-catching sign, Guignard sought to implement an original formula: good meat grilled over wood, served with a single vegetable—potatoes—in a pleasant setting and with the emphasis on good quality at the right price. With passing years, the Hippopotamus style developed and took shape in the new restaurants which opened in Paris and the provinces. See Exhibit 2.1 for a menu in five languages.

For the consumer, the Hippopotamus emblem represented not only a product, but also a certain setting, created by a simple, natural decor

This case was written by Jacques Horovitz, Professor of Service Management at IMD, Lausanne, Switzerland, for CPA, France. All rights reserved. Used by permission. For conversion purposes, use five FF as approximately equal to U.S. $1, Canadian $1.35, £.65, 140 pta, 1.6 DFL, and SF 1.2.

Exhibit 2.1
Hippopotamus Menu

HIPPO ATOUT 98,50 F

ENTRÉE Œufs pochés à la ciboulette ou Carpaccio de tomates fraîches ou Saucisse de Morteau ou Rillettes aux deux saumons	OU DESSERT Glaces ou Sorbets ou Mousse au chocolat ou Crème caramel
LE PLAT Accompagné d'une pomme au four ou de pommes allumettes ou de haricots verts (servis à volonté).	Bavette ou Brochette en duo de bœuf et d'agneau ou Chef salad ou Chili con carne
BOISSON	Pichet (31 cl) de Vin d'Anjou rouge ou 1/2 Eau minérale (50 cl) ou Tourtel Pur Malt sans alcool (25 cl) ou Stella Artois (33 cl)

HIPPO SPECIAL 98,50 F

STARTERS Poached eggs with chives or Carpaccio of fresh tomatoes or Morteau sausage or Potted double salmon spread	OR DESSERT Ice cream or Sorbet or Dark chocolate mousse or Caramel cream
MAIN COURSE Accompanied by a baked potato or matchstick potatoes or green beans (as much as you like).	Beef tenderloin or Beef and lamb brochette duet or Chef's salad or Chili con carne
BEVERAGES	Pitcher (31 cl) of red Anjou wine or 1/2 Mineral water (50 cl) or Tourtel alcohol-free beer (25 cl) or Stella Artois (33 cl)

Exhibit 2.1 *(continued)*

HIPPO SPEZIAL 98,50 F

VORSPEISEN	ODER NACHTISCH
Verlorene Eier mit Schnittlauch	Milcheis
oder Carpaccio von Rohen Tomaten	oder Sorbet
oder "Morteau"-Wurst	oder Mousse au chocolat
oder Pastete mit zwei Lachssorten	oder Karamellpudding
HAUPTGERICHT	Lendensteak
Als Beilage, wahlweise, eine gebackene Kartoffel	oder Rind-Lamm-Duo am Spiess
oder Streichholzkartoffeln	oder Chef-Salat
oder grüne Bohnen.	oder Chili con carne
GETRÄNK	Karaffe roter Anjou-Wein (31 cl)
	oder 1/2 Flasche Mineralwasser (50 cl)
	oder Tourtel ohne Alkohol (25 cl)
	oder Stella Artois (33 cl)

HIPPO ATOUT 98,50 F

ANTIPASTI	O DESSERT
Uova in camicia alla cipollina	Gelati
o Carpaccio di pomodori freschi	o Sorbetti
o Salsiccia affumicata di Morteau	o Mousse al cioccolato fondente
o Rillettes ai due Salmoni	o Crema al caramello
PRIMO	Punta di petto
Contorno: una palata al forno	o Spiedino, duo di manzo ed agnello
o patatine fritte o fagiolini	o Insalata dello Chef
(a volontà).	o Chili con carne
BEVANDE	Caraffa (31 cl) di Vino d'Anjou rosso
	o 1/2 Acqua minerale (50 cl)
	o Tourtel analcolico (25 cl)
	o Birra Stella Artois (33 cl)

HIPPO ESPECIAL 98,50 F

ENTREMESES	O POSTRE
Huevos escalfados con cebolleta	Helados
o Carpaccio de tomates frescos	o Sorbetes
o Salchicha de Morteau	o Mousse de chocolate negro
o Chicharrones de dos salmones	o Crema de caramelo
EL PLATO	Solomillo bajo
Acompañados con una patata al	o Pincho en "dúo" de vaca y cordero
horno o patatas paja o judías verdes	o Ensalada del chef
(a voluntad).	o Chile con carne
BEBIDA	Jarra (31 cl) de Vino de Anjou tinto
	o 1/2 Agua mineral (50 cl)
	o Tourtel sin alcohol (25 cl)
	o Stella Artois (33 cl)

Exhibit 2.1 *(continued)*

HIPPO HIT 59,50 F

Main course:
Steak Surprise
or Beef and Lamb brochette duet
or Country Sausages with Brittany salt
accompanied by baked potatoe or matchstick
potatoes or green beans.

Beverages:
Glass of Anjou wine (12.5 cl) or 1/2 Mineral water
or Stella Artois beer (33 cl).

WINES

RED ANJOU WINE (31 cl) _____ 32,50 F
CÔTES DU RHÔNE ROUGE (31 cl) _____ 36,00 F
GLASS OF CÔTE DE BROUILLY (12.5 cl)___ 17,50 F

STARTERS

POACHED EGGS AND CHIVES_____ 28,50 F
CARPACCIO OF FRESH TOMATOES _____ 29,50 F
VEGETABLE TERRINE_____ 35,00 F
SLAB OF DUCK FOIE GRAS _____ 49,50 F

FROM THE GRILL

With a selection of sauces
MINUT SIRLOIN STEAK_____ 69,50 F
It's just as delicious when well cooked (180 g).
TENDERLOIN STEAK _____ 79,50 F
*For those who love their meat slightly cooked or rare
(170 g).*
THICK-CUT STEAK _____ 89,50 F
*Cut from the heart of the rump-steak, thick and lean
(180 g).*
T.BONE STEAK _____ 109,00 F
*American style, with the fillet and sirloin
on either side of the T.Bone. Two qualities of meat
in one serving (400 g).*
ENTRECÔTE STEAK_____ 94,50 F
A mouth-watering cut even when well cooked (250 g).
"VILLETTE" STEAK _____ 229,00 F
*For two famished people who like their meat cooked
the same way (1 kg approx.).*

LAMB CUTLETS_____ 89,50 F
At Hippo, they come in threes (3 × 80g).
RIB OF BEEF _____ 99,50 F
*An individual thick rib of beef that melts in your
mouth (330 g).*
PRIME CUT OF BEEF _____ 88,50 F
Long, distinguishable by its texture and flavour (190 g).
HIPPO MIXED GRILL_____ 89,50 F
*Rich brochette: lamb, beef, smoked bacon, duck, grilled
medium rare. Served with tomato slices, lettuce and gar-
nished to choice.*
BUTCHER'S SPECIAL _____ 98,00 F
*As its name implies, this is strictly for professionals.
Thick and delicious (260 g).*
CHILI CON CARNE _____ 64,00 F
*This recipe is as hot as the Mexican sun: kidney beans,
beef and a spicy and aromatic sauce.*

Cooked to choice:
very rare, rare, medium, well done.

CHEESES

"BRIE DE MEAUX" WITH WALNUTS _____ 32,50 F
ROCAMADOUR GOAT CHEESE _____ 29,00 F

DESSERTS

DARK CHOCOLATE MOUSSE _____ 24,50 F
FLOATING ISLAND _____ 26,00 F
APPLE UPSIDE-DOWN TART _____ 37,50 F

ICE CREAMS

COUPE DÉLICE_____ 26,50 F
*Three scoops of your choice: rum-raisin, vanilla, choco-
late, chestnut, or chocolate-mint.*
CHOCOLATE OR COFFEE LIÉGEOIS_____ 37,50 F
*Chocolate or coffee ice cream topped with a sauce of the
same flavour and whipped cream.*
FROZEN NOUGAT _____ 35,00 F
*Nougat mousse, nougat candy and grilled hazelnuts with
raspberry sauce.*

SHERBETS

COUPE BOLSHOÏ_____ 34,00 F
Lime sorbet with a zest of vodka.
COUPE "AUX TROIS FRAÎCHEURS"_____ 28,50 F
*Three scoops of your choice: raspeberry, lime, apple or
coconut.*

SERVICE INCLUDED (16%/H.T.).

to which plants, materials (stone and brick), colors in keeping with the mood of the restaurant (red, black, and white), and pleasant lighting all contributed. Added to this was a special sort of service: the staff who received the customers and served at the tables were smiling young women. The menu held no surprises and the customers knew the prices before they ordered.

THEME RESTAURANTS

Hippopotamus belonged to the theme-restaurant sector in which it was a forerunner. Some years ago, restaurants tried to shake off their competitors and to acquire fame by making the most of specialties. The adoption of an original theme allied to a product and a setting was a recent development in the restaurant business. The first was Courte Paille; then came Hippopotamus. Others followed: Chantegrill, Amanguier, Cour St. Germain, the Bistro Romain. The basic concept behind this type of restaurant was the offer of a limited menu, the quality and presentation of which remain constant and 100 percent predictable.

The Market

According to a study carried out under the auspices of the European School of Business (EAP) in France[1]:

> The restaurant business has undergone a marked decline . . . in at least three European countries: France, Great Britain, and West Germany. In this climate of recession, steak houses, taken as a whole, have performed well and have enjoyed a bigger growth than that of commercial restaurants generally.

> In this sector, two categories live side by side: the independent restaurants and the chains. The share of chains is growing steadily in relation to that of the independent restaurants.

> In Great Britain, the chains are very big in size and controlled by the big hotel/restaurant/brewery groups. In Germany, the chains are few in

[1] École Européenne des Affaires (European School of Business), Paris Chamber of Commerce and Industry.

number and average in size; in France the chains are average in size and are either independent or controlled by the hotel/distribution groups. The names/logos are numerous. . . . In France a selectivity stage is now being reached: a certain number of ill-fitting concepts are disappearing (e.g., Churrasco), and the chains that have managed to perfect an effective concept are developing at a very rapid rate. [See Exhibit 2.2]

HOW HIPPOPOTAMUS FUNCTIONS

The identity of Hippopotamus was colored very much by the personality of its chairman, Christian Guignard, who held 50 percent of the capital, on an equal basis with the Casino group. He had a very strong determination to succeed and to innovate and had used modern management techniques to develop his business. In his marketing he had practiced a policy of institutional communication in which humor was present, and he used the services of an advertising agency.

In the heart of the company an Integrated Data Processing Center collected and exploited the encoded data coming up daily from the units. The cash registers were connected to microcomputers, which were themselves linked up with a central computer. Questions about purchases, investments, and advertising, marketing, and the expansion of the chain were settled at the head office, called Hippoconseil, to show the top

Exhibit 2.2
Categories of Theme Restaurants in France

Category	Type of Location	Chain Names
Top of the range	Center of Paris Starting up in the provinces	Hippopotamus, Cour St. Germain, Amanguier, Bistro Romain
Middle of the road	Edge of main roads and in small- and medium- sized towns	Courte Paille, Chantegrill
Budget	Town centers	Pizza Pai Pizza del Arte

management's intention to bring down-to-earth assistance to the individual restaurants and to remain in contact with them.

The Hours

Hippo restaurants were open to the public seven days out of seven, 365 days a year, from 11:30 A.M. to 1:00 A.M. Nevertheless, most of the units, with the exception of the four largest, closed after lunch to open again 2½ hours later. The working hours were staggered between 7:00 A.M. to 4:00 A.M. according to the job and the schedule. Everyone had two days off per week. These were rarely Saturday and Sunday.

One-third of the sales were made at lunchtime; two-thirds in the evening. The rotation of staff was five per day, but could rise to six or seven on the weekend.

The Market

In Paris there was a restaurant almost every 10 meters, which meant that competition was fierce and things had to be right the first time. The customer was present every day and his or her sanction was immediate. The consumer judged the quality of a restaurant according to the following criteria:

- The setting and atmosphere of the restaurant
- The welcome
- The waiting time before a table became available
- The waiter/waitress service
- The quality of the food
- The attention given to the customer in the restaurant
- The price paid
- Consistency in the overall quality of service

At Hippopotamus it was estimated that a satisfied customer would mention the restaurant to, perhaps, three people, while a dissatisfied one, on the other hand, would mention it to at least 11 people. The restaurateur's job was made up of a thousand details. The customer accepted the situation as normal if none of these was overlooked. If a single one was neglected, the customer was dissatisfied.

Hippopotamus' Clientele

At Hippopotamus one customer in seven was new every day (14 percent). The average age remained constant, which meant that the clientele had changed. The results of a market study provided the following information:

- On the whole, the age of the customers varied between 25 and 49 years with significant differences for:

    Hippo-Citroën, the clientele of which is very young—18 to 24 years (30 percent)

    Les Halles, target 25 to 34 years (46 percent)

    The Champs-Elysées Roundabout, with the target group 35 to 49 years (49 percent)

- Their educational standard is quite high: 59 percent had had some kind of higher education. This was particularly true of

    Hippo-Citroën (65 percent)

    St. Germain Maubert (70 percent)

- As for the sex of the customers, the only significant result concerned Saturday lunchtime, when the proportion of men to women was more balanced. Otherwise males predominated.

- As far as age was concerned, the lunchtime customers tended generally to be older (35 to 49 years), and this was the same during the week (42 percent) as on Saturdays (41 percent).

- In the evening the age of the customers varied. It was rather higher on Mondays (47 percent, 25 to 34 years) and rather younger on Saturdays (33 percent, 18 to 24 years).

- Hippopotamus customers generally came from quite a high socioeconomic category. Professions of householders were:

    businessmen and senior managers (38 percent)

    middle managers and staff (43 percent)

- The customers interviewed (in particular at the Montparnasse-Maine Hippo and at the Opera Hippo), when in active employment, belonged predominantly to the middle class (45 percent).

- On Monday evenings there was a larger proportion of middle managers/staff, which probably reflected the fact that cinema seats were cheaper then.

- There is a greater representation of the upper class in the three Champs-Elysées Hippos.

- Students met in the biggest numbers at Montparnasse (26 percent), with very few at the Champs-Elysées Roundabout (8 percent).

RUNNING A RESTAURANT

The Actors

According to the size of the unit, the manpower ranged between 50 to 100 people, who served from 600 to 1,300 meals a day. The chain's restaurants operated, broadly speaking, in the same way. (See Exhibit 2.3.) In the small restaurants the post of chef did not exist; it was the grill operator who did this job. The existence and number of deputies to the manager was also dependent upon the size of the establishment.

The main duty of the grill operator was to cook the meat. The grill assistant prepared the accompanying vegetables and trimmings. The kitchen junior prepared everything which was not the main course: starters, desserts, coffee. The leader supervised the hostesses. The hostesses played

Exhibit 2.3
Unit Organizational Chart

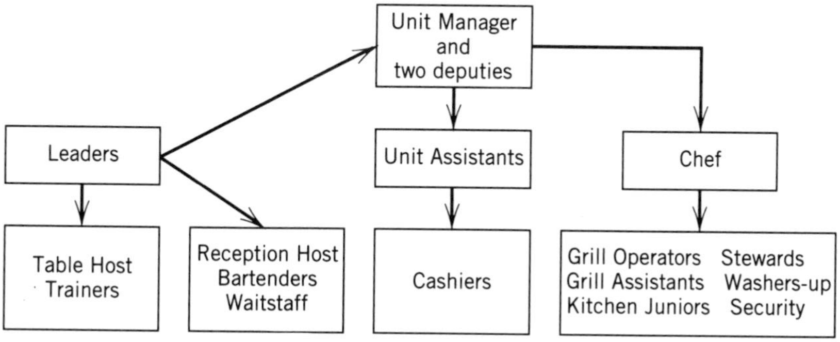

an important role as far as the service was concerned. There were the reception hostesses and the hostesses who waited on tables.

The hostess trainee was appointed to become a table hostess. She learned the job and saw to the cleaning of the premises. The steward kept the stocks of crockery, table linen, food, and drink. It was estimated that about 90 percent of the personnel were trained on the job.

In the restaurant business the human factor plays a role of paramount importance. The quality of the service depends upon the professionalism of all the employees, those who see to the cleaning as much as those who prepare the meals, wait at table, greet customers, and work out the bill. The attainment of a constantly high level of quality is dependent upon the actors' being constantly motivated.

Remuneration of the Restaurants' Personnel

One part of the personnel received a fixed pay, while the other received a remuneration that was linked directly to the turnover. The salaries of the manager, his deputies, and his dining room and reception staff were governed by a calculation based on 15 percent of takings received under the heading of "service." The unit manager, who reported directly to the Chairman, could reserve a percentage of the total of the 15 percent for monthly, variable bonuses, which were paid to the most deserving. The pay of the kitchen staff and the cashiers was fixed.

"Barometer" readings measuring the level of customer satisfaction were taken into consideration when determining the profit sharing of the restaurant managers. Broadly speaking, salaries at Hippopotamus were higher than the average in the restaurant business.

Recruitment

The working conditions in the restaurant business had led to a very high annual turnover of personnel, on the order of 300 percent. At Hippopotamus this figure had been reduced by half, but efforts were being made to reduce it still further.

The unit manager himself carried out the recruitment of personnel for his restaurant. Restaurant managers and deputies were recruited by the Human Resources Manager of the group.

Other Specific Features of the Chain

- Each restaurant had the benefit of contributions made by the group's culinary research laboratory.

- The purchasing department at the head office negotiated prices with the suppliers so as to obtain the best possible terms. It subsequently forwarded the list of these suppliers and the prices agreed upon to the restaurants. These then got their stocks directly from the suppliers.

- The restaurant put in its order for the day at about 3:00 A.M. Generally it did not get more than one-half day's stock in advance. The meat delivered was checked as soon as it was received, and was returned to the supplier if it was not up to standard or not what had been ordered.

- The cakes and pastries served in the chain's Parisian restaurants came from the group's confectionery laboratory, Cuisine-Pâtisserie Services (CPS).

- The chain's restaurants had layouts that were similar in a number of ways. Their three focal points were designed and created by the group's architect and decorator:[2]

  The bar–reception–dining room

  The kitchen

  The cashier's desk–secretarial office

SERVICE QUALITY PROGRAM

Hippopotamus had important advantages: the locations of the restaurants on excellent sites, the architectural designs of the establishments, and the welcome and atmosphere to be found there. All this meant that the chain had made a name for itself on the market as a point of reference. The price for the quality of service given seemed right, but the number of customers had dropped slightly. Studies showed that the level of customer

[2] The architect and decorator belonged to the architecture and works company, SATRA, which the group created in 1985 and of which it was the chief customer. SATRA had the job of making the necessary studies and creating the new restaurants, while at the same time improving and maintaining the existing ones.

satisfaction stood at 77 percent and that, if this were 100 percent, the turnover could be increased by a third.

The personality of the Chairman was an asset. He was a young man whose charisma was acknowledged by all. He was dynamic and strong-willed, and he intended to lead the company to success. He was determined to examine lucidly the threats looming on the horizon. He went through all the possible factors that might be throwing the company off balance:

- He was alone and at that time he had not yet formed any real management team. He now needed help in guiding and inspiring all the individuals who made up the company.
- There was a shortage of driving forces, or at least they were not always in keeping with the company's philosophy.
- Were the practical values of Hippopotamus in danger of disappearing from its culture because they had not been formalized or passed on?
- The expansion had generated a compartmentalization and lack of communication. The Chairman knew that those who had been with the company for some time were sorry not to have direct contact with him anymore and that they were perhaps no longer as enthusiastic as they had been. Some wastage of human resources seemed likely.
- There was no real personnel policy as far as salaries, recruitment, training, or communication were concerned.

To sum up, Guignard wondered whether his business was going to be in a position to forge ahead with the same dynamism while remaining faithful to its image. Would it be able to keep its customers?

Finally he selected some priorities and decided to take steps that would, he hoped, answer the following four questions:

1. How to avoid letting the Hippopotamus tradition die as the company grew?
2. How to remain the best when faced with the growing competition?
3. How to pass on the company's culture to new colleagues?
4. How to motivate the scattered teams to work toward the same objective?

The actions destined to answer these questions were contained in the Service Quality Program that Guignard drew up using the services of a consulting firm specializing in quality problems.

Description

Guignard invited his executives to a meeting he had carefully prepared, and he put before them the issues on which he was going to ask them to work. The objective was to implement the Service Quality Program within three months.

A few weeks before, a market research study had been carried out. A survey covering 1,325 customers in nine establishments had revealed the level of satisfaction of the clientele, their profile, and their expectations. This study had presented the opportunity for the company to define accurately the product and the service it wanted to put on the market.

The plan proposed by the Chairman to his executives was as follows:

1. To work out a service agreement
2. To formulate standards of service quality, that is, to write down the know-how of Hippopotamus
3. To communicate the standards to everyone
4. To train all the teams
5. To improve the quality of the service
6. To innovate

To Work Out a Service Agreement

A committee composed of members of the top management and unit managers clarified and carefully worked out "the promise to the customer." The following was going to constitute the basic reference text. Each word had been carefully weighed:

The Sources of Success: Hippo's Promise to Its Customers

To always be able to have a good meal centered around a red meat, grilled, always tender, always fresh, always tasty, and chosen from a wide range of good-quality cuts at the right price.

To always be served generously and to enjoy, at your own speed, a
meal—meat and accompanying vegetables of your choice—the
preparation and presentation of which are flawless.

To always be welcomed warmly, known and recognized, put at ease,
guided, and then accompanied to your table with a pleasant manner,
good humor, and simplicity.

To relax in an atmosphere that is always cheerful, in a clean, tidy
restaurant with a warm decor.

Hippopotamus' promise conveyed without any ambiguity the originality of the company's formula, its comparative advantage (why go to Hippopotamus rather than somewhere else), and the principal dimensions of the
service. Through this promise, the company stated its position to the
outside world. It served as a point of reference for the quality charter and
its formalized expression in measurable standards.

To Formulate Standards of Service Quality

On the basis of Hippopotamus' promise, measurable standards of service
quality were defined, on two levels:

- On the level of the restaurant chain taken as a whole, general
  standards were drafted by a working group made up of individual
  restaurant managers, who put them to the top management.
- On the level of the service of each individual restaurant, the general
  standards, once formulated, were presented to more specialized
  groups so that they could define the standards applicable to each job:
  reception, bar, waitress service, kitchen, and general organization.

In total, 60 people belonging to all levels of the hierarchy and to all
the departments in the company were involved in working out the service
quality standards. It took six months for the document to be finalized.
In the last analysis it was a lot more than an instruction manual. It was
the product of 20 years' experience, and it expressed all the know-how
and originality of the chain.

The quality standards, as presented in the document, were suggested
by the stages through which the customer passed when he or she came

for a meal at Hippopotamus: the customer arrives and enters, is greeted, waits, is accompanied to table, orders, is served, eats/drinks, pays, and leaves.

At each of these stages the points in the promise were gone through so as to define what this promise meant for the customer (the result expected), what had to be done to give him or her satisfaction (tasks), and the resources to be used (methods and processes).

To Communicate the Standards to Everyone

The service quality standards were given to each member of staff and subsequently to newcomers. They were put up in the departments of the individual restaurants (out of sight of the customers). Any training undertaken was centered around these standards.

To Train All the Teams

The implementation of the Service Quality Program required wide-ranging training operations. This training was carried out in two phases. First of all, 250 people were trained by outside training specialists. (A training of this kind was also given to the members of the executive board.) Then the rest of the personnel were trained by in-house training specialists in the restaurants and at Hippo School.

First Phase: Training by Outside Training Specialists   This meant a big investment, and was considered essential for the success of the program. It concerned those with leadership responsibilities.

The 250 people took part, in groups of 30, in a residential Quality Seminar lasting five days. The Chairman and the Human Resources Manager attended each of the seven seminars personally, speaking at the beginning and the end.

The teaching method involved, essentially, trainee participation. It used the study of cases (specially devised at Hippopotamus), exercises with Hippopotamus data, and role plays with video cameras and debriefing. The following is a very brief résumé of the content of the Quality Seminars:

• The Hippo promise and quality standards

- Communication of the standards to someone else (training methods in the field)
- Improvement of current service quality: presentation of the tools required to "hunt the mistake," and how to lead a Quality Group
- The contribution to be made by the satisfaction barometer recently introduced

The objective was that, back at his or her unit, the course participant would constantly ask himself or herself questions concerning the way to reach the standards, would be convinced of his or her responsibility to pass on the quality message, and would be able to lead in-house meetings on this theme.

An appraisal of the Quality Seminars eight months later showed that the entire message had been conveyed and that each participant had fully understood that the prime objective was to satisfy the customer. Each now knew what was expected and what he or she had to do.

It seemed that the numerous exchanges that took place during the seminars and the mixture of participants gave a new dynamism to the discussions between individuals and improved relations between the different departments such as the kitchen and dining room.

As a result of the contacts made between the different hierarchical levels and the communication between the provincial restaurants and the Parisian ones, everyone acquired a much better understanding of the company's organization and the spirit of Hippopotamus as a group.

Second Phase: Training by In-House Training Specialists   In-house training specialists took over from the Quality Seminars and were given the responsibility of providing training for the people who had not attended one. Hippo School was created as a means of continuously communicating the service quality standards to colleagues at all levels. The training specialists were line executives who, after participating in the Quality Seminars, were given specific training in teaching skills.

Hippo School had training rooms equipped with audiovisual material at its center in Paris. Seminars of one or two days were organized there: for example, two-day seminars for table hostesses, and one-day seminars for the kitchen juniors and the washers-up.

Three subjects figured prominently in the program: the presentation of Hippo's promise to its clientele, the quality standards, and role plays intended to convey unequivocally the importance of the customer. Hippo School had an extension in each unit where managers participated in the training of the teams using the teaching aids specially devised for this purpose.

To Improve the Quality of the Service

Improve the Quality of the Service through In-House Communication
In Hippopotamus' line of work it was necessary to win over not only the customer, but also the personnel. The Service Quality Program inevitably had to be diffused through in-house communication. This was done in several ways.

A Quality Campaign   The communication of the standards was reinforced by humorous posters put up in the restaurants. Every month the Human Resources Manager sent to all the personnel a copy of the Quality Letter, the purpose of which was to inspire and communicate total quality to all levels within the company. (See Exhibit 2.4.)

Quality Group Activity   Working groups were set up in every unit. Their aim was to "hunt the mistake" in order to reach a "zero-fault" level. The groups operated under the responsibility of the unit's manager, with management personnel, and on a voluntary basis.

The Hippo Quality Contest   This was a means of spurring on the units. It revitalized and rewarded the individuals and units reaching excellence. The Quality Cup was awarded ceremoniously to the most deserving. This was the occasion for a dinner at Maxim's for the winners.

The Quality Committee   This authority included certain members of the chain's top management including the Chairman. It was expected to meet to help solve the problems coming from the units in the hunt-the-mistake process.

The "Promise of Human Resources to Our Customers"   The quality of the service was transmitted through the quality of the personnel and their motivation. The Chairman decided that human resources would also be

Exhibit 2.4
Example of a Quality Letter

H I P P O Q U A L I T Y

I N A U G U R A T I O N O F H I P P O S C H O O L

18 A P R I L, 16.30: O U R T R A I N I N G S C H O O L
has brought together in its premises at the
Bastille 135 people representing all the colleagues
of the Hippo Group

I T I S A G R E A T N E W S T A G E

ITS GOAL: TO ALLOW US TO REACH, TOGETHER, THE 95
PERCENT LEVEL OF CUSTOMER SATISFACTION!!!

H I P P O S C H O O L, I T W O R K S.

From 19th May, groups of 15 colleagues are going to attend the school,
following on from one another at the rhythm of one group for one to two
days per week in order to LEARN WITH THE HELP OF 15 IN-HOUSE
TRAINING SPECIALISTS why and how we must SATISFY OUR
CUSTOMERS EVERY HOUR OF EVERY DAY.

---

a priority and that a recruitment and training policy was to be worked out. A new Human Resources Manager had been taken on at that time.

To obtain the maximum level of support for the company project, the Human Resources Manager in turn made promises to the in-house customers: the personnel. This pledge was drawn up in five points:

The Promise of Human Resources to Our Customers

1. to be available to welcome them in a kindly manner with good humor and without reserve
2. to assist them in legal and social matters, in questions of insurance, and other administrative formalities
3. to give them every support in order to have quality personnel (promotion, training, and recruitment)
4. to inform them about the life of the group and the human potential at Hippo
5. to give them precise and rapid answers (within 24 hours)

In line with this promise, important training and recruitment activities were forecast for unit managers and their deputies.

Improve the Quality of Service by Regularly Assessing It   To improve service quality, one has to be able to measure it. Hippopotamus therefore used the following measuring tools.

The Satisfaction Barometer   This enabled the level of customer satisfaction to be assessed. Every three months a survey was carried out on 400 customers in each of the 17 restaurants, in the course of a week. Forty questions—concerned with concrete and precise points, such as the dress and behavior of the receptionists and waitresses, the cleanliness of the establishment, the quality of the food and drink—were thus put to the customers.

Careful study of the 7,000 completed questionnaires led to the setting up of the Hippo barometer, which helped the company to evaluate the cost of inadequate quality, focus improvement efforts on the most sensitive points as far as customer satisfaction is concerned, and reward those giving the best performances.

The Quality Audit   The aim was to help a unit improve its service quality. It worked on the principle that the manager of one restaurant audits another. It represented the help given by one manager to his or her colleague.

Two managers never audited one another. The results were communicated only to the manager whose restaurant had been audited. It was in no way an inspection.

To carry out the audit, a manager had a checklist specially designed for the purpose. The manager filled this in after making one or several visits to the restaurant and after having a meal there. The checklist was used by restaurant managers for their own unit.

The Hippo Suggestions Table   In the course of a month, a manager systematically and punctually invited eight customers to dine at his restaurant. This allowed him to make a qualitative assessment of customer satisfaction between each quarterly barometer reading.

To Innovate

To succeed, Hippopotamus had to be constantly seeking new ways to improve its service. Here is an example of innovation: In the course of the surveys carried out on the clientele, it became apparent that the customer was occasionally dissatisfied with the time he or she had to wait before a table became available. Action was therefore taken:

> The reception hostesses were asked to tell the customer truthfully how long he will have to wait. If the actual waiting time proved longer than anticipated, he or she was to be offered a free drink.
> Ideas regarding possible ways of livening up the waiting time were constantly being studied.

By putting this point in the Service Quality Program, the Chairman of the Hippopotamus chain wanted to emphasize that stringency, that is, the strict application of exact standards, had to be combined with flexibility and creativity in order to reach the desired objective: excellence.

APPLICATION OF THE SERVICE QUALITY PROGRAM

The description of the program showed the means put at the disposal of leaders and management, but what happened next in the field? Each unit manager was quite free to work out his or her own strategy, and each did so in his or her own way.

The Experience of the Restaurant Hippo-Citroën

It was the most spectacular. This case was special in as far as the restaurant had recently been taken over by a new manager, who had been given the task of boosting an establishment the results of which were falling. Fifty percent of the unit's personnel (about 100 people) underwent quality training: 40 percent attended the Quality Seminar; and 10 percent went on a course at Hippo School. The Hippo-Citroën manager explained what happened:

> Returning from the Quality Seminar, a manager has his head full of ideas. There was a great deal of thought about a profession which is concerned with doing things and wanting to do things. There were some very strong messages. We were shown tremendous tools. . . . On getting back, I wondered how we were going to use all this, if we were ready to digest everything, if it wasn't too much.

But the manager of Hippo-Citroën was convinced that the program was good and fully justified, for at the seminar he rediscovered things that he had been trying to do or that he was already doing to a certain extent.

The first decision was to have a meeting room converted into what he baptized the Quality Sanctuary. This was equipped with the teaching material and audiovisual aids necessary for personnel training. Messages were stuck up on the walls; Hippopotamus's promise to the customer, and Hippo-Citroën's plan of action for the implementation of the Quality Program.

However, such a plan of action could not be worked out immediately. First of all, the manager devoted a lot of time to meetings with his management personnel. It was then that he became aware of the following phenomena:

There is now a common language: each person can see where he stands in his particular job. The posts which have been described and commented upon have gained in depth; they have been identified and developed; their standing has been increased. Everyone is now able to describe his duties. He knows the vocabulary and concepts to be able to explain what he does (which was not the case before for a lot of the personnel). He feels that he can get on, that the company is offering him more than just a salary.

Communicating took a lot of the Hippopotamus manager's time. He became aware that he had to delegate a certain number of tasks to his colleagues if he was to cope. The following actions were taken.

Communication of "the Standards" In the Quality Sanctuary the standards were communicated to all the personnel with the visual tools worked out by the group.

Coaching Coaching was started in the field. This step, in conjunction with the theoretical training and the Quality Group meetings, seemed both natural and indispensable for the attainment of the appointed goal. The coaching was carried out by the hierarchy (indeed, colleagues) who fulfilled their management role in a more educational way than previously. In the kitchen, in the dining room, at the bar, and at reception, the manager showed how something was to be done by doing it himself. He got others to do it, and explained what could be improved. "When a remark was made during the service, a few minutes were taken afterwards to discuss the matter." The Hippopotamus manager noted: "The staff are more receptive to instructions, and they really understand them."

The Quality Group Meetings As a complement to theoretical and on-the-job training activities, service quality problems were dealt with in the Quality Groups. Four groups were created, with about 10 people in each group:

- Bar/reception group
- Product group
- Dining room service group
- Citroën information bank

The Quality Groups' objective was to hunt the mistake. For the manager of Hippo-Citroën, the terms used were important: they highlighted the fact that it was not a question of man-hunting or fault finding, but a common search for solutions in order to improve the running of the company.

What Happened at a Quality Group Meeting?

1. The agenda was given to the participants a few days in advance.

2. There were about 10 participants. They volunteered to be members of the Quality Group.

3. At every meeting there was a chairman, who must have attended the Quality Seminar, an observer, and a reporter, who took the minutes. The unit manager was almost always present at the meetings. The Hippopotamus manager pointed out, "At the beginning nobody wanted to take the minutes; people were afraid of not knowing, of making spelling mistakes. Now they all volunteer." The minutes played an important role. Through them the entire personnel was kept informed of the decisions taken to remedy the problems under discussion, and the actions decided upon subsequently to be followed up and monitored.

4. Number and length of the meetings: an hour once a fortnight in the restaurant's slack period, that is, the afternoon.

5. Subjects tackled. A few examples from Hippo-Citroën:
- With the Dining Room Service Quality Group: food served luke-warm to the customer; orders taken down badly worded; and crockery breakages.
- With the Bar/Reception Group: the problem of the discrepancy between the number of bottles of champagne charged to the customer and the number charged by the supplier.

6. The method for conducting the meeting was simple. It was the method of Ichikawa and that of Pareto and was explained during the Quality Seminar. It allowed solutions to be found relatively quickly, with the consensus of a group where several levels of hierarchy were represented. The chairman went around the table and asked each member of the group what, in her or his opinion, the possible causes of error were, and the chairman listed the causes on a board. When he went around the table a second time, the participants indicated the importance they attributed to

each of the causes listed. This meant that they could then concentrate on
the two or three causes judged by the group to be essential. For example,
to resolve the problem of the champagne discrepancy, the group agreed
that the principal sources of error were:

- Too large a goblet for the capacity indicated
- A lack of precision in pouring out the appropriate measure of champagne

7. Going around the table for the third time, the chairman drew
together the solutions put forward by each participant. In the final phase,
two decisions to be made were noted (in this case:

- The replacement of glasses that were too big by smaller glasses to
  serve well-filled to the customer's satisfaction
- Staff training; how soon and by whom)

The Hippo-Citroën manager stressed the following points:

To make the meeting as effective as possible, figures need to be given
so that one can put one's finger on the financial consequences of the
mistake; for the badly measured-out champagne it's a turnover loss of
so much per month and so much per year. You also have to think about
the customer and the impact that the solutions considered will have on
the quality of the service.

It is important too that the group members get the feeling that they
have made the decisions themselves. The hunt-the-mistake process also
serves to show the personnel that there is a permanent check on what
is happening in the company.

For their part, the employees expressed the following opinions:

It's good that time's taken to talk about our problems. We have a better
idea of what we've got to do. We think more about the customer's
opinion. Here you don't get the impression that you're just a number.
I've been learning more about the job, and yet I've been in the restaurant
business for a long time.

8. General meetings: For the implementation of the Quality Program
and the relaunching of his restaurant, the manager of Hippo-Citroën felt
the need to organize meetings to which the unit's entire personnel would

be invited. The meetings provided him with the opportunity to remind everyone of the company's objectives, to point out the good work done by the Quality Groups, and to sustain enthusiasm. The participation of the Chairman of the company and the Human Resources Manager in these meetings was a reminder that the unit was part of a group and that the latter helped and advised.

The manager of Hippo-Citroën believed that his restaurant benefited substantially from these general meetings. (The last one was filmed, and a lot of people expressed their views in it.) They contributed to the creation of a good atmosphere, a common language, an internal cohesion, and a feeling of belonging.

9. The results of the implementation of the Service Quality Program at Hippo-Citroën:
- Growth in the level of customer satisfaction:
    October = 75%
    February = 85%
    May = 98.5%, the best score in the group
- Growth in revenue (+5 percent) and therefore corresponding increases in pay

10. The unit no longer needed to have recourse to advertisements for personnel recruitment. The salaries were on display in the restaurant.

The achievement of Hippo-Citroën had repercussions within the group and, at the request of the Human Resources Manager, the unit's manager gave a presentation of his plan of action to the managers of the other restaurants and the Chairman of the company. It goes without saying that such a step had its own impact on the state of mind of Hippo-Citroën's personnel: the restaurant was becoming a point of reference.

The Point of View of Hippo-Wagram's Manager

The results of the Hippo-Wagram unit, unlike those of Hippo-Citroën, were already very satisfactory. They were the best in the chain. For several years the restaurant's personnel had been the most stable in the group, and the manager was anxious to maintain this situation by taking precautionary measures. In this unit, small-group and general meetings were already taking place.

Here is the opinion of Hippo-Wagram's manager:

> As far as motivation is concerned, the positive benefits of the Quality Seminar have been extraordinary. A seminar of this type organized outside the company increases the participants' potential. Meeting people from different units is enriching and encourages a group spirit and consequently the sense of belonging, . . . but personnel motivation is not something to be done for [only] a few days each year.

> The Quality Program has allowed us to develop an attitude that was already present; we have subsequently changed certain things in the field. We think more in customer terms. . . . We've done things in a more standardized—and at the same time, more rational—way. Before it was more intuitive.

The actions associated with the Quality Program were like those at Hippo-Citroën:

- Communication of the standards to the restaurant's personnel and to newcomers
- Hunting the mistake through the organization of three Quality Groups meeting once a month

The mistakes dealt with were, for example, meat sent back, errors in the bill, running out of an item on the menu, problems concerning the changeover of staff, and the clearing of tables. Some very important work was done at the reception level to make the waiting time given to the customer by the hostesses exact.

The Service Quality Program suggested a comparison between units with reference to the satisfaction barometer, for this would give the results of all the units of the chain and lead to a grading process and rewards:

> This comparison is not always possible, for the clienteles are not the same and their expectations differ. . . . The important thing is that a unit should be able to measure itself against its own achievements.

The Hippo-Wagram manager considered the Service Quality Program to be one of the tools of human resources management. "Others, like the

annual individual interview, are equally necessary. The program is not an
end in itself, but it has built up a state of mind."

A Few Opinions Collected within the Company

A year after the launching of the Service Quality Program, the consulting
firm specializing in quality problems, whose services the Chairman of
Hippopotamus used, audited the program and its implementation in the
company. Discussions held with about 30 people belonging to the different
units brought to the fore the positive repercussions and the difficulties.

Positive Repercussions of the Quality Program That Have Been Cited

The unit managers considered that Hippo School, the prime function of
which was to diffuse the standards, contributed a lot more in other ways
as well:

> "The personnel who go through Hippo School understand the general
> organization of Hippopotamus."

> "They become aware of the importance of each person's role."

> "They can stand back from the unit in which they live and be enriched by
> the experience of others; they come back with something in their heads."

> "Hippo School gives them an extra motivation to reach a better level
> of quality. For the grill assistants/operators it's a plus."

> "The definition of quality standards and precise objectives binds the
> teams together. Everyone is in agreement over the essentials. It's the
> basis of the profession; it's logical. Anyone who doesn't believe in logic
> isn't with it."

> "There are exceptions, but, by and large, everyone's focusing more on
> the customer."

> "Everyone knows what he has to do and tries to come as close as possible
> to the service quality standard. There is a determination in people, a
> better team spirit."

> "Now there are railings and landmarks. . . . Anyone straying from
> the quality standard gets brought back into line by the team. The girls

know what to say when the food comes out of the serving hatch, and a hostess told *me,* the manager, that I was below standard."

Difficulties Mentioned by the Personnel Consulted   Certain unit managers took quite a while to consider service quality as a priority and to believe in it.

"I didn't have enough time; there was the problem of management being understaffed."

"It isn't always easy to get standard communication groups meeting together because you first have to find a slot in the schedule that everyone can make."

"The team turnover means that you're forever having to start all over again."

When they talk about hunting the mistake, certain unit managers say,

"We don't always have the time to meet."

The results of the Hippo barometer, especially the first, came as a shock to a few units.

"Some people wept at the results."

"The results aren't precise enough; for example, when people talk about the quality of the starters, we don't always understand exactly what is wrong."

"We'd rather use the Hippo barometer to measure our own restaurant over a period of time than compare ourselves to other units, for we are not in the same districts. The different clienteles don't have the same expectations."

The automatic control quality audit has its supporters and its opponents:

"It's dangerous."

"I have learnt something."

"I'm not going to stab a pal in the back."

"The person who was to do it for me never came."

"We realize that it takes several months (three to four) for certain habits to be formed, like the introduction of the hostesses by their first name, the indication of the exact waiting time, speed in producing the bill. We also realize that, if these three points are satisfactory in a restaurant, all the rest will be, for they are the most difficult to achieve."

CONCLUSION

The Service Quality Program was wanted by the Chairman, who followed its progress very closely. Practically every individual in the company was approached. It involved a very big financial investment—FF 4.5 million for the first year—and it was similarly expensive in terms of human effort, but it produced results.

As Far as the Commercial Situation Is Concerned

The overall customer satisfaction level went up by 10 points between October and May from 77 to 87 percent. Survey results of other satisfaction ratings are shown in Exhibit 2.5.

As Far as the In-House Situation Is Concerned

Although these results were more difficult to measure in concrete terms, there was no doubt that the company had grown in dynamism and had improved the performances and the potential of its human resources. By giving precise objectives, by making everyone understand the importance of his role, by reinforcing the feeling of belonging to a company that's different, by providing training, the Service Quality Program brought back enthusiasm and gave a noticeable boost to the culture of the company.

The staff turnover did not come down sufficiently, 1.26 as compared with 1.50, but the figure 1.00 was being targeted. However, it was easier to manage, thanks to the existence of training tools.

Finally, the formalization of the Hippopotamus quality standards made it easier for the company to get franchisees. It met the expectations of the chairman, Christian Guignard, who wanted the group to refocus its efforts and have better assets at its disposal prior to launching into a

Exhibit 2.5
Customer Satisfaction Survey Responses

	Satisfied (%)	Unsatisfied (%)
Price:		
Too expensive	5	26
Somewhat expensive	37	37
Just right	58	37
	100	100
Word of Mouth Heard:		
Very often	21	4
Frequently	39	17
Sometimes	31	43
Never	9	36
	100	100
Visits to Hippopotamus:		
Less than once a week	32	44
One to two times a week	15	15
Two to three times a week	38	25
More than three times a week	5	5
First time	10	11
	100	100
Success of Hippo Formula:		
Come more often	19	11
Come same as before	70	36
Come less often	11	53
	100	100

Note: Numbers do not always add to 100 because of nonresponses.

new phase of expansion. Nevertheless, it was recognized that the process was cumbersome and would take a long time to set up, and that its practical application needed to be very closely supervised. The Service Quality Program was put into practice at a rate which fluctuated from 20 to 80 percent depending on the restaurants, and the results of the satisfaction barometer seemed to mirror in the same way the extent to which the program was being implemented in the units.

Part II
The Marketing Environment

Case Three

The São Paulo Hotel

Laurel J. Walsh and Robert C. Lewis

Both the city of São Paulo and most of Brazil had been enduring a wave of economic turmoil for a number of years. The value of the Brazilian cruzado relative to the American dollar had continued to decline. "Hyperinflation," now at 15 to 50 percent a month, had run as high as 900 percent in some years. A newspaper could double in price overnight, and in one year a television set went from 20,000 to 190,000 cruzados (about $320 at the time). In one weekend, airfares had gone up 33 percent and postal charges 64 percent. This, in turn, had stimulated the threat of an international banking crisis, with Brazil targeted as the developing world's largest debtor. As a result of this instability, the government had imposed strict regulations on importation and on the flow of money across Brazil's borders.

All forms of international commerce had decreased. Pressures to "buy Brazilian" diverted attention from potential imports that had so far managed to survive strict regulations. High unemployment caused by factory shutdowns created labor problems, particularly in São Paulo which had previously boasted high employment. Strikes had swept the country, shutting down much of the oil and steel industries. With a presidential election soon to be scheduled, the economy experienced a pre-election slowdown led by cautious investors awaiting the new administration (recent administrations had been corrupt and/or ineffective in resolving the economic crises). Local elections showed a sharp shift toward leftist parties: One candidate was promising to open the borders to all kinds of international trade to attract the attention of foreign investors. In the hotel industry competition was tighter than ever.

This case was written by Laurel J. Walsh, International Strategies, Inc., Boston, and Robert C. Lewis, University of Guelph, Ontario. All rights reserved. Some data and names have been disguised. All monetary figures are in US$ unless otherwise noted.

THE CORPORATE MARKET

São Paulo was a Brazilian city with over 12 million people in its greater metropolitan area. It had its sights set on being the second largest city in the world by the year 2000. Despite this huge size, the hotel business had always been relatively lean. Now, due to a decline in foreign business travel, the city's hotels discovered that they needed to target Brazilian travelers if they hoped to achieve an acceptable occupancy of their historically underutilized rooms.

Compounding the problem was the relocation of many corporate headquarters from downtown São Paulo, where the São Paulo Hotel was located, to the Paulista area on the outskirts of the city, 10 to 15 minutes from downtown, and to the Faria-Lima area, which was 10 miles farther from the downtown area than was Paulista. This was due to the outgrowing of available space and expansion, rather than any undesirability of the downtown area.

Major room-night-producing companies such as DuPont, Embratel, Rohm and Haas, L'Oréal, and Hewlett-Packard (one of São Paulo Hotel's largest accounts) moved to newly developed office buildings in Paulista, while others like Monsanto planned to relocate soon. The exodus to the Faria-Lima area was somewhat slower due to the higher cost of office rental, but growth there was steady. Despite the shift of business, downtown São Paulo continued to host the banking community, major airline companies, other types of industries located within walking distance of the São Paulo Hotel, and smaller companies that were moving into the vacated offices.

The São Paulo Hotel was severely impacted by the economic crunch along with all the other hotels. Since the hotel had relied heavily on the international business traveler in the past (Exhibit 3.1), management

Exhibit 3.1
Geographic Origins of the Business

	Percent Occupancy		
Geographic Source	Last Year	Present Year	Next Year's Forecast
North America	18.2	14.9	12.8
Latin America	15.1	11.1	11.1
Europe	16.7	16.3	13.2
Brazil	42.4	54.6	58.5
Other	7.6	3.1	4.4

recognized that a different style of operation would be required to handle Brazilian business.

Since the needs and wants of the smaller Brazilian companies were not clearly defined and more hotels were now vying for fewer customers, the sales effort was recognized as challenging. A salesperson could no longer rely on a few major client companies to produce the bulk of the business, and was forced to explore dramatically different approaches to direct selling, as well as making multiple visits to more smaller companies.

The decreasing demand for hotel rooms was further aggravated by some changes in airline routes. Major airlines had begun to schedule additional morning and evening flights to accommodate corporate and government officials flying to or from Rio de Janeiro or Brasília (the capital) for the day. By encouraging same-day, round-trip customers, the airlines allowed the traveler to save the cost of a night's accommodation. This deprived the city's hotels of considerable revenue, particularly from Rio, which was only a 50-minute shuttle. The trip to Brasília, an hour and a half, was equally conducive to day trips.

THE GROUP MARKET

Corporate accounts were not the only type of business for which São Paulo hotels were actively competing. Brazil boasted over 10,000 associations in the country, but only 150 to 200 could be considered major convention producers worthy of pursuit. In addition, volume and/or cyclical business from the association market was not significant. The Maksoud Plaza Hotel regularly undercut any other hotel and was therefore understandably the first choice of the association market. Association decision makers generally ranked the São Paulo Hotel as their second or third choice, although historically it was chosen most often as convention headquarters amid stiff competition.

Nonbusiness groups were usually one-shot deals from other countries and were largely controlled by wholesale agents in Rio. These were usually typical tour groups, and the agents bargained hard for volume wholesale rates.

São Paulo convention business was focused at two major facilities with one other center at Brazil's largest hospital. The Ibeuratera Convention Center was located near Viracopos International Airport, a 15- to 20-

minute taxi ride from downtown São Paulo. It was situated in a densely populated residential area and was the smaller of the two centers.

The Anhembi, the largest convention facility in Brazil, had a 3,500-person capacity and housed all large exhibitions. Since international trade had declined, it was primarily the site of trade shows within the country. The Anhembi was located 20 minutes from downtown in a poor residential neighborhood. Several attempts to build a hotel near this facility had proven futile. Shuttle buses were used to transport people from hotels.

São Paulo, along with Brasília, competed with two other major cities for convention business. Until a facility was built in the east coast resort town of Recife, São Paulo had been known as the "only game in town." The city of Rio de Janeiro also had a municipal convention center that was promoted and supported by Embratur, the national tourist bureau. Regardless of location, convention facilities and activity were embedded in politics and difficult to control.

SÃO PAULO AS A DESTINATION

São Paulo suffered from a poor self-image in regard to its ability to attract either the leisure or the business traveler. In the past, the hotel association, the city, and the airlines had each attempted to promote São Paulo as a shopping or cultural attraction, but all had failed or aborted their efforts before any positive results could be seen. State officials pessimistically wondered, "Who would want to come to São Paulo? It's such a dirty, large city."

The São Paulo Hotel was quite active in organizing a convention and visitors bureau. Hoping to receive government support through the Embratur, a government tourism agency, the hotel suffered a major setback when the financial backing went to Rio.

The role of Embratur was to promote Brazil as a destination to visitors from outside the country. Its management was only marginally effective, and it was further hindered by poor tourism infrastructures in the many cities having potential for foreign visitors. These cities lacked organized sightseeing and had few if any buses, taxis, or car rentals. Airfares were expensive. The national airline, Varig, was favored by the government and influenced airline routes.

THE SÃO PAULO HOTEL

The São Paulo Hotel was a 25-story, 407-room hotel with three restaurants, a lounge, pool, discotheque, health club, and an extensive shopping arcade of international shops. It was managed by an international hotel company with a strong international reservations system. Its location in the heart of the business district, as well as its close proximity to Viracopos International Airport, made it attractive to the business market. However, a newer airport, Guarulhos International, was considerably farther away.

The hotel opened its doors 15 years ago and was initially very successful. Now, however, occupancy was down to 51.4 percent with an average rate of $70.80, in comparison with the previous year's occupancy of 53 percent (average rate $86.73) and the year before that with an occupancy rate of 54.5 percent (average rate $96.59). Percentage changes in year-to-year average rate and occupancy are shown in Exhibit 3.2, the breakdown by market segment is shown in Exhibit 3.3, and Exhibit 3.4 shows a comparison with projections by segment.

Exhibit 3.2
**Year-to-Year Average Rate/Occupancy
Change Percentages**

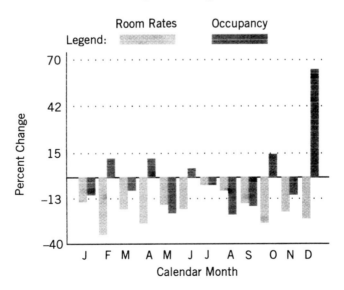

Exhibit 3.3
Profile by Market Segment (Based on 10 Percent Sample)

	All Guests	EBS*	FIT (Commercial)	Company Mtg.	FIT (Social)
Occupancy:					
Occupied rooms	8,033	3,280	2,376	783	484
Percent of total	100.0	40.8	29.6	9.7	6.0
Complimentary	127	0	54	2	42
Registrations:					
Number	3,510	1,166	1,090	279	261
Percent of total	100.0	33.2	31.1	7.9	7.4
Expenditure Averages (U.S.$):					
Room rate (per occupied room)	58.52	54.95	69.92	40.88	63.69
Charge per day (occupied room)	75.21	69.29	90.80	49.00	81.45
Nonroom charge per day	16.69	14.34	20.88	8.13	17.76
Charges per stay	188.03	194.01	217.92	151.93	179.19
Revenue Estimates (U.S.$, 000s):					
Total revenue**	660.0	226.2	237.5	42.4	46.8
Room revenue***	462.7	180.2	162.4	31.9	28.2
Nonroom revenue†	186.4	46.0	75.1	10.5	18.6
Percent of total revenue	100.0	34.3	36.0	6.4	7.1
Room revenue as percent of total	70.1	79.7	68.4	75.2	60.3
Nonroom revenue as percent of total	29.9	20.3	31.6	24.8	39.7
Rate Category:					
Percent rack	26.7	0.9	65.9	1.1	53.6
Percent discount	73.3	99.1	34.1	98.9	46.4
Stay Patterns:					
Length of stay (days)	2.5	2.8	2.4	3.1	2.2
Guests per room	1.1	1.0	1.1	1.1	1.3
Percent advance reservation	91.3	94.9	85.0	98.2	78.2
Percent walk-in	8.7	5.1	15.0	1.8	21.8
Average lead time (days)	6.8	7.3	7.6	4.8	9.3
Percent commissionable	21.3	6.3	23.6	3.9	24.1
Percent direct	79.6	86.1	69.6	96.8	58.6
Percent CRS††	11.7	8.8	15.4	1.4	19.5
Percent first visit	60.4	36.1	61.9	69.9	76.2

* EBS = Executive Business Service.
** Average charges per stay × registrations.
*** Noncomplimentary rooms × room rate.
† Total revenue − room revenue.
†† Corporate reservations system.

Exhibit 3.3 *(continued)*

Nonbusiness Group	Convention/ Congress	Package	Tour Series	Flight Delay Overflow	Airline Crew	Incentive
461	330	151	735	7	25	13
5.7	4.1	1.9	0.9	0.7	0.3	0.2
20	3	0	0	0	3	3
325	122	138	35	69	16	9
9.3	3.5	3.9	1.0	2.0	0.5	0.3
53.21	48.27	70.82	86.09	48.92	22.98	48.81
68.39	62.93	117.24	116.65	57.75	60.80	54.17
15.18	14.66	46.42	30.56	8.83	37.81	−5.36
143.62	201.38	211.03	384.95	57.75	97.28	92.09
46.7	24.6	29.1	13.5	3.4	1.6	0.8
23.5	15.8	10.7	6.3	2.8	0.6	0.5
23.2	8.8	18.4	7.2	0.6	1.0	0.3
7.1	3.7	4.4	2.0	0.5	0.2	0.1
50.3	64.2	36.8	46.7	82.4	37.5	62.5
49.7	35.8	63.2	53.3	17.6	62.5	37.5
0.0	2.5	46.4	0.0	0.0	0.0	0.0
00.0	97.5	53.6	100.0	100.0	100.0	100.0
2.1	3.2	1.8	3.3	1.0	1.6	1.7
1.5	1.3	1.8	1.6	1.2	1.2	1.2
99.4	90.2	96.4	100.0	100.0	93.8	100.0
0.6	9.8	3.6	0.0	0.0	6.3	0.0
6.0	4.1	4.2	7.9	1.0	0.0	3.7
74.2	18.9	29.7	100.0	1.4	0.0	22.2
86.5	77.0	86.2	65.7	100.0	87.5	100.0
12.9	12.3	10.1	34.3	0.0	6.3	0.0
94.2	79.5	78.3	85.7	100.0	62.5	100.0

Exhibit 3.4
A Comparison with Projections (Based on 10 Percent Sample)

	Projected		Actual		Variance	
Segment	Number	Pct.	Number	Pct.	Number	Pct.
FIT* (commercial)	3,174	38.7	2,376	29.6	−798	−25.1
EBS**	2,852	34.8	3,280	40.8	428	15.0
Convention/Congress	773	9.4	330	4.1	−443	−57.3
Company meeting	718	8.8	783	9.7	65	9.1
FIT* (social)	384	4.7	484	6.0	100	26.0
Nonbusiness group	133	1.6	461	5.7	328	246.0
Package	79	1.0	151	1.9	72	91.1
Incentive	48	0.6	13	0.2	−35	−72.9
Airline crew	30	0.4	25	0.3	−5	16.7
Flight delay/overflow	0	0.0	57	0.7	57	NA
Tour series	0	0.0	73	0.9	73	NA
Total	8,191	100.0	8,033	100.0	−158	−2.0

* FIT = free independent traveler.
** EBS = Executive Business Service.

Room rack rates (U.S.$) were as follows:

Single	$ 95	$110	$132
Double	$105	$126	$147

All rooms had modern conveniences such as direct-dial telephones, air-conditioning, private baths, and small refrigerators. There was a deluxe Presidential Suite, 33 one-bedroom suites, and a Penthouse Suite offering a panoramic view of São Paulo. The Grand Ballroom could accommodate 340 banquet-style, and there were other meeting rooms with capacities of 140, 80, and 60.

The São Paulo Hotel had undergone a face lift in recent years. The main lobby was modernized, as were the banquet rooms and executive floors. One hundred fifty of the guest rooms were also renovated. The Roof restaurant was closed due to its unprofitability. The plan was to replace it with two meeting rooms.

The hotel offered an assortment of distinctive dining experiences ranging from the casual to the elegant. The Tavern was remodeled to resemble an old English pub and transformed into one of São Paulo's hottest discos in the evening. Native Brazilian cuisine was served in the Grill Colonial, which catered to the luncheon businessman. The Varavida Bar, located on the pool's terrace, was an informal yet chic lounge frequented by the "in" São Paulo crowd. All of the food outlets gained a reputation for superb cuisine among business and pleasure travelers alike.

Meeting and banquet facilities were versatile in both the hotel and its recently completed convention center. This addition featured state-of-the-art audiovisual systems in the new auditorium/exhibition foyer.

Other amenities included concierge service, beauty shops, laundry and valet service, and a business center. Travelers pressed for time frequently contacted the business center for information or assistance in making appointments, sending faxes, and arranging secretarial, copying, and translation services. The hotel also developed an executive credit card for the purpose of encouraging food and beverage spending in the hotel.

The hotel had a toll-free 800 number as part of its computer reservations system (CRS). The volume of calls was low, about 100 a month, and was almost entirely generated from FIT commercial business; about 60 percent of the calls were converted into reservations. São Paulo was the major contributing source for the business of all market segments, but Rio contributed heavily for FIT, package, nonbusiness, and Executive Business Service (EBS) groups.

Company meetings were predominantly of São Paulo origin and were almost entirely controlled within the city. This type of business was very cutthroat. Most hotels would do anything to sell a room and, in fact, offered various different rates depending on how low they had to go to get the business.

COMPETITION

The 177-room Caesar Park was the first hotel built in the Paulista region. It boasted a long-standing, favorable reputation in the community. One of its selling features was the Presidential Suite, which was often in demand by heads of state governments and other prestigious visitors. The Caesar Park had three food-service outlets, all of which were very well received.

Meeting facilities consisted of five rooms with a maximum banquet capacity of 300. The rack rates (U.S.$) were as follows:

Single	$158–195
Double	$188–240
Suite	$345–675

The new 250-room Transamerica Hotel was to open soon and be positioned to attract the "training-related" group market. It had state-of-the-art audiovisual equipment, closed-circuit television, and other training facilities. In contrast to the São Paulo Hotel, the Transamerica was to be a midrange hotel competing for the specialty groups market. Proposed rack rates were unknown.

The Maksoud Plaza Hotel was owned by a well-known Lebanese real-estate developer. It had an impressive appearance with an atrium lobby, French restaurant, unique Scandinavian coffee shop, auditorium, and disco. The owner was a prominent local "wheeler-dealer" who favored lavish, international entertainment and who bartered free hotel rooms for business-related favors.

The Maksoud Plaza was a 371-room hotel with 50 suites, a heated swimming pool, and a 420-seat theater located in the Paulista area. It featured a health club, executive service center with office facilities, and 40 meeting rooms with the latest in meeting equipment. Rack rates (U.S.$) were as follows:

Single	$150–183
Double	$173–210
Suite	$310–390

Maksoud's quality of service and plant maintenance was declining as the hotel grew older.

The Eldorado Boulevard Hotel was situated in the downtown region, approximately seven miles from the airport. It was a 136-room property with 21 suites and the following rack rates (U.S.$):

Single	$ 90–105
Double	$108–162
Suite	$210–255

There were two food outlets accessible by a street entrance. Function space consisted of only two rooms with a maximum capacity of 200 people.

The Mofarrej Hotel was a beautiful new property under construction in Paulista by a wealthy São Paulo businessman. Each guest room was to be equipped with the latest in modern technology including American programmed television, conference calls, and video checkout. The property was intended to be a "monument" to the wealthy and was unlikely to operate profitably. It was to be operated by Sheraton.

The 252-room Brasilton Hotel was only a short distance from the São Paulo Hotel and was constructed by the same owners to absorb the São Paulo Hotel's overflow. It was more attractive to a price-sensitive guest than the São Paulo Hotel was, and had the following rack rates:

Single	$138–150
Double	$150–175
Suites	$242–272

In the current competitive climate, the Brasilton took a survival stance in the battle for room nights. It had two fine restaurants, the Braseiro and the Taverna. Banquet facilities included a maximum banquet capacity of 520 people. This hotel also had a good reputation with the local community.

The 500-room Hotel Ca d'Oro was also located close to the São Paulo Hotel and was owned by a local Italian restaurateur. Its success in attracting a strong base in the training market allowed the construction of a new wing, which made the property very competitive. Rates were "negotiated."

Holiday Inn, the second international hotel company to enter the São Paulo market, planned to open a 232-room "Crowne Plaza" hotel near Paulista. More upscale than the typical Holiday Inn, the Crowne Plaza was expected to fall into the deluxe range.

The location of the hotels is shown in Exhibit 3.5. The Caesar Park, the Maksoud Plaza, and the Ca d'Oro were all members of the consortium entitled Leading Hotels of the World.

CONCLUSION

The most resounding echo of competition in São Paulo was the result of vicious price-cutting by the hotels. The Maksoud Plaza practiced a bazaar

Exhibit 3.5

Map of São Paulo with Location of Hotels

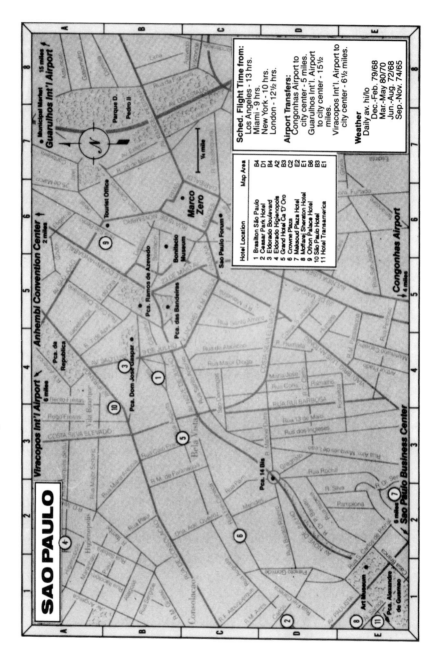

style of rate negotiation where the philosophy was "anything to fill the room." Other hotels were quick to follow suit for fear they would lose out on the available business.

Because it was almost entirely controlled within the city, corporate meeting business tended to be the most frequent benefactor of the cutthroat price war. Many hotels consistently quoted rates that were as little as 40 percent of their minimum rack rate in order to capture the corporate function booking, even though they gave the appearance of maintaining rack rates. For example, Maksoud was known to offer corporate rates in the $60 range, while Ca d'Oro had offered a $50 rate to company meeting groups.

Competitive occupancy figures and business mix are shown in Exhibit 3.6.

Future business prospects did not appear dismal for the São Paulo Hotel, just highly competitive. The Maksoud Plaza had recently become the new social gathering spot for the elite of São Paulo. By investing heavily in lavish, international entertainment, the Maksoud family succeeded in overtaking the São Paulo Hotel as the place to be seen. The Mofarrej was expected to follow suit in head-to-head competition with the Maksoud Plaza. Neither of the owners was particularly concerned with profit; image appeared to be the primary concern.

Once a stable property, the São Paulo Hotel was apparently in need of a new, clearly defined identity to compete effectively in the intense environment. The economy was not projected to bounce back quickly, and the available pool of rooms continued to increase in an already diluted market.

The ownership and the management of the São Paulo Hotel recognized that strategic marketing was the only tonic for survival in a highly competitive market. Given their limited resources, they wondered how to segment and position themselves in the current marketplace, in addition to what their product strategy should be. Exhibit 3.7 shows the demand analysis projected for the following year, while Exhibit 3.8 shows abstracts from the new marketing plan.

Exhibit 3.6
Competitive Occupancy and Business Mix

	São Paulo	Maksoud Plaza	Caesar Park	Brasilton	Eldorado	Ca d'Oro	Total
				Last Year			
Number of rooms	407	421	177	252	157	500	1,914
Annual occupancy (%)	53	65	62	68	50	55	58
ARR $	87	102	75	59	63	72	
Market Segment (% occupancy):							
FIT (commercial)	75	70	60	74	65	75	71
Group (commercial)	15	12	30	4.7	11	15	14
FIT (social)	5	8	5	3.2	9	5	6
Group (social)	5	10	5	18	15	5	9
				Present Year			
Available Rooms:							
Number	407	421	177	252	157	500	1,914
Percent of total	21.3%	22.0%	9.2%	13.2%	8.2%	26.1%	100.0%
ARR $	71	87	74	57	54	71	
Occupancy:							
Percent	51.4%	74.6%	59.3%	64.9%	57.0%	40.1%	56.5%
Room nights	76,424	114,634	38,311	59,695	32,664	73,182	394,910
Percent of total	19.4%	29.0%	9.7%	15.1%	8.3%	18.5%	100.0%

Exhibit 3.7
Projected Demand Analysis

	São Paulo		Maksoud Plaza		Caesar Park		Brasilton		Eldorado	
Annual occupancy rate (%)	50		59		62		64		52	
Available rooms	407		421		177		252		157	
Room nights	148,555		153,665		64,605		91,980		57,305	
Market Segment	RN	% Occ.	RN	% Occ.	RN	% Occ.	RN	% Occ.	RN	% Occ.
FIT (commercial)	53,179	71.4	64,715	71.2	25,264	62.8	43,736	74.1	20,562	69.5
Group (commercial)	4,916	6.6	5,896	6.5	3,302	8.2	2,774	4.7	800	2.0
FIT (social)	14,678	19.7	11,094	12.2	7,773	19.3	1,888	3.2	3,839	13.0
Group (social)	1,708	2.3	9,246	10.2	3,886	9.7	10,630	18.0	4,378	14.8
Total	74,481	100	90,951	100	40,225	100	59,028	100	29,579	100

	Ca d'Oro (August)		Crowne Plaza (August)		Mofarrej (August)		TransAmerica (November)		Total	
Annual occupancy rate (%)	59		42		37		23		55	
Available rooms	450		232		250		250		2,596	
Room nights	164,250		35,032		37,750		15,250		768,392	
Market Segment	RN	% Occ.	RN	% Occ.	RN	% Occ.	RN	% Occ.	RN	% Occ.
FIT (commercial)	74,115	76.4	9,319	62.7	9,204	64.6	2,007	57.2	302,181	71.3
Group (commercial)	2,141	3.2	1,090	7.3	1,284	9.0	351	10.0	23,554	5.6
FIT (social)	14,123	15.3	1,195	12.9	3,060	21.5	799	22.8	59,789	14.1
Group (social)	4,941	5.1	2,530	17.0	612	4.3	351	10.0	38,362	9.0
Total	97,020	100	14,854	100	14,240	100	3,508	100	423,886	100

Exhibit 3.8
Marketing Plan Abstracts

To: Senior Vice President of Marketing, Corporate Office, NYC
From: Director of Marketing, São Paulo Hotel

Following a meeting held on September 4 with Luis Filipo on our marketing plan and strategy, here are some thoughts and additional promotional ideas for the São Paulo Hotel. All these ideas are subject to your agreement.

Introduction

There is no doubt that the São Paulo Hotel will physically enjoy a renewed image with the outstanding renovated lobby and Lobby Bar. One can already hear very favorable comments from guests realizing the hotel has undertaken a serious effort to upgrade its facilities. This factor is critical to supporting any marketing actions.

However, one very essential point to consider and one that will play a tremendous role in our overall performance is "service." São Paulo Hotel offers a good service; marketing-wise we are convinced "service" will differentiate us from any other existing or new hotel in town.

The following ideas are suggested for achieving these specific objectives:

- Consolidate and secure our present market share despite new hotels.
- Anticipate the reaction to be caused by new hotel, and minimize the impact as much as possible.
- Create new business opportunities.

These ideas focus on major market segments, aside from some others geared to the market in general.

I. Executive Floors (Top Class)

The last advertising campaign had the Executive Floors as a theme. Since then, these floors have been promoted through sales personnel. Your advertising budget limitations will not allow continued advertising of this unique service. Therefore, two ideas could be developed to consolidate the image and promotion of these floors.

A) Executive Floors Brochure   This brochure will include detailed information on the Executive Floors and the service provided. It is far more than a nice room and a lounge that we are offering, and this could be clearly stressed in a single

Exhibit 3.8 *(continued)*

brochure. The brochure could be distributed by sales personnel when introducing this service, as well as be included in the preferential mail (sales and management correspondence). The brochure would only be utilized for direct mail when felt convenient. The layout could be a three-panel format and printed by your print shop.

B) *Icaro International* Now that the Executive Floors will have been completed for two years, we could develop a celebration promotion by offering a bonus to Varig International passengers through its Icaro in-flight magazine international edition. It is difficult to precisely establish the volume of incremental business this program could generate since we cannot exactly know the volume of Varig International passengers that normally utilize the Executive Floors. We estimate 0.5%, which would translate into 600 to 700 room nights a year.

II. FIT (Commercial/Social)

A) *Frequent Traveler Program* This program for FIT commercial and social business would consist of a progressive discount for a total of six visits within a period of four months (January through April).

FIT guests, upon checking out the first time, will be handed the program brochure showing the program content. On each of the next five stays, he will be granted a specific discount according to the following schedule: 2nd stay, 10% off the rack rate; each additional stay, an additional 5% off, up to the 6th stay at 30% off.

The average length of stay of FIT commercial guests is 2.35 nights, which means an average 20% discount will be granted over a total of 16.6 nights throughout six visits. Note that the purpose is to minimize the loss of FIT business to the newcoming hotels and to ensure the FIT guest loyalty to the São Paulo Hotel as much as possible.

The cost for this program will only be that of producing the Frequent Traveler brochure. The program will not be available for the Executive Floors and will not be commissionable.

B) *Microcomputer for Guests* As an additional service to the guests, a room could be set up with a microcomputer and technical program for the use of guests. The computer could be easily obtained from a local manufacturer such as Itautec on a promotional basis, and this could be promoted as one more service. Most executives nowadays require permanent access to a computer for their data

---

Exhibit 3.8 *(continued)*

---

processing, and it could be a meaningful tool. We could have this available on a trial basis.

C) Interior Sales Coverage   Since three years ago, the 3,570 annual guests from the state interior have increased to this year's 5,857 guests. It is clear that there is an excellent potential from that area. Sales coverage in major towns should be intensified by planning trips for next year. Rio production has also increased from 6,491 guests to 9,192, which also indicates the need for a continued and expanded coverage of that market.

D) Service Committee   Along the lines of permanent monitoring of service, a rotating "service committee" could be created where members are selected from staff supervisory level and changed every month. This committee would meet twice a month or at department head meetings, to report on what they observed. No department head should be part of the committee. This initiative would help in monitoring quality and would show employees our permanent concern with their performance.

E) Transportation Project   Considering our location problems vis-à-vis the existing airport, the São Paulo Hotel together with the Brasilton and Ca d'Oro could establish a free transportation service to and from the intracountry Congonhas Airport only for hotel guests. If feasible, this would mean the hotels in this part of town (versus Maksoud, Caesar, Mofarrej, and Crowne Plaza) will be offering a unique service. If you agree with this idea, a meeting between the three hotel managers could be arranged to discuss the project, and we could obtain a quotation from a ground transportation agent and clearance from the airport authority.

III. Executive Business Service (EBS)

The EBS business represents a significant share of our business mix and, despite our efforts to control it, we are always bound to see it moving to competitive hotels. The research New York is conducting to define a new modus operandi for this segment will be a very important step in establishing a new strategy. While we have some thoughts on this particular item, we prefer to wait for the research results before making any decision on the rate concessions. Nevertheless some other actions can be taken to help secure this business. For example:

Exhibit 3.8 *(continued)*

A) EBS Stuffer   Aside from a special rate, there is a variety of other services and attentions we provide EBS accounts such as speedy check-in, checkout, late checkout, room upgrade, credit, executive card, etc.

Many times the accounts do not seem to visualize the convenience of such facilities and therefore regard the EBS program as a rate concession only. A stuffer on this program's privileges can be distributed by sales personnel on their calls and by the front office staff to EBS guests. This will show that we offer things to EBS customers that most hotels in town do not.

B) Executive Card   The Executive Card program is coming along fairly well. Over 700 cards are already distributed; however, this volume can be greatly expanded. The marketing plan for next year includes a specific program for this; however, it will not be carried out due to advertising budget limitations. We would like to propose a different approach to promote this program:

1. A personal visit with you would be planned for top existing and potential accounts that could provide us with more business. The president or top executives of these accounts would be visited as a courtesy and upon the visit handed an Executive Card. This could open doors to two things:
   a. Allow for eventual interest in the card program for other company executives upon recommendation by the top man.
   b. Attempt to expand the business from these accounts with the top man approbation.
2. Intensify the card promotion in São Paulo by sales personnel and at the front desk for checking in/out guests.
3. Make sales trips to Brasília, Porto Alegre, Belo Horizonte, and Rio to promote the card, plus ads in those cities.

IV. Package

Thirty-seven percent of Package business is booked in São Paulo and 24 percent of these guests originate from here. Seventy-two percent of all package reservations are booked by guests directly. Aside from the ongoing packages promotion, we thought of creating a new package called "Acredite se quiser" labeled according to the quite popular program on TV, "Manchete" (the American "Believe It or Not").

This package, which would include the basic contents of the usual weekend package, could be promoted through the normal channels. However, we could

Exhibit 3.8 *(continued)*

try a different approach and have it displayed in one of São Paulo's largest supermarkets, The Eldorado, just like any other product. The gimmick is that it is not usual to see this kind of promotion in such places. However, the Eldorado receives daily hundreds and hundreds of visitors (potential buyers) who, being from São Paulo, would be easily reached to be sold a weekend package. The idea may sound fancy, but it could produce weekend business. Obviously, there would be some costs involved like producing the flyer and the display. Similar displays could be placed in other shopping centers in town.

Another type of package could be arranged with a microcomputer manufacturer. Courses in microprocessing could be promoted on weekends at the hotel. Computers are now in fashion, and we could get some manufacturer interested in joining this program, including rooms for participants from other cities.

V. Food and Beverage

With the closing of the Roof restaurant, the hotel is left with a limited number of options for entertainment. Aside from the beautiful Lobby Bar and the refurbished theater, the only outlet left is the London Tavern.

We believe that a Brazilian popular music program could be organized by occasionally having typical Brazilian singers perform at the London Tavern during the week. Something along the lines of a "Cafe Concerto" where one could hear nice Brazilian music by traditional artists. This should not be a profit-minded program but a PR and sales promotion approach toward the local community and one that could help establish the hotel image.

Conclusion

I know there is a lot to discuss about these ideas, and eventually some may not be applicable for various reasons. However, one has to realize that under present circumstances and in view of the money limitation for broader advertising, the objective of these thoughts is to take advantage of the momentum whereby the hotel looks physically renewed, and to stress this by as many promotional actions as possible.

Case Four

Victoria Station Restaurants

Robert C. Lewis

In 1969, Richard Bradley, a former investment broker, Robert Freeman, a former in-flight service supervisor for Pan American Airlines, and Peter Lee, a former Sky Chef cost analyst, had two things in common: they were 1963 graduates of the Cornell Hotel School, and they wanted to organize a quality operating business enterprise where operations were critical to success. Bradley, Lee, and Freeman felt they had the ability to operate nearly any type of business, but wanted to obtain maximum leverage. The restaurant opportunity presented itself first. They finally decided on a limited-menu theme restaurant in the mid-priced market. After much discussion the concept of Victoria Station was agreed on, based on the elements they considered crucial for success: concept uniqueness, quality control, and financial control.

BACKGROUND

Concept Uniqueness

Victoria Station was designed for the growing number of singles, couples, and families who liked to eat out but who could not afford high prices. Victoria Station featured prime rib of beef served in a unique railroad atmosphere of boxcars converted into restaurants. The interiors of the boxcars were refurbished to retain as much authenticity as possible includ-

This case was written by Robert C. Lewis, University of Guelph, Ontario. All rights reserved.

ing railroad equipment and memorabilia. Old baggage carts were used as room dividers and tables. Prime rib was displayed in large glass-front refrigerators in the central bar area.

Gas lights, a red English telephone booth, and a London taxi were placed in front of the restaurants, which depended largely on the unique exteriors to draw customers. Prime rib was the major menu drawing card. At the time, it was usually sold only in expensive restaurants whereas steak and lobster restaurants were plentiful.

The first restaurants seated about 150 persons. Male college students were used as waiters, while young women provided cocktail service. The atmosphere at a Victoria Station was very relaxed. It was possible for a couple to enjoy a prime-rib dinner, which represented approximately 70 percent of orders, with salad and wine for approximately $15.00 including tip. The average lunch check was $4.00 without tip.

No advertising or paid promotion was utilized, and the restaurants relied entirely on initial publicity before opening and on word-of-mouth advertising for their marketing success. Simply being open for lunch, particularly in downtown areas, was considered by management to be a form of advertising for couples or family dinner business.

Quality Control

Management felt that its first job was to ensure uniformly high quality at all locations. Beef was cut to specification, and Victoria Station used controlled-portion filets and top sirloin butts. Produce and most service items and accessories were purchased locally from an approved purveyor list. A computerized checking system verified that unapproved vendors would be brought to management's attention.

Execution was a matter of strong management supervision to ensure strict adherence to standards, which were defined in a comprehensive operations manual. Appearance, food preparation and service, beverage preparation and service, atmosphere, equipment maintenance, safety, inventory control, and other matters were set down in detail, together with complete job descriptions for all managers. A checklist was the basis for determining whether the manager and his two assistants would be eligible for a semiannual performance bonus. Failure to qualify for the performance bonus eliminated an individual from participation in the profitability bonus.

Financial Control

Financial control was maintained through detailed reports. Daily meal counts, sales receipts and expenditure reports, and sales breakdowns for food, wine, and other beverages were tallied for each waiter at both lunch and dinner. Daily inventories were taken. A profit-and-loss statement was prepared monthly for each restaurant. Computer operations provided financial analysis of similar-sized restaurants by region, budget and actual variance, man-hours, revenues per seat, and revenues per square foot.

Meat costs represented 70 percent of food costs and management constantly monitored meat prices. Prices were following an upward trend, and it was felt that there would be an increase of 12 to 18 percent over the next 12 months. This emphasized the need for a well-executed cost control program.

1973

By late 1973, the initial phases of the development strategy had been completed. President Bradley and Vice Presidents Freeman and Lee were preparing for the next growth phase by developing operating controls and reporting procedures to maintain profits, while continuing to open new units. Victoria Stations numbered 17 by that time, with an additional five under construction, and 10 more committed to or being designed. The financial community described the Victoria Station growth record as most impressive. The stock was selling at about $18.00 a share with a price/earnings ratio of approximately 59 times 1972 earnings. Analysts felt that the price was justified based on past and anticipated growth, but was dependent on a continued record of growth in the number of units and profitability. The annual report for the year ending March 31, 1973, contained the following statements:

> It is gratifying to report that fiscal year 1973 was unquestionably the most successful in the history of Victoria Station. In many ways 1973

was truly a spectacular year, particularly for so young a corporation. Challenges, often severe and frequently beyond our control or that of any lone corporation, also abounded during fiscal 1973. Sharply rising costs in virtually all areas, frequent frustrating construction delays, and significantly increased competition, often from vastly larger organizations, were major problems we faced most of the year. Nevertheless, we close out 1973 by all standards a far stronger company than we were 12 months ago. Perhaps the true measure of 1973 is the height of our achievements, given our rapid rate of growth and the challenges created by it and a host of other factors. . . .

At a meeting of the company's officers, the following remarks were made in regard to the future:

> We have built the foundations for a much larger company. The cost controls, quality controls, and organization we have installed are intended for the future. If we were planning to stay at our present size, these expenditures would not be necessary. The financial community has high expectations for Victoria Station. They expect fast, steady, profitable growth. How fast does growth have to be to satisfy them and our investors? The real question, however, is how fast does it have to be to satisfy ourselves? How much should we sacrifice day-to-day operations to maintain growth just to please others? Should we be concerned that we are losing our objective?

1976

In June 1976, the company operated 46 Victoria Station restaurants. Prime rib was 51 percent of sales, and the restaurants were a popular rendezvous for dinner, cocktails, and lunch. Three other restaurants with diversified themes in the San Francisco Bay Area were additions to the company's business: Thomas Lord's was designed after an English sporting tavern; The Royal Exchange in the financial district had an English stock exchange atmosphere; and Quinn's Lighthouse, located in a renovated Coast Guard lighthouse, featured seafood as well as beef entrees. The company also operated the Plantation Gardens restaurant on the island of Kauai, Hawaii.

Atlanta, Georgia, was the location of the most radical diversification. Quinn's Mill restaurant resembled an old grist mill and featured an expanded menu, including appetizers, which no other Victoria Station property served. The restaurant had a spectacular lakeshore location.

Victoria Station had gained national recognition. A television network special cited its restaurants, among all the so-called theme restaurants, as models of effective execution. *Business Week* featured Richard Bradley in a two-page article. Bradley was also named "Man of the Year" by the Multi-Unit Food Service Operators Association at its annual convention.

Marketing

With competition increasing, management was determining the necessary strategy that would enable it to dominate the industry in the years to come. The company established a marketing department to increase sales growth in existing properties. The present Director of Human Resources, Harlow White, also took on the job of Director of Marketing. He felt that the company was not using its marketing information to best advantage and that restaurants were losing marketing opportunities because they did not know how to generate additional business. White's view of the reasons for the company's success was as follows:

> It was product definition that made us do so well. We concluded that we were selling a product that was more than a piece of meat on a plate, more than an ounce and a quarter shot in a 13 ounce glass. It was a total experience. The general ambience of the restaurant, the quality of the product, the size of the portions, and the architecture of the place all contributed.

Success had been attained without paid advertising, except for direct-mail announcements at the time of each restaurant's opening. While the restaurants were under construction, management sought TV and press coverage for free publicity. Prior to opening, lists of prospective customers were obtained from country clubs, banking contacts, and the American Express mailing list for a direct mailing to some 20,000 persons. Management felt that the food, service, and atmosphere offered would provide the best advertising by word of mouth.

It was also felt, however, that some primary research should be conducted to determine the market segments attracted to the restaurants. A market research firm used in-house interviews to establish a consumer profile and geographic target markets. In addition, awareness and trial levels and customer perceptions were obtained from telephone interviews. It was found that customers tended to be under 35, college-educated, and married, with annual incomes of $20,000 or more.

Customers most often mentioned food (71 percent), atmosphere (65 percent), and service (24 percent) as what they liked about Victoria Station. Over two-thirds saw the restaurants as specializing in red meat, and one-third mentioned prime rib as the specialty. Total awareness of Victoria Station was found to range from 71 to 84 percent of the sample in the three cities surveyed, while unaided awareness ranged from 5 to 16 percent. From 38 to 51 percent of the sample had patronized Victoria Station, while 32 to 41 percent listed themselves as current patrons. Five to 8 percent named Victoria Station as their most patronized restaurant. These figures were all considerably below those of the leading competitors in each city, showing that there was considerable potential for improvement.

Management was most surprised when the survey showed that atmosphere was such an important perception for the respondents, as they had put so much emphasis on the quality of the food product. They felt that success could not be based on atmosphere because this attribute was vulnerable to erosion from competition. This led them to decide that advertising emphasis should stress the food, and a billboard campaign was developed featuring "Perhaps the Finest Prime Rib Ever." Brochures were printed with food pictures and the same tag line. Radio advertising emphasized the food, and then the atmosphere. Local managers were not involved in advertising policy decisions.

Competition and Strategy

The limited-menu theme restaurant was highly in vogue by 1976, much of it targeting the singles market. Victoria Station, however, concentrated on the dinner business of couples and families. There were a number of imitators, as well, using the boxcar dining concept. Large companies also joined the theme restaurant fray. Pillsbury acquired Steak & Ale, a 100-unit English pub concept. General Mills bought the 180-unit Red Lobster seafood chain and planned other concepts. Far West Services operated theme restaurants under the names Reuben's, The Plankhouse, Moonraker, and Reuben E. Lee. Saga was operating Velvet Turtle, Black Angus, and The Refectory. All of these concepts competed broadly in the Victoria Station market segment.

Victoria Station's policy had been to build only in areas with a population of 1 million or more, as this was considered the level necessary to maintain consistent volume. In 1976–1977, management changed this policy and started building in areas of lower population in places like Virginia, Maryland, and Canada.

Management also recognized that, on any given night, customers' desires in food type would vary. To capture the same market in these cases, it was decided that a second but different restaurant was appropriate for expansion in selected market areas.

Other multiunit operators were beginning to build larger units that enabled them to produce higher-volume levels with lower fixed-cost percentages. Accordingly, Victoria Station increased the size of its new units to 300 seats wherever possible. It was found, however, that after the initial opening rush, sales tended to slacken. Advertising was planned to counteract this.

The pricing of menu items was changed from the previous one-price policy throughout the country to one of regional pricing, based on perceived value in local markets. The company strongly fought any price increases, as management's strategy included a high price-per-value offering. At some locations, both prices and portion sizes were reduced.

By the end of 1976, management's future plans envisioned at least 150 Victoria Stations in North America. They were still unsure how large a population was required to support a Victoria Station. As costs of construction increased, plans were made to put more emphasis on the food product and less on the decor. The threat of competition from large, sophisticated operators was omnipresent; management's challenge was to be prepared to meet it.

1978/1979

In 1978, almost 100 Victoria Stations throughout the country were grossing up to $1.5 million a year, on average. However, beef prices had started to rise in 1976 and were continuing an upward trend. Nevertheless, 1978 fiscal-year revenues had increased 32 percent over 1977 to $101.2 million, and earnings had risen 20 percent to almost $5 million.

In 1979, sales increased 18.5 percent to $120 million, but income declined 30 percent to $3.3 million. The profit slide was attributed to a decline in customer counts, partly due to the 1979 gasoline crunch and general economic malaise.

1980

In fiscal year 1980, Victoria Station experienced the first loss in its 10-year history, accumulating sales of $128 million while losing $1.2 million. The average unit volume slipped to $1.3 million. The year 1980 also marked the beginning of a series of turnaround efforts.

Brunch

In 1979, the chain offered brunch in 34 units across the country, but the concept did not catch on in the Southwest, so it was discontinued in that area. In January 1980, the chain started to add brunch to carefully selected restaurants in the East, Midwest, and West, where management believed customers would be predisposed to accept it. Management expected to have brunch in one-third of the 103 units by September and, ultimately, in about 60 units. Senior Vice President of Marketing Paul Sheppard said that brunch would be added only in those units with above-average performance, and would be discontinued if the unit failed to sell 125 to 150 brunches per Sunday. Besides a fruit bar, there was also a "Station Master's Counter" where eggs Benedict, quiche, scrambled eggs, eggs Florentine, lox and bagels, sauteed mushrooms, and prime rib carved to order were available. "All you can eat" was $7.95 for adults, $3.95 for children under 12, and free for children under five. Food costs were higher than the chain's standard 40 percent, but the company looked to build high margins on items like dessert.

Price Reductions

In July, after a quarter of even revenues but a loss of $663,000 compared to net earnings of $876,000 the year before, Victoria Station began changing menu prices, instituting new promotions, and converting some of its less profitable units to new concepts. The company implemented price reductions in many of its units to improve traffic. Plans were to increase them again gradually while concurrently upgrading the product offerings to reflect a proper price/value relationship. Menu offerings were reevaluated, as was the total Victoria Station dining experience.

Barbeque Ribs

To broaden its traditional customer base, the company promoted all-you-can-eat barbecue beef ribs for $6.95 in a special heavily advertised summer campaign. The eight-week "Have I Got a Barbecue for You" campaign raised the customer count about 30 percent, according to executives, after they had been down 15 percent. The rib promotion gave people a good reason to come back, according to Sheppard.

New Concepts

Three units were closed for renovations and repositioning. According to President Bradley, each was in a good restaurant market but had become inappropriate for the standard Victoria Station concept. One unit was reopened as Mules, featuring sandwiches in a pub atmosphere. Another was reborn as a limited-menu, medium-priced French cafe and bar called Bistrot Les Halles. The third reopened in Toronto as an eastside New York–style saloon called The Temperance Grill at Yorkville. Bradley said that other marginal units might be converted to one of the new concepts in the future.

Game Hens

In the fall of 1980, Victoria Station rolled out a promotion to introduce a "gourmet" game hen entree. Similar to a Cornish hen, it had been pretested in 16 cities. Sheppard, now Executive Vice President, said that while Victoria Station would probably not attempt to shed its image as a prime-rib house, there would be a subtle deemphasis of prime rib on the menu. The game hen promotion was designed to draw new customers into the restaurants without actually shedding the prime-rib image. The promotions were also calculated to allow the company to restructure its menu while broadening the base of its traditional customer demographics.

Personnel Changes

The chain reduced its regional manager team from 19 to 14. It also hired a new advertising agency, Bozell and Jacobs, and established a network of 12 public relations companies across the country. Jon Rose, formerly with Bozell and Jacobs, was named Marketing Director; Laura Phillips, who had been with the National Restaurant Association, was named Public Relations Director; and Victoria Victory, former Field Marketing Manager, was named Director of Advertising. Peter Lee, Executive Vice President and one of the founders, resigned for personal reasons. The position Vice President for Corporate Development was eliminated and its occupant also resigned. Also eliminated were the positions Director of Corporate Projects, Director of Architecture, and Director of Engineering and Construction.

Despite the personnel changes, Sheppard said there was a new enthusiasm among the company's employees, a good deal of which was due to the success of the barbecued-rib promotion. Sheppard would not predict the financial future of the company, saying only that he was optimistic and that the year was one of transition and rebuilding.

In December, Richard Bradley, President, CEO, and one of the founders, announced his resignation as soon as a successor could be found. He continued as Chairman. No reason was given. Also in December, Victoria Station suspended its quarterly dividend. Sheppard, who was now spearheading the turnaround and was a candidate for the President's slot, stated, "I am looking for other significant [personnel] cuts, both in the field and at headquarters, to expedite specific fourth-quarter goals."

The Menu

The menu was quietly expanded from seven to 15 items. "By January, we will have a new format menu with 20-plus items," Sheppard said. The items were to include fish, shellfish, and a variety of casserole dishes. Sheppard said that the new menu emphasis away from red meats, combined with the decreased cost of red meats, could speed a possible turnaround.

An outside observer visited a Victoria Station restaurant in December 1980 and made the comments contained in Exhibit 4.1.

Exhibit 4.1
An Observer's Comments on One Particular Victoria Station

Victoria Station is a theme restaurant, serving American food and offering a unique fun dining experience. Though this location is superb, the setting is unattractive. The restaurant is situated in a large, bare parking lot with little landscaping. Improvements such as plusher surroundings could help stress its theme.

The theme of Victoria Station is a British railroad station, reflected in both the indoor and outdoor decor of the restaurant, which consists of British railway artifacts. From the time reservations are made to the time of departure, the mood is effectively set for an exciting dining experience in a railroad boxcar.

First Impressions

Upon arrival, one can see several adjoining train cars that form Victoria Station. They look like old-fashioned train cars. They are muddy red in color and sit on steel railroad tracks. There is even a red caboose! At the foot of the entrance is an old-fashioned red telephone booth. Along the outside of the train cars are black steel railroad traffic lamps.

One enters the restaurant through the caboose and is greeted by a friendly hostess. Above her head is a small-scale model of the restaurant protruding from the wall. The hostess suggests a seat at one of the cocktail tables while waiting for a dinner table. On the cocktail tables are jars of cheddar cheese and baskets of crackers. Friendly waitresses quickly return with the cocktail of choice.

There are two flaws with the cocktail system. One is the television at the bar, which takes away from the restaurant's atmosphere. The other is that waitresses bombard the customer too frequently, a bit too eager to take an order, which becomes annoying.

Atmosphere and Artifacts

As one awaits a seat for dinner, everywhere he looks are different sections, or "depots," all having signs, decorations, or contraptions dealing with train sched-

Exhibit 4. *(continued)*

ules, passengers, or train cars. Also noticeable is the steel of the outside decor continuing inside, which gives the feeling of continuity and realism and the sense that one is really in a train station. Placing the cocktail tables in the center of activity gives the customer a chance to get into the mood of the place. One feels like he is people-watching at a train station.

Looking up, one can see that a busy decor prevails. There are two large skylights. Large steel beams support the ceiling. A ladder leads to a high loft where trunks, duffle bags, and beer drums are loosely scattered under a sign reading "Baggage Claim." Plants hang from the barnboard rafters. Even the bar is involved in this decor: there are screened box compartments filled with wines and connected to the rafters.

The kitchen's food-pickup window also resembles a train stop, as it is decorated with copper lamps and headed with a depot name. The cooks are dressed as train conductors in blue-and-white overalls and caps.

A customer sits in one of the dining cars to have dinner. Each dining car has separate compartments, which are individual tables made of barnboard. Before sitting down, you can hang your coat on a steel spike coatrack. The tables are set with a simple red tablecloth and traditional silverware, dishes, and glasses. Each dining compartment has its own small traffic light, which is dim enough to set a romantic atmosphere for two. On the wall is a picture of an old train or a train schedule. At the end of the car is a framed layout design of a train.

Busboys, waiters, and waitresses are dressed in simple street clothes and employ typical American service. The menu is a piece of paper burned around the edges, shellacked onto a slim, rectangular piece of wood, headed "NOTICE." All foods are listed under "Tracks" or "Platforms." Track One is a choice of "Engineman's Soup" or "Baggage Cart Salad Bar." Platform Two is the entree list, Platform Three is vegetables, and Platform Four is desserts and beverages. The bottom of the menu states management's goal: to provide the customer with the best food and service available. Management urges complaints if the customer is not satisfied.

Final Impressions

Victoria Station has some good points as well as some flaws. The aisles in each dining car are very narrow. There is no room for the waiter or waitress to put the meals down before putting them on the customer's table. A greater problem is that parties on one side of the car are very close to those on the other side,

Exhibit 4.1 *(continued)*

limiting the privacy of the experience. Another fault is the limitation of the menu; it is geared toward the American steak-and-potato customer. The limited menu and the high prices make the restaurant dependent on its unique atmosphere.

Victoria Station is not a typical family restaurant. One would not want to bring children here, since prices are high and there are no children's portions. The restaurant is geared toward the night-out group, specifically couples, who want high-class atmosphere, food, and service. The entire property is dimly lighted, which sets a romantic mood. Dress ranges from smart casual to three-piece suits.

Victoria Station has the usual promotional items such as matchbooks, postcards, and napkins, all headed with the restaurant's trademark. They also have items such as gift certificates, food coupons, and promotional material for private parties, conventions, and birthday parties.

The atmosphere of Victoria Station is busy like a train station, yet it is unrushed for the customer. There is a comfortable amount of time between courses so one can relax, chat, and digest. Management seems to attempt to play on the imaginative, fun side of the customer, while still maintaining high-quality standards of good food and service.

Victoria Station is as close to a railway station as a restaurant could be. Although there are several flaws in the layout and service, the restaurant is a most enjoyable one. The facilities are clean and well tended; the staff is well trained, well mannered, and hospitable; the food is superb; and the atmosphere is unusually delightful.

1981

By 1981, it appeared that Victoria Station was getting back on track. An article in *Restaurant Business* outlined the past problems:

It was inevitable. Victoria Station followed a story line all too familiar to developing restaurant chains. Its mis-steps included:

- Over-expansion—opening too many new units in too many new markets in too short a time span.
- An inflexible approach to interior and exterior design.

- An over-reliance on a red meat–based menu.
- An insufficient reservoir of trained, competent unit management.

At the same time, these internal mistakes were compounded by such external factors as skyrocketing food, energy, and labor costs and a rapid shift in the tastes of the dining-out public.

. . . Losses have continued through the first two quarters of fiscal 1981, but the chain's current management believes the downward trend, while continuing through the third quarter, will be arrested in the fourth quarter and reversed in the first quarter of fiscal 1982. According to Paul Sheppard, "We'll break even at the end of fiscal 1981 and be much better positioned for 1982, when we'll be up again. It's not a matter of *wanting* to be up; we *have* to be up."

Today, Victoria Station is in the hardest phase—the turnaround—of the so-called "chain restaurant life-cycle." Management has attacked a variety of problem areas and devised a program to return the chain to its past successes, with these key elements:

- A halt in unit expansion.
- Reorganization of the management structure at every level.
- Increased cost controls at each level, watched on a daily basis.
- The addition of new menu items.
- Changes in its menu pricing strategy.
- New marketing and promotional techniques to hold the traditional customer base while expanding the chain's appeal.
- The closing of some units, remodeling and conversion of others.

A sense of urgency exists in the chain's headquarters as well as in the field; public optimism and private worry characterize chain employees; the entire corporate staff is aware that decisions they make now will determine whether the chain continues to exist.[1]

The departure of Bradley was believed to signal the beginning of a change from "entrepreneurial" to "professional" management. Sheppard was the front-running candidate for President, and the current direction

[1] "Getting Back on Track," *Restaurant Business* (January 1, 1981), p. 23. Other parts of this section also draw from this article.

of the chain came primarily from him. Sheppard stated, "There will be absolutely no new units built until we see concrete, ongoing evidence that the numbers have changed."

The major problem seen to be facing the company was falling customer counts caused by a declining price-per-value perception of Victoria Station. Bradley, however, defended the chain's history.

> . . . We were also caught in some other binds not of our making. First of all, the economy was getting squeamish. Our segment was impacted first, and the results have hung on longer. We were in a rising cost environment which we couldn't control and were unable to pass on those costs through increased menu prices because of customer resistance. Also, customer spending habits and tastes were changing. We may have made tactical errors, but I disagree with critics who claim our theme is outdated. Decor is not the determining factor—price, food quality, and service are all more important than decor.

Sheppard agreed: "After 10 years, I think it is safe to say that the decor concept has withstood the test of time."

An all-out attempt was made to bring customers back into the restaurants. Better cost controls, improved communications, and a cut in support-service expenses were instituted, in addition to attempts to make the company more responsive both from the bottom up and from the top down. To attract more customers and adjust the poor consumer perception of price per value, the company inaugurated "Operation Rollback," during which prices in two-thirds of the restaurants were decreased anywhere from 11 to 22 percent. This caused some additional problems, however. Victoria Station had cut prices to the point where they further eroded profit margins. According to Sheppard,

> Operation Rollback created some problems in that we established a new base from which we had to raise prices. Although we brought the customers in because of the program, it did have some long-lasting unfortunate consequences. We're still trying to get to where we should have been in relationship to the price of beef.

However, the company also saw positive effects in preparing the chain for a return to higher customer counts. According to Bradley, "Rollback made us return to the basics—service, food, quality, and attitude. Today we can go after more customers with the confidence that we can handle them."

The new emphasis could be seen at Victoria Station headquarters, where a second-floor office was emblazoned with a large sign reading, "War Room." Walls were covered with performance charts for each unit. The room had a large conference table at which department heads met regularly. If a unit was in good shape, it was left alone, but the wall charts highlighted any apparent difficulties so that they could be addressed promptly. The focus was on results. Said Sheppard,

> Each manager reports weekly. That includes sales and food and labor costs for both the current week and the next week's objectives. By keeping an eye on those figures and comparing them to objectives almost daily, we can see where the problems are and move on them immediately. We have already succeeded in lowering our food costs six points in 60 days through unit level controls coupled with our changed price strategy. Our purchasing is better, our pricing is more equitable on our new menu items, and labor hours are scheduled more tightly. We are managing the company on a daily basis.

Menu changes were made to reduce the image of a "prime-rib palace," which more or less excluded from the customer base those persons who did not eat beef. Shrimp Victoria or teriyaki chicken with prime rib or top sirloin, and shrimp Victoria with teriyaki chicken replaced the 23-ounce "Owner's Cut" of prime rib with its high food cost. "The response has been excellent," said Sheppard, "and we anticipate more additions to the menu along those lines—items we haven't been known for in the past which the customer is looking for today."

Other additions included an "Inflation-Fighter's Special" at lunch for $2.95, a teriyaki chicken breast with rice or an artichoke, and spinach quiche with salad. A children's menu was also introduced. "The door is open," said Sheppard. "We're not locked into anything." Added Sheppard, "Today, we're looking for a wider customer base, and I feel we're succeeding. We're less skewed toward one customer and attracting more families, seniors, and non–red meat eaters."

In referring to the game hen promotion, an item which remained on the regular menu, Jon Rose, Vice President of Marketing, said, "It's a good new product with a good food cost. And the message is, 'Victoria

Station has something different, good, and inexpensive, and it's not red meat.' " According to Rose, the hen promotion did not generate customer count increases, but it was not expected to. "We just wanted to get across the message that we're changing. Our new-item promotions are designed to communicate to the public that Victoria Station is diversified and affordable."

Sheppard decentralized marketing and promotional activities and hired six public relations firms across the country to help create a less chainlike image. Some units were closed and others remodeled or repositioned. According to one corporate executive, "I think all we need is time. If the lenders are willing to give us that time, we'll make it. If not, I just don't know what will happen."

Sheppard was generally seen as the man to get most of the credit if the company made a turnaround. In January, the Board of Directors named Sheppard Chief Operating Officer, reporting only to the board, with all divisions reporting to him. His rise was seen as meteoric in the nine months since he had left Marriott Corporation as Vice President of International Operations.

THE GUARD CHANGES

Nation's Restaurant News (March 16, 1981) carried the following news item:

Collins New CEO at Victoria Station

Larkspur, Calif.—Terrance A. Collins has joined financially troubled Victoria Station as president and chief executive officer. He was president of General Foods Burger Chef chain for four years. Collins, 39, replaces Richard Bradley who resigned last October. Bradley was the last of the 90-unit specialty dinnerhouse chain's founders to leave the company. But he remains board chairman.

Collins makes the transition from the fast food segment to a dinnerhouse chain with this switch. He has 13 years experience in the fast food business, first as western regional vice-president for McDonald's and, since 1977, as head of the 900-unit Burger Chef hamburger chain. . . .

Collins' task as the new president will be to pull the ailing restaurant chain into full financial recovery. However, company officials pointed out that for the month of December, the company showed its first operating profit in 15 months.

The March 28 issue of *Nation's Restaurant News* carried these items:

Victoria Station Reorganizes

Larkspur, Calif.—A tremendous reorganization of Victoria Station is underway, along with extensive menu testing and marketing programs.

Currently, four new menu programs are ongoing at various Victoria Stations throughout the country. All the menu changes are designed to appeal to a large segment of the population.

Victoria Station had been recognized mostly as a roast beef and red meat dining facility. "Because of the limited appeal menu, people weren't coming as frequently," a spokeswoman said, adding that the trend in dining is toward a lighter diet and less red meat. An extensive selection including lighter fares and many "stack-type" items is being pilot tested for use in other Victoria Stations. Among the items featured are, "It's a Crock" (soup), "There's No Tamale" (chile nachos, quesadillas, Mexican pizza), "Quiche Me Quick" (artichoke and spinach or crab quiche), and "Network" (seafood).

To date, the new menu has been "extremely successful" in so far as cocktail and dinner business has improved greatly, the spokeswoman said.

The second ongoing promotion features Dungeness crab from Oregon. When first introduced last month in Dallas, the item went over so well that an additional 40,000 pounds had to be shipped to the restaurant the first week. The number of units in which this promotion will be featured will depend on the supply of the crab. The third promotion, "All you can eat B-B-Q chicken and ribs," will be featured in southern California. A fourth promotion, "the inflation-fighters luncheon," will be used in most of the Victoria Stations in the western region of the country, and on a limited basis in the east. It offers a choice of a cheeseburger with french fries, an artichoke and spinach quiche with soup of the day, or teriyaki chicken breast with rice pilaf for $2.95. For an additional $1.25, the customer has unlimited use of the salad bar.

The pilot programs are in the initial stages, the spokeswoman said, explaining that it is too early to know how extensive their use will be throughout the chain.

Victoria Station Testing All-Day Menus in 3 Units

Larkspur, Calif.—In its later effort to improve customer counts and stimulate repeat business, Victoria Station has introduced experimental all-day menus in 3 of the chain's 99 units. The chain traditionally has used separate lunch and dinner menus.

The new menus offer a wide variety of items at price points that appeal to a larger segment of customers, marketing vice president Jon Rose said.

. . . "Preliminary results are very positive," Rose said. He said the test would run for at least three months before the company would judge the success of the experiment.

The new menus are printed on a huge roll of butcher shop brown paper and are left on the roll and handed to customers as they enter the restaurant.

Collins—Victoria Station's Mystery Man

Larkspur, Calif.—. . . Although sources say he appeared to be happy at Burger Chef, Collins decided it was the right time for a change. "Aside from the fact that he was well compensated, Terry apparently felt that he could make a real contribution at Victoria Station," a high-level source said. "It was a challenge. I'm not a safe player," Collins said, in a 1977 interview for the Burger Chef publication, *Scene.*

. . . Collins is currently involved in a period of assessment at the chain and is scheduled for a two-week cross-country trip to visit many of the company's 99 units. "He's a very one-on-one person," Victoria Station vice president of marketing Jon Rose says. . . . "He wants to make sure he's fully aware of everything before making any major decisions."

What those major decisions may be is still unclear. And chain officials note that many of the "hard decisions" have already been made. "[Collins is] joining a company that is fairly on its way to recovery," Rose says.

Many of those decisions have been made by executive vice president and COO Paul G. Sheppard. . . . Under Sheppard, management ranks have been pared [both at] headquarters and in the field. His turnaround strategy, centered around decreasing the operational expenses while increasing customer counts through menu expansion and heavy promotion, appears to be showing some signs of success. . . . Overall customer counts are reportedly up over last year and sources say the chain stands a good chance of showing a profit in the final quarter.

Despite the modest improvements, some analysts maintain that very serious problems remain. "Efforts have been made to change the format and the menu, and they've done some good creative advertising, but nothing seems to stick," says Edward M. Tavlin, an analyst with Prescott, Bull and Turben.

"They've got a very heavy capital expenditure in each unit, requiring high unit volumes and they have been impacted in a large part by circumstances beyond their control [rising red meat prices]," he said. "The unit itself is more of a novelty type," he continued, "and the big question is whether it can stand the test of time."

. . . Collins is the lead role in a play that is still being written. The play is about survival. Whether that drama turns into a triumph or a tragedy is yet to be determined.

By June 1981, Victoria Station's menu had a completely new look both in format and in menu offerings. The changes, rolled out nationally during that month, were aimed at broadening the chain's market appeal by offering more variety and lower-priced items. The menu was leather-bound with a printed insert instead of the boards that had been used in the past, but it still had a train motif and theme. It contained new appetizers, a wine list, special house drinks, and a half dozen more entrees. The changes had been tested in 10 markets.

Appetizers, which had not generally been on previous menus, included potato skins, nachos, and zucchini. New entrees were boneless filet of salmon, stuffed shrimp, an 8-ounce cut of prime rib, teriyaki beef kabob, and Shrimp Diana, which was shrimp baked in wine, cheese, garlic, and bread crumbs. The new entrees included a starch accompaniment, which previously one had to order separately.

Although the new items had lower prices, management expected the check average to remain the same, at about $14.00, because there were more items to choose from, such as appetizers and drinks. These were expected to offset the lower-priced entrees in the total check. The company was also testing all-day menus in three of its units. These menus included such items as soup, salad, chili, nachos, quesadillas, artichoke-and-spinach quiche, crab quiche, and seafood. The new menu quickly improved food-cost figures, according to Rose.

Also introduced in 1981 was a new wine program. After careful study over a year's time, three core wine lists were designed for various sections of the United States and Canada. A special feature was a carefully selected group of California and imported wines available by the glass as well as by the bottle. An extensive training program in wine identification, appreciation, and service was initiated. A special handbook was developed for employees that included a description of the basic elements of wine and the steps in the production of wine from the vine to the bottle. Also included were a glossary of wine terms, features of wine service, and suggestive selling and merchandising techniques. "Wine of the Month" and "Manager's Selection" were also featured. "From the patron's point of view," said Rose, "the opportunity to try before you buy, and sampling a wine or two by the glass before ordering a bottle, provided an easy and inexpensive way to compare wines and develop a certain expertise."

In the fiscal quarter ending June 1981, the chain reported a net profit of $703,000 on sales of $30.1 million, as opposed to a net loss for the first quarter of $1.2 million on the same amount of sales. According to Collins, the positive results where due to a continued cost control program, the new expanded menu, and elimination of several marginal properties. He also stated that the results provided firm evidence that the strategies initiated over the past year were moving the company toward a gradual, planned return to long-term profitability.

Thousands of dollars were invested in capital improvements to upgrade units. Banquet facilities were being added, and, in some locations, windows were put in to give a lighter, more open appearance.

NEW MARKETS

In October 1981, Victoria Station announced that it was making a major push to obtain group business. Ken Bracken, Manager of Field Marketing, stated,

> We are going after the tour and travel, corporate and local group business
> as a major project. It's a lucrative market and in many areas we see a

great shortage of rooms where meals and liquor service are available for groups of 20 to 80 persons.

A new "tour and travel menu package" was put together, to be sold at major travel shows such as that of the American Bus Association. The move was accompanied by the creation of a new national group sales staff. According to Bracken, "We hope to add several million dollars a year in sales." Group business was solicited in off-hours when the restaurant was not normally open with a "Rent a Restaurant Rent-Free" program. The chain also worked with various local attractions such as the Boston Children's Museum and the Museum of Transportation. "Working with local attractions," said Bracken, "helps build business for us and for them."

Advertising was put into the programs for major sports events, with discount coupons. Local sports teams were asked to select their favorite charity and sponsor fund-raising dinners at Victoria Station restaurants. The following year Victoria Station planned to take part in the Jerry Lewis Muscular Dystrophy fund-raising appeal. "Now that we have turned around, we can do these things," said Bracken.

END OF THE TUNNEL

By the end of 1981, Victoria Station was seeing an end to its financial woes. In the quarter ended September 13, it reported profits of $391,000 on sales of $30.4 million, compared with a loss of $1.6 million for the same period a year earlier. Sheppard explained the turnaround:

> The target was brought into range primarily through far better controls in food and beverage and attention to detail at the unit level. We've cut our costs by hedging beef requirements, and by better short- and long-range negotiating in our purchasing. Being able to broaden the menu, offering an expanded dinner selection and a broader price structure, has also helped. [However, customer counts are] probably close to even with last year's [counts—19 percent below what they were the last profitable year, 1979].
>
> It's not something that happens overnight. We're hoping that, with the changes we're making, we'll answer that question [of not bringing more

people in through the front door]. [The intention now is to] appeal to every market, from the secretary to the businessman and local family business.

Collins stated it this way:

Victoria Station is now competing in a tougher marketplace, but we are successfully competing. The basic concept on which our system was built has now withstood the test of over a decade of operation and two years of adversity. We have turned the corner back to profitability, expanded our demographic appeal, and tightened our management and control mechanisms where necessary. We cannot promise miracles. Our return to prosperity will be gradual, but it will be steady—and planned.

1982

1982 saw Victoria Station double the size of its lunch menu and revise the dinner menu once again, after a year of testing in markets from Cincinnati to Portland. The company went from a limited lunch menu to a much broader menu that included lower-priced items; an "Express Lunch" section promising complete service within 30 minutes; and other special sections including Mexican dishes, appetizers, soups, and meals for the calorie-conscious.

"Historically," Rose said, Victoria Station has not drawn "clerical workers and nonexecutives." The lunch changes are an effort to bring in all types of people and expand the chain's demographic base. Four more Inflation-Fighter items were added, as well as rainbow trout and an item called "Stuff a Wild Potato," which was a baked potato, split and loaded with a Mexican-, Italian-, or California-style filling.

The soup selection was expanded to seven, and included such items as Tomato Florentine, Golden Gate Mushroom, and Southern-Style Chicken Gumbo. The salad bar now had four ways in which it could be ordered. Appetizers from the dinner menu were also added to the lunch menu.

The dinner menu was revised as well. The salmon dish was dropped in favor of Alaskan King Crab, and a shellfish sampler was added. Shrimp Victoria was reinstated in place of Shrimp Diana.

Rose said the changes would be reflected in a small increase in the average check, but the purpose was primarily to increase meal counts. "We want to expand the customer's perception of Victoria Station," he said.

THE GUARD CHANGES AGAIN

In May 1982, the Board of Directors, in a tightening-up process, eliminated the positions held by Paul Sheppard and Jon Rose. Collins, in addition to retaining his titles of Chairman, President, and CEO, also took on Sheppard's position of COO. It was reported that he was anxious to take more direct control in his greatest area of expertise, operations. Victoria Victory continued as Marketing Director.

In July 1982, Collins resigned from the company in a dispute with the Board of Directors over the company's future course. Richard Niglio was named as his replacement. Niglio had been Vice President and General Manager of the fast-food and restaurant division of International Multifoods, and had started with that company as President of the Mr. Donut division. He was a 1964 Yale graduate with a degree in economics who had begun his career at the J. Walter Thompson advertising agency. From there he became Director of National Advertising and the Vice President of Marketing for Kentucky Fried Chicken (KFC). At age 26, he had taken over as President and CEO of KFC's troubled H. Salt fish-and-chips division, and took it from a loss to a profit.

Niglio, 39, commenting on his appointment, said that most likely what Victoria Station needed was a simpler "repositioning from a marketing point of view," to include greater menu development. Niglio's reputation was that of a "fixer." With strengths in marketing, advertising, and franchising, he had helped to patch up a number of troubled operations in a 15-year career as a food-service executive. Collins, the trade press noted, had had a similar reputation.

Fiscal year 1982, for the year ending March 28, showed a $7 million turnaround, from 1981's $6.3 million loss to 1982's net earnings of $1.2 million. Although Collins had rolled out a broader menu, the improvement was due to "totally improved" operational controls, according to a company spokesperson.

1983

Nation's Restaurant News of January 3, 1983, reported the following:

Discounting Strategy Backfires

Larkspur, Calif.—Victoria Station, wounded by a now-abandoned discounting strategy and suffering from an ongoing decline in meal counts, has posted a $1.2 million loss for the second quarter ended September 12. Revenues were $25.5 million, compared to $30.4 million a year ago.

For the first 24 weeks of fiscal 1983, the loss was $1.1 million vs. earnings of $1.1 million for the previous year. Revenues were $52.4 million compared to $60.4 million.

Along with the probability of damage to its image from discounting, president and CEO Richard Niglio pointed to the slump in customer counts as the basis for the troubles.

Niglio's strategy for both short- and long-term recovery is based on revamping the company's marketing structure and philosophy. Included in the short-term moves are the replacement of some dinner items with more fresh fish; the elimination of the company's field marketing staff, which had been heavily involved with discount and coupon promotions; and creation of a broadcast-oriented media campaign to boost seafood sales.

For long-term reversal of the meal count decline, the company is constructing an entirely revamped menu which will feature a wider selection of entrees with a greater range of prices.

Other changes, which Niglio characterized as "a significant change in strategic direction for the company," include an overhaul and repositioning of the Victoria Station concept and format and its reintroduction to the marketplace through a high-impact television advertising effort. Niglio declined to give any further details of his newly conceived battleplan.

In July, Victoria Station reported a net loss of $8.3 million for the fiscal year ending April 3, compared with net earnings of $1.21 million in fiscal 1982. Revenue declined to $112.3 million from $123.9 million the year before. The company reported that it was testing various menu modifications in hopes of reversing a drastic decline in customer counts. "We're very hopeful the economy will improve, and that we will experience some of that improvement," said a spokesperson. He indicated the chain was concentrating on test markets in the Southeast, where broader menu offerings had been introduced and eventually would be deployed in other major markets.

The menu changes were "not necessarily a deemphasis of beef, or an emphasis on seafood, but involve a realignment of items to offer broader appeal with something for everyone." Victoria Station was proceeding cautiously in rolling out new menus, "not from financial restraints, but because of efforts to maintain quality as it shifts to new concepts."

In November, Victoria Station reported a net loss of $1.06 million for its second quarter ending September 18 on revenues of $23.09 million. The company also said that it had reached an agreement in principle with its lenders that included a restructuring of loan payments and a plan to sell off up to 35 of its restaurants over a three-year period. The latter was part of a corporate strategy to achieve greater market penetration through more effective allocation of company resources. Proceeds from the sale would be used to support the introduction of a new menu and new merchandising concepts for working-capital purposes and to repay debt.

1984

Nation's Restaurant News of March 27, 1984, reported the following:

Vic Station Looks to Bonkers to Help Cut Staggering Losses

Larkspur, Calif.—Victoria Station is opting to trade boxcars for burgers in its newest strategy to overcome staggering, ongoing losses. While reporting a $1.95 million net loss on revenue of $30 million for the third quarter ending January 8, the 97-unit chain disclosed plans to jump on the upscale burger bandwagon with conversion to a new concept, Bonkers.

The company said it anticipated conversion of a significant number of its restaurants to the fast-growing segment, starting with two units. Bonkers will feature a new exterior and interior design, while the traditional railcar concept will continue in non-converted units. . . . [The announcement] came one day after American Values, a Bermuda-based investment company and Victoria Station's biggest stockholder, sold most of its interest in the company.

Richard Niglio said that converting the company's restaurants to a new concept may "substantially impact long-term profitability." The concept included a retail bakery and a self-serve format. Burgers, hot dogs, soups, salad bar, and other items comprised its menu. "The Victoria Station concept, as originally conceived, was outmoded," declared Niglio, "but we have breathed some life into it." Results were being felt. Customer counts were up in the last half of fiscal 1984. Now a revolution was rising in the form of Bonkers.

Niglio felt that the new concept was the key element in a long-term solution that would return the company to profitability. Said Niglio,

We are very enthusiastic about Bonkers, and may convert a significant number of units to the concept. We were looking for a home run concept. We considered the fern bar concept, but there is too much capital investment involved and the segment is too mature. Upscale, adult fast food is a new segment. Customers are trading up from fast food; there's erosion from the dinner house segment. I see long-term growth.

The baby boom has grown up on fast food. A big bulge of the population is growing older and, though they still enjoy fast food, the baby boomers want more ambience and a higher quality product. There has been a lot of banter about this, but I believe it is true.

The check average at Victoria Station is $15; fast food checks average a few dollars. There is a hole of $4 to $6 between these two ranges that is yet to be filled. Bonkers is an adult fast-food hamburger restaurant. It is a fun food place. Alcoholic beverage sales are under 20 percent. We can get that up four or five points, and we will, but we want to keep it fun. It's an unstructured dining experience, very informal. There are no rules. It's self-serve like fast food.

The Bonkers theme combined the nostalgia of the 1950s with the flair of the 1980s. The exterior was reminiscent of an East Coast diner of the fifties era, with stainless steel trim and neon highlighting. The concept was aimed at appealing to a broad range of customers. Baby boomers were the main target, but the restaurant was expected to do well with their kids as well. For parents, it was a change from fast food, and they could order a drink if they wanted. Niglio felt that Bonkers' prices and good value would attract seniors as well. The half-pound "ultimate hamburger," ground fresh from quality raw product and complete with buns made on the premises and "add-it-yourself" trimmings, was priced at $3.75.

The company planned to open 10 to 15 Bonkers in 1984. All units would be conversions of Victoria Stations and would disguise the boxcars, at a conversion cost of under $300,000. The check average was $5 to $6. The company expected a unit to do over $2 million annually. Food costs were lower (about 30 percent) than for a Victoria Station, as were labor costs, largely due to the self-service aspect.

Niglio's summation of his attack against Victoria Station's problems was three-pronged: First, changes to the Victoria Station concept; second, the rollout of Bonkers as a long-term solution; and third, the disposal of unprofitable operations. "We've come up with a long-term solution and the financing to do it," he said. "We are excited about the future." Exhibit 4.2 describes the Bonkers concept.

The future, however, did not bear out the promise. Cash-strapped and unable to nail down a crucial $5 million loan it needed to appease its banks and to carry out more Bonkers conversions, Victoria Station tried to formulate a new survival strategy. The prospect of bankruptcy had pervaded the company, as evidenced by Niglio's golden-parachute move to guarantee his minimum $200,000 annual salary through 1987 if the company succumbed to its financial ailments or his contract was otherwise breached.

The company had been able to sell only a few of its restaurants that it had put on the block and was facing lower-than-anticipated sales. The reportedly high-grossing Bonkers units were facing reluctance by outsiders to finance the conversions. For fiscal year 1984, net losses were $6 million on sales of $101.5 million, a revenue decline of 9.6 percent from 1983.

Exhibit 4.2
The Bonkers Concept

Victoria Station
Customers Go Bonkers!

Bonkers for the future

During the past fiscal year, the Company developed "Bonkers Burger Grill & Bar" to enter this emerging adult hamburger business. The first unit was converted from a former Victoria Station restaurant and opened in Southern California in March of 1984. Bonkers was conceived as a contemporary, hamburger-specialty establi·hment which offers simple, top quality foods and beverages at readily perceived low prices in a casual, fun atmosphere. The results of the initial restaurant have exceeded projections by a wide margin, and the Company plans to convert several additional locations to the new Bonkers concept over the next two to three years.

Bonkers for a new look

In the transition to Bonkers, both the interior and exterior of the original train-themed Victoria Station restaurant are completely remodeled so that the boxcars and other railroad elements virtually disappear. An entirely new facia is built completely around the boxcars and caboose which comprise the existing structure. Windows and

Bonkers for burgers

As the kids of the McDonald's generation have grown up and become more sophisticated, their food tastes and eating-out preferences have been changing. They have become young adults, and they are no longer content with the plastic decor and prepackaged fast food that they happily consumed as children. While very value-conscious, they are seeking more interesting eating-out experiences and, most importantly, fresher, higher quality food. However, they have not lost their taste for hamburgers. Thus, an entirely new market segment of the foodservice industry is emerging — the "adult gourmet hamburger" market. The potential size of this new business promises to be substantial, and it seems to appeal to a much broader segment of the population than the young adults for whom it was originated. The concept seems attractive to just about everyone — from budget-conscious single parents and retirees, to vested business-men looking for a quick lunch, and trendy young pacesetters out for an evening of fun.

Exhibit 4.2 *(continued)*

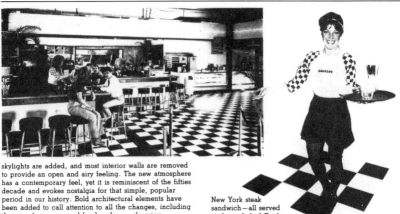

skylights are added, and most interior walls are removed to provide an open and airy feeling. The new atmosphere has a contemporary feel, yet it is reminiscent of the fifties decade and evokes nostalgia for that simple, popular period in our history. Bold architectural elements have been added to call attention to all the changes, including the use of neon, curved hard surfaces, gleaming metallics, bright graphics, and colors. Night or day, it is truly difficult to pass by a Bonkers restaurant without looking and stopping.

Bonkers for fresh food and fun

The Bonkers menu, served all day, is relatively simple to prepare and offers the high quality and level of variety that are expected by today's discerning customers at reasonable, attractive prices. The Bonkers specialty is a half-pound, freshly ground pure beef hamburger, grilled to order in the open kitchen, and served on a large sesame-seed bun that is baked fresh every hour in Bonkers' own bakery. Customers garnish their own burger with a variety of dressings and fresh produce which are laden on convenient condiment bars. Other items on the menu include the popular and abundant 59-item salad bar, a hefty New York-style hot dog, a marinated teriyaki chicken sandwich, and a

New York steak sandwich—all served on home-baked Bonkers buns. Beef ribs, a smaller children's burger, and side orders such as chili, special fries, and thick homemade milkshakes and malts complete the Bonkers menu. Oversized, freshly-baked cookies and brownies are available to take out from the bakery in addition to ice cream cones. The fun atmosphere at Bonkers is enhanced by a friendly, lively young staff, an attractive, open bar specializing in beer by the bucket, blended drinks and fruit-based cocktails, and a fifties-style jukebox playing beloved oldies.

Bonkers for success

Bonkers is designed to be fun, exciting, memorable, highly recommendable, and priced right for the frequent restaurant-goer of today and tomorrow. It has an obvious appeal to contemporary casual lifestyles and delivers the high levels of quality and freshness which consumers are demanding. In short, Bonkers is the restaurant with a hint of the 50's, which is styled for the 80's and 90's—styled for success.

1985

Nation's Restaurant News reported the following:

July 22: Victoria Station Narrows Net Loss

Larkspur, Calif.—Victoria Station Inc. said it narrowed its annual net loss to $5.26 million for the year ended March 31 from $5.76 million from 1984. Revenue declined 8%, to $93.8 million. The company is retrofitting some of its steak houses into Bonkers dinnerhouses and closing others.

November 4: Victoria Station Faces New Hitch

Larkspur, Calif.—Victoria Station Inc., facing a $3 million operating loss for its second quarter because of disappointing sales in its dinnerhouses and new Bonkers hamburger restaurants, said a complex plan to renegotiate leaseholds and restructure its debt load is vital to the company's continued viability.

The company completed a balance sheet restructuring last April amid hopes that the Bonkers concept would boost sales and profits while it exited from the steakhouse business.

November 11: Victoria Station Losses Mount

Larkspur, Calif.—Victoria Station Inc., hobbled by poor sales in both its old dinnerhouses and its new Bonkers restaurants, lost $3.21 million in the second quarter ended Sept. 15, almost twice as deep a loss as that of the year-ago quarter, $1.65 million. Revenue slumped 12%, to $20.1 million.

1986

Nation's Restaurant News published the following items:

March 10: Restaurant Unsure of Negotiation Outcome

Larkspur, Calif.—Victoria Station said that current negotiations with lessors, lenders and other parties over lease and debt restructuring are "vital to the continuing viability" of the company. But, it added, it can offer "no assurances" about the outcome of the negotiations.

Once a leading theme dinnerhouse chain, Victoria Station has been buffeted in recent years by huge losses, the latest coming in the third quarter ended Jan. 5, when the beleaguered chain posted a net loss of $19.1 million on revenues of $22.3 million.

Victoria Station has shuttered 34 of its 91 restaurants since last May. It took a $17.6 million charge for closing 29 of the units in the most recent quarter. The ongoing closings and sales of restaurants, including four of its seven Bonkers burger outlets, put Victoria Station in violation of its loan agreements.

Victoria Station's nine-month losses totaled $24.3 million, compared with a $3.7 million loss for the same period a year ago.

June 2: Victoria Station Files Chapter 11 Petition

San Francisco—No longer confident it could keep creditors at bay and pressed to find additional capital after losing more than $40 million in four years, Victoria Station, Inc. has filed for protection under Chapter 11 . . . .

. . . Officials of the company said they had taken the unusual step of filing a reorganization plan with a petition for protection, a step that could substantially shorten the reorganization process . . . . The 45-unit railroad themed chain, which closed 46 of its restaurants and laid off about 2000 of its employees during the past year . . . lists company assets of $36.4 million and liabilities of $34.2 million.

The small mountain of paperwork . . . covered the parent Delaware corporation and 11 subsidiaries, including eight doing business as Victoria Station in as many states; Euston Station in New York; Railhead Restaurants in Texas; and Bonkers, of California, the company's ill-fated "gourmet" burger concept.

Founded in San Francisco in 1969, the steak, prime rib and seafood chain by the mid-70s was considered by many to be on the fast track to success . . . . However, skyrocketing red-meat prices, a drop in the consumption of such meat by most Americans in recent years and an aging concept has left the company fighting for its life. It lost $19 million between April 1983 and March 1985 and reported $23 million on losses during the first nine months of fiscal 1986.

Victoria Station officials have amazed industry observers for years with their ability to come up with new funding and fight off creditors . . . . Much of the miracle workers' efforts were wasted.

The snake-bitten company plowed a good deal of its new resources into the development of Bonkers Burger Grill and Bar. The '50s-themed burger restaurant seemed just the ticket for the clean conversion of Victoria Station units, but like many other concepts born during "gourmet" burger mania, it fell by the wayside, taking much of the chain's future with it.

RETROSPECTIVE

The following is excerpted from comments in *Restaurant Business,* printed in the July 20, 1987, issue:

For six long and painful years, the troubled publicly-owned company struggled with various strategies and schemes to stage a turnaround. In the end, all efforts proved futile. Victoria Station just took a long time to die.

"In retrospect, I think Victoria Station needed a priest, not a doctor," says former president Richard Niglio. "I think it is a miracle the company didn't go into bankruptcy before it did."

Victoria Station has closed all but 12 or 14 of its units. Remaining units have been located on the east coast, so headquarters have been moved to the premises of a unit in Darien, CT. Mike Colonna, for years a regional manager, has taken the reins as president. Niglio left at the end of April to become chief executive of Darien-based Child Care Centers of America, a chain of day-care centers.

According to Niglio and to several observers, what happened to Victoria Station could easily happen to another company. Like the stories other failed chains have to tell, this is the tale of a company that expanded too fast, was too heavily leveraged, and was too closely tied to a single very identifiable theme.

Niglio was convinced that the long-term solution to Victoria Station's problems was to allocate funds from the mature dinnerhouse market to a segment with growth potential. Thus Bonkers, an upscale fast food restaurant, was born. As late as June 1985, Victoria Station was planning aggressive franchising of Bonkers. A vice president of franchising was named and an additional $5 million in new financing was arranged.

A lot of other companies saw potential in the idea of adult fast food, and the so-called gourmet burger niche turned out to be too small for all the players jostling to get in. Six Bonkers were opened in all.

The question is, why did all Victoria Station's attempts at repositioning fail? Other companies have made the transition from one concept to another without going into bankruptcy.

Today, Freeman is president of San Francisco-based California Restaurants. Bradley operates Mexican restaurants in Hawaii, and Lee is a business man in the San Francisco area, assembling and distributing laser-disc video jukeboxes.

The bigger question, however, asked by many industry observers, was where, when, and how did Victoria Station management, or managements, lose sight of where it was going? Was Victoria Station's defeat really due to all the external forces that were blamed along the way, or was management(s) their own worst enemy?

Part III

Operational Strategies

Case Five

Andy's Barbecue Restaurants

Roger Kerin

In May, Andrew Johnston, President of Western Foods, Inc., commissioned a market research study to examine consumer attitudes toward Andy's Barbecue Restaurants, its restaurant division, and barbecue in general in order to determine the optimal type of restaurant for Andy's. According to Mr. Johnston, the focal question to be addressed in the research was: "Can Andy's appeal to more families to increase its dinner traffic for the purpose of generating $750,000 in sales per outlet, a 25 percent operating profit, and an ability to withstand intense competition?"

THE RESTAURANT BUSINESS

Since 1985, Western Foods, Inc. had operated five restaurants in a major southwestern metropolitan area. Each restaurant specialized in barbecue sandwiches and barbecue plates as its main product, although some locations offered steaks. The price, cost, and gross margin of menu items are shown in Exhibit 5.1. Andy's restaurants used a cafeteria style for food service; table service for dinner had been introduced at two restaurants on a limited experimental basis. Each restaurant also offered a take-home service. This service accounted for 25 to 30 percent of the total sales, which were currently about $600,000 per location.

This case was originally written by Roger Kerin, Professor of Marketing, Southern Methodist University, Texas. All rights reserved. Used by permission. Names and some facts have been disguised.

Exhibit 5.1
Price, Cost, and Gross Margin of Menu Items

	Size	Price ($)	Food Cost ($)	Gross Margin ($)
Lunch:				
Beef	Regular	2.90	.90	2.00
	Jumbo	3.75	1.30	2.45
Ham	Regular	2.90	.93	1.97
	Jumbo	3.75	1.34	2.41
Sausage	Regular	2.90	.70	2.20
	Jumbo	3.75	1.02	2.73
Beef Po Boy		3.90	1.25	2.65
Ham Po Boy		3.90	1.30	2.60
Big Tex (beef, ham, cheese, vegetables)		4.90	1.65	3.25
*Dinners:**				
Beef	Alone	6.90	2.15	4.75
	w/salad	7.50	2.38	5.12
Ham	Alone	6.90	2.18	4.72
	w/salad	7.50	2.41	5.09
Sausage	Alone	6.90	1.90	5.00
	w/salad	7.50	2.13	5.37
Ribs	Alone	6.90	2.28	4.62
	w/salad	7.50	2.51	4.99
Big Tex	Dinner	7.50	2.40	5.10
	w/salad	7.90	2.63	5.27

* Dinners include a vegetable, sauce, and toast.

In the previous two years, Andy's had consciously moved away from the fast-food "barbecue joint–truck stop" image common among competitive outlets. Subsequent efforts to establish itself as a quality barbecue restaurant had resulted in an expanded menu, salad bars, and improved outlet decor. Concurrent with this move was a decline in lunch sales that had not been offset by increased dinner sales.

Andy's was the largest chain of barbecue restaurants in the metropolitan area. It was also the only barbecue restaurant open seven days a week (11:00 A.M. to 10:00 P.M.) for both lunch and dinner service. Competitive truck-stop-type, fast-food, barbecue-only outlets were open five days a week from 11:00 A.M. to 2:00 P.M.

The five Andy's restaurants currently averaged a gross profit of 60 percent of sales with a 20 percent operating profit. It was Johnston's policy to allocate 2.5 percent of sales to advertising and sales promotion annually. Promotion had typically included some radio advertising, complimentary dinners, and direct mail to residents in the trade areas surrounding the restaurants.

Published statistics indicated that 746 restaurants were currently located in the metropolitan area served by Andy's Restaurants. Combined, the restaurants were generating $622 million in sales annually. Of these restaurants, there were 75 specializing in barbecue in the metropolitan area served by Andy's. Previous research commissioned by Western Foods indicated that barbecue as a separate food group accounted for 5 percent of restaurant dollar sales volume in the city, or $31.1 million at the present time.

THE RESEARCH STUDY

In early August, Johnston received the results of the commissioned research. Excerpts from the report are presented in the Appendix to this case.

Reaction to the Study

On August 19 of the current year, after having reviewed the results of the study, Johnston prepared a statement of implications from the study results for his management team (Exhibit 5.2). At that time, he asked Oscar Miles, an independent marketing consultant with a Ph.D. in Marketing, to work with Andy's on strategy development.

A September 4 meeting brought together Johnston; Clark Tully, the Director of Outlet Operations; Tom Smith, Director of Marketing; and Oscar Miles, the marketing consultant. During the course of their meeting, the group reexamined the research results, outlined seven generalizations from the research, and stated a number of strategic considerations. The generalizations were:

1. Barbecue is a specialty food with a rather modest demand, yet a demand of sufficient magnitude to justify being in that business.
2. Barbecue is eaten significantly more at lunchtime than at dinner.

Exhibit 5.2

Andrew Johnston's Summary of Research Results

Date: August 19

To: Clark Tully, Director of Operations
      Tom Smith, Director of Marketing
      Oscar Miles, Marketing Consultant

Subject: Research Report

I have had a chance to examine in greater depth the results from the research agency study. As I see it, the overall implications of the study are:

   I. *Barbecue is not a particularly favorite type of food; however, it is sufficient to build a successful restaurant business.*
      a. Compared with the general frequency of eating out at lunch and dinner where approximately 40% eat out twice or more per week, and another 40 to 50% eat out once per month up to twice a week, only 28% eat barbecue five or more times a year at Andy's. More precise figures on frequency are needed to get a fix on market potential!
  II. *Barbecue is far more popular for lunch than dinner.*
 III. *Reasons why barbecue is more popular at lunch than at dinner and how to change:*
      a. Women and children together are more influential than men, and they are the least favorable toward barbecue (these two statements need to be supported).
      b. Barbecue is "filling"—The report does not expand on the consequences of being "filling," but I would assume "hard to digest" may be the same as "filling," and no one likes this—particularly women and children at night when they don't have after-lunch activities to help digestion.
         If the above is valid, perhaps some of the following would help to overcome the objection and expand the market—a market that Andy's is well ahead of the competition in capturing:
      (1) Is steak any less filling or hard to digest? Is it just meat? Type of meat? Amount of smoke and its effects?
      (2) Seek counsel of doctors to determine how they might help.
      (3) Are chicken and ham less difficult? If so, promote.
      (4) Offer some variety, perhaps other than barbecue or meat.
      (5) Barbecue considered tasty; build on it. Also reasonably priced, informal, friendly people, quick service at lunch.

Exhibit 5.2 *(continued)*

---

c. Characteristics desired by dinner consumer differ from lunch consumer, which probably explains why restaurants have difficulties being successful at both. A number of dinner restaurants appear to be successful at both; perhaps Andy's can be also. The following suggestions might serve as a beginning; cafeteria for quick service at lunch; dinners at night with sandwiches offered; family style to be "leader" as it fits informal perception, and it fits Andy's and barbecue—different yet similar to "All You Can Eat." Also: add baked potato and steak at night, not at lunch; add a fish and shrimp at night (frozen); perhaps corn on the cob in husk at night and heated in a microwave. Special recruitment and training of waiter/waitress/hostess at night, as friendliness is important.

Keep working on "informal" interior decor that is barbecue but attractive and comfortable. Attempt to define what is informal. Similarly, work on exterior.

Price evening food higher, particularly dinners, but sandwiches too if salad is included—one reason for calling [it] "Plate" at lunch.

d. Continue to exploit takeout. Andy's dollar sales of 25–30 percent far exceeds average barbecue of 10 percent. This is probably due to food packaging, separate takeout facility. More can be done.

I would like to schedule a meeting for September 4 to discuss the research report and consider strategic options. I have asked Oscar Miles of Miles and Friedman to consult with us on these matters.

---

3. Barbecue is significantly more popular with men than with women and children.

4. The three primary characteristics at lunch are quality of food, quick service, and waiting time. The three primary characteristics at dinner are quality of food, friendly service, and table service.

5. Barbecue is perceived to be tasty, informal, moderately priced, middle-class, and pretty good for dinner.

6. Females make the decision or influence where to eat 60 percent of the time.

7. At all times a balance must be maintained among marketing, production, and finance.

The strategic considerations were:

1. Since desired sales volume requires more than a heavy lunch business, sales at night and weekends must be developed.
2. Since women find barbecue only moderately desirable, and since they are major decision makers in selecting an evening and weekend restaurant, a special program needs to be developed to appeal to them, and it must be determined more precisely why they like barbecue less than other foods.
3. Special emphasis should be placed on the primary characteristics that are desired by customers and that are different at lunch and dinner. At dinner they are quality food, friendly service, and table service.

After the meeting, Miles voiced several opinions on Andy's. He viewed the situation as one requiring rethinking the positioning of the restaurants. Miles commented that "Andy's has consciously moved away from the hard-core barbecue eaters who seek a barbecue joint. This alienation has resulted in a loss at lunch."

Having discussed Andy's communication efforts with the firm's management group, Miles concluded that Andy's had been only moderately active in any communicative effort.

> What had been done, however, aimed primarily at communicating Andy's as offering quality barbecue [according to Miles]. Since the barbecue market is very thin, I suggested that further efforts in this direction would result in diminishing returns. Andy's should expand its market base by repositioning or repackaging in a manner that makes Andy's a logical alternative for evening and weekend dining.
>
> How should Andy's be positioned is the question to be answered. Should it be as a family dinner restaurant or as a barbecue lunch restaurant? Once a position is adopted, then a communication effort must be designed to convey the proper message.

On September 25, Johnston and his management team met again with Miles. They addressed themselves to the following: (1) What should Andy's position be? (2) How should Andy's package or get into that position?

(3) How should Andy's communicate this position to potential customers?

(4) How could Andy's evaluate the effectiveness of the first three steps?

At the conclusion of the meeting, Johnston summarized the opinions of those present:

> It is recognized that developing a different position at lunch and dinner requires very careful handling so as not to destroy both of them. The message communicated has to point up the fast-food specialty food by cafeteria service while at the same time communicating the idea that Andy's is a logical alternative for evening dining—being informal, and offering friendly table service. Still further, the evening communication must include a strong message to women, since they are so influential in selecting the evening eating spot. A number of suggestions were made including the following: add chicken on the evening menu and keep the atmosphere warm and informal with such things as wooden floors, old chairs, checkered tablecloths, and perhaps candles or lantern-type lights. Special attention should be given to the menu, with such additions as soup, cheese, sandwiches, and wine being considered as well as fruit and salad. Also available should be one or two vegetables (such as asparagus) that particularly appeal to women.

The next day, Tom Smith, Director of Marketing, contacted LaRouche, Markham, and Smit (LM&S), a local advertising agency. After briefing them about what had transpired in the meetings, he sent them a copy of the market study and requested a short advertising proposal.

On October 16, LM&S submitted both a review of the research as they saw it and a short advertising proposal. Both of these are shown in Exhibit 5.3.

Reaction to the LM&S Proposal

Receipt of the LM&S proposal produced a controversy among managers of Andy's management ranks. Smith supported the proposal in its entirety, citing the reevaluation of research results as his major reason. Andrew Johnston was uneasy with the positioning aspect of the LM&S proposal. According to Johnston,

> Were we to accept the positioning of LM&S, we would be scrapping the positioning we worked out with Oscar Miles and returning to the

positioning that previous advertising programs used and which were unsuccessful. The fact that were we to accept their positioning, the marketing, media, TV, strategy, and first quarter is attractive: however, since that positioning is unacceptable, it reminds me of the insurance salesman who asked if I was interested in a tax-free bond and although I said no, he continued to tell me how desirable it was.

Clark Tully displayed mixed feelings about the LM&S proposal and again raised the issues of outlet image and lunch-versus-dinner patronage. His thoughts on these subjects were outlined in a memo to Andrew Johnston (Exhibit 5.4).

Oscar Miles impressions of the LM&S proposal were contained in a letter to Tom Smith. A summary of this letter is shown in Exhibit 5.5.

Exhibit 5.3
LaRouche, Markham, and Smit Research Review and
Advertising Proposal

Research Findings

1. Granted, Andy's appears to be the most popular barbecue restaurant. However, this preference is far from overwhelming—particularly since Andy's has more locations and thus exposure than direct competition; also the survey was conducted in the trading areas served by Andy's units.

	Percent Respondents for:	
Where to Eat BBQ for	*Lunch*	*Dinner*
No indication	37	51
No preference	22⎱ (59)	17⎱ (68)
Andy's	16⎰	12⎰
All others	25	20

Specifically, the major finding from this research is not that Andy's was apparently preferred by more respondents than any other barbecue establishment. In our judgment, the major finding is that around *two-thirds of all respondents had no favorite whatsoever*. This indicates a low level of awareness overall, particularly in response to a guided question.

Exhibit 5.3 *(continued)*

2. In barbecue, as in virtually every consumer marketing case, heavy users (12 times per year or more) emerge as the dominant force in the market. These users are conservatively estimated to account for 77 percent of all consumption occasions.

| | | | Projected | Total Projected | |
Criterion	#	Percent	Factor	Occasions	Percent
Heavy users (12+ times/yr)	141	47	12 times	1,692	77
Medium users (6–11 times/yr)	26	9	8 times	208	9
Light users (1–5 times/yr)	100	33	3 times	300	14
Nonusers (0)	33	11	0	0	0
Totals				2,200	100

It is the attitudes toward trial and usage of Andy's by the heavy user segment that will be the most critical in successfully marketing the properties.

3. The attitudes of heavy users indicate that they are not necessarily convinced that Andy's offers "the best barbecue in the city." It suggests, though, that there is a basis for receptivity to this claim if effectively presented and if satisfactory trial ensues. Heavy-user attitudes also indicate that they are quite satisfied with the current menu selection and do not think that Andy's should offer more than barbecue.

| | Heavy Users | |
Andy's	Agree	Disagree
Has low-quality food	9%	80%
Has sufficient variety	76%	11%
Should offer more than BBQ	15%	67%

Accordingly, a move to broaden the menu and change the basic character/appeal of Andy's would meet resistance from the most important market segment.

Exhibit 5.3 *(continued)*

---

4. Further, research reveals that, while there may be some reluctance on the part of some family members to dine out on barbecue, there is a low incidence of their refusal to do so.

Everyone would eat barbecue	80%
Female would *not*	7%
Children would *not*	10%
Male would *not*	3%

5. While the wife plays an important role in dining-out decisions, it is hardly an overwhelming one, as the male is almost equally important.

Decision Made By	Percent
Male, primarily	36
Female, primarily	41
Both, jointly	22

Thus, it has been noted that women play a role in 63 percent of decisions. But it should also be pointed out that men play a role in 58 percent of them.

6. Overall, then, it may be concluded from the research that: (a) Andy's offers a basically good product as is; (b) while relative preference versus direct competition is good, awareness is poor in the absolute; (c) a fundamental change in Andy's menu selection that would reposition the restaurants is not necessary and runs more risk of being harmful than being beneficial; (d) while barbecue may not be the most preferred food for dining out, neither would it be rejected out of hand as an alternative; and (e) men and women exhibit about equal sway in the dining-out decision, so neither should be ignored in advertising planning (particularly when the men will tend to be more receptive).

Proposal

Our proposal is consistent with the researcher's recommendations in the following areas: (a) communicate that barbecue is good for dinner; (b) communicate this proposition to women; and (c) develop carryout opportunity.

The LM&S proposal departs from the researcher's recommendation to "stress that barbecue need not be sloppy/too spicy." Rather than deal with a

---
Exhibit 5.3 *(continued)*

---

negative—removal of which is not viewed as a compelling motivation—we have chosen to accentuate the positive.

The objective of Andy's new marketing program should be to increase traffic by: (a) gaining a larger share of the existing market for barbecue restaurants and (b) increasing the propensity among the current barbecue market to have barbecue when dining out at night. This would be accomplished by: (a) forcefully establishing Andy's positioning as a superior barbecue restaurant among barbecue users, preempting direct competition; (b) delivering the product (food, atmosphere, and service) to support this positioning; and (c) introducing the concept that Andy's is appropriate and good for nighttime dining . . . an alternative to be considered.

Positioning

1. Clearly and firmly position Andy's as a barbecue restaurant of superior quality.
2. Exploit and develop existing favorable perceptions regarding barbecue—informal, hearty/masculine, tasty and friendly, quick service.
3. Accept those perceptions about barbecue which are not necessarily positive, and would be inactionable without compromising Andy's fundamental identity—spicy, somewhat downscale, moderately expensive, not "neat," limited selection.

Overall Advertising and Promotion Strategy

Invest all of next year's advertising and promotion budget toward current users of barbecue in order to: (a) stimulate new user trial of Andy's; (b) profitably increase frequency among current users; and (c) avoid short-term price cutting that subsidizes current users without realizing any long-term benefits.

Insure that all efforts are consistent with Andy's positioning as a barbecue restaurant of superior quality.

Creative Strategy

The primary objective of advertising for Andy's will be to convince the barbecue market that Andy's is a superior barbecue restaurant. This will be accomplished by distinctive, memorable advertising directed toward the quality of the barbecue from the standpoint of raw material selection and preparation. These product

Exhibit 5.3 *(continued)*

points will believably support the position that Andy's is the "Best Barbecue Restaurant in the City."

The secondary objective is to introduce the concept that Andy's is appropriate and good for nighttime dining. This will be accomplished by direct copy suggestion. It will be further supported by reference to the Family Platter. In addition, the opportunity to expand carryout business will be exploited.

Execution will strongly rely upon barbecue's inherent appetite appeal (among current barbecue users) and will be consistent with Andy's quality positioning.

Media

Andy's media objective should be to stimulate new users' trial of Andy's and to increase frequency among current users. This can be achieved as follows: (1) generate broad awareness of Andy's among the current barbecue market; (2) heighten introductory impact at the outset of the program; and (3) establish key message delivery to the most propitious time of day and day of week for dining-out decisions.

Exhibit 5.4

Clark Tully's Reaction to the LM&S Proposal

To: Andrew Johnston
From: Clark Tully
Date: November 7
Subject: Andy's Marketing & Promotional Strategy

Perhaps beginning back in February, we have been wrestling with the question of exactly what kind of restaurant Andy's should be, to which market (or markets) it should be directed, and where we should go from there. Since then we have gone from the research report to the present LM&S proposal. All have been dealing with the same problem, namely how to market Andy's. During each phase, several important related questions have been raised, but all of the reports and memos share some similarities and common themes. I will try in this memo to pull my thoughts together on them and state how they may relate to any future action.

1. *Image*—What is Andy's "image" now in the minds of its customers? What has it been, and have we done anything to change it? This seems

Exhibit 5.4 *(continued)*

to be so important to us that we commissioned a marketing survey to find out. Its specific purpose, among others, was aimed at answering the question: "Can Andy's establish an identity that would separate it from the ordinary barbecue market and increase its nighttime and weekend patronage?" The key word to me seems to be *identity* or *image.* Not surprisingly, the report confirmed that Andy's had a pretty good image or identity overall—not exactly great but good.

To me, the problem is how to build on a good established image so that you can expand and grow. Also, what improvements can you make on along the way? From this report, the desirable improvements seemed to be table service, more variety, and more atmosphere so that we would attract more families and, in particular, so that we would appeal to women and children. Certainly, maintaining consistent food quality was at the top of any list. The question of repackaging or repositioning Andy's was discussed. It was felt that in the past, Andy's had always been promoted as a good–great barbecue restaurant and that further efforts in this area would not produce any significant results. Based on limited experience, I would have to accept that premise since I do not know what has been done prior to my joining Andy's two years ago.

But, in thinking of "repositioning," I believe we have to realize the fact that Andy's is a specialty barbecue restaurant and that people come to Andy's primarily because they want barbecue. Unless you completely change into another type of restaurant, this must be the basis for all action. In other words, I think for anyone to try Andy's, they must like barbecue, since that is our specialty and that is what Andy's has been known for since it has been in business. I think sometimes we try to get away from this in attempting to find ways to appeal to everyone.

I believe as long as we are a barbecue restaurant, we may just have to accept the fact that we are not going to appeal to everyone. Maybe doing $600,000 sales per year is excellent for a product with the limited appeal of barbecue. Therefore, I do not think you can "repackage" Andy's image into something other than a barbecue specialty restaurant—if you do, you are pretending we are something we are not. Now certainly, you can appeal to people and attract new customers by offering things like better atmosphere and decor, a salad bar, and table service—if that's what they want—but *only* if they like barbecue or at least want to try it to begin with.

My point remains, then, that we must build on Andy's established image and find ways to strengthen and improve it. Although I agree with

Exhibit 5.4 *(continued)*

the ideas of emphasizing table service and so on, I think that what we are really doing is improving and adding to what we do best and strengthening people's perceptions about Andy's.

2. *Lunch versus Dinner*—It has become obvious through all the discussions that one particular area in which Andy's has not been successful is the attracting of evening business. Perhaps we are trying to buck a fundamental trend of the market which is that barbecue is just not a type of meal people eat in the evenings. I believe that we raised this question before and still decided that we must find ways to attract more people in the evenings. *If* barbecue is not particularly attractive as an evening meal, then it would seem that the only way to attract customers is to offer other varieties of food, atmosphere, and so forth. However, I believe that as long as Andy's is a restaurant whose specialty is barbecue (and has been known as such for many years), then we should be careful about changing that image or perception in order not to drive away our primary customers who came specifically for barbecue.

I have collected some data that gives a rough indication of our sales breakdown between lunch and dinner. This information was taken from sales records kept by various managers. (I believe the records are reasonably accurate.) On the average, we get about 50% of our revenue by 2 P.M. and about 40% after 5 P.M. Although I do not have any data, I guess that most of the evening business is done between 5 P.M. and 7:30 P.M. I think this information shows that obviously we do a great deal of our business at lunch, but we do now pick up a good bit in the evening. Perhaps the spread is not as lopsided toward lunch as you would have thought, but considering that we get half of our revenue in about three hours, it does leave room for much improvement the rest of the time we are open. Again, I do not think we want to lose our lunch business by getting away from the fact that we do specialize in barbecue.

Relating all of this to the present marketing implications, I would say that it would be appropriate and consistent to promote Andy's as a good barbecue restaurant—still emphasizing barbecue—that is good for dinner. I do not think we want to get away from the fact that we are a specialty restaurant. No matter how hard we try to get people in at any time, they will not come if they don't like barbecue; to go all out to please them at the expense of losing barbecue eaters would, in my opinion, be a mistake.

3. *Advertising and Promotion*—Finally, I must say something about advertising and promotion in general, as they relate to growth. Certainly, you

Exhibit 5.4 *(continued)*

must have a good operation in order to advertise to the public. You can never stop improving the operation, but, at the same time, you must keep your name in front of the public. This does not necessarily have to involve large amounts of money, but rather a consistent coordinated effort that lets people know about Andy's. I do not think that we have had such a consistent program since I have been here. I believe that the lack of a long-term advertising program has contributed to the present problems. As the marketing survey showed, even in areas close to Andy's locations, there was a significant number of people who had not heard of or been in an Andy's, or who had not even tried barbecue. Thus, I believe that any reasonably constructed advertising program will, in the long run, benefit Andy's regardless of the exact message.

So, I am not necessarily disagreeing with the LM&S proposal, because I think that any advertising or promotion help at this stage would be beneficial. Certainly, advertising is only a part of the overall strategy—the other more important part is the opportunity to provide the food and service on which to build business. Since it has been decided to concentrate on a message different from just "Andy's serves great barbecue," that seems simple enough to change. However, I say once again we should realize that Andy's is, and is known by the public as, a specialty barbecue restaurant. We should thus orient all our efforts around the fact that customers come primarily because they like barbecue.

Exhibit 5.5

Oscar Miles's Reaction to the LM&S Proposal

Dear Tom:

The following remarks summarize my initial impressions of the LM&S proposal. These remarks are designed to stimulate discussion and should be interpreted accordingly.

Positioning

LM&S maintain that Andy's should position itself as "a BBQ restaurant of superior quality." Obviously, this position is almost directly opposite to the position we desire. I feel that Andy's has little to gain from this [the former] position because:

1. This is not a unique selling point for a BBQ restaurant—everyone can say that!
2. I believe that the BBQ market is relatively narrow. Greater sales opportunities exist in expanding Andy's customer base.

Exhibit 5.5 *(continued)*

---

3. Andy's must cultivate female/family dining. By emphasizing the "best BBQ" position, we may further remove ourselves from this market.

Marketing Strategy

LM&S maintain Andy's can increase store traffic by:

1. Gaining a larger share of the existing market for BBQ restaurants.
2. Increasing the propensity among the current BBQ market to have BBQ when dining out at night.

In terms of gaining a larger market share of BBQ restaurant users, I believe that the cost of converting Andy's noncustomers for BBQ to Andy's customers will be extremely high, relative to the opportunity cost of converting the female/family evening dining market to Andy's customers. In other words, we will have greater success if we focus on the restaurant market. My feeling is that it will be easier to get a fraction-of-a-percent market share from the restaurant market (which is obviously larger than the BBQ restaurant—a subset) than, let's say, 1 percent of the BBQ restaurant market. Economics favor a larger customer base.

The second strategy concerning our increasing the propensity among BBQ users to consume at dinner seems more reasonable if the position is family dining, rather than BBQ dining.

Overall Advertising and Promotion Strategy

LM&S maintain that all promotional expenditures should focus on current BBQ users to:

1. Stimulate new user trial of Andy's BBQ.
2. Increase frequency among current users.
3. Avoid short term price-cutting, and so forth.

Media Strategy

Their strategy to "generate broad awareness of Andy's BBQ among current barbecue market" is noteworthy. If previous research has any credibility, Andy already has broad awareness. That does not appear to be our problem. The remaining three strategies seem appropriate, providing the positioning controversy is resolved.

These remarks are based on my initial impressions of the LM&S proposal. I think we should discuss this proposal at greater length. In the meantime, I will try to schedule a meeting with Andrew.

APPENDIX A5   EXCERPTS FROM RESEARCH
COMMISSIONED BY ANDY'S BARBECUE RESTAURANTS

Methodology

Study Sample and Data Collection   A quota sampling technique was used to select households located within a two-mile radius of five Andy's Barbecue Restaurants. Fifty households were selected from each trade area. Three hundred personal interviews were completed.

Household Classification Scheme   For purposes of analysis, households were classified according to the extent to which they (1) ate away from home generally, (2) ate barbecue, and (3) ate at Andy's. The classifications were "heavy," "medium," "light," and "never." A definition of each category is shown in Table A5-1.

Results

Restaurant Selection Criteria   Reasons for selecting a restaurant for lunch and dinner vary considerably, as shown in Table A5-2. For all households in the sample, the major reasons for selecting a restaurant for lunch were: (1) waiting time, (2) food quality, (3) friendly personnel, (4) quick service, and (5) price. The major reasons for selecting a restaurant for dinner were: (1) food quality, (2) friendly personnel, (3) table service, (4) atmosphere, and (5) type of food. Some variation in selection criteria for lunch and dinner by type of use was also evident.

Eating-Out Decision Making and Popularity of Barbecue   Table A5-3 presents data on respondents' decision making and eating habits. Among respondents, 36 percent stated that the man makes most of the decisions to eat out, 41 percent that the woman makes most of the decisions, 22 percent that the decisions are made jointly, and 1 percent made no response.

The second part of Table A5-3 shows that most people (80 percent) in the sample think that everyone in the household would eat barbecue for dinner. Those most against barbecue for dinner are the children (10 percent) and the women (7 percent). In those households where

Table A5-1

Respondent Frequencies for Eating Out, Eating Barbecue, and Eating at Andy's

Frequency	n	Percent of Sample
Number of Times Eat Lunch at a Restaurant		
Twice per week or more (heavy)	123	41.0
Once per month (medium)	119	39.7
Less than once per month (light)	40	13.3
Never	15	5.0
No response	3	1.0
Number of Times Eat Dinner at a Restaurant		
Twice per week or more (heavy)	118	39.3
Once per month (medium)	154	51.3
Less than once per month (light)	23	7.7
Never	5	1.7
Frequency of Eating Barbecue at a Restaurant		
12+ times per year (heavy)	141	47.0
6–11 times per year (medium)	26	8.7
1–5 times per year (light)	100	33.3
Never	30	10.0
No response	3	1.0
Frequency of Eating at Andy's		
5+ times per year (heavy)	86	28.7
3–4 times per year (medium)	29	9.7
1–2 times per year (light)	86	28.7
Never	93	31.0
No response	6	2.0

women and children have a major influence in dining decisions, barbecue has less of a chance as an alternative for dinner. Overall, the data in Table A5-3 have implications for Andy's promotional activities. In almost 63 percent of the decisions on eating out, women are involved either as the major decision maker or as an equal decision maker. Women also are less fond of barbecue for dinner than men are. This suggests the need for some

Table A5-2

Rankings* of Restaurant Selection Criteria by Type of User for Lunch and Dinner

Selection Criteria	Heavy	Medium	Light	Total
Lunch				
Convenient location	5	7	6	7
Quick service	3	4	7	4
Waiting time	2	1	1	1
Friendly personnel	4	3	3.5	3
Price	6	6	3.5	5
Atmosphere	11	10	9	11
Liquor	14	15	14	14
Food quality	1	2	2	2
Food quantity	8	11	10	9.5
Food variety	10	8	8	8
Table service	7	5	5	6
Overall decor	12	12	12	12
Type of food	7	5	5	6
Cafeteria service	13	13	13	13
Take-out service	15	14	15	15
Number of households	123	119	40	282
Dinner				
Convenient location	13	13	13	13
Quick service	12	11	11	11.5
Waiting time	8	6	4	6
Friendly personnel	2	2	2	2
Price	11	9	8	9.5
Atmosphere	4	5	5	4
Liquor	10	12	12	11.5
Food quality	1	1	1	1
Food quantity	9	10	9	9.5
Food variety	7	7	7	7
Table service	3	3	3	3
Overall decor	6	8	10	8
Type of food	5	4	6	5
Cafeteria service	14	14	14	14
Take-out service	15	15	15	15
Number of households	118	154	23	295

* Rankings are based on an average rating given to each selection, where 1 = most important and 15 = least important.

Table A5-3
Respondent Decision Making about Eating Habits

Decision Variable	Number	Percent of Sample
Who Makes Most Decisions to Dine Out		
Man	109	36.3
Woman	123	41.0
Joint man/woman	65	21.7
No response	3	1.0
Who in the Household Would Not Eat Barbecue for Dinner		
Everyone would eat BBQ for dinner	240	80.0
Female of household would not	21	7.0
Children of household would not	30	10.0
Male of household would not	9	3.0

attitude change strategies directed at women to sway their perceptions of barbecue.

As a whole, the respondents perceive barbecue as being very filling, middle-class, moderately expensive, moderately sloppy, very tasty, rather spicy, somewhat for kids, and pretty good for dinner.

Consumer Perceptions of Barbecue Restaurants

In addition to obtaining data on overall perceptions of barbecue, it was necessary to gather data about consumer perceptions of barbecue restaurants. Respondents think that barbecue restaurants are quite informal, moderately expensive, middle-class, rather clean, quite family oriented, and having a good atmosphere. The data, when analyzed by type of user, indicate that the "heavy" user perceives barbecue restaurants as being less clean than other user types perceive it. Although the differences are slight, the "light" user perceives barbecue restaurants as more informal, less expensive, lower-class, less clean, less family-oriented, and with a poorer atmosphere than the "heavy" user perceives them. This pattern does not exist in the general perceptions of barbecue as food.

Table A5-4 reports the ratings for statements concerning Andy's. Respondents were asked to relate their degree of agreement or disagreement

Table A5-4

A Comparison of Andy's Rankings with General Selection Criteria

| Selection Criterion | Importance for* | | Likert Statement | Percent Responses** | | | | |
	Lunch	Dinner		SA	A	U	D	SD
Convenient location	I	U	Andy's is conveniently located.	49.2	35.4	9.8	4.7	.8
Quick service	I	U	Andy's has quick service.	29.6	46.6	20.2	3.2	.4
Waiting time to get in	I	I	Andy's waiting lines are too long.	2.8	8.7	17.2	47.4	13.8
Friendly personnel	I	I	Andy's personnel are unfriendly.	1.6	11.1	30.0	43.5	13.6
Price	I	U	Andy's has reasonable prices.	9.9	47.8	26.1	11.1	5.1
Atmosphere	I	U	Andy's has a good atmosphere.	11.1	57.9	22.6	7.1	1.2
Quality of food	I	I	Andy's has low-quality food.	6.7	6.7	24.9	45.1	16.6
Variety of food	U	I	Andy's offers a sufficient variety of foods.	9.2	20.3	31.5	31.5	7.6
Overall decor	U	I	Andy's does not have a good interior appearance.	9.6	50.6	27.3	10.3	2.4
			Andy's does not have a good exterior appearance.	5.5	14.6	21.3	45.8	12.6

* Based on Exhibit 5A.2. I = important, U = unimportant.

** SA = strongly agree, A = agree, U = undecided, D = disagree, SD = strongly disagree.

121

with each statement. The ratings in Table A5-4 suggest that respondents believe that Andy's is conveniently located, has quick service, does not have long lines, has friendly personnel, has a good atmosphere, does not have low-quality food, has a sufficient variety of foods, and has a good interior and exterior appearance. Respondents are somewhat uncertain, however, as to the amount of food for the price, the reasonableness of the price, and whether or not Andy's should offer more than barbecue as the main food.

Focusing on dinner, the data show that while Andy's is conveniently located and has quick service and reasonable prices, these criteria are relatively unimportant for dinner. Thus, while Andy's is perceived quite positively on these dimensions, consumers do not think them important criteria for dinner restaurant selection.

The criteria perceived as being important, and in which Andy's is doing fine, are length of waiting time, friendly personnel, good atmosphere, and quality of food. The criteria perceived as being important for dinner, and in which Andy's is not perceived as doing well are: the offering of sufficient variety of food (40% disagree that Andy's is offering such variety), having a good interior appearance (60% agree that Andy's does not have one), and having a good exterior appearance (21% agree that it does not have one).

Case Six

Carden Park Hotel and Resort

David Bowie

When Carden Park formally opened, John Broome's ultimate vision of creating Europe's premier hotel, golf, sports, and leisure resort finally came true. Although the development was not entirely complete, the first stage was: a championship golf course and golfing academy, a luxury hotel, and extensive corporate hospitality and banqueting facilities were ready to welcome guests. One of the finest management teams in the United Kingdom had been recruited to cater to top international business and leisure customers, who were expected to enjoy the luxurious facilities and high-quality service that the resort promised. Broome's vision was to see Carden Park as "an example of perfection where guests can work and relax in complete peace." Following a high profile public relations and marketing campaign, Broome was quoted as confidently expecting a 90 percent occupancy from day one.

In a short time, however, Carden Park was suffering both from disappointing sales and from unkind rumors and gossip, as was Broome himself. The hotel was not achieving target sales, some members of the management team had left, and a number of the local traders were complaining that their bills remained unpaid. Broome's dream was rapidly turning into a nightmare. What were the reasons for Carden Park's current problems, and what actions could now be taken to ensure that Carden Park survived and prospered? he wondered.

This case was written by David Bowie, M.B.A., while he was Visiting Lecturer in Hospitality Marketing at Sheffield Hallam University, England. He is now Senior Lecturer in Marketing, Oxford Brookes University, England. All rights reserved. Used by permission.

JOHN BROOME—A CONTROVERSIAL ENTREPRENEUR

Although his father was the headmaster of an English prep school, John Broome was a natural entrepreneur. He demonstrated his risk-taking acumen for property development, and surprised his family and friends, when he bought a large, detached house in Chester for £2,200 at auction. Broome was 16 at the time and only had savings of £122 in his Post Office account. Thankfully his family rallied around and agreed to help pay for the property—on condition that he carried out the conversion work and agreed to pay the family back when the property was sold. Broome succeeded in his first venture and enjoyed the thrill of property speculation. By day he became a history and geography teacher at his father's prep school, and by night he developed his rapidly expanding property business. By the time he was 24, Broome's property company, J L B Investments, had made its mark. At 25 he became the youngest-ever Conservative Councillor in Chester, but continued developing his company, which, within a few years, owned nearly 200 properties in the area.

In 1971, aged 28, Broome married Jane Bagshawe, whose family owned Alton Towers in nearby Staffordshire. Alton Towers was one of England's first stately homes to be opened to the public by the 18th Earl of Shrewsbury in 1860. In 1923, Bagshawe's grandfather was among a group of businesspeople who bought Alton Towers and further developed the facilities to encourage more visitors to the house and grounds. The estate was taken over by the Ministry of Defence during World War II and, unfortunately, the house suffered from neglect, leaking roofs, and wet rot. After the war Bagshawe's father, Dennis, eventually acquired the controlling interest in the estate, restored the gardens, opened Alton Towers to the public again, and continued to improve the facilities. With its attractive gardens, boating lake, and cable-car system, Alton Towers was a popular place to visit in the 1950s and 1960s.

After marriage, Broome took an active interest in his father-in-law's business. He obtained the franchise for the company's first "ride" attraction in 1973 and then successfully developed the concept of a theme park with a wide range of popular attractions. In the next 15 years, he installed Britain's first double-loop roller-coaster "The Corkscrew"; an "Adventure-land" for youngsters and a "Fantasy World" with a "Black Hole" roller-coaster for older children and adults. A "Log Flume" and hi-tech monorail system followed, and the biggest fast-food restaurant in Europe was built to cater to the 2 million visitors whom Alton Towers attracted each year. Although the local Staffordshire Moorlands District Council did not find Broome the easiest of developers to deal with—there were comments that he tended to apply for planning permission after a new facility had been constructed—many people recognized Broome as a charismatic and visionary leader in U.K. tourism. By the late 1980s, his energy and vision had transformed Alton Towers into Europe's premier leisure park, and he was awarded a CBE[1] in recognition of his significant contribution to tourism in Britain.

In 1987, Broome won a competition for the best land use for some property owned by the Gas Board and, for £1.5 million, he bought the site of its redundant power station at Battersea Park—one of London's most famous landmarks. While retaining the shell of the "listed" power station, his intention was to develop a major leisure and amusement park with the backing of a consortium of banks led by Security Pacific. This was an exciting, high-profile project that attracted considerable public and media interest. Indeed, Mrs. Thatcher attended a press conference on the site and gave the venture her support. By 1990, the projected development costs had risen from an estimated £135 million to over £300 million, and Broome's backers began to express concern about the escalating costs. Broome decided to adapt the original concept to enhance the viability of the scheme by providing conference and exhibition facilities and two hotels, with over 1,600 bedrooms, on part of the adjoining land at Battersea Wharf, land that he did not own. There was some local concern about his proposals, and meanwhile two rival developers had put forward alternative schemes.

Earlier, in 1987, Broome had bought Carden Park, once a great country estate in Cheshire, which was located adjacent to his family's private country residence Stretton Hall. Although Carden Park's magnificent old

---

[1] A CBE (Companion of the British Empire) award is given by the British Government to a citizen for outstanding services to the Country. There are several different categories of award, dating back many centuries, and most are linked to the monarchy. Recipients attend an awards ceremony at Buckingham Palace and receive their "honors" from the Queen.

hall had been destroyed by fire over 50 years earlier, and the parkland had suffered considerable neglect since the estate fell into disrepair, Broome had a dream of restoring Carden to its former glory.

With so many projects requiring such considerable funding, Broome had to raise more capital. Although Alton Towers was sold to the Madam Tussaud's Group in 1990, Broome's backers in the Battersea Park project were not prepared to invest the additional sums required and, finally, that venture collapsed. As a result of these events, Broome was now able to concentrate his considerable charm and entrepreneurial skills on developing Carden Park. To do this, he was able to raise £23 million, as a sole trader, and commit very little of his own resources.[2]

THE CONCEPT

Although Broome frankly admitted he did not have a hotel background, he had traveled extensively throughout the world staying in the top resorts and hotels and gaining firsthand experience of their facilities, standards, and service. During his research Broome was particularly impressed with the luxury American resorts, especially Boulders Inn near Phoenix, Arizona. With no alternative land-use constraints and few planning restrictions, the Boulders Inn development had been able to take advantage of the large tracts of land available. Situated in the sunny, dry, and warm climate of the Arizona sun belt, Boulders, with its two championship golf courses and extensive leisure amenities, was an impressive resort. The development was beautifully landscaped to complement the natural sandstone rocks and had been designed to be ecologically and environmentally sensitive despite being built on the grand American scale. The accommodations, set in nearly 400 acres, provided guests with luxurious facilities in individual two-story villas. The rooms were extremely spacious with large, panoramic windows, and each villa had extraordinary, giant-sized verandahs with spectacular views. A high staff/customer ratio impressed visitors and provided an efficient service, epitomized by the competent buggy service that ferried guests around the resort. Broome, equally impressed with the

---

[2] For conversion purposes, use one English pound (£) as approximately equivalent to U.S. $1.50, Canadian $2.10, FF 7.8, DM 2.3, and 190 pta.

style and quality of Boulders and the fact that the resort was so busy, wished to emulate the Phoenix operation at Carden Park.

Broome believed it was essential to provide guests with a wide range of facilities and activities and to offer customers the choice of being able to opt for different service levels according to their needs. Most of all, he believed that it was important to offer customers excellent value, and "the pursuit of affordable excellence" became the public mission statement at Carden Park. This concept of choice extended to the dining arrangements, where guests would enjoy dining in the elegance of one of Europe's finest restaurants; preparing a meal for themselves in their very own "butler's pantry"; or even dining in their own suite with a butler, maid, and chef catering exclusively to them. The resort facilities at Carden Park were also designed to provide guests with an unrivaled choice of different sporting and leisure activities, but, while Broome wanted to provide the ultimate European resort experience, he did not believe in cutting corners. The foundations of Carden and its infrastructure were built to the highest specifications. For example, the drainage and irrigation systems and the design and landscaping of Carden's golfing facilities were exceptional.

GOLF

In the 1980s a combination of factors had contributed to a surge in golf's popularity. Television coverage, including by the new satellite channels, of the major international tournaments promoted golf throughout the year to consumers enjoying greater affluence and increased leisure time.

In 1987, in an attempt to reduce farming surpluses and diversify the usages to which agricultural land could be put, the U.K. government advised local authorities that appropriate development of poorer-quality farmland would be considered more favorably. The relaxation in planning conditions coincided with an internal survey carried out by the English Golf Union (EGU), which estimated that at least 400 new golf courses were needed in England by the year 2000. The Royal and Ancient Golf Club of St Andrews (the R&A) investigated the situation and produced a 1989 report, "The Demand for Golf," which suggested that as many as 700 new courses were needed. The R&A based their projections on the

1989 ratio of the number of golf facilities to the country's population, as shown below.

Ratio of Golf Courses to Population in 1989

Scotland	1 : 12,000
England	1 : 36,000
Eastern USA	1 : 20,000
Australia	1 : 10,000

The R&A's target of 700 new courses was based on a playing facility-to-population ratio of 1 : 25,000. The reasons for choosing this ratio for England was that the target compared favorably with ratios in other countries where there was an equilibrium between supply and demand. Although the projected provision of new courses was considered to be ambitious, the golf authorities believed it was a realistic target.

The Sports Council, keen to promote the development of golf, provided advice to would-be entrepreneurs. They produced "Study of Golf in England," a report suggesting that successful projects in the past had been developed as low-cost, low-risk projects with simple golf facilities. After finding suitable land and gaining planning permission, developers were advised that they should open half a dozen holes to start generating revenue as soon as possible. It was recommended that during the start-up stage, developers should charge extremely competitive prices to encourage use of an embryonic golf course. Indeed, clubhouse facilities should be limited to changing rooms only. As the low-priced golfing facility became more popular and revenues increased, the surplus would be reinvested in additional holes and finally in the provision of clubhouse facilities. As the facilities improved, it was suggested that fees could be increased and the surplus reinvested. This trading formula provided a simple but effective route for entrepreneurs to develop popular and profitable golfing facilities.

In the five years between 1989 and 1994, farmers put forward speculative proposals hoping to realize substantial profits. The EGU estimated that there were 1,800 planning applications for golfing facilities. In 1989, the value of agricultural land with planning permission for golf was between £3,000 and £5,000 per acre, approximately twice the value of similar farmland. Typical land prices for a 150-acre golfing site, suitable for an 18-hole golf course, ranged from £450,000 to £750,000. The Sports Council estimated that an 18-hole commercial golf operation could achieve 50,000 rounds of golf per annum. At an average green fee of £10 (allowing for concessions), this could generate £500,000 annual turnover including a value-added tax of 17.5 percent. Other activities like the bar, catering, and professional's shop should be self-financing, and the average club expenditure on a course could be less than £200,000 annually.

Leisure and property developers were obviously attracted to golf developments that were ostensibly put forward as leisure and recreation developments but which increasingly became ancillary elements to mixed residential housing developments. Although this was termed "the Trojan Horse" phenomenon by the English Heritage Foundation, the development of executive-style houses and time sharing was a fundamental element in the successful financing of major golf projects. John Broome, always one to take advantage of opportunities, felt the time was ripe to tap into this phenomenon.

CHESTER AND THE CHESHIRE PLAIN

Carden Park was approximately 10 miles south of historic Chester in the Cheshire Plain, 30 miles from Liverpool, and 40 miles from Manchester. Exhibit 6.1 shows a location map. The county was 2,331 square kilometers and had a population of just under 1 million people. North Cheshire was part of the Mersey Belt connurbation stretching from Liverpool to Manchester, a heavily industrialized area with a catchment population of over 4.5 million residents.

The county was subdivided into four separate areas. The west, which included Chester, was an "EC assisted area," largely dependent upon old declining industries, and with large tracts of derelict land and high unemployment. East Cheshire, which included Congleton, was relatively prosperous: a high level of new firms were forming, key science-based industries were located in the area, and it was home to the prosperous business community of Manchester. The rural south relied on dairy farming and suffered from the closure of dairies. The fourth area was a north/south

Exhibit 6.1
Carden Park Location Map. [From Carden Park brochure.]

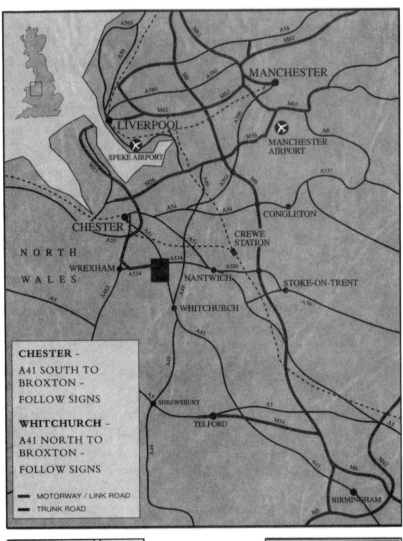

BY ROAD	
CHESTER	15 mins
CREWE STATION	20 mins
LIVERPOOL	40 mins
MANCHESTER AIRPORT	40 mins
MANCHESTER	50 mins
BIRMINGHAM	75 mins
BY RAIL	
CREWE STATION TO LONDON	2 hrs

central corridor running from Warrington to Crewe. This corridor had become a major transport access for the motorway and rail system. The M6 highway carried traffic from Birmingham and the south/southwest, to the northwest and Scotland; a similar route was followed by the main-line railways.

Over 60 percent of Cheshire people lived in the industrialized towns, 20 percent in rural communities, and 10 percent each in the suburbs and historic towns. Cheshire industry relied on chemicals (Fisons, ICI, Shell), engineering (Vickers), motor vehicles (Vauxhall), and textiles. The county was regarded as one of the most prosperous in northern England.

The mean annual temperature of Cheshire and Lancashire varied between 8°C and 10°C, with extreme temperatures varying from +15°C to −15°C in January and from +5°C to +30°C in July. Annual sunshine was approximately 1,550 hours, and average yearly precipitation was about 800 millimeters. The number of snow days each year varied from 15 to 30 and was higher farther inland, but snow lay on the ground an average of only 10 days per year. Exhibit 6.2 provides further details of the climate in the northwest.

Historic Chester

The ancient walled city of Chester had been founded by the Roman Legions in A.D. 79 and retained much of its Roman and medieval heritage. The main city thoroughfares had been laid out by the Romans, and the largest Roman amphitheater ever uncovered in Britain lay just outside the medieval walls. Chester had been the largest port in northwest England in medieval times, when the city exported cheese, candles, and salt. From Viking raiders to Norman conquerors, from Cromwell and the two-year siege of Royalist Chester to the industrial revolution, the city offered a rich and colorful history. Chester had become a honey-pot tourist destination, with thousands of European, American, and Japanese tourists enjoying the sights of the historic city every year. Chester had also become a world-famous shopping center featuring "The Rows," a network of tiered galleries of medieval and modern shops offering the best of British shopkeeping.

Visitors to Chester enjoyed a wide choice of good-quality accommodations including one of the most highly rated hotels in the North of England—the Chester Grosvenor. Owned by the Dukes of Westminster

Exhibit 6.2

Climate in Northwestern England. [From The Meteorological Office, Climate of Great Britain (Lancashire, Chesire, and Isle of Man). Crown copyright—reproduced with the permission of the controller of HMSO.]

Preston, Lancashire, Cheshire	Jan.	Feb.	Mar.	Apr.	May	June	July	Aug.	Sep.	Oct.	Nov.	Dec.
Monthly Rainfall (mm)												
Average	87	62	53	63	68	71	86	113	108	99	98	97
Maximum	144	164	121	108	126	126	144	314	200	254	207	219
Minimum	11	11	22	3	14	17	28	7	12	35	33	23

Manchester Airport	Jan.	Feb.	Mar.	Apr.	May	June	July	Aug.	Sep.	Oct.	Nov.	Dec.
Hours of Monthly Bright Sunshine												
Average	42	62	117	140	184	190	160	157	123	96	57	41
Maximum	71	98	169	190	252	285	279	259	197	136	89	65
Minimum	11	34	63	94	120	119	102	89	69	62	24	16

since it was built in 1866, this stylish Victorian four-"red"-star hotel[3] won the Egon Ronay Hotel of the Year Award in 1993. The hotel had an informal Parisian-style brasserie, a gourmet restaurant that had been awarded three AA rosettes for the quality of the cuisine, generously proportioned bedrooms with high-quality furniture, and extremely high levels of courtesy and professionalism from smartly uniformed staff. The Grosvenor had an enviable tradition of catering to royalty, VIPs, businesspeople, and tourists. Accommodation prices ranged from £135 per night for a single (room only) and £199 for a double, to £434 for the master suite. The à la carte gourmet dinner menu was priced from £37.00.

The Chester Moat House (150 bedrooms) and the Best Western Mollington Banastre (64 rooms), both four-star hotels with extensive banqueting and conference facilities, also offered high standards of accommodation and service, and at competitive prices. Moat House prices ranged from £60 to £99 for a single room including breakfast, and the Mollington Banastre, which had an excellent health club with a large swimming pool, charged from £77 to £85. A few miles outside Chester, just over the border in Wales, a newly built four-star hotel—St David's Park with 121 rooms—was even more price-competitive. A single room with breakfast ranged from just £56 up to £79. The owners of St David's had opened a golf club at nearby Northrop in June 1994 and now offered a full range of exciting golf and leisure packages at great value prices.

There were at least 10 three-star hotels in the Chester area, including the highly acclaimed Crabwall Manor—a 48-bedroom luxury countryhouse hotel refurbished in the traditional English style.

Cheshire also had a good selection of golf clubs for both residents and visitors. The clubs, memberships, and green fees are shown in Exhibit 6.3.

CARDEN PARK

Conservation and a high regard for the community and environment were at the top of John Broome's priorities in the design and restoration of

---

[3] In the United Kingdom the Automobile Association (AA) awards hotels star ratings based on the level of comfort, facilities, and service: one star for modest establishments to five stars for the most exclusive and luxurious hotels. The AA awards prestigious "red" stars to the finest hotels in each star rating. In 1995, there were 121 British hotels out of 4,000 listed establishments with red stars. Twenty-one hotels had been awarded four red stars, and only 13 had been awarded five red stars. Restaurants are awarded comparable "rosettes."

Exhibit 6.3

List of Cheshire Golf Clubs. [From *The Royal and Ancient Golfers Handbook*, 1994. Copyright Pan Macmillan.]

Name*	Number of Members	Public Fees (£) When Available	
		Weekday	*Weekend*
Alder Root	450	16	18
Alderley Edge	382	18	22
Astbury	700	25	
Birchwood	1,069		
Chester	840	21	26
Congleton	425		
Crewe	628	27	
Davenport	600	24	
Delamere Forest	400	25	35
Eaton	550		
Ellesmere Port	350	5	6.30
Frodsham	550	18	25
Helsby	600	20	
Heyrose		18	23
Knights Grange	Public	3.40	5.10
Knutsford	250	15	20
Leigh	700	25	32
Lymm	625	20	
Macclesfield	600	17	20
Malkins Bank	Public	5.30	6.30
Mere	650	45	
Mottram Hall Hotel	Pay and play	30	35
New Mills	350		
Oaklands	630	16	21
Portal	100	Summer 30	Winter 20
Poulton Park	360	16	18
Prestbury	725	27	
Queens Park	Public	3.30	4.25
Reaseheath College	120	3	
Runcorn	535	16	20
Sandbach	390	16	
Sandiway	300	30	35
Shrigley Hall	540	22	28
The Tytherington	700	25	40

Exhibit 6.3 *(continued)*

Name*	Number of Members	Public Fees (£) When Available	
		Weekday	Weekend
Upton-by-Chester	750	20	25
Vicars Cross	650	20	
Walton Hall	Public	4.50	5.50
Warrington	875		
Widnes	800	20	30
Widnes Municipal	Public	n/a	n/a
Wilmslow	770	30	40

* This list does not include clubs affiliated with the English Golf Union but not registered with the R&A.

Carden Park. The rebuilding of the estate started in 1988, and over 14 miles of dry stone wall were repaired, 27,000 trees were planted, and new drainage was installed for over 1,000 acres of parkland. Thousands of tons of earth were moved and grassed over to form an attractive natural bank designed to obscure from view the estate's roads and car movements. Over 25,000 pheasants and 15,000 deer were introduced to enhance the resort's natural setting. Europe's most northerly commercial vineyard was set up on the gentle slopes behind the woodland lodges of the hotel. The 10 acres of Carden Park's vineyard grew the Seyval Blanc grape, which produced a dry Chablis-style wine and compared exceptionally well with wines produced in more traditional wine-making countries. The estate produced over 32,000 bottles of wine per annum, which was offered as the house wine in the resort's restaurant and was served at banqueting and hospitality events. Exhibit 6.4 provides a plan of Carden Park and its facilities.

Golf

The 18-hole, 6,775-yard par-72 championship golf course, designed by Alan Higgins and John Garner and constructed by Brian Pierson, Ltd., had an advanced irrigation and drainage system to allow play throughout the year. Set in 140 acres, six of the holes were in Carden Park's superb undulating parkland; six in a mature, contoured woodland setting; and six designed around natural water features. Each of the holes had its own unique identity and offered a challenging test for golfers of every ability.

Exhibit 6.4
Plan of Carden Park. [From Carden Park brochure.]

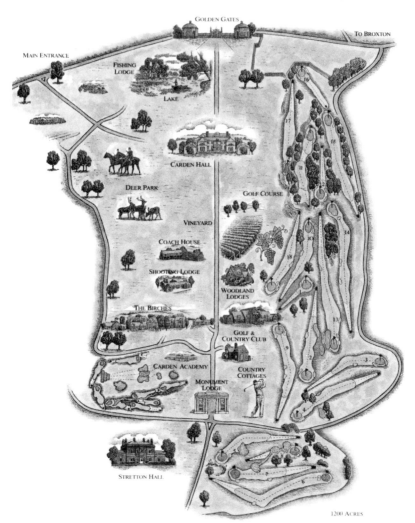

A buggy track provided access throughout the course, and 60 of the very latest state-of-the-art buggy carts were to provide a transportation system.

In addition to the championship course, the Carden Golf Academy offered a delightful nine-hole executive par-3 course, three driving ranges—one under cover—an international game arena, a pitching area, and a putting green. Broome claimed that the academy had the finest golf tuition center in Europe, with the very latest in split-screen, video teaching technology. Expert advice and coaching were offered to every standard of golfer from the novice and inspired amateur to the seasoned professional and even international players. Exhibit 6.5 provides details of the Championship Golf Course, and Exhibit 6.6shows details of the Carden Academy.

The professional's golf shop provided a computerized booking facility, a huge selection of top-name golf clubs and equipment, and expert advice given to guests on how to select the most appropriate equipment.

The decor and design of the attractive clubhouse subtly emphasized Broome's high regard for environmental concerns. The interior design used natural timbers, red brick, and white plaster to create a modern yet traditional ambience. The comfortable, deep-seated sofas and armchairs, covered in rich traditional fabrics, and open log fires created an informal, elegant atmosphere. Facilities included a spacious, open, planned lounge area; reception and golf shop; superbly appointed changing facilities, spike bar, and brasserie restaurant/coffee shop; and a top-fashion shop with English and Scottish country-style garments.

The fees for membership in Carden's Golf Club were £570 to join and £540 for the annual subscription. The green fee, at £35.00, was among the highest for a new club in England.

Croquet

One of the finest croquet lawns in the world was set out on the grounds in front of the Birches Hotel and Restaurant. Indeed, the lawns were of such a high standard that the World Croquet Championships were played at Carden Park early in its first year. This most quintessential of English summer games was offered as just one of over 20 outdoor leisure pursuits and sporting activities for corporate and individual guests.

Outdoor Pursuits and Sports

Country sports at Carden Park included game shooting, clay-pigeon shooting, archery, falconry, and trout fishing—both lake and stream. The equestrian center provided country riding, expert tuition, dressage, eventing, and even carriage driving. There was lawn tennis on a championship course, bowls, boules, mountain biking and cycling, hot-air ballooning,

Exhibit 6.5
Carden Championship Golf Course. [From Carden Park brochure.]

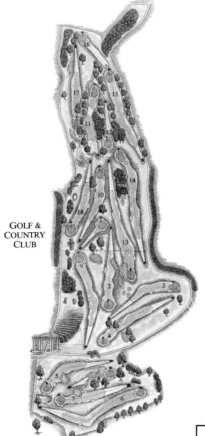

18-HOLE CHAMPIONSHIP GOLF COURSE

- DESIGNED AND BUILT TO BLEND TOTALLY WITH THE LANDSCAPE

- SUPERB PARKLAND SETTING

- 6 HOLES IN PARKLAND, 6 IN WOODLAND AND 6 AROUND NATURAL WATER FEATURES

- UNIQUE IDENTITY TO EACH HOLE

- MOST ADVANCED IRRIGATION AND DRAINAGE SYSTEM ALLOWING PLAY ALL YEAR ROUND

- BUGGY TRACK THROUGHOUT THE WHOLE COURSE

- A TEST FOR PLAYERS OF ANY ABILITY

- ON COURSE PLAYERS AND GUESTS CHANGING FACILITIES AND LOUNGE

- THE VERY LATEST BUGGY CARTS

Membership available

GOLF &
COUNTRY
CLUB

Hole	Par	Length(Yds)	Hole	Par	Length(Yds)
1	3	175	10	4	363
2	4	387	11	4	278
3	4	411	12	3	200
4	4	454	13	5	585
5	4	380	14	5	570
6	5	553	15	4	396
7	4	461	16	3	169
8	3	229	17	4	380
9	5	477	18	4	360
OUT	36	3527 yds	IN	36	3301 yds

Exhibit 6.6
Carden Golf Academy. [From Carden Park brochure.]

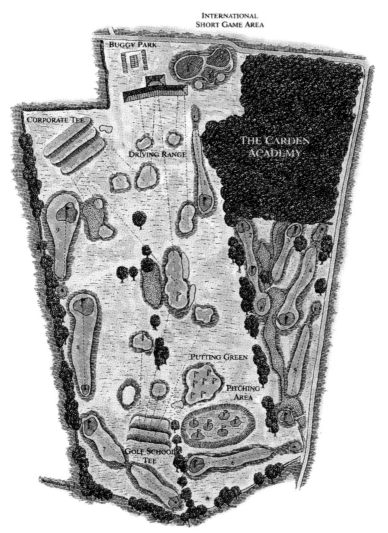

an exciting four-wheel-drive rally course, quad bikes, and an orienteering course. For those who preferred more gentle pursuits, there was an 18th-century pleasure walk through the gardens and grounds, or sightseeing and shopping in nearby Chester. Indeed, the sporting facilities at Carden Park were of such a high international standard that the resort would have hosted the croquet, equestrian, and shooting events in the 2000 Olympics if Manchester had won its bid to host the games.

Health-and-Beauty Spa

A five-star-standard health-and-beauty spa with a specially designed fitness pool (approximately 8.5 meters long), steam room, trimnasium, jacuzzi, and sauna solarium complemented the outdoor activities. A comprehensive beauty clinic with facials, top-to-toe body treatments, massage, and makeup was provided by Clarins of Paris. These facilities were provided in the Birches Hotel, but Broome had plans to build a new £5 million Olympic-sized swimming pool, leisure center, and sports hall.

The Birches Hotel

The Birches Hotel had been carefully designed to complement the nearby old houses and farm buildings built during earlier centuries. The public areas, overlooking the croquet lawns, were housed in two single-story red-brick octagonal rotundas with striking, pitched roofs. Exhibit 6.7 shows an artist's impression of the hotel. Originally the plans provided for a larger reception and foyer area, but Broome needed to adapt the design to make some cost savings. Although the guest reception and lobby area—housed in one of the buildings—was smaller than in most luxury hotels, it had been designed for convenience to enable guests to check in

Exhibit 6.7
The Birches Hotel: An Artist's Impression. [From Carden Park brochure.]

and drive to their suites with a minimum of fuss. The guests' electronic room key card doubled as a swipe card and could be used to bill any activity throughout the resort.

A few yards away in the other "rotunda" was the restaurant. Access between the buildings was by a covered walkway. Le Croquet was described in Carden Park's brochure as one of Europe's finest restaurants. The stylish circular room; the elegant china—an unreleased Villeroy and Boch design—and Palomo Picasso cutlery; the attractive setting with views overlooking the croquet lawns, deer park, and Welsh hills; the elegant drapes, subtle lighting, live band or piano music, and feature wrought-iron "band stand" dance floor—all this created an intimate ambience for fine dining. Andrew Mitchell, formerly the chef to the Aga Khan, was appointed to ensure that the international brasserie-style cuisine rivaled the best of French gourmet restaurants, and Victor Scapetti, "Waiter of the Year," was hired for his finesse and skills in customer care. With such excellent cuisine and service in such a wonderful venue, the set dinner menu, at £17.50, provided exceptional value for money. A proposed lounge and bar area had been eliminated due to space requirements.

The hotel accommodations and two woodland lodges were designed around Mediterranean-style garden courtyards. The accommodations included:

Number	Accommodations	Comprising
68	Ambassador	Double/twin bedroom
		Dressing area/butler's pantry
		Luxury bathroom
12	Earl	Lounge in addition
2	Duke	Lounge with dining area in addition
1	Prince of Wales	Four-poster bedroom
		Fitted kitchen

Exhibit 6.8 provides details of Carden Park's pricing structure.

The two-story modern brick villas ("country cottages") were built with pitched roofs, each housing approximately six suites. Broome believed that people, when staying away, were looking for something more than they had in their own houses: "Today, people's houses are full of electronic

Exhibit 6.8

Carden Park's Pricing Structure. [From Carden Park brochure.]

DELUXE AMBASSADOR

Single Occupancy	*Double Twin*
£85.00	*£125.00*

EARL SUITE

Single Occupancy	*Double Twin*
£125.00	*£150.00*

DUKE SUITE

Single Occupancy	*Double Twin*
£175.00	*£200.00*

PRINCE OF WALES SUITE

Single/Double Occupancy (exc boardroom facility) £250.00
Single/Double Occupancy (inc boardroom facility) £450.00

*All the rates for hotel rooms include VAT at the current rate
and are inclusive of full English breakfast.*

WEEKEND BREAK

Single Occupancy
£50.00 per night Inclusive of Full English Breakfast & VAT

Double/Twin Occupancy
£80.00 per night Inclusive of Full English Breakfast & VAT

ROOM SUPPLEMENTS

Earl Suite £30.00, Duke Suite £50.00, Prince of Wales Suite £130.00

COUNTRY COTTAGES TARIFF

From 1st January–31st December

Cherry Cottage from £237.00 to £460.00 Sleeps 4
Firtree Cottage from £237.00 to £460.00 Sleeps 6

CONFERENCE AND BANQUETING FACILITIES

*Carden Park has a wide range of conference and banqueting facilities.
Please contact Kate Webster or Judy Jones for more details.*

Exhibit 6.8 *(continued)*

Child Accommodation and Meals Policy

Children up to the ages of 12 sharing their parents room stay at £20.00 per child

including full English breakfast

(Maximum 2 children)

A minimum of 2 children occupying their own room do so at a 20% discount of the adult rate.

Children up to 8 years—meals are charged at 50% discount of the adult rate.

gadgets, and hotel rooms have to offer something different." Broome insisted on installing the latest technology in every suite with a state-of-the-art high-definition television, video, CDI, CD, hi-fi, telephone and fax entertainment and communications system, including CDs, tapes, and videos. The luxury suites, with spacious lounges, tastefully decorated and furnished with Regency-style reproduction furniture, fine art prints, books, and ornaments, and feature fireplaces with real log fires, created an exclusive ambience.

Villa facilities included stylish bathrooms, with pressed-steel baths, elegant tiles, and the finest range of complementary toiletries; individual dressing rooms; a butler's pantry complete with kitchen equipment, fridge, wash-up area, and utensils; a minibar; and a trouser press, and iron/ironing board. Of course, a 24-hour room-and-valet service was readily available, with butlers and housemaids on hand to cater to guests' every requests.

Banqueting, Conference, and Corporate Hospitality Facilities

The Old Shooting Lodge, Pavilion, Coach House, and Prince of Wales Suite each provided a flexible range of facilities suitable for business and private entertaining. The Shooting Lodge, with its old brick and plaster walls, great open fireplace, timbered ceiling, and full-length windows, was a multipurpose room suitable for meetings, private dinners, and as a reception room for the Pavilion. The Pavilion, really a marquee, housed in a temporary brick-and-timber structure, could comfortably seat 150 people at attractive tables of 10. The Coach House comprised four smaller conference rooms, catering between 12 and 40 delegates, depending upon the room and whether the event was boardroom or theater style. The Prince of Wales Suite was designed exclusively for the chairmen, chief

Exhibit 6.9

Carden Banqueting and Conference Layouts. [From Carden Park brochure.]

**THE SHOOTING LODGE
AND PAVILION**

- PERFECT SETTING FOR CONFERENCES,
  SEMINARS, EXHIBITIONS, PRODUCT LAUNCHES
  AND CORPORATE HOSPITALITY OF ANY TYPE
  FOR UP TO 200 PEOPLE

- FLEXIBLE USE OF BUILDINGS

- REMOVABLE SIDE OF PAVILION ALLOWS
  ACCESS FOR LARGE EXHIBITS

- SUPERB GREAT OPEN FIREPLACE, TIMBERED
  CEILING AND FULL LENGTH WINDOWS

- EN-SUITE KITCHEN FACILITIES MAKE IT IDEAL
  FOR PRIVATE PARTIES, WEDDINGS, BANQUETS
  AND A FULL RANGE OF SOCIAL FUNCTIONS

- THE SHOOTING LODGE AND PAVILION CAN BE
  USED SEPARATELY OR TOGETHER.

- WINE TASTING EVENINGS

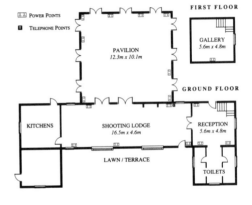

THE SHOOTING LODGE
Boardroom style- 24c (Using Mahogany Table)
Boardroom style- 50c (Using covered tables)
Reception-   80c
Dining-   24c (Using Mahogany Table)
Dining-   50c (Using covered tables)

PAVILION
Boardroom style- 60c
Theatre style-   160c
Banqueting-   150c (round tables of 10)
Reception-   200c

executives, and diplomats of top international corporations and governments. The boardroom could seat 16 executives and was linked to the hotel's most luxurious private suite. See Exhibit 6.9 for the banqueting and conference layouts.

Carden Park was actively promoted as an ideal venue for corporate hospitality and incentive travel occasions. Indeed, Broome believed the marketing was so important that he appointed Nick Smith, who had been Chief Executive of the Consort Hotels marketing consortium, to head up the campaign. The combination of the outstanding sporting and activity facilities and the excellent catering facilities made Carden a natural choice for top companies wishing to impress customers or reward employees. The Carden Park "incen-

Exhibit 6.9 *(continued)*

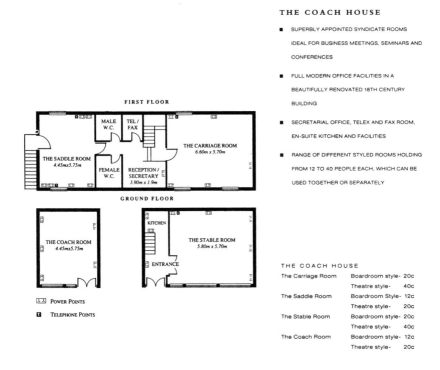

THE COACH HOUSE

- SUPERBLY APPOINTED SYNDICATE ROOMS IDEAL FOR BUSINESS MEETINGS, SEMINARS AND CONFERENCES

- FULL MODERN OFFICE FACILITIES IN A BEAUTIFULLY RENOVATED 18TH CENTURY BUILDING

- SECRETARIAL OFFICE, TELEX AND FAX ROOM, EN-SUITE KITCHEN AND FACILITIES

- RANGE OF DIFFERENT STYLED ROOMS HOLDING FROM 12 TO 40 PEOPLE EACH, WHICH CAN BE USED TOGETHER OR SEPARATELY

THE COACH HOUSE

The Carriage Room	Boardroom style-	20c
	Theatre style-	40c
The Saddle Room	Boardroom Style-	12c
	Theatre style-	20c
The Stable Room	Boardroom style-	20c
	Theatre style-	40c
The Coach Room	Boardroom style-	12c
	Theatre style-	20c

tive team" created tailor-made programs for each client down to the finest detail. Carden Park quickly developed a reputation for excellent corporate hospitality—in particular, for product launches. Companies like Ciba-Geigy, Toyota, Honda, Molnlycke, and Ford enjoyed using the venue and endorsed the quality of Carden Park's service and facilities.

THE GOLF HOLIDAY MARKET

An *Economist* Intelligence Unit Report, "Golfing Holidays," suggested a key feature of the golfing holiday market in the United Kingdom was that golfers made their own booking arrangements. Travel agents were rarely used when booking a domestic holiday, primarily because the commission income was relatively low. Consequently, there was little data available on the size and value of the golfing holiday market. Most golfers arranging a break in the United Kingdom booked their accommodation directly with the establishment and arranged tee-off times directly with the courses. Destinations and resorts were chosen on the basis of prior knowledge, reputation, recommendation, and golfing magazine articles. Specific details were often obtained in the classified advertisement sections of media like *Golf World, Golf Monthly,* and *Today's Golfer.*

Golfing holidays could be divided into two categories: holidays to learn golf and holidays to play golf.

There had been a rapid growth in the number of golf schools and golf school holiday packages in both the United Kingdom and overseas. These packages included golf tuition, hotel accommodation, and board. Tuition was recognized as an important feature in learning the game of golf, and new as well as more experienced golfers regarded the costs of a weekly golf school as a reasonable investment in learning the game. Women golfers in particular enjoyed the golf school experience, and more than half of the attendees in some schools were women. The success of a golf school was dependent on the reputation of the professional who was actually teaching.

Golf playing holidays could be characterized as short, informal golf breaks in the United Kingdom; more organized golfing breaks, probably linked to a society outing; longer-duration, longer-haul golf holidays in overseas resorts; and casual golf, which is played as part of a general overseas holiday.

GOLFING HOTELS AND RESORTS

Scotland

Many of the famous courses and resorts in Scotland were well known by individual players both in the United Kingdom and throughout the golfing world. Scotland had a wide range and choice of courses and accommodation establishments. At the "home of golf"—St Andrews—there was a four-"red"-star hotel (the Old Course) and another four-star hotel (the Forte Grand); three three-star hotels and two two-star hotels; and dozens of small guest houses, as well as bed-and-breakfast establishments. The variety of accommodation enabled the resort to cater to every type of golf enthusiast.

Scotland boasted two genuine five-"red"-star golfing resort hotels: Gleneagles and Turnberry. Gleneagles was synonymous with golf. Scotland's premier hotel, unique in every way (their brochure rightly claimed "there's only one Gleneagles"), had developed a reputation for excellence during the last 65 years and had become a celebrated venue for the rich and famous. Gleneagles was open all year with four golf courses. The new leisure center, with its lagoon-shaped pool, gym, squash court, and health spa, housed in a magnificent, contemporary glass building set within the woods, provided a perfect holiday retreat. The elegant and famous hotel with its courteous and professional staff commanded a premium price. Two-day golfing breaks, including dinner, bed and breakfast, and two rounds of golf, were £315 per person in the winter and £360 in the summer. The hotel's accommodation prices ranged from £125 for a single room and breakfast in the winter, to £1,000 for the Royal Lochnagar Suite at any time of the year. Exhibit 6.10 shows some operational details.

On the west coast, the Turnberry Hotel and its two world-famous golf courses had hosted the 1994 Open championship. Housed in a fine Edwardian building with grand, elegant, and comfortable public areas, Turnberry also had the additional leisure facilities that were expected in a golfing resort hotel—its swimming pool even had an underwater sound system.

Exhibit 6.10

Gleneagles Hotels PLC Accounts. [From Gleneagles Plc Audited Accounts.]

	£ (000s)
Turnover	17,833
Pretax profit	4,224
Interest paid	2
Nontrading income	3,435
Operating profit	791
Depreciation	899
Taxation	973
Trading profit	1,690
Audit fees	20
Directors fees	159
Wage costs	5,515
Number of employees	549

Both Gleneagles and Turnberry had extensive conference and banqueting facilities and relied on large corporate events to fill the hotels in the autumn, winter, and spring seasons. Both hotels were marketed through the Leading Hotels of the World consortium and benefited from their long established reputations as luxury resort destinations.

England and Wales

Since its opening in 1988, the St Mellion Nicklaus Course in Cornwall had attracted international players and enthusiastic amateurs and had truly become one of Europe's great new courses. Apart from the golf, St Mellion's provided 24 hotel rooms, bars and restaurants, five banqueting and conference suites, and 30 self-catering lodges. Prices for one night, including dinner, bed and breakfast for two people, and golf, ranged from £96 in the winter to £189 in the summer.

In the Mid-Glamorgan area was another example of an impressive, and very welcoming, facility called Bryn Meadows. In summer, the two-night dinner, bed, and breakfast rate was £137.50, including free use of the leisure facilities and 18 holes of golf each day.

Whitbread's Country Club Hotels, mostly over 100 bedrooms, and with extensive banqueting, conference, and leisure facilities, targeted the corporate business and leisure market most effectively. The hotels were located close to major commercial centers and benefited from Whitbread's sophisticated marketing strategy, which included a central reservation system, in-company referrals, a cost-effective brochure distribution network linked to the other Whitbread hotel chains, and selling direct through travel agents. Golfing-break prices, based on staying a minimum of two nights and including dinner, bed and breakfast, and one round of golf, ranged from £69 per night in the winter to £98 per night in the summer.

Some of the old established golf clubs had also seen opportunities for further developing their facilities. At Wentworth in Surrey, Willy Bauer, formerly the General Manager at the luxury Savoy Hotel in London, was recruited to develop the club's facilities. Bauer had spent £17 million investing in the club, including £10 million on the clubhouse. He employed a Michelin-starred chef, Ian McAndrew, to improve the catering, and increased revenue to seven times its previous level. Catering sales alone were projected to rise to £4 million.

Exhibit 6.11
Hanbury Manor Operating Statistics. [From *Caterer & HotelKeeper* (February 1994).]

	1992	1993
Average room occupancy	48%	57%
Achieved room rate	£108	£103
Turnover	£5.87 m	£6.4 m

An English Tourist Board paper entitled "Golfing Hotels" published details of a survey carried out a few years earlier on the occupancy statistics of 10 golf hotels. The survey indicated that the average room occupancy of the golf hotels was, at 65 percent, significantly higher than the English average. However, it was also observed that most English golfing hotels were rated three-star and had quite modest AA-quality percentage guide ratings. There were few four-star, and only one five-star, golfing hotel resorts in England and Wales.

The only five-star English golfing hotel was Hanbury Manor near Ware in Hertfordshire, which opened in August 1990. This elegant, Jacobean-style mansion house, built in 1890, was converted to a 96-bedroom hotel by Paul Leach, the multimillionaire house builder. Early operating statistics are shown in Exhibit 6.11.

The cost of converting the mansion; building additional accommodation, conference, and leisure facilities; and improving the golf course was £28 million. In 1992, the business turned in a pretax loss of £2.76 million, and in 1994, Leach sold Hanbury Manor to Whitbread's Country Club Hotels group.

Overseas Golfing Holidays

The "package holiday" trend in the 1960s of Britons and other North Europeans flying cheaply to the Mediterranean sun created unprecedented building opportunities for developers, especially in the regions of the Costa del Sol in Spain and the Algarve in Portugal. Developers soon realized that the demand for golf was another great opportunity, and by the early 1990s several dozen golf courses had been constructed in the Costa del Sol and at least 16 in the Algarve. Virtually all of these developments were linked to hotel, apartment, time-share, and villa housing, which helped to make a profitable return on the huge capital investments. Both regions had officially rated, five-star luxurious, modern golfing hotel resorts, including Quinta Do Lago, owned by Venice-Simplon-Orient-Express, which was the finest hotel in the Algarve. Price for a British Airways seven-night holiday at Quinta Do Lago ranged from £589 per person in January to £999 in the high season. This included accommodation, breakfast, and free car hire; green fees ranged from £17 to £23 per round.

The Costa del Sol was famous for excellent courses providing challenging golf in spectacular surroundings. The officially rated five-star Don Carlos Hotel, set in a 130-acre private estate and close to the beach in fashionable Marbella, provided international guests with first-class facilities at reasonable prices. A similar British Airways seven-night holiday cost £589 in January and £797 in the peak season with unlimited free golf.

Despite suffering from the problems of overpriced green fees and a poor tourist image following the excesses of the rapid overdevelopment, both the Costa del Sol and the Algarve remained popular golfing holiday destinations, especially for a shorter 2/4 night break. One of the reasons these resorts were popular was that they scored highly on the other ingredients—the weather, food, bars, accommodation, sightseeing, and (for some) the nightlife—that were essential to the success of any golf holiday.

France, especially northern France, had also become a popular destination for short golfing breaks from southern Britain. The reasons were simple to understand. There was the ease of access; the uncrowded, peaceful, low-cost, easy-to-play (nonchampionship) courses; the appeal of French hotels, family-run pensions, and self-catering *gittes;* and the love of French cuisine and wine. These factors helped to explain why France was an attractive destination for Britons. However, France was not noted for its luxury golfing resorts.

The international boom in golf had affected many of the exotic tourist destinations of the world, and luxury hotel chains forged links with golfing resorts to offer their guests quality holidays. The Far East was also witnessing considerable interest in the game. From Thailand to China to Tokyo, golf courses were springing up both for holiday golf and as tourist leisure resort destinations, creating a new market for exotic, packaged golfing holidays.

The real challenge to the European golf resorts came from the United States and in particular from the southern East Coast. Myrtle Beach in South Carolina was promoted internationally as the ultimate golfing resort. There were 80 golf courses within a 20-minute drive from the beach center and literally hundreds of accommodations and food establishments. The five-star Radisson Resort complex, set in a 145-acre private plantation beside the beach, and the four-star Litchfield Resort and Country Club, set in 4,500 acres of private grounds, both offered excellent facilities at competitive prices. A British Airways seven-night holiday at the Radisson ranged from £639 in January to £1,059 in the peak season, and the Litchfield prices ranged from £509 in the low season to £865 in the summer. Green fees ranged from £6 to £29 depending on the course and season. Florida—with the appeal of Orlando and the attraction of the coastal resorts of Miami Beach, the Florida Keys, Palm Beach and Fort Lauderdale, Daytona and St. Augustine, and the Gulf of Mexico—was also a popular destination, especially for golfers who wanted to holiday with their families.

Exhibit 6.12 provides weather comparisons of different overseas resorts from the British Airways Golf Holidays brochure.

THE ENVIRONMENT

In the winter of 1991, the U.K. economy entered into a period of deep recession, which devastated many British companies, especially in the hotel and leisure industry. The demand for both business accommodations and leisure breaks declined and hotel occupancy dropped dramatically, as did achieved room rates. Hoteliers were forced to drop their prices and offer discounts. Unfortunately, those companies that had borrowed to their limit saw their debt-to-equity ratio rise dramatically as hotel and leisure property values fell.

The number of hotel and leisure companies put into liquidation in the early 1990s rose significantly and, in particular, major new hotel, golf, and country club developments suffered. See Exhibit 6.13 for some of the effects.

By 1994, some of the major hotel groups were announcing improved trading results as the United Kingdom slowly emerged from recession.

Exhibit 6.12
Popular Overseas Golf Resort Climate Details. [From British Airways Golf Holiday brochure.]

Average Daily Max Temperature °C/Monthly Rainfall (mm)/Daily Sunshine Hours

Average	Jan	Feb	Mar	Apr	May	June	July	Aug	Sep	Oct	Nov	Dec
Algarve												
Temp°C	17	18	20	22	25	28	31	32	29	25	20	17
Rainfall	59	38	69	31	24	7	2	1	18	44	58	66
Sunshine	6	7	7	9	10	12	12	12	9	8	6	6
Barbados												
Temp°C	28	28	29	30	31	31	30	31	31	30	29	28
Rainfall	66	28	33	36	58	112	147	147	170	178	205	96
Sunshine	10	10	10	9	9	8	8	9	8	8	8	9
Bermuda												
Temp°C	20	20	20	22	24	27	29	30	29	26	23	21
Rainfall	112	119	122	104	117	112	114	137	132	147	127	119
Sunshine	5	5	6	7	8	9	10	9	8	6	5	5

Costa del Sol

Temp°C	17	18	19	21	24	27	30	30	28	24	20	17
Rainfall	83	75	59	40	23	13	2	5	15	55	115	98
Sunshine	6	6	7	7	9	11	11	10	8	7	6	5

Florida

Temp°C	21	22	24	27	30	32	32	32	31	28	24	22
Rainfall	74	94	96	67	98	156	186	182	177	91	59	74
Sunshine	7	8	8	9	10	9	8	8	8	8	8	7

South Carolina

Temp°C	14	15	19	23	27	30	31	31	28	24	19	15
Rainfall	95	89	108	75	115	142	156	144	146	78	61	82
Sunshine	6	7	8	9	10	10	10	9	8	8	7	6

Exhibit 6.13

List of Golf, Hotel & Country Clubs in Receivership, 1994. [From Colin Hegarty, Financial Performance of U.K. Golf Developments (Golf Research Group England, 1994).]

Club	Hotel Facilities	Number of Members
Brunstone castle	No	150
Castle Coombe	Yes	300
Langton Hall	No	N/A
Malton	No	N/A
Manor of Groves	Yes	350
Patshull Park	Yes	?
Peterstone	N/A	N/A
Quietwaters	Yes	375
Shrigley Hall	Yes	540
Slaley Hall	Yes	Pay and Play
Stavertone Park*	Yes	N/A
Thoulstone Park	No	N/A

* Bought out of receivership on November 18, 1993.

While room occupancies began to increase, achieved room rates were still "difficult" and price competition remained a feature of the trading environment.

Colin Hegarty of the Golf Research Group published an annual survey, *The Financial Performance of UK Golf Developments.* In the 1994 report, Hegarty noted that out of 350 new golf facilities, 12 were in receivership, approximately 20 were in extreme financial difficulty, and a further 20 were in some financial difficulty. The report suggests that about one-third of the new golf developments surveyed were not viable. With 77 new golf courses opening in 1994, and 40 in 1995, the supply of courses was beginning to exceed current demand. The report also detailed the decline in membership takeup in the first year when a new golf course opened. To obtain 100 percent membership occupancy of an 18-hole golf course, the maximum number of players permitted a handicap was 1,000 players. The Golf Research Group's survey revealed that the average occupancy of new courses opening in England had fallen from 72 percent in 1989 to 64 percent in 1993, and the average daily green fee for new clubs had risen from £11.27 to £16.25 in the same period.

It was suggested that many of the hotel and golf developments had not been properly researched. A detailed demographic survey of the catchment area and a rigorous analysis of both the supply and quality of existing and planned hotels, and the supply and quality of existing and planned golfing facilities, were not always evident. In particular, some golfing officials suggested that the separate components of a hotel facility and a golf facility needed to be independently financially viable, and any cross-selling between the different divisions should be seen as an added element to the sales mix rather than as part of the core concept of the development.

CONCLUSION

Within a short time after opening, John Broome was experiencing difficulties in a number of areas. Some of the adaptations to the design concept—for example, the lack of space in the reception foyer, the inadequate bar facilities in the hotel, and the very small sized swimming pool compared with the glossy photograph in the brochure—were perceived by customers as a drawback to staying at Carden. In particular, the difficulty of walking from the bedrooms to the public areas was off-putting, given the vagaries of the unpredictable English climate. Indeed, while the facilities were excellent for company product launches, the Shooting Lodge and temporary marquee did not provide banqueting and conference organizers with the quality of facilities that competitors offered. There were also comments that Carden was too far from the center of Chester to attract the local business and corporate market.

The marketing of Carden had not really been that successful. Unfortunately the management team changed frequently. While consultants came and went, providing additional marketing expertise, some of Broome's ex-advisors commented that he was quite selective in acting upon their professional advice. Carden also suffered from the lack of a U.K. and international marketing network to push sales in the opening launch period.

In many ways Carden's attractive brochure raised customers' expectations too high, and the new resort had difficulty delivering the expected standards. The glossy literature emphasized the quality, luxury, and five-star standard throughout the resort; however, despite discussing a star rating with the AA, Broome did not actually apply for one. Given the AA's strict criteria for awarding five-star ratings, the problems of outside access to Carden's accommodation villas, and the limitations of the public foyer and function areas, it was improbable that the AA would have awarded Carden a five-star rating. Indeed, Carden still required considerable additional investment to complete the facilities. Apart from the proposed Olympic-standard swimming pool and leisure center, there were plans to build a major banqueting and conference complex and to rebuild the derelict site of old Carden Hall to provide 80 additional leasing units. Additional plans included 25 new woodland lodges, providing a further 150 bedrooms. Meanwhile, 10 of the 83 suites technically open at Carden had not been completed, a fire certificate had not yet been awarded, and, due to a cost-cutting exercise, only 12 golf buggies had been ordered.

There were difficulties with the Chester Council Planning Committee. From the beginning of the project, some local people and councillors were concerned that Broome would try to re-create Alton Towers at Carden. Broome, a tall and big man but in many ways an amiable personality, appeared to have little time for the planning regulations. While none of his local critics denied the quality of his schemes, there was considerable apprehension about his approach. One Labor Councillor, Christine Russell, recalled that Broome's original plan for Carden was to build a new Palladian mansion for his family. Then the idea turned into a country-pursuits-and-educational center, then to a self-catering complex, and finally to a hotel, golf, and leisure resort.

Again, the energetic Broome would build first and apply for planning permission afterwards—for example, an implement shed became a catering outlet—which naturally upset the planners. Although the council was kindly disposed to local employment initiatives (a local dairy had recently been closed with the loss of over 100 jobs), there was little trust between Broome and the planners. These difficulties resulted in inconvenient planning restrictions, such as the number of major events that could be hosted at Carden (limited to two each year) and nonmembers and nonresidents not being permitted to dine in Le Croquet.

The local concerns about Broome's financial problems were well known, and many small suppliers complained about the extended credit terms Broome took. Broome and his wife had sold Stretton Hall to provide additional funding for Carden. The cost of the development to date was approximately £22 million. The Bank of Scotland had provided a loan of £15 million and the main contractors of Carden's building program, Pochins, had agreed to convert their outstanding invoices of £2.7 million into loan stock. Given Broome's flamboyant lifestyle, his charming wealthy wife, his London flat, his Sunseeker boat *Willangina IV* moored in Majorca, and his lavish parties, some people were not really sure whether Broome was exceptionally rich or whether the cost of financing Carden was creating excessive financial burdens for him. Unfortunately for his creditors, Broome had set up the business of Carden Park as a sole trader (sole proprietorship), and so no financial information about Carden's viability was available.

Exhibit 6.14
John Broome's Quality Statement. [From
Carden Park brochure.]

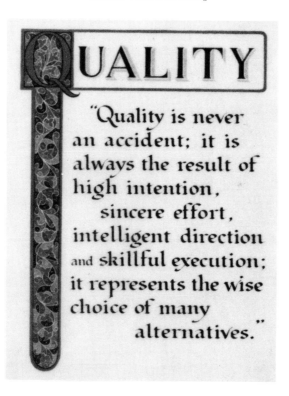

"Quality is never an accident; it is always the result of high intention, sincere effort, intelligent direction and skillful execution; it represents the wise choice of many alternatives."

Councillor Russell commented that "Broome has sometimes been his own worst enemy," but meanwhile Broome made light of the problems and was quoted as saying, "The Park is going from strength to strength. . . . I am totally confident about the future." Privately, however, Broome wondered as he looked at his own statement of quality (Exhibit 6.14).

Case Seven

The Log Cabin Restaurant

Lee J. Acham and Robert C. Lewis

"It's not the way it used to be," said Richard (Dick) Smith, owner of the Log Cabin Restaurant. He was referring to the most frequently heard comment from customers about the restaurant since he had acquired it. He was growing tired of hearing this. Although he knew that things would be different with a new owner, he did not expect the change in ownership to bring about a decline in sales. "Sales have been declining about 5 percent per year over the last two years," said Smith. He and his manager Keith Simms were examining the previous year's earnings statement (Exhibit 7.1) in the dining room of the Log Cabin.

> I'm thinking about changing the name of the restaurant, said Smith. I believe a name change is what this restaurant needs to breathe new life into it. The essence of the new concept will remain unchanged with the focus on steaks; the seafood and barbecue will be maintained. The new name, Carson City Steakhouse, will position us as a steak house. In our primary trading area there is only one other steak house, the Outback. I think there is room in Jupiter for a quality, neighborhood steak house and that we can compete with the Outback.

The Outback Steakhouse was one of the hottest restaurant concepts in the country at the time, and its growth had been phenomenal. The first Outback Steakhouse opened in Tampa, Florida, in March 1988. Six years later there were over 200 Outback restaurants with systemwide revenues estimated at over $644 million. The editors at *Inc.* magazine

This case was written by Lee J. Acham and Robert C. Lewis, University of Guelph, Ontario. All rights reserved. Some names have been disguised to protect confidentiality.

159

Exhibit 7.1
The Log Cabin's Statement of Earnings. [From company records.]

	Past Year ($)	*Previous Year ($)*
Revenue:		
Breakfast sales	265,990	226,481
Lunch sales	218,796	229,795
Dinner sales	551,047	607,392
Bar sales	181,152	200,754
Employee meals	(5,443)	(49)
Senior citizen discounts	(116)	(19)
Coupon discounts	(32,328)	(108)
Complimentary meals	(2,813)	0
Miscellaneous sales	26,123	6,026
Totals	1,202,408	1,270,272
Cost of sales	470,466	462,717
Payroll expenses	451,598	444,860
Gross profit after payroll	280,344	362,695
Controllables	296,304	271,692
Controllable profit	(15,960)	91,003

selected the owners of the Outback as their "Entrepreneurs of the Year." A brief overview of the company is given in Exhibit 7.2, and a portion of its menu is shown in Exhibit 7.3.

HISTORY OF THE LOG CABIN

The Log Cabin was a casual-theme restaurant located about one mile north of Indiantown Road, on Route A1A in the town of Jupiter, on the southeast coast of Florida. The building's wooden structure was reminiscent of an authentic lodge circa the early 1800s. On entering the dimly lighted restaurant, one walked past the host/hostess stand and into a small waiting room. There were numerous plaques on the walls of this room, signifying the Log Cabin's achievements in local chili cook-offs, as well as autographed pictures of well-known actors who had performed at the nearby Jupiter Theatre. On one side of this waiting room was the bar and lounge, which

Exhibit 7.2

Synopsis of the Outback Steakhouse. [From Jay Finegan, "Unconventional Wisdom," *Inc.* Magazine (December 1994) pp. 44–59.]

Founders:	Robert D. Basham (Operations), Chris T. Sullivan (RealEstate), and J. Timothy Gannon (Food) were the founders. Each founder's area of expertise is indicated in parentheses. The three have a combined 60 years of experience in the restaurant industry with major national dinner house chains Steak & Ale, Bennigan's, and Chili's. Sullivan and Basham built the Bennigan's chain from 32 to 140 units in three years.
Concept:	The theme of the restaurant was inspired by the Australian Outback. The walls of the Outback Steakhouse are decorated with boomerangs, Aboriginal art prints, Foster's beer signs, and travel posters. The concept's initial success was due in part to America's interest in Australia in the late 1980s. At that time the movie *Crocodile Dundee II* was a box office hit.
Marketing:	The target market is adults aged 25 to 54, a segment that will comprise over two-thirds of the population by the year 2000. According to Nancy Schneid, Marketing Vice President, the Outback is a lifestyle type of restaurant. In her own words, "The Australian attitude is fun, friendly, and active." Advertising on television occurs primarily during professional and college sports events including football, basketball, and hockey.
Menu:	The menu features almost all signature items such as Bloomin' Onion and Victoria's Filet. According to Timothy Gannon, it is imperative to add new items to the menu in order to maintain interest in the concept. As a result, he is always looking for such items, e.g., he is experimenting with lobster appetizers.
Service:	Dinner only but no reservations are taken.
Food costs:	39% of sales. The high food cost can be explained by the fact that everything is made from scratch.
Seats:	220.
Weekly customers:	3,800 persons.
Average check:	$16.00 including the bar.
Average sales:	$3.2 million per restaurant.

Exhibit 7.3
The Outback Steakhouse Menu

Aussie-Tizers

G'day mate! Start your ticker off with one o' those wonders from down under!

Bloomin' Onion*
An Outback Ab-original from
Russell's Marina Bay $4.95

Kookaburra Wings*
Known as Buffalo chicken wings here
in the States. Mild, medium, or hot $4.45

Grilled Shrimp On The Barbie
Seasoned and served with Outback's
own Remoulade sauce $5.95

Aussie Cheese Fries
Aussie chips topped with Monterey
Jack and Cheddar cheeses, bacon
and served with spicy ranch dressing...$4.95

Walkabout Soup*
A unique presentation of an Australian
favorite. Reckon! .... Bowl/Cup...$2.95/$1.95

Gold Coast Coconut Shrimp
Six colossal shrimp dipped in
beer batter, rolled in coconut,
deep fried to a golden brown
and served with marmalade sauce........$5.95

Down Under Favorites

Heaps of hearty traditions from the shoreline to deep in the never never. Every one's a beaut. Too right!

Jackeroo Chops
Two 8-ounce center cut pork chops served with
cinnamon apples and a choice of potato $10.95

Alice Springs Chicken*
Grilled chicken breast and bacon smothered
in mushrooms, melted Monterey Jack
and Cheddar cheeses, with honey mustard
sauce. Served with Aussie chips.................$9.45

Queensland Chicken 'N Shrimp*
Seasoned and grilled, over fettuccine
Alfredo, topped with a light lemon sauce.....$9.95

Brisbane Shrimp Sauté
Seasoned and sautéed with mushrooms,
over fettuccine in a light herb butter sauce ...$9.95

House or Caesar Salad with
any Down Under Favorite $1.95

Land Rovers

Our steaks are fair dinkum — absolutely genuine — USDA cuts. It was one of those three dishes that had Max was so mad about!

The Outback Special*
A 12-ounce center-cut sirloin, seasoned
and seared to perfection $11.45

Prime Minister's Prime Rib
A tempting, 16-ounce cut, roasted slowly...$15.45
12-ounce cut $13.45
8-ounce cut $11.45

Victoria's Filet*
A 9-ounce tenderloin $14.95

The Michael J. "Crocodile" Dundee
A 14-ounce New York Strip $15.45

The Melbourne
A 20-ounce porterhouse –
it's bonzer! $17.95

Rockhampton Rib-Eye
A 14-ounce rib-eye steak.......................$14.95

Land Rover Entrees are served with
a choice of House or Caesar salad, bushman
bread and choice of jacket potato, Aussie
chips, or fresh steamed veggies.

Grilled Shrimp On The Barbie with
any Land Rover Favorite.......................$4.75

Grilled On The Barbie

Cheers! Get a real taste of the ol' outback, seared to perfection over an open flame.

Chicken On The Barbie
Seasoned and grilled breast served
with BBQ sauce and fresh veggies $7.95

Ribs On The Barbie
Danish baby back ribs, smoked
and grilled, with Aussie chips
and cinnamon apples $10.95

Drover's Platter*
Generous portion of ribs and chicken
breast on the barbie with Aussie
chips and cinnamon apples....................$11.95

Botany Bay Fish O' The Day
Fresh catch, lightly seasoned and
grilled, with fresh veggies $10.95

House or Caesar Salad with
any Grilled On The Barbie Favorite...........$1.95

allowed smoking; on the other side was the main dining room, which served as the nonsmoking section. Total seating capacity was 165 seats. The decor was rustic, with wooden furniture used throughout. This countrylike atmosphere was highlighted by many period antiques, including bucksaws, wooden toys, and cast-iron cookware.

The restaurant was built and opened for business by Liz and Johnny Cartwright in 1982. It was one of only three restaurants in Jupiter at that time. In addition to its award-winning chili, the Log Cabin was renowned locally for its barbecued ribs and chicken, which were first "smoked" and then finished to order over real wood charcoal. The restaurant had built its reputation on using mostly fresh ingredients, in recipes that were either created by the Cartwrights or passed on by family members. For example, the barbecue sauce was created by Liz, while the baked beans and cole slaw were made with recipes from Johnny's mother. The overall theme of the menu was best described in the words of Johnny and Liz, "We try our best to give good old home cooking consistently, day after day, at a reasonable price." A 1992 Zagat survey (a highly reputed ongoing national restaurant review) of restaurants in South Florida seemed to verify that the Cartwrights were successful in this regard (Exhibit 7.4). "The restaurant," in the words of one customer, "was a local institution." The local Chamber of Commerce confirmed the reputation of the Log Cabin as "the place to go for breakfast."

As owners, Liz and Johnny knew most of their regular customers by name, and also created a familylike atmosphere among their employees. As one employee put it, "We used to be one big family—we would even have our spats!"

THE NEW OWNER

Richard Smith received a B.S. degree from Florida International University and an M.B.A. degree from Emory University. From 1980 to 1983, he worked with a consulting company, specializing in real estate and hospitality consulting for the eastern United States, South America, and the Caribbean. From 1983 to 1988, he was Senior Vice President of Real Estate for a publicly traded hotel company that owned and operated 68 hotels. In 1988 he formed his own company, Hospitality Consultants of America, Inc. (HCA). HCA provided management, consulting, brokerage, appraisal, and insurance services to lenders and equity holders of hotels, time-share condominiums, restaurants, apartments, and senior assisted-living facilities. Smith managed the operations of HCA from his Palm Beach office with a corporate staff of one, a controller. Additionally, HCA utilized several consultants on an "as needed" basis.

Exhibit 7.4

Excerpt from Zagat's Survey of South
Florida Restaurants

	F	D	S	C
	18	17	17	$15

Log Cabin, The*/S
631 N. A1A (U.S. 1), Jupiter, 746-6877
*U – "Go for breakfast, and go hungry" is the inside
word on this "quaint" Jupiter American; at lunch and
dinner you'll also find "cheap but good" barbecue and
a panoply of fried foods that, if not great, are both
affordable and filling.*

EXPLANATION OF RATINGS AND SYMBOLS

FOOD, DECOR and **SERVICE** are each rated on
a scale of 0 to 30 in columns marked **F, D** and **S:**

   0–9 = poor to fair
   10–19 = good to very good
   20–25 = very good to excellent
   26–30 = extraordinary to perfection

The **COST** column, headed by a **C**, reflects the
estimated price of a dinner with one drink and tip.
As a rule of thumb, lunch will cost 25 percent less.

An **Asterisk (*)** after a restaurant's name means the
number of persons who voted on the restaurant is too
low to be statistically reliable; **L** for late means the
restaurant serves after 11 PM; **S** means it is open on
Sunday; **X** means no credit cards are accepted.

By way of **Commentary,** we attempt to summarize the comments of the Survey participants,
occasionally retaining a prior year's comments
where appropriate. The prefix **U** means comments
were uniform; **M** means they were mixed.

The Palm Beach Cafe

In 1993 HCA acquired the 145-seat Howard Johnson Restaurant on the
island of Palm Beach, about 25 miles south of Jupiter. Smith remodeled
the restaurant, changed its decor and menu, and renamed it the Palm
Beach Cafe. In 1994, the Palm Beach Cafe's gross sales were $1.4 million.

The restaurant offered complete meal "deals," which were a big attraction for senior citizens. The majority of the Palm Beach Cafe's clientele were seniors who lived on the island and found the restaurant conveniently located. Smith acknowledged that the success of the Palm Beach Cafe was partly due to its location, but more importantly to the value offered to customers, most of whom were on fixed incomes.

Jay's Family Restaurants

Smith was always looking for opportunities to invest, and eventually he bought 28 units of Jay's Family Restaurants with his partner Ralph Meade. The 28 freestanding restaurants in South Florida annually generated sales of approximately $30 million. The Jay's concept was essentially a full-service diner and coffee shop and was well known in South Florida for its breakfast and its senior citizen discounts. Seniors were offered 10 percent off the regular menu prices every day of the year and were the chain's largest customer group. The menu was broad in its appeal (something for everyone), with limited substitutions and special orders. Portions were large, and most items were purchased wholesale, were preportioned, and were ready to cook. Additionally, the standardized recipes facilitated preparation. The chain's financial success, as measured by its controllable profit, was based on high customer counts and strong cost controls. The operating philosophy of the original founders of the Jay's chain often resulted in their managers being very strong in back-of-the-house operations as compared with the front of the house.

Smith was primarily involved in the financial aspects of the operation of Jay's, while Meade oversaw the operations. Within two years all 28 Jay's Restaurants were sold for a profit in excess of $2.5 million.

ACQUISITION OF THE LOG CABIN

Dick Smith then acquired the Log Cabin Restaurant from Liz and Johnny Cartwright. After 13 years in the restaurant business, the Cartwrights had decided to sell the Log Cabin and enjoy the many benefits of living in Florida. The acquisition of the Log Cabin brought the total number of properties in HCA's portfolio to six. HCA had management contracts for a 50-room motel, the foodservice operation of a senior care facility, and the rooms division of a time share property. These properties were all located in South Florida. Additionally, the company owned a rental apartment complex in West Palm Beach as well as owning the Palm Beach Cafe. Smith's primary role was to ensure that each property was meeting its financial objectives. Each property had its own management team and reported directly to Smith.

Smith's original plan for the Log Cabin when he first acquired the restaurant was to pattern it after the Cracker Barrel Old Country Store. The latter was a concept that flourished in the late 1980s and continued to grow in the 1990s throughout the southeastern part of the country. In a survey conducted by *Restaurants & Institutions (R&I)* magazine in February 1994, Cracker Barrel was rated the number 1 chain in family dining by American families. For its fiscal year ending 1995, sales per Cracker Barrel Store were over $4 million with equally strong sales in all three "day parts" (breakfast, lunch, and dinner). The Log Cabin's highest-ever sales, by comparison, were $1.7 million. In the year prior to the acquisition by Smith, sales were $1.4 million.

Smith especially liked the idea of the country-store-themed gift shop, which was a part of Cracker Barrel's philosophy, especially as there were no Cracker Barrels in the immediate area. The gift shop, located on the way to the dining room, accounted for 22 percent of total sales at a typical Cracker Barrel restaurant. Smith felt the gift-shop idea could work well with the Log Cabin and would be a perfect fit with the theme. However, the implementation of the idea at the Log Cabin never went beyond a single glass showcase that contained postcards, bottles of barbecue sauce, and "Log Cabin" T-shirts.

Smith had acquired the Log Cabin with the objective of achieving cash flows and profits that were similar to a Jay's Restaurant. The typical operating percentages for a Jay's Restaurant were: 30 percent for cost of goods; 30 percent for payroll cost; 20 percent for controllable expenses; and 20 percent for controllable profit, that is, profit before taxes, rent, and depreciation. Through his association with Jay's, Smith had access to the purchasing leverage of a multi unit chain. "I saved 10 percent on purchases alone," Smith said, as he talked about how the purchasing power of Jay's impacted favorably on his decision to acquire the Log Cabin. Prior to the sale of the Jay's chain in 1993, Smith successfully negotiated a competitive contract with another major national distributor for the majority of the Log Cabin's food products. To achieve his objective of running the Log Cabin like a Jay's, Smith hired Keith Simms, an experienced Jay's General Manager, to be the new General Manager of the Log Cabin. Simms was responsible for the daily operations and reported directly to Smith.

THE AREA

The town of Jupiter (with an estimated year-round population of 27,291) is located in Palm Beach County, one of the fastest-growing counties in the state of Florida. Exhibit 7.5 is a map of the area, showing the relevant competition for the Log Cabin. The county grew by an estimated 54,720 residents between 1990 and 1993. According to the 1990 *Census Handbook* for Florida, the largest increase in population in the county during the 1980s was in the 40 to 49 age group. This segment almost doubled in size, from 50,558 residents in 1980 to 98,277 residents in 1990. A Chamber of Commerce representative indicated that the local demographics mirrored that of

Exhibit 7.5
Map of the Jupiter (Florida) Area

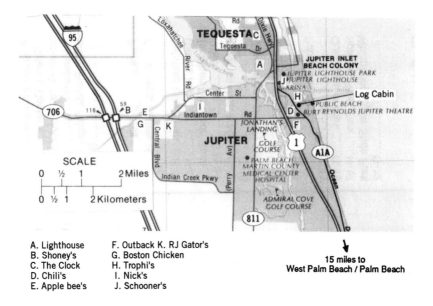

A. Lighthouse
B. Shoney's
C. The Clock
D. Chili's
E. Apple bee's

F. Outback
G. Boston Chicken
H. Trophi's
I. Nick's
J. Schooner's

K. RJ Gator's

15 miles to
West Palm Beach / Palm Beach

the county at large, with a noticeable increase in the number of young families moving into the area. In 1995 the median household income for Jupiter was $38,211 and the median age was 38.2. The Town of Jupiter had recently approved the construction of a 6,000-home development, a branch campus of Florida Atlantic University, business uses, and a major-league baseball spring-training facility for the Atlanta Braves, all on 2,000 acres of the town's southwest corner. This was expected to further enhance the attractiveness of the area and draw more visitors.

The estimated population of Palm Beach County was 918,223 in 1995. This usually grew to about 1.1 million during the winter months—or "season," as it was commonly called—from December to March (roughly 18 weeks). During season, it was not unusual to have to wait at least 45 to 60 minutes to be seated for dinner at some of the more popular eating places.

The restaurant industry in Palm Beach County was a billion dollar business. According to *Restaurant Business* magazine, in 1993 the total eating-place sales in the county were $968,483,000, and the Restaurant Growth Index (RGI) was 117. This RGI value indicated that the market growth potential for the region was above the national average. When supply equals demand, the index is 100, and when the market is saturated the index falls below 100.

The region's resistance to economic downturns could be attributed to a number of factors, including a steadily increasing population, the absence of large manufacturing companies, a vibrant tourist industry, and a large senior citizen base. Despite the significant number of senior citizens in the county (estimated at over 300,000 in 1990), the percentage of seniors in the total population was declining and, in fact, decreased from about 41 percent in 1980 to 38 percent in 1990. According to the Palm Beach County Convention and Visitors Bureau, the total number of visitors to the county in 1995 actually increased by more than 200,000 over 1992.

THE DEVELOPMENT

Smith adopted a hands-off approach and left the day-to-day operations to Meade when he first took over the Log Cabin Restaurant. Meade's priority was to learn both the front-of-the-house and the back-of-the-house aspects of the operation and to develop a specifications manual. Since the restaurant had been a family-run operation for 13 years, there were no formal training procedures for either part of the operation. Most of the recipes were in the heads of the previous owners and cooks, and few if any were formally recorded. One of the first tasks was to record every recipe and procedure according to current standards. The first draft of the "Spec Book," as it was commonly called, was completed in about a week. At some future time, the plan was to cost the menu to arrive at an ideal food cost.

Initially, only minor changes were made to the recipes and the menu. For example, several of the homemade salad dressings were replaced with ready-to-use substitutes. The savings that could be realized from using these products were substantial, and Smith did not think that customers would recognize any differences. Recipes for meat loaf and pot roast that were successful at the Palm Beach Cafe were introduced at the Log Cabin. As time progressed, other changes were made to the menu; most involved removing items that were not big sellers like the chili and the Virginia Ham and Eggs country dinner. Exhibit 7.6 shows a copy of the dinner menu, which was presented in a typical plastic binder.

Although Smith did not formulate a written marketing plan, he directed the marketing efforts toward increasing awareness of the Log Cabin through advertising in the local newspapers. One major initiative was to build an early-bird business, that is, to increase business in the early, nonpeak part of the day. Early birds at the Log Cabin were similar to the meal "deals" at the Palm Beach Cafe, and were designed primarily to attract seniors who liked the idea of paying one price for a complete meal, including a nonalcoholic beverage. This initiative, which proved to be successful at the Palm Beach Cafe, allowed the customer to choose from among at least 12 entrees that were all equally priced. Each entree was bundled to include a soup or salad, rolls, a special dessert, and tea or coffee. Prior to Smith's acquisition of the Log Cabin, the restaurant did not offer early-bird specials. Exhibit 7.7 shows an Early Bird Menu.

Various promotions were directed at all three day parts to increase sales. For example, one breakfast promotion featured a large selection of country pancakes with a choice of homemade syrups, an idea Smith got from the International House of Pancakes (IHOP). A $4.99 hot lunch buffet with salad bar was introduced to stimulate lunch business, but was discontinued a few months later. A "Sizzlin' Steaks" promotion was run

Exhibit 7.6

Log Cabin's Dinner Menu

❀ STARTERS ❀

Mozzarella Sticks 4.25
Deep fried to perfection and served with chunky marinara sauce.

Cabin Cheese Fries 3.95
Golden brown french fries topped with shredded cheddar cheese and bacon bits.

Spare Rib Basket 4.99
Half slab of honey roasted barbeque ribs

Baby Back Basket 5.99
Half a rack of our genuine baby back ribs

Shrimp Scampi 5.95
Gulf shrimp sautéed inour own zesty garlic sauce

Blooming Onion 4.95
Colossal spanish onion lightly dusted then fried up crispy and served with our own special dipping sauce

Catfish Basket 4.95
Our famous local catfish lightly breaded and deep fried

Stuffed Mushrooms 5.25
Mushroom caps stuffed with crabmeat, baked and topped with our own Bernaise sauce

Dolphin Fingers 4.95
A cabin specialty since 1978! Served in our unique breading. A real treat!

❀ CABIN SALADS ❀

House Salad 2.99

Grilled Chicken Caesar Salad 5.95

Sliced Steak Salad 6.25

Fresh Fruit Salad 5.95

❀ HOT SANDWICHES ❀

Bar-B-Q Pork or Beef 4.95

Log Cabin Burger with Cheese & Bacon . 5.95

Grilled Chicken with Cheese & Bacon 5.95

Steak Sandwich 7.95

Fried Fish Sandwich 5.95

Grilled Dolphin 6.95

Served with french fries and cole slaw.

❀ DESSERTS ❀

Bread Pudding with Whiskey Sauce 2.95

Apple Cobbler à la Mode 2.95

Platte County Pie 2.95

Homemade Rice Pudding 1.95

Ice Cream 1.75

❀ SOUPS & SUCH ❀

Baked Onion Soup 2.95

Soup of the Day 2.25

Brunswick Stew 3.25

❀ COUNTRY VEGETABLES ❀

APPLE SAUCE · COLE SLAW
COUNTRY GREEN BEANS · CREAMED SPINACH
VEGETABLE OF THE DAY · HUSH PUPPIES
FRENCH FRIES · BAKED BEANS
MASHED POTATOES · RICE
BAKED POTATO

Any of the above 1.25

❀ CABIN FAVORITES ❀

Liver and Onions 7.95
Calves liver served with sauteed onions.

Grilled Chicken Breasts 9.95
Two boneless breasts of chicken lightly seasoned and cooked over our wood grill.

Old Fashioned Pot Roast 9.95
Slow cooked, fork tender and served with natural gravy.

Sirloin for Two 24.95
A 26 oz. Top Sirloin sliced by our chef.

Includes house salad, rolls and butter,
and any two country vegetables.

Exhibit 7.6 *(continued)*

❀ SIZZLING STEAKS ❀

Fresh Sautéed Mushrooms 1.25

All of our steaks are hand cut USDA Choice.
Cooked over Orange Wood and Florida Oak and lightly seasoned.

Bearnaise Sauce 1.25

Top Sirloin .... 12 oz. 12.95
A boneless lean cut from a choice top butt. The steak lovers steak.

New York Strip .... 16 oz. 15.95
A true "boneless" New York Sirloin well-trimmed. A long time favorite of many.

Delmonico (Rib Eye) .... 14 oz. 14.95
A rich steak taken from the rib section and charbroiled. This steak has a heavy fat marbling, and is very flavorful.

Filet Mignon .... 9 oz. 15.95
A well-trimmed tenderloin steak wrapped in bacon. Butter-tender and delicious.

Prime Rib (Friday & Saturday) ..... 12 oz. 14.95
A limited amount is cooked daily. 18 oz. 16.95
We do run out so please understand.

Porterhouse .... 24 oz. 16.95
A great steak combining the best of both worlds: filet and New York Strip.

Includes house salad, rolls and butter and choice of
baked potato, french fries, real mashed potatoes, or our famous baked beans.

❀ CABIN COMBOS ❀

Dolphin & Sirloin 13.95
Scampi & Sirloin 15.95
Chicken & Sirloin 12.95

Substitute Petite Filet add 2.95

❀ BROILING INSTRUCTIONS ❀

PITTSBURGH .... Black Outside, Raw, Cool Center
RARE .... Red, Cool Center
MEDIUM RARE .... Red, Warm Center
MEDIUM .... Pink, Hot Center
WELL .... Cooked Thoroughly

❀ SEAFOOD ❀

All of our seafood is fresh daily

Grilled Dolphin 11.95
Lightly seasoned or blackened.

Okeechobee Frogs Legs 15.95
Available sauteed or fried.

Gulf Coast Jumbo Shrimp 12.95
Available as scampi or deep fried.

Grilled Swordfish 13.95
Center cut lightly seasoned on the grill.

Okeechobee Catfish 10.95
Hand dipped and lightly fried-tender sweet.

Includes house salad, rolls and butter
and choice of rice or potato.

OLD FASHIONED ❀ REAL PIT BAR-B-Q ❀

Danish Baby Back Ribs 13.95
small, tender, tasty - a full rack.

Bar-B-Q Chicken 8.95
Cooked slow - you'll love this one!

Spare Ribs 10.95
the traditional rib for barbeque.

Bar-B-Q Sampler 12.95
Includes chicken, baby back ribs, spare ribs, chopped beef and sliced pork.

Chicken & Rib Platter 10.95
A generous portion of chicken & spare ribs.

Includes cole slaw, rolls and butter,
and choice of baked beans or french fries.

Exhibit 7.6 *(continued)*

WINE LIST

WHITE WINES

Bin #			Bottle	Glass
11	Chardonnay, Estrella River, Prop. Reserve, CA.	V	12.95	2.95
12	Chardonnay, Grand Cru Vineyards, CA	V	15.95	
13	Chardonnay, Kendall Jackson, Vintn. Reserve, CA.	V	19.95	
14	Sauvignon Blanc,, Montpellier Vineyards, CA.	V	13.50	
15	Chateau de Vire, Macon, Prosper Maufoux, France	V	19.95	

RED WINES

21	Cabernet Sauvignon, Estrella River. Prop. Reserve , CA.	V	12.95	2.95
22	Cabernet Sauvignon, Woodbridge. R,. Mondavi, CA.	V	14.50	
23	Cabernet Sauvignon, Grand Cru Vineyards, CA.	V	15.95	
24	Merlot, Grand Cru Vineyards, CA	V	14.50	
25	Merlot, Forest Glen, CA.	V	19.95	
26	Beaujolais Villages. Prosper Maufoux, France	V	18.95	

BLUSH WINES

31	White Zinfandel. Estrella River Prop. Reserve, CA	V	12.95	2.95

OUR PREMIUM HOUSE WINES

Estrella River "Proprietors Reserve"
California

Chardonnay	Cabernet Sauvignon	White Zinfandel
Glass: 2.95	Glass 2.95	Glass: 2.95

OUR CALIFORNIA SPARKLING WINE

Armstrong Ridge, Brut
Glass 2.95

Exhibit 7.7
Log Cabin's Early-Bird Menu

to capture a larger share of dinner customers. Most of these promotions were advertised in the local print media and were often accompanied by a coupon offering, for example, a specified dollar amount off an item. On the whole, these promotions were marginally successful. An example of the "Sizzlin' Steaks" promotion is shown in Exhibit 7.8.

Smith devoted a considerable amount of his time to improving the physical appearance of the restaurant. The outside porch was enclosed to

Exhibit 7.8
Log Cabin's "Sizzlin' Steaks" Promotion

make better use of the seating; this area was either too hot or too cold for customers prior to being enclosed. Several antiques were imported to add to the Log Cabin's already impressive collection. These included slot machines, an old Coca-Cola vending machine, and a life-size statue of a native American Indian.

After about a year, as a result of declining customer counts and sales in that part of the day, the decision was made to discontinue serving

Exhibit 7.9
Average Weekly Sales for the Log Cabin by Day Part and Season.
[From company records.]

Day Part	Check Average* ($)	Weekly Food Sales— Jan, Feb, Mar, and Dec ($)	Weekly Food Sales— Apr–Nov ($)
Breakfast	4.52	8,400	3,500
Lunch	7.17	5,300	3,500
Dinner	12.75	14,800	8,900
Total Sales		28,500	15,900

* Check averages do not include the bar. Weekly bar sales ranged from $3,200 for out of season to $4,000 in season.

breakfast except on weekends. Smith had noticed a negative trend in breakfast sales during the previous two months. Typically, 60 percent to 70 percent of total breakfast sales were achieved on the weekends. Exhibit 7.9 shows the breakdown of weekly sales by day part for the past full year, separated by season. Smith admitted that the way the customers were informed, simply by not opening for breakfast one morning, was poorly handled. Not only did he lose his weekday breakfast business, but some customers believed the restaurant was permanently closed. One employee commented that, for weeks afterward, several cars still pulled into the parking lot during the weekday mornings.

Overall, customers were described by servers as mostly locals and middle-aged. Their feedback was solicited by means of comment cards that were available at the host/hostess stand. Reviews were mixed, for the most part, and focused on the food quality and the service. Specific comments from customers during the past calendar year are included in Exhibit 7.10.

THE COMPETITION

There were dozens of eating places in Jupiter, ranging from quick-service restaurants like McDonald's and Taco Bell to higher-priced, more upscale restaurants like Charley's Crab and Sinclair's American Grill. Competition intensified after Smith acquired the Log Cabin. Several nationally recog-

Exhibit 7.10

Specific Customer Comments. [From company records.]

- Change the barbecue. It needs to be shredded and cooked like they used to cook it.
- Bartender/Waiter—excellent job.
- Serve fresher food, less greasy.
- Not change a thing.
- Our server was great! Also we love the new addition—great atmosphere—just got better!
- The service was very prompt, and very professional.
- Try to go back to the way it was as far as the chicken, potatoes, and beans! Something's changed!!
- Keep the waitress and not serve rubber pancakes, deep-fat-fried bacon, and overcooked sausage. It tasted as if it had been reheated, not freshly cooked.
- Terrible grade of beef, very stringy and fatty.
- Please take the time and tell your people what a great job they have done.
- The waitress, Dana, and the busboy, Al, were fantastic. The food was great, the atmosphere was excellent.
- Keep it pretty much the way it is (you did a great job on the porch).
- No coffee refills, two tables seated after me served before me.
- Pork fatty, chicken overcooked.
- Keep serving unlimited biscuits with breakfast during the week, and serve quality bacon instead of thin, fatty kind.
- Not change the original Roast Pork gravy recipe. What I had last night was awful. I was so disappointed.
- We used to be regular customers but only come on occasion to see if any better—it never has changed, so we will wait a few months and see again. It was great under prior ownership, what happened?
- Pick a better quality of meat! Our server was nice and helpful!

Note: Questionnaires were not collected systematically. There is no data on how many or over what period these were collected.

nized, casual restaurants opened in Jupiter, including Applebee's, Boston Market, and Chili's. "Even Boston Market, which recently opened, is stealing some of our business," Smith commented. According to Smith, competition in the area could be divided into two segments, breakfast and lunch/dinner. A competitive analysis provided by management is shown in Exhibits 7.11 and 7.12.

CONCLUSION

"I think a dinner house concept is the only way to go," said Smith,

and that's the intention with the Carson City Steakhouse. The margins are a lot higher than at breakfast, and the hours of operation are less demanding. There are very few concepts today that serve all three day parts equally well, Cracker Barrel being the exception. People usually don't consider eating dinner at the same place that they eat breakfast because they don't perceive the breakfast place to be good enough for dinner.

The motifs of the new concept are western, gold rush, and gambling. I am working with a restaurant consultant from Atlanta on the design, and the Log Cabin will be used as the pilot store. If it is successful, the plan is to expand it in the way that the Outback Steakhouse did. I have investors who are willing to invest in this new concept and, unless I can be convinced otherwise, I will go ahead with my plan.

The plan he was referring to was, of course, to change the name and the concept from the Log Cabin to the Carson City Steakhouse.

Exhibit 7.11
Breakfast Competition to the Log Cabin

Restaurant	Value*	Quality*	Ambience*
Lighthouse	+	=	−
Shoney's	+	−	−
The Clock	=	=	−

* +, superior to the Log Cabin; −, inferior to the Log Cabin; =, equal to the Log Cabin.

Exhibit 7.12

Lunch and Dinner Competition to the Log Cabin

Restaurant (Year Opened)	Type	Segment	Independent or Chain	V**	Q**	A**	Price Range***
Lighthouse (1950)	Diner	Midscale	Indep.	+	−	−	$7.50–12.99
Shoney's (1991)	Family restaurant	Midscale	Chain	−	+	−	$5.99–8.49
The Clock (1992)	Family restaurant	Midscale	Chain	+	−	−	$2.95–6.99
Chili's Grill & Bar (1992)	Tex-Mex	Casual theme	Chain	=	−	=	$4.75–9.95
Applebee's Neighbourhood Grill & Bar (1993)	American	Casual theme	Chain	+	+	+	$4.69–9.49
Outback—D* (1991)	Steak house	Casual theme	Chain	+	+	+	$7.95–17.95
Boston Market (1994)	Cafeteria-style	Quick-service	Chain	−	−	−	$2.59–5.59
Trophi's—D* (1988)	Italian	Casual theme	Indep.	=	+	=	$7.95–13.95
Nick's Tomato Pie—D* (1992)	Italian	Casual theme	Indep.	+	+	+	$8.95–16.95
Schooner's (1984)	Seafood	Casual theme	Indep.	+	+	+	$4.95–19.99
RJ Gators Neighbourhood Sea Grille & Bar (1986)	American	Casual theme	Chain	+	=	+	$4.95–11.95

* D, open for dinner only.
** V, Q, and A refer to value, quality, and ambience, respectively; +, superior to the Log Cabin; −, inferior to the Log Cabin; =, equal to the Log Cabin.
*** Price range is the range in menu-item prices on the lunch and dinner menu, not including appetizers.

Keith had heard all this before, mostly in silence. This time he decided to speak up:

Is changing the name a solution, or just a bandaid? Why did you buy the restaurant in the first place when you knew it was doing well and felt it could do even better? What has changed since then? I suggest we consider our strategy before we blindly change the name.

Case Eight

Positioning Holiday Inn Worldwide

Robert C. Lewis

Mike Leven, President of Holiday Inn Worldwide, had an amused look on his face as he read the letter printed as a paid advertisement in *Hotel & Motel Management,* from Henry Silverman to Robert Hazard (see Exhibit 8.1). The dispute between Silverman and Hazard was over franchisees and "flag-switching," a phenomenon that had become quite prevalent in the United States, in which hotel franchisees switch from one company to another.

Leven was amused because he had been the instigator of these wars. As former president of Days Inn, during which time he more than doubled the number of franchise properties under the Days Inn flag, he had run full-page ads attacking the franchise competition to gain converts. One of these ads, in fact, trumpeted, "The Holiday Is Over. Days Inn: America's Waking Up to Us." Now, here he was an officer of one of the very companies he had attacked.

When he was President of Days Inn, Leven's Chief Executive Officer (CEO) and boss was Henry Silverman, so he knew a little bit about Henry's policies. But what really caught his eye was the second paragraph of the letter. Silverman, now CEO for Hospitality Franchise Systems (HFS) with five hotel brands (two more—Super 8 and Park Inns—were later added to the Days Inn, Howard Johnson, and Ramada brands), followed a policy of separating the brands, as well as some of the products, with separate marketing programs and different 800 numbers.

This case was written by Robert C. Lewis, University of Guelph, Ontario. All rights reserved. Some aspects have been altered to make the case more focused.

Exhibit 8.1

Paid Advertisement in *Hotel & Motel Management*

HOSPITALITY
FRANCHISE
SYSTEMS, INC.

339 JEFFERSON RD. P.O. BOX 278, PARSIPPANY, NEW JERSEY 07054-0278
PHONE (201) 428-9700
FAX (201) 428-6057/8

TRUTH IN ADVERTISING

Mr. Robert C. Hazard, Jr.
Chairman and CEO
CHOICE HOTELS INTERNATIONAL

Dear Bob:

No, Bob, we don't specialize in negative advertising -- instead we are committed to the truth.

Fact: All three of the franchisees you mentioned in your advertisement in this publication who converted from Choice to Days Inns, Howard Johnson and Ramada have made or have committed to make significant investments in their properties in order to upgrade to meet their new franchisor's standards. These licensees informed us that they were unwilling or unable to make the investment under their former Choice flags due to, among other reasons, their concern about reservation volume being split among seven brands.

Bob, what we are saying in our advertising is that our policy of separate brand identity for Days Inns, Howard Johnson and Ramada is our **comparative difference** with Choice. It is what our customers tell us they want - **separate brands**, each with a clearly articulated **impact policy** and with **distinct marketing/advertising programs** and **different 800 numbers.**

Fact: Smith Travel Research merely points out various chains' market share of travelers based on total rooms in the chain*. Of course your market share went up: you increased the size of your systems. HFS could make the same claim; since 1990 our three brands have grown by more than 20%. Our customers, however, could care less; what they are solely interested in is how we are doing **for them.** As long as our **call volume** and **room nights booked per available room** continue to **increase** every year, as they have, then we're on the right track.

Bob, if you will allow me to have the last word, we're not being negative but rather we're running a comparative advertising campaign. It's the kind of advertising that makes a distinction between companies and allows buyers to make a choice. It's a highly respected tradition in the advertising world and one that's particularly appropriate in our industry today. We're happy to offer customers real choices, not manufactured statistics, and let them decide.

Best regards.

Sincerely yours,

Henry R. Silverman
Chairman and CEO

---

* Source: Smith Travel Research letter dated May 6, 1992.

Exhibit 8.2

Choice Hotels International's Seven Brands and Fourteen Products.

[From Choice Hotels International franchise flyer.]

Choice Hotels International

Hotel Brands:			
Sleep Inns:	limited-service, economy hotels	**Rodeway Inns:**	limited and full service, upper-priced economy hotels
Comfort Inns and Suites:	upper-economy, limited-service hotels and all-suite hotels		
		Econo Lodges:	limited-service, mid-priced, economy hotels
Quality Inns, Hotels and Suites	mid-priced, full-service inns and and limited-service all-suite hotels	**Friendship Inns:**	lower economy, limited-service hotels
Clarion Hotels, Suites, Resorts, and Carriage House Inns:	upscale hotels, all-suite hotels, resorts and boutique inns		

Hazard's group, Choice Hotels International, took the opposite course. All seven Choice brands, which had 14 different products (see Exhibit 8.2), were advertised together with one 800 number and were all lumped together in the Choice 2001 reservation system as well as in the Apollo, Datas II, Pars, and Sabre airline systems. The idea, of course, was that a customer could be "switched" to a different brand or product[1] if another one wasn't suitable (Exhibit 8.3).

"That makes sense," thought Leven, "but was that the real issue?" Presumably, each brand identified its own market segments and established its own position in the marketplace. Naturally, there was some overlap but, it seemed to Leven, if there wasn't some clear distinction between brands as well as products in the product line, then what you would end up with was a totally confused customer. It wasn't exactly as if you could go to a store shelf and compare brands and their product lines by reading the ingredients and noting the prices. Leven recalled how Howard Johnson,

---

[1] The terms *brand, product,* and *product line* can be confusing. As commonly used and used here, a brand is a brand name that identifies a set of products called the product line. Thus, Chrysler Corporation has four car brands—Chrysler, Dodge, Plymouth, and Eagle. The brand Chrysler has a product line with different products such as Neon, Intrepid, Cirrus, Sebring, Concorde, LHS (and maybe something else by the time you read this).

Exhibit 8.3
Choice International's Statement on Lumping Brands and Products

WHAT'S IN A NAME? EVERYTHING, IF IT MEANS VALUE, COMFORT AND RELIABILITY TO THE WORLD'S TRAVELERS. AND OUR NAME SAYS IT ALL. CHOICE HOTELS INTERNATIONAL IS NOW THE WORLD'S LARGEST LODGING FRANCHISOR AND STILL GROWING. CHOICE HAS EMBARKED ON A GLOBAL EXPANSION PROGRAM THAT INCLUDES NEARLY 3,000 HOTELS OPEN AND UNDER DEVELOPMENT. OUR GUESTS CAN CHOOSE FROM MORE THAN A QUARTER MILLION ROOMS OR SUITES AROUND THE WORLD. WHATEVER THE LOCATION, PRICE OR SERVICE LEVEL, WE HAVE A PRODUCT FOR THE TRAVELER AND HOTEL OWNER. FROM TOKYO TO TUSCALOOSA, OVER AND OVER AGAIN, TRAVELERS CHOOSE CLARION, QUALITY, COMFORT, SLEEP, RODEWAY, ECONO LODGE AND FRIENDSHIP INNS, THE SEVEN BRANDS THAT MAKE UP THE CHOICE HOTELS INTERNATIONAL FAMILY. WITH THESE PROVEN PRODUCTS, CHOICE HAS A FRANCHISE BRAND TO MATCH EVERY BUSINESS STRATEGY.

when it was a division of Prime Motor Inns, advertised its product line (see Exhibit 8.4). "How in hell," thought Leven, "could anyone know one from the other?"

HOLIDAY INN WORLDWIDE

Holiday Inn Worldwide had over 1,700 hotels around the globe and was growing, with one brand name and six products in its product line. Unlike Choice and HFS, all carried the Holiday Inn logo (see Exhibit 8.5).

Holiday Inn was the original and staple product of Holiday Inn Worldwide and accounted for the vast majority of the properties. Holiday Inn Crowne Plazas numbered 80 worldwide with plans to grow to 200 over the next five years—100 in the United States and 100 internationally. Holiday Inn Garden Courts numbered 30 but were only in Europe and

Exhibit 8.4
Howard Johnson's Former One Brand, Five Products under Prime Motor Inns

Exhibit 8.5

Holiday Inn's One Brand with Six Products

THE HOLIDAY INN
FAMILY OF HOTELS
─────────────
We offer different Holiday Inn hotels to meet your needs
on different types of travel occasions:

Africa. Holiday Inn Express, introduced in 1990, had over 100 properties in the United States and Mexico and was growing. Crowne Plaza Resorts was a new product in 1993, with five hotels in Florida, South Carolina, Mexico, and St. Thomas. SunSpree Resorts was also new in 1993. One was in Lake Placid, New York; two were in Florida; and one was on the Côte d'Azur in France. The two resort products were believed to have high growth potential. Slightly over 200 of the over 1,700 properties were company-owed and/or managed. The rest were franchised.

"I wonder," thought Leven, "how our products are really positioned? I mean, *we* know how they're positioned, but does the customer know? When you're a multiple-brand or multiple-product company, or both, how do you differentiate one from the other and identify its appropriate target markets?

"Wow," thought Leven, "I wonder how other industries do it. The classic branding and product-line company, with a brand and product for each and every market segment, is Procter and Gamble. How many products does the Crest toothpaste brand include? Fluoride, tartar, mint, gel, push button, stand up, and more, and all kinds of combinations. Funny, I don't have any problem buying toothpaste—I know just what I want. Now, how can we get our hotels positioned the same way?"

Leven picked up a folder on his desk that contained copies of ads from Holiday's current campaign. (Exhibit 8.6 shows one of these.) All

Exhibit 8.6
Holiday Inn's Corporate Advertising

WE'RE ALL
AROUND THE

WORLD

AND JUST AROUND
THE CORNER.

Wherever you travel you can count on finding the warm welcome and friendly service of a Holiday Inn° hotel. From San Francisco to Springfield, from Rome to Beijing, we're ready and waiting to make you feel at home. In fact, we're in over 1,700 locations in more than 50 countries. Which means we'll always be near. No matter how far you go.

STAY WITH SOMEONE YOU KNOW.°

FOR RESERVATIONS CALL THE HOLIDAY INN WORLDWIDE RESERVATION OFFICE NEAREST YOU.

of them were identified simply by the Holiday Inn name and sunburst logo, and accommodations could be reserved at any one of them by calling the same 800 number. Yet these ads were intended to represent over 1,700 locations and six products worldwide.

Leven then looked at an ad that a New York franchisee was running (see Exhibit 8.7). This ad identified both a Holiday Inn and a Crowne Plaza—both as not just upscale, but luxurious. Leven knew that prior expectations had a great deal to do with eventual customer satisfaction. What, he wondered, would be the expectations and resultant satisfaction at these two properties based on this ad? "Are we positioning both brands as luxurious? Does either one meet that condition? Does one differentiate from the other?"

Exhibit 8.7
Holiday Inn's Franchisee Ad

Go From Plane to Luxurious.

In a matter of minutes. The Holiday Inn Crowne Plaza–LaGuardia Airport and The Holiday Inn-JFK Airport offer luxurious rooms exquisite restaurants, spectacular meeting rooms and state-of-the-art health facilities, without Manhattan prices or hassles. Shouldn't luxury be a convenience?

1-800-HOLIDAY

CROWNE PLAZA®
LAGUARDIA AIRPORT
Ditmars Blvd., E. Elmhurst, NY 11369
718-457-6300

JFK AIRPORT
144-02 135th Ave., Jamaica, NY 11436
718-659-0200

Stay With Someone You Know.

WHAT THE OTHERS DO

Leven decided he was too familiar with his own products to be totally objective at this point. He asked his secretary, Hilary, to get him some files on the competition. He decided to try to view these as a consumer.

Choice International

Choice Hotels International saw itself as clearly defined by price, although with considerable overlap (see Exhibit 8.8).[2] Remembering a friend complaining to him about paying $100 at a Comfort Inn in Erie, Pennsylvania, last summer, Leven wasn't so sure. He knew that the Econo Lodge, Rodeway, and Sleep brands were quite different products, but they were all positioned in the economy class according to Choice. "That's okay," he thought, "all Crest toothpastes aren't the same even at the same price, but how does the customer know which hotel to choose when calling the 800 number? Maybe," he laughed to himself, "we should put flavors on our products."

Then there was the overlap of Comfort, Quality, and Clarion. True, prices would vary by location, but as a consumer, Leven wondered if he could save $20 by staying at a Quality instead of a Clarion and have the same expectations and the same price value? Mike remembered how General Motors had messed up its brand lines in the 1980s by duplicating parts and overlapping prices.

Leven looked again at Choice's definitions of its brands (Exhibit 8.2) and noted that, for example, Rodeway Inns offered both limited and full-service "economy." As he looked at the other definitions, he thought, "Interesting. I know these products but how does the average customer sort them out?"

"Choice was trying, however," thought Leven, as he looked at their *Plan for consistency* (see Exhibit 8.9). "I wonder if that will do the trick."

---

[2] The price segment categories shown in Exhibit 8.8 are those commonly recognized by the hotel industry in the United States.

Exhibit 8.8

Choice Hotels' Brand and Product Positioning Strategy. [From Choice Hotels International franchise brochure.]

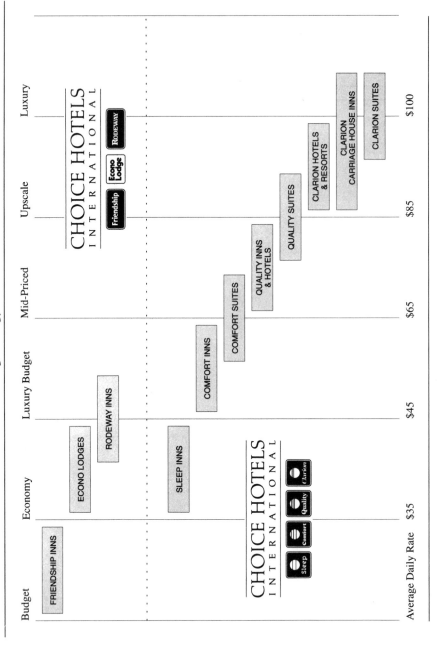

Exhibit 8.9

Choice Hotels' Plan for Consistency, a Brand-by-Brand Summary of Upcoming Changes. [From Choice Hotels.]

AMENITY/CHANGES

BRAND	Guest Satisfaction Guarantee	Free Continental Breakfast	Free Local Phone Calls	In-Room Coffee	Free Newspaper	Capital Improvements	Higher Minimum QA scores?
Sleep Inn	one-year test	required	required	N/A	N/A	no change	no change
Comfort		required	required	recommended	recommended	no change	no change
Quality	one-year test	N/A	required	no change	required	20% renovated by 1995	yes
Clarion	N/A	N/A	required	required in renovations	required in renovations	20% renovated by 1995	no change
Econo Lodge	N/A	N/A	recommended	N/A	N/A	10% renovated by 1995	yes
Friendship	N/A	N/A	required	recommended	recommended	100% renovated in five years	yes
Rodeway	N/A	required in renovations	required	required in renovations	required in renovations	25% renovated by 1995	no change

SOURCE: Choice Hotels
N/A- Not Applicable

Hospitality Franchise Systems

HFS had four brands and 11 products according to one of their ads (see Exhibit 8.10). Or was it five brands and 12 products (including Park Inns)? Three brands—Super 8, Park Inns (not shown in Exhibit), and Days Inn—had just one product, each in the economy sector. At one time a budget concept called DayStop had been inaugurated by Days Inn. Days Inn franchisees, however, complained about cannibalization, and the effort was abandoned.

The Howard Johnson brand had four products: Plazas, Hotels, Lodges, and HoJo Inns (see Exhibit 8.11). All but the last were typically full-service hotels but positioned to different markets. Mike recalled, however, a recent news item that HoJo Inn expansion was being halted and that many of the inns would be converted to something else. According to Eric Pfeffer, Howard Johnson's President, research showed that 80 percent of American travelers believed HoJo was synonymous with Howard Johnson and expected HoJo Inns to be full-service lodging facilities complete with meeting rooms and swimming pools. "Now there's a case in point," thought Leven.

After separating Renaissance into a brand of its own, the Ramada brand had three products according to its franchise brochure—Hotels, Inns, and Limiteds (see Exhibit 8.12)—unlike its ads (see Exhibit 8.10), which showed five. Mike could remember the confusion that resulted

Exhibit 8.10
HFS Advertises Three Brands and Five Products

1-800-I-GO-HOJO

1-800-2-RAMADA

1-800-325-2525

1-800-800-8000

1-800-2-RAMADA

1-800-I-GO-HOJO

Exhibit 8.11

Howard Johnson's One Brand, Four Products. [From Howard Johnson franchise brochure.]

ONE BRAND, THREE CONCEPTS.

Howard Johnson Plazas and Hotels — Positioned in the top half of the mid-price market, these high rise, full service hotels offer complete amenities including restaurants, room service, lounges, meeting facilities and indoor pools and spas.

LAKE BUENA VISTA, FL ▶

Howard Johnson Lodges — Also typically full service properties, these hotels cater to the mid-to-lower half of the mid-price market and are usually low rise buildings with outdoor pools.

CLIFTON, NJ   ▲

HoJo Inns — The most successful new launch in the history of the economy segment, and the fastest growing economy chain in 1991, this concept emphasizes quality accommodations and everyday low prices.

MCDONOUGH, GA ▶

when Ramada tried to go upscale luxury with the Renaissance product which was incongruous with the basic Ramada product.

"The Ramada distinction seems a little better than the Howard Johnson one," thought Leven,

> discounting the ad. Yet, between the two, there are 'inns' at two different levels. To me, an inn is some quiet little place in the country. I wonder what the consumer thinks an inn is? Somehow, Holiday *Inn* doesn't seem to have the same problem. I wonder why?

Exhibit 8.12

Ramada's Three Major Products. [From Ramada franchise brochure.]

MAXIMIZING THE MID-PRICE MARKET

Ramada Hotels — These first class properties offer the best in amenities. Multiple restaurants, lounges with live entertainment, spa facilities with whirlpools and exquisite meeting rooms all contribute to the mid-priced luxury of Ramada Hotels.

◀ **KISSIMMEE, FL**

LONG BEACH, CA ▼

Ramada Inns — Well positioned at the heart of the mid-price market, Ramada Inns combine full amenities, including a restaurant, pool, lounge and meeting facilities, with a value that out performs our competition.

SAN DIEGO, CA ▼

Ramada Limited — Targeting value-conscious travelers, this new *limited feature* concept, introduced in November 1991, concentrates on quality rooms without the complications of food and beverage service.

One thing, at least, is that all five HFS brands are marketed separately. The consumer need never know that they all have the same parent organization. Of course, no Choice brand carries the Choice name either.

Sheraton and Hilton

Sheraton and Hilton, like Holiday, carried the parent name on their brands. Sheraton brands numbered only 2, if you could call them brands. Sheraton owned or managed properties were Sheraton Hotels, although they tended to be identified by their location such as the Sheraton Manhattan or Sheraton Jeddah, or Sheraton Gateway for airport hotels, or by whimsy such as the Sheraton Palace in San Francisco. Although some of these properties varied widely in quality or type (such as convention), they all were called "hotels," and all were positioned and advertised together with one 800 number.

Under the same 800 number, but more recently advertised separately, were Sheraton Inns (Exhibit 8.13). These were largely franchised properties located outside of major cities. The product varied widely, but they were largely midmarket properties. Because of the variations between "hotels" and "inns," which had hurt the hotel image, Sheraton tried to differentiate them. Leven wondered if the customers knew the difference between an inn and a hotel. Instead, he felt, they probably saw Sheraton as one brand name with varying levels of product that could be confusing. Hilton, Leven felt, did the same as Sheraton and was pretty much in the same category.

Marriott

Marriott had four brands (Exhibit 8.14). The upscale brand was Marriott with three products—hotels, suites, and resorts. The hotels varied considerably from Marriott Marquis, large convention hotels, to a basic Marriott hotel. Again, there was considerable variation in product, but most were company-managed and the Marriott standard consistency was evident; that is, people usually knew what they were going to get at a Marriott, Leven felt.

Marriott's other three brands were distinctively different, each aimed at a specific market segment and often franchised. Two of them, Courtyard and Fairfield, had been developed after extensive consumer research of the specific segments they hoped to attract, and both had been largely successful.

Although sometimes advertised together, as shown in Exhibit 8.14, Marriott brands were usually advertised separately and often by individual hotel in the upscale brand, and each brand had its own 800 number. Internally, however, in the corporate reservation system (CRS), reservationists had the ability to switch over to another brand if necessary to find what the customer wanted.

Like Sheraton, Hilton, and Holiday, Marriott used the parent name on all brands but downplayed it for the three lower-level brands. Marriott had made a conscious decision to capitalize on the well-respected brand equity of its name but still position the different products individually as unique brands.

Exhibit 8.13
Sheraton's Ad to Differentiate Its Inns from Its Hotels

Most inns give you a good price.
We just make it worth more.

More service is what you'll find at Sheraton Inns. Besides affordable
rates, we have room service, meeting space, restaurants, pools, comfortable rooms
and of course, ITT Sheraton quality.
If you join ITT Sheraton Club International, you can enjoy late check-out,
upgrades when available and earn ClubPoints. ClubPoints can
be redeemed for awards and free travel. And right now we have SureSaver Business
Rates that are 5%-30% off of our regular rates. They're available
Sunday through Thursday with no advance reservation or purchase requirement. As
you can see, we're making it very easy to find a good value.
*Simply contact your travel professional or **800-325-3535.***

A whole lot of Sheraton **Sheraton** *Jnn* *at just a slice of the price.*

ITT Sheraton

Exhibit 8.14
Marriott's Product Line

Marriott...
The Right Choice

Whenever you travel, there's a Marriott that's right for you.
Each of our chains is unique. And they
all offer the hospitality and service you've come to trust.
Marriott. The Right Choice Every Time.

HOTELS · RESORTS · SUITES

Full Service Accommodations
1-800-228-9290

Moderate Priced Lodging
1-800-321-2211

Extended Stay Lodging
1-800-331-3131

Economy Lodging
1-800-228-2800

International

"Again, I'm too familiar with these products," thought Leven. "I think I need to look at some I'm not so familiar with." He recalled seeing a Sofitel and Novotel in Paris—four-star and three-star brands of Groupe Accor of France—under the same roof but with different entrances, although the brands were marketed totally separately. All Accor brands, six in all, were company managed but none carried the Accor name. "Interesting," he thought, "I have no problem differentiating those two brands."

Leven picked up an ad for the Ashok Group in India (see Exhibit 8.15). He didn't know any of these hotels. "What do these three brands mean to me?" he wondered. "Can I tell an Elite from a Classic from a Comfort? Do these names determine my expectations? Some of

Exhibit 8.15
Ashok Differentiates Three Products under One Brand Name

Some of our hotels are priceless.
Some are thoughtfully priced.

The Ashok Group gives a new dimension to hospitality with a multiple choice of hotels.

Ashok
ELITE
HOTELS

☐ Ashok Hotel, New Delhi
☐ Hotel Samrat, New Delhi
☐ Hotel Ashok, Bangalore
☐ Hotel Airport Ashok, Calcutta
☐ Kovalam Ashok Beach Resort
☐ Lalitha Mahal Palace Hotel, Mysore

The Ashok Group

India's host to the world

Ashok
Classic
HOTELS

☐ Hotel Kanishka, New Delhi
☐ Qutab Hotel, New Delhi
☐ Hotel Janpath, New Delhi
☐ Ashok Country Resort, New Delhi
☐ Hotel Agra Ashok
☐ Bharatpur Forest Lodge
☐ Hotel Kalinga Ashok, Bhubaneswar
☐ Hotel Bodhgaya Ashok
☐ Hotel Jaipur Ashok
☐ Hotel Jammu Ashok
☐ Hotel Khajuraho Ashok
☐ Hotel Madurai Ashok
☐ Temple Bay Ashok Beach Resort,Mamallapuram
☐ Hotel Manali Ashok
☐ Hotel Pataliputra Ashok, Patna
☐ Laxmi Vilas Palace Hotel, Udaipur
☐ Hotel Varanasi Ashok

Ashok
Comfort
HOTELS

☐ Hotel Ranjit, New Delhi
☐ Lodhi Hotel, New Delhi
☐ Ashok Yatri Niwas, New Delhi
☐ Hotel Aurangabad Ashok
☐ Hotel Lake View Ashok, Bhopal
☐ Hotel Brahmaputra Ashok, Guwahati
☐ Hotel Hassan Ashok
☐ Hotel Donyi Polo Ashok, Itanagar
☐ Hotel Japfu Ashok, Kohima
☐ Hotel Pondicherry Ashok
☐ Hotel Nilachal Ashok, Puri
☐ Hotel Ranchi Ashok
☐ Hotel Pinewood Ashok, Shillong

Exhibit 8.16

Forte's "Branded Products." [From John Connell, *Forte Hotels Rebranding Exercise, 1991.* Copyright 1992, Glasgow Caledonian University, Glasgow. All rights reserved. Used by permission.]

VENUE GUARANTEE

The best hotel brand in meetings, training, conferences
and exhibitions worldwide. Quality charter.
Professional management.
Comprehensive facilities. The widest choice of venues.

Your changing needs

People need different things from our hotels. Their needs change over time.
Our branded products reflect this. All are easy to buy and easy to understand.
A complete service our guests will value.

The only complete guide to short breaks featuring the United
Kingdom and Europe. One comprehensive leisure programme
ideal for the independent traveller. Superb choice. Fixed prices.
No seasonal supplements. No supplements for single rooms.
Easy to book. Guaranteed flexibility.

INCENTIVE GUARANTEE

The best in leisure incentives delivering success for all
business strategies. Outstanding variety of leisure rewards
across a wide range of hotels and restaurants.
Year round flexibility. Stylish, easy to use presentation material.
Programme to suit all budgets.

BUSINESS GUARANTEE

Our guarantee of priority at 280 hotels worldwide, designed to
meet the exacting needs of the experienced traveller on business
or leisure. Room priority. Dedicated reservation number.
Flexibility to change or cancel. Express check-out.
Overnight parking. Complimentary daily newspaper.
No membership. No fees.

Exhibit 8.17

Forte's Product Lines. [From John Connell, *Forte Hotels Rebranding Exercise, 1991.* Copyright 1992, Glasgow Caledonian University, Glasgow. All rights reserved. Used by permission.]

The new strategy for our hotels

OUR BRANDS *will consist of purpose-built modern hotels, each brand catering for a different set of customer needs by providing a different level of facilities and service.*

Forte Travelodge: our roadside budget accommodation brand offering simple, modern rooms conveniently situated along major routes. It will encompass the existing Travelodge networks in the UK and North America, as well as new properties on the Continent where construction begins this year.

Forte Posthouse: our branded UK chain of accessible, modern hotels offering comfortable rooms and providing good restaurant and meeting facilities at highly competitive prices. It will comprise many of the three star properties presently trading under the Post House and Crest names.

Forte Crest: our branded chain of high quality modern business hotels specialising in personal recognition and service. Most of the properties will be situated in major city centres throughout Europe. Forte Crest will incorporate some of the best existing Crest and Post House hotels as well as a number of other properties in our portfolio.

FORTE
Travelodge

FORTE
Posthouse

FORTE
CREST

Exhibit 8.17. *(continued)*

OUR COLLECTIONS *will be different from our brands insofar*
as they will bring together a range of individual properties, each
with its own name, style and character. Like the brands, each
collection will appeal to a particular set of customer needs.

Forte Heritage: our collection of traditional British inns offering a unique combination of comfort, personal hospitality and character. Forte Heritage will include properties such as the White Horse at Dorking and the Black Swan at Helmsley.

Forte Grand: our collection of first class international hotels offering traditional European standards of comfort, style and service. Forte Grand will include hotels such as The Waldorf in London, The Randolph in Oxford and the Grand Hotel in Nuremberg.

Exclusive hotels: the Exclusive portfolio presently includes sixteen hotels such as the Hyde Park Hotel in London, the Georges V in Paris, the Ritz in Madrid and the Plaza Athénée in Paris and New York. These internationally renowned names represent the finest hotels in the world, and will continue to be promoted in their own right with subtle Forte endorsement.

each carry the Ashok name, some do not. Am I confused? I'm really not sure."

Finally, Leven turned to the United Kingdom's Forte Hotels, which he knew had been through a rebranding strategy in 1991. Forte had a myriad of different property types, and nobody had known really what they had, as all had been identified only by "THF" or "Trusthouse Forte," the company's previous name. Forte wanted to make it easier for customers to choose the hotels they needed. They grouped the hotels as follows:

Physical characteristics	Modern or traditional
Service style	Formal or informal
Location	City center or out-of-town
Principal use	Business or leisure

At the same time, Forte created "branded products" that defined what customers receive and the level of service for distinct segments of the market. These are shown in Exhibit 8.16. After considerable research using a wide range of segmentation variables and some internal soul searching, Forte Hotels defined market segments with the products to match them. This was intended to lead not only to greater clarity of customer expectation, but also to greater product consistency as all hotels had to meet the standards set by the product brands that were grouped within three price bands. The resulting six product lines, which Forte calls three brands and three collections, are shown in Exhibit 8.17, and their positioning is shown in Exhibit 8.18.[3]

BACK TO HOLIDAY INN

With all this in mind, Mike Leven turned back to the job at hand. Obviously, there were many ways to try to position a multiple-brand or multiple-product hotel company, but which one works the best? In essence,

[3] All information about Forte Hotels is taken from John Connell, *Forte Hotels Rebranding Exercise, 1991.* Copyright 1992, Glasgow Caledonian University, Glasgow. All rights reserved. Used by permission.

Exhibit 8.18

Forte's Positioning Map. [From John Connell, *Forte Hotels Rebranding Exercise, 1991.* Copyright 1992, Glasgow Caledonian University, Glasgow.]

Hotel Positioning

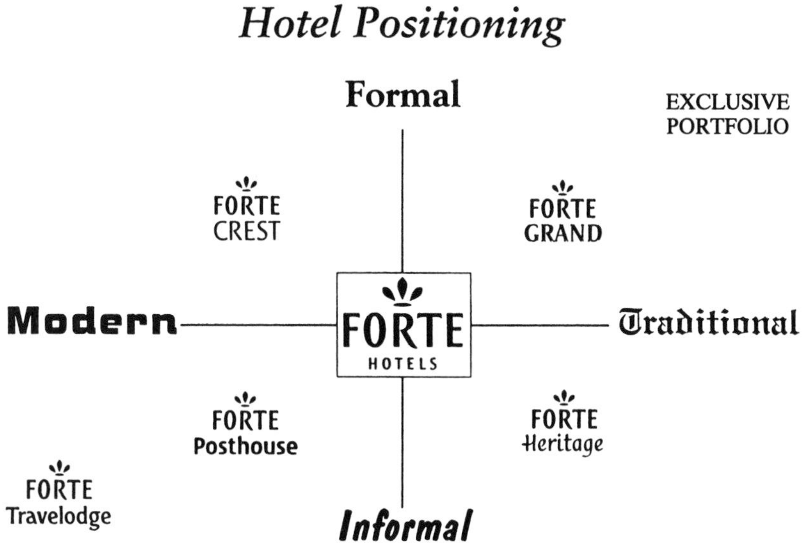

Mike felt, there were a number of issues. These included facilities, service levels, services offered, quality, operations, and many others. The issue that concerned Mike now, however, was a marketing one—how to position each product (should they be different brands?) so as to create the right consumer expectations; that is, how to make the consumer's choice clear depending on the purpose of the trip.

Allied with this were the three basic tenets of positioning: creating a clear image; differentiating from the competition and, in this case, from the other products; and promising the benefits that the target market wants for this particular choice, and which could be fulfilled.

Leven got out a copy of the latest Holiday Inn Worldwide Directory to see just how the company was defining its product line to the consumer. These are shown in Exhibit 8.19. He then looked at some of the listings and their facilities and amenities (Exhibit 8.20). "Other than the logos," he thought, "how do you tell some of them apart? Surely not by the

(Text continues on p. 215.)

Exhibit 8.19
Holiday Inn's Product Lines' Facilities

THE HOLIDAY INN PORTFOLIO OF HOTELS
We offer different Holiday Inn hotels to meet your needs on different types of lodging occasions:

✿ HOLIDAY INN® HOTELS
The traditional Holiday Inn hotel offers dependable service and attractive facilities at an excellent value. In addition to a warm and friendly staff, you can expect to find these and other features:
• Lobby/Reception area
• Full-service restaurant
• A range of meeting facilities including small, medium to large rooms
• Room service
• Swimming pool (at most hotels)
• Fitness facilities (optional)
• Holiday Inn Executive Club Rooms (An option available only in Europe/Middle East, Africa & Asia Pacific)
Holiday Inn hotels are highlighted throughout this directory with the symbol ✿.

❦ HOLIDAY INN CROWNE PLAZA®
Located in major cities, resort destinations and near international airports worldwide, these distinguished hotels provide enhanced services and amenities for todays discriminating business and leisure travellers. You can expect to find these and other features at Crowne Plaza hotels:
• Elegant lobby with bar
• Finely appointed rooms with enhanced amenities
• Several dining facilities, often including a specialty restaurant
• Extensive meeting facilities
• Business services or business center
• Fitness facilities/pool/sauna
• Extended room service hours
• Crowne Plaza Club, Executive Level (The Americas and Asia/Pacific regions)
• Executive Board Room
Holiday Inn Crowne Plaza locations are highlighted throughout this directory with the symbol ❦.

ⅲ HOLIDAY INN GARDEN COURT℠
Located in Europe and South Africa, mainly in smaller towns and near larger cities, these comfortable hotels are competitively priced for leisure and business travellers. The Holiday Inn Garden Court hotels feature:
• Reception area
• Informal bistro style restaurant featuring local specialities and bar
• One to five meeting rooms
• Fitness or leisure facility
Holiday Inn Garden Court locations are highlighted throughout this directory with the symbol ⅲ.

⌒ HOLIDAY INN EXPRESS®
A simplified version of Holiday Inn hotel, with locations in the U.S., Mexico and Canada. Offering full-sized guest rooms and an economy-priced package of facilities and services. Holiday Inn Express hotels feature:
• Lobby/Great Room
• Complimentary Breakfast Bar
• Free local phone calls
• One or two small meeting rooms
• Swimming pool (optional)
• Fitness room (optional)
Holiday Inn Express locations are highlighted throughout this directory with the symbol ⌒.

❦ HOLIDAY INN CROWNE PLAZA® RESORT
Crowne Plaza Resorts are located in premier resort destinations worldwide. Designed for the more selective traveller, Crowne Plaza Resorts appeal to those who expect an outstanding resort experience and demand value. Each resort has its own unique personality and offers extensive meeting and recreational facilities and services. The following is a listing of the special features you will find at Holiday Inn Crowne Plaza Resorts:
• Attractive guest rooms with enhanced amenities
• Unique architecture, dramatic lobby and public areas
• Elaborate swimming pool with generous deck
• Several dining and beverage outlets—specialty, casual, poolside, etc.
• Retail outlets
• Leisure services/Concierge desk
• Daily events calendar and activities coordinator
• Full range of facilities & planned activities appropriate to the location
• Sports activities and on-site or nearby tennis/golf
• Full-service exercise facilities, sauna/whirlpool
• Extensive meeting facilities, including outdoor function area
Holiday Inn Crowne Plaza Resort locations are highlighted throughout this directory with the symbol ❦.

⬥ HOLIDAY INN SUNSPREE RESORT℠
Located in preferred vacation destinations around the world, SunSpree resorts provide an activity-rich, true resort experience at a great value. They offer an extensive choice of recreational features and services drawing on the surrounding attractions. Sunspree Resorts are designed to enhance your leisure travel with facilities and services such as these:
• Distinctive architecture, inviting lobby and public areas
• Full-service restaurant and family-oriented casual food service
• Markettessen℠ – half-deli, half-market food and beverage concept.
• Enhanced exercise facility
• Unique pool designs
• Children's Activities Program complete w/scheduled daily activities
• Special access to tennis and golf facilities
• Meeting facilities
• Daily events calendar and activities staff
• Gift shop and arcade
• Free local phone calls
Holiday Inn SunSpree Resort locations are highlighted throughout this directory with the symbol ⬥.

Exhibit 8.20

Holiday Inn's Directory of Amenities and Sample of Individual Property Listings

These special symbols and abbreviations appear in the directory:

Ⓗ Holidome–Holidome indoor recreation center offers indoor pool, whirlpool, sauna, exercise equipment, and free games.

❋ Resort–Hotels located in areas that have extensive recreational and entertainment facilities.

Ⓢ Seniors–Participating hotels offer at least a 10% discount off the non-discounted room rates for members of the American Association of Retired Persons (including National Retired Teachers Association, National Council of Senior Citizens).

ᴾᵀ Preferred Senior Traveler–Participating hotels offer 20% off the single person non-discounted room rates and a 10% discount at hotel restaurants.

♿ Wheelchair Accommodations–Hotel rooms equipped to accommodate wheelchairs.

▨ Some of our hotels have the Visual Alert System for use by the hearing impaired.

🎾⛳🏓 Tennis, Golf, Raquetball– These activities are available either on premises or within 5 miles of the hotel.

🏊 Indoor Pool–Swimming pool indoors; may or may not be heated.

♨ Whirlpool/Sauna–A whirlpool and/or sauna is available on premises.

Ⓧ Fitness Center–Health and exercise area, either indoor or outdoor, may include all or some of the following: exercise equipment, spa, whirlpool/sauna, jogging trail, etc.

🐾 Pets–Pets allowed (may have kennels)

🚫 No Pets–Pets not allowed (usually due to local laws/ordinances).

✈ Airport Transportation–Transportation to and from local airport (restricted hours/fees may apply).

♪ Live Entertainment–Entertainment available in the lounge or restaurant.

FRANKFURT   **GERMANY**

1. FRANKFURT
   Conference Center
   ☎ 069/68020
   ℍ𝑜𝑙𝑖𝑑𝑎𝑦 FAX 069/6802333
   𝑆𝑛𝑛 TELEX 411805
   CROWNE PLAZA Mailander Strasse 1
            6000 Frankfurt/
            Main 70
Directions: Offenbach, Direction Frankfurt City Centre.
Attractions: Dwtn. Rail Station 3 km. • Exhibition 4 km. • Airpt. 14 km.
Facilities: Mtgs. to 400 • 19 Meeting Rooms. Parking DM 17/Ngt.
Features: Gourmet Rest. (Closed Sunday) • Coffee Shop • Garage • Lady Executive Rooms • Executive Suites • No Pool • Bariner Rooms.
Misc: Tax/Svc Chg Included. Breakfast DM 29.

Ⓢ♿♨Ⓧ   **FRACT**

🛏 **2. FRANKFURT-Langen**
      (06103) 5050
      FAX (06103) 505100
      Telex 4032293
      Rheinstrasse 25-29
      6070 Langen
Directions: Motorway A5/A661 Exit Langen.
Attractions: Frankfurt Centre/Fair Area 20 km. • Frankfurt Airpt. 12 km. • Located in City Centre. • Historic Buildings Nearby.
Facilities: 90 Rms. • 4 Flrs. • Mtgs. to 12 • Free Parking.
Features: Bistro • Bar.
Misc: Tax/Svc Chg Included. Breakfast DMK 18.

♿♨Ⓧ🛏   **LGNGE**

✿ **3. FRANKFURT-Main-Taunus-Zentrum** ⊞
      06196/7630
      FAX 06196/72996
      TELEX 40725
      Main-Taunus-Zentrum 1
      6231 Sulzbach
Directions: Direct to Hwy. A66 Frankfurt-Wiesbaden. Hwy. 66 Exit Main-Taunus-Zentrum.
Attractions: Dwtn. Frankfurt/Fairground/Airpt. 15 min.
Facilities: 289 Rms. • Free Parking • Conference Facility up to 350.
Features: 3 Rests. • Summergarden • Executive Rooms.
Misc: Tax/Svc Chg Included. Breakfast DM 22.

♿🏊♨   **FRASB**

MONTREAL (Cont.)   **QUEBEC**

3. MONTREAL-Metro Centre
   ☎ 514/842-8581
   ℍ𝑜𝑙𝑖𝑑𝑎𝑦 FAX 514/842-8910
   𝑆𝑛𝑛 505 Sherbrooke St. E
   CROWNE PLAZA Montreal, PQ H2L 1K2
Attractions: Dorval Int'l Airpt. 8 mi. • Mirabel Int'l Airpt. 28 mi. • Adj. Metro • Fine BTQS.
Rests. Nearby • Easy access to Convention Centre/Shopping Area/Olympic Stadium/Amusement Park & Botanic Gardens • Greyhound 1 blk.
Facilities: 318 Rms. • 23 Flrs. • Mtgs. to 350 • Indoor Parking $9/Ngt/Maximum Clearance 6 ft.
Features: Dining Room • 2 Bars • Suites/Executive/Deluxe Floor Avail.
Misc: G.S.T. 7%.

Ⓢᴾᵀ🏊♨Ⓧ♪   **YULRH**

QUEBEC CITY (Cont.)   **QUEBEC**

✿ **2. QUEBEC CITY-Ste Foy**
      418/653-4901
      FAX 418/653-1836
      3125 Hochelaga St. Ste-Foy
      Quebec, PQ G1V 4A8
Directions: Exit Hochelaga off Henri IV Blvd. Autoroute 73 Exit 136.
Attractions: Quebec Airpt. 4 mi. • Plaines d'Abraham & Parliament 4 mi. • Dwtn/Old Quebec 5 mi. • Shopping Malls 1/2 mi. • Aquarium 1 mi. • Skiing 15 mi.
Facilities: 233 Rms. • Mtgs. to 250.
Features: Rest. • Lounge • Gift Shop • Down & Out Rooms.
Services: Gueste-Day Valet Service • Sightseeing Tours.
Misc: TAX 7% & 4%.

Ⓢᴾᵀ♿🎾⛳🏓🏊Ⓧ🛏✈   **YQBST**

Exhibit 8.20 (continued)

 7. FORT LAUDERDALE-Plantation
305/472-5600
FAX 305/370-3201
1711 N. University Dr.
Ft. Lauderdale, FL 33322
Directions: I-95 or FL Tnpk. Exit Sunrise Blvd. W 12 mi.
Attractions: Int'l Airpt. & Port Everglades 5 mi. • Sunrise Music Theatre/Mall 1 blk. • Central Park 2 mi. • Home of Motorola/Amex/Racal Milgo/Bell South/Encore/Sawgrass Mills Mall.
Facilities: 335 Rms. • Mtgs. to 700.
Features: Palm Court Grille Rest. • Club Mirage-High Energy Lounge • Suites Avail.
Misc: TAX 9%.

FLLPL

 8. FORT LAUDERDALE-I-95 Airport
     (Port Everglades Area)
305/584-4000
FAX 305/791-7680
2275 SR 84
Fort Lauderdale, FL 33312
Directions: I-95 Exit #27, SR 84 West 1 Blk, FL Tnpk. Exit #54 (St Rd #84).
Attractions: Ft. Lauderdale Airpt. 3 mi. • Beaches 5 mi. • Port Everglades. Shuttle Avail. (Nominal Fee) 3 mi. • Joe Robbie Dolphin Stadium 10 mi. • Galleria Mall 8 mi. • Convention Center 3 mi. • Atlantis Water Kingdom 3 mi.
Facilities: 4 Flrs. • Ext. Corridor.
Features: Toucan's Rest. • Lobby Lounge • Poolside Tiki Bar • 2 Pools • Port-Side Gift Shop • Suites Avail.
Services: Free Airpt. Shuttle 6am to Midnight.
Misc: TAX 9%.

FLLAP

 **9. HOLLYWOOD-Downtown**
305/927-3341
FAX 305/925-1695
1925 Harrison Street
Hollywood, FL 33020
Directions: Hollywood Blvd. to 20th Ave. South 1 Blk. to Harrison St.
Attractions: Airpt. 5 mi. • Beach 1 mi. • Dog Track 1 mi. • Horse Track 2 mi. • Jai Alai 3 mi. • Atlantis Water World 3 mi. • Miami Dolphin Stadium 5 mi. • Miami Heat 12 mi.
Facilities: 6 Flrs. • Ext. Corridor • Meeting Rooms.
Features: Terrace Rest. • Inn Place Lounge • Poolside Tiki Bar • Pool Patio • Meeting Rooms.
Misc: TAX 9%.

HWODT

 10. HALLANDALE
305/456-8333
FAX 305/456-8333 EXT. 302
101 Ansin Blvd
Hallandale, FL 33009
Directions: Interstate 95, Exit #21 (Hallandale Beach Blvd), 1st Traffic Light "U" Turn Right on Ansin Blvd.
Attractions: Gulf Stream & Calder Thoroughbred Racing 2 mi. • Ft Lauderdale/Hollywood Int'l Airpt. 4 mi. • Beach 2 mi. • Hollywood Greyhound Race Track 3 mi. • Joe Robbie Stadium 5 mi. • Miami int'l Airpt. 14 mi.
Facilities: 98 Rms. • Mtgs. to 60.
Features: Outdoor Pool • Sleeper Sofa in all King Rms. • Refrig/Microwave Oven Avail.
Misc: TAX 9%.

HALFL

1. SEATTLE-Lynnwood
206/775-8030
FAX 206/774-0344
4117 196th Street S.W.
Lynnwood, WA 98036
Directions: From I-5 Southbound, Exit 181 turn Right onto 196th St. From I-5 Northbound, Exit 181 turn Left on 44th Ave; then Right on 196th St. (Behind Denny's).
Attractions: Alderwood Mall 1 mi. • Boeing 747 Tour Center & Paine Field 6 mi. • Univ. of Washington 15 mi. • Edmonds Ferry Dock 4 mi. • Sea-Tac Airpt. 30 mi. • Seattle Dwtn. & Space Needle 20 mi.
Facilities: 46 Rms. • Mtgs. to 10 • Int. Corridor.
Features: Indoor Jacuzzi Swim Spa • Guest Laundry Room • Jacuzzi Rooms Avail. • Refrig. & Microwave • Cable TV/Showtime.
Services: Car Rental.
Misc: TAX 8.2%.

LYNEX

5. LAKE BUENA VISTA
407/239-4500
FAX 407/239-8463
13351 S. R. 535/P.O. Box 22184
Lake Buena Vista, FL 32830
Directions: I-4 Exit 27 (South) on SR 535.
Attractions: Disney World 1 1/2 mi. • Airpt. 15 mi.
Facilities: 507 Rms. • 6 Flrs. • Ext. Corridor.
Features: Family Fun Resort • All Standard Rooms w/2 Queenbeds/Hairdryer & In-Room Safe • All Rooms Kitchenette With Refrig/Microwave/Coffeemaker • Maxine's Rest. • Lounge • Pinky's Diner • Heated Pool/Whirlpools • Playground • Kids Eat Dinner Free • Fitness Facility (7/93) • Nightly Family Bingo & Karaoke Party.
Services: Camp Holiday-Free Supervised Activities For Kids 2-12 • Ticket Sales • Licensed on-Site Child Care • Free Scheduled Disney Shuttle • 24 hr. Security.
Misc: TAX 10%.

DISBV

 **6. MAINGATE AREA**
     (To Open 4th Quarter 1993)
407/396-7100
FAX 407/396-6822
4311 W. Irlo Bronson Mem. Hwy.
Kissimmee, FL 34743
Directions: I-4 to Exit 25A, 5 mi. on Left.
Attractions: Disney/Epcot/MGM 5 mi. • Sea World 10 mi. • Universal Studios 12 mi.
Facilities: 173 Rms.
Features: Heated Outdoor Pool • Playground • Game Room • Kiddie Pool • Picnic & Shuffleboard Area.
Services: VCP's and Video Rentals.
Misc: TAX 11%.

DISKE

7. DISNEY WORLD AREA-Maingate
407-396-7300
FAX 407/396-7555
7300 Irlo Bronson Memorial Hwy
Kissimmee, FL 34747
Directions: I-4 Exit 25B (US 192 West).
Attractions: Closest Holiday Inn to Disney 1 mi.
Facilities: 529 Rms. • 2 Flrs. • Ext. Corridor • Free Parking.
Features: Family Vacation Resort • 3 Heated Pools/3 Whirlpools/3 Lighted Tennis Courts/2 Playgrounds/2 Heated Kiddie Pools/Video Arcade • Free Live Family Enter. • Home of Nikki the Bird/ Zucchini the Magical Clown/The Dean & Cindy Puppet Show • Guest Laundry • Nikki's Gift Shop • 3 Themed Rest. • Kids 12 & Under Eat Free Yr. Round (with or without Adult).
Services: Free Scheduled Disney Shuttle • Car Rental • 24 Hr. Security • Guest Service/Ticket Desk.
Misc: TAX 11%.

DISWE

2. SEATTLE-Downtown Area
206/464-1980
US 800/521-2762
CANADA: Zenith 8804
206/340-1617
1113 Sixth Avenue
Seattle, WA 98101
Directions: 6th and Seneca St.
Attractions: Airpt. 17 mi. • Convention Center/Bus. Dist. 1-3 blks. • King Dome 1 mi. • Waterfront 6 blks.
Facilities: 415 Rms. • 34 Flrs. • Mtgs. to 460 • Int. Corridor • Valet Parking Only (Limited Space Avail.) Parking $12/day.
Features: Parkside Cafe • Parkside Rest. & Lounge • No Pool • Executive Floor Avail.
Misc: TAX 15.2%.

SEADT

Exhibit 8.20 *(continued)*

GUADALAJARA — MEXICO

(52) 363 41034
FAX (52) 363 19393
TELEX 684004
CROWNE PLAZA **Lopez Mateo #2500**
Guadalajara, Jal 31214
Attractions: Dwtn. 6 mi. • Airpt. 10 mi. • Adj.
Guadalajara's largest Shopping Centre • Golf 2 mi. •
Chapala Lake 28 mi. • World Trade Centre & Expo
Guadalajara 1/2 mi.
Features: Jacarandas Gourmet Rest. • La Fuente (24 Hour) Coffee Shop
• Gourmet Rest. "El Kiosko" • Lobby Bar • La Fiesta Night club • Outdoor Pool •
Playground • Putting Green • Tobacco Shop • Beauty Parlor • Concierge FLoor • Gym
• Suites Avail. • HBO.
Misc: TAX 10%.

GDLMX

JUAREZ — MEXICO

(52) 162 96000
FAX (52) 162 96020
Paseo Del Triunfo De La Republica 3745
CD. Juarez Chihuahua CP 32310
Attractions: Int'l Airpt. 7 mi. • El Paso TX Border
Bridge 3 mi. • Dwtn. 1.5 mi. • Commercial Center Adj.
• Financial Center Adj. • El Paso TX 4 mi.
Facilities: 148 Rms. • Mtgs. to 80 • Free Parking
Panoramic Elevators.
Features: Outdoor Pool/Gardens • In-Room Movies.
Misc: TAX 10%.

JUAEX

HUATULCO — MEXICO

(52) 958 10044
FAX (52) 958 10221
CROWNE PLAZA RESORT **Blvd. Benito Juarez No. 8**
Bahia Tangolunda
Bahias de Huatulco,
Oaxaca 70989
Attractions: Airpt. 20 km. • Marina 1 mi. • Full
Service Beach Club & Watersports 1/4 mi. •
Tango Lunda Beach 300 yds • Historical/
Archaeological Sites In Oaxaca 200 mi. • Dwtn. 3 mi. • Professional Golf Course Par 72 1 mi.
Facilities: Mtgs. to 120 • Free Parking.
Features: 3 Rest/4 Bars • 2 Pools • 135 Oceanview Suites • Servibar • Hairdryer •
Safe Deposit Box • Sofabed • Shopping Arcade w/Travel Agency • Boutique • Drugstore.
Services: 24-Hour Room Service • Car Rental • Doctor Service • Catering.

HUXMX

MAZATLAN — MEXICO

(52) 691 32222
FAX (52) 691 41287
TELEX 66876
Calzada Camaron Zabalo 696
Mazatlan Sinaloa 82100
Attractions: Int'l Airpt. 12 mi. • Aquarium 3 mi. •
Dwtn. 5 mi. • Bull Fight Arena 2 mi. • Shopping Zone 1/
2 mi. • Fishing Fleets 5 mi. • In Front of Famous 3
Islands. On the Beach • Bus Station 3 mi.
Facilities: 204 Rms. • Mtgs. to 600.
Features: Speciality Rest. • Seafood Rest. • Deep-Sea Fishing • Gardens • Suites Avail.
Misc: TAX 10%. Golf Pkgs. Avail. Affordable Mexico Holidays.

MZTMX

MONTERREY (Cont.) — MEXICO

2. MONTERREY

(52) 831 96000
FAX (52) 834 43007
TELEX 382009
CROWNE PLAZA **Ave. Constitucion Ote 300**
Monterrey, Nuevo Leon 64000
Attractions: Dwtn. Airpt. 15 mi. • Walking Distance to Shopping/Business Dist. & Govt.
Offices • Convention Centre 5 mi.
Facilities: 408 Rms. • Mtgs. to 1200 • Free Parking.
Features: 2 Rests. • Breakfast/Lunch/Dinner Buffets • 2 Bars • Night club • Gym • Tennis
Court • Gift Shop • Hairdryers • Mini-Bars in Rooms • Concierge Floors Have VCR •
Free Video Club • Suites Avail.
Services: 24 Hour Room Service • Business Center • Travel Agency • Car Rental.
Misc: TAX 10%. Corp. Rates.

MTYPL

---

3. MONTERREY
(52) 832 96000
Av. Eugenio Garza Sada #3680
Monterrey, Nuevo Leon 64310
Directions: Facing Eugenio Garza Sada in front of Commercial Centre Plaza, La Silla, Hwy. 85. Hwy.
54, Exit Eugenio Garza Sada.
Attractions: Mariano Escobedo Int'l Airpt. 15 mi. • Tec of Monterrey 1 mi. • Shopping Centre
Walking Distance • Dwtn. Business Area 4 mi. • Planetarium 5 mi.
Facilities: 141 Rms. • Mtgs. to 80 • Panoramic Elevators.
Features: Four Story Bldg. • Fecade Mexican Colonial Style • All Rooms w/Balconies • Spanish
Hacienda & Modern Atmosphere • Outdoor Pool • In Room Movies • Direct Dial Phones.
Misc: TAX 15%.

SINGAPORE — SINGAPORE

1. SINGAPORE-Royal

(65) 737-7966
FAX (65) 737-6646
TELEX RS21818.
CROWNE PLAZA **25 Scotts Rd.**
Singapore 0922
Directions: City Centre at Jct. Orchard & Scotts
Rd.
Attractions: In the Main Shopping & Enter. Area
• All Local Tourist Attractions Mins. away • Airpt.
($20 taxi ride) 20 km.
Facilities: 493 Rms. • Mtgs. to 300 • 7 Meeting
Rooms.
Features: Luxurious Rms. & Suites • 4 Rests. •
Bar • Outdoor Pool • All Rooms Have IDD
Phone • Sprinklers • Fitness Center • Squash/
Badminton Court • Room Safe.
Services: 24-hr. Room Service • Business Centre.
Misc: Svc Chg 10% Local Prevailing Tax.

SINSN

---

2. SINGAPORE-Park View
7338333
FAX 7344593
TELEX 55420
11 Cavenagh Rd.
Singapore 0922
Attractions: City & Shopping Centre/Orchard Rd. 3 min walk • Presidential Palace 5 min walk •
Museum 8 min • Airpt. 30 min • Chinatown 10 min • MRT (Tube) 5 min walk • Zoo 30 min.
Facilities: Banq. to 200 • Car Park.
Features: New Orleans/Indian/Chinese Rests. • Lounge • Cafe Rest. • Outdoor Pool • Mini Bar •
IDD Phones • 24 Hour In-House Movies • Shopping Arcade • No Pets • Suites • Executive Floor •
Handicap Room • Safe.
Services: 24-hr. Room Service • Concierge Desk • Business Centre.
Misc: Tax 4% Svc Chg 10%.

SINPV

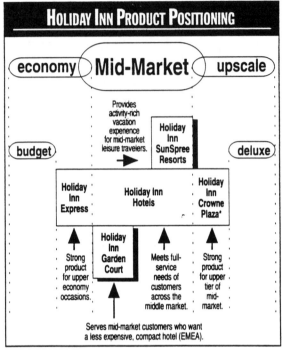

*Includes hotels and resorts.

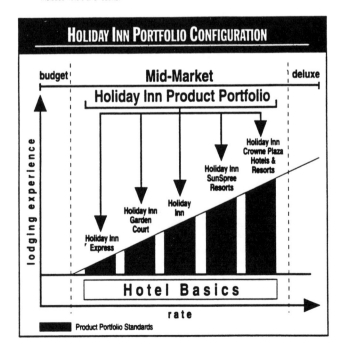

Exhibit 8.22
Holiday Inn Worldwide's Product Line

Holiday Inn Hotels

Category: Full-service hotels catering to the middle-market segment.

Description: From big cities to small towns, from airports to industrial parks, Holiday Inn Hotels are known throughout the world for dependable service and attractive facilities. Not surprisingly, Holiday Inn Hotels account for an impressive 10 percent of the total lodging market supply in the U.S. Average number of rooms: 150 to 300.

Amenities: Restaurants, lounges, swimming pools, and meeting and banquet facilities.

History: The first Holiday Inn Hotel opened in Memphis, TN, in 1952.

Status: 1,558 hotels in the Americas; 131 hotels in Europe, the Middle East and Africa; 57 hotels in the Asia/Pacific region, for a total of 1,746 properties worldwide representing 336,943 rooms.

Projections: Aggressive growth in key regions, with an emphasis on changes that work to ensure Holiday Inns' high quality standards. Americas division president, Michael A. Leven, predicts the net growth for Holiday Inn Hotels to be about 100 properties in the next five years.

Conclusion: A strong recognition factor, both domestically and internationally, ensures Holiday Inn Hotels a consistently strong consumer base. This product is, and will continue to be, the recognized leader in the middle segment of the lodging market.

Exhibit 8.22 *(continued)*

Holiday Inn Garden Court Hotels

Category: Small, three-star European hotels.

Description: Located in secondary European towns and cities, these competitively priced properties were created to meet the needs of business and leisure travelers seeking modern, inexpensive accommodations with guaranteed standards. Average number of rooms: 100.

Amenities: Restaurant and bar, exercise rooms and meeting rooms.

History: Introduced in 1987.

Status: At present there are 14 Garden Court Hotels in operation.

Projections: An additional 100 Garden Courts are scheduled to open over the next five years in Europe, the Middle East and Africa. At present, there are no plans to expand the brand into the U.S.

Exhibit 8.22 *(continued)*

Holiday Inn Crowne Plaza Hotels

Category: Business-class hotels catering to executive travelers.

Description: Business-class, business-friendly properties offering tastefully appointed guest rooms, comprehensive meeting facilities and extensive business services, with locations in urban, airport and some sub-urban areas. Average number of rooms: 250 to 500.

Services: Health club (whirlpool, sauna, exercise equipment); business center (message, fax, copying and secretarial services); extended room-service hours; expanded meeting facilities; on-site convention services, manager and professional meetings staff; executive boardrooms; concierge; fine restaurants; and, at many Crowne Plazas, private executive floors featuring a lounge, turndown service, etc.

History: Introduced in 1983.

Status: 39 hotels in the Americas, 25 hotels throughout Europe, the Middle East and Africa, and 10 properties in the Asia/Pacific region. Total: 74 hotels representing 24,740 rooms.

Projections: Development plans call for a significant increase in Crowne Plaza properties over the next several years. According to Americas division president Michael A. Leven: "We expect to go between 150 and 200 in the next five years."

Progress Report: Due to their key locations (downtown areas and business districts within major cities) and targeted business amenities, Crowne Plaza occupancy rates have continued on an upward trend despite reports of sluggishness throughout the lodging industry. High guest ratings have been a constant.

Conclusion: A strong product with an international following that has enjoyed excellent success over the last 10 years. With the acceleration of global travel, Crowne Plaza hotels, with their high-recognition profile, will continue to see high levels of occupancy in the upcoming decade and beyond.

Exhibit 8.22 *(continued)*

Holiday Inn Crowne Plaza Resorts

Category: Upmarket, full-activity resorts.

Description: Located in prime resort destinations, Holiday Inn Crowne Plaza Resorts are "marquee" properties that deliver a full-service resort experience. Average number of rooms: 200 to 300.

Amenities: A selection of restaurants and shops, as well as extensive meeting space, complete fitness facilities, concierge services, supervised children's activities, a wide range of destination-specific recreational activities and nightly entertainment offerings.

History: In September 1992, the first Holiday Inn Crowne Plaza Resort—Sugar Bay Plantation—opened on St. Thomas, U.S. Virgin Islands. A month later, Holiday Inn Crowne Plaza Resort-Bays of Huatulco opened in Huatulco, Mexico.

Status: In addition to St. Thomas and Huatulco, Holiday Inn Crowne Plaza Resorts has opened three other properties: Crystal Sands in Hilton Head, SC; Indigo Lakes in Daytona Beach, FL; and Pier 66 in Ft. Lauderdale, FL. By year's end, the Princess Beach in Curacao and the Baraloche, Argenta in Italy will also have opened, bringing the total number of Crowne Plaza Resorts to seven.

Conclusion: A new brand extension that has, in a short period of time, garnered exceptional interest, especially from existing resort properties looking to convert.

Exhibit 8.22 *(continued)*

Holiday Inn Express

Category: Upper economy/limited service.

Description: A streamlined version of the traditional Holiday Inn full-service property, the Holiday Inn Express hotel features a distinctive tower for easy product identification from the highway. Although mostly located along interstate highways, they are also located in secondary markets, suburbs and airports. Average number of rooms: 100.

Services: Free local phone calls; express check-out; complimentary Breakfast Bar.

History: October 1990—Three company-owned properties open; February 1991—First franchised property opens.

Status: 110 hotels throughout the U.S. and Mexico as of September 1993.

Projections: By Jan. 1, 1994—140 hotels; by Jan. 1, 1996—500 Holiday Inn Express hotels throughout the U.S., Mexico and Canada.

Progress Report: The fastest growing segment in the Holiday Inn portfolio, with excellent guest response. Nine out of 10 guests polled in recent surveys indicated they intend to return.

Conclusion: According to Americas division president Michael A. Leven: "Holiday Inn Express is a wonderful example of a market-driven product which has managed to be successful despite tough economic times. The hotels have proven to be an exciting financial success for our franchisees because they provide the right product, in the right place, at the right time."

Exhibit 8.22 *(continued)*

Holiday Inn SunSpree Resorts

Category: Middle-market, full-service resorts.

Description: Located in popular vacation destinations near themed attractions, beaches, mountain areas and lakes, SunSpree Resorts are designed to provide value-conscious families with a comfortable, affordable, "total" vacation experience. Physically, SunSpree Resorts have a "sense of arrival" entrance/themed gateway. Average number of rooms: 100 to 250.

Amenities: Guest-services desk, organized children's programs, destination-specific recreation options, restaurant and a "Marketessan" foodservice operation offering both take-out and sit-down service.

History: On Feb. 8, 1993, the first Holiday Inn SunSpree Resort was announced at Lake Buena Vista, Orlando, FL, with its grand opening following in June. This hotel, which had operated as a traditional Holiday Inn hotel since 1991, became the prototype for developing SunSpree Resorts.

Status: The Grandview Holiday Inn Resort and Conference Center in Lake Placid, NY, became the second U.S. SunSpree Resort to open, while the Holiday Inn SunSpree Resort Nice-Port Saint Laurent, France, is the first European property to fly the SunSpree flag. SunSprees in Guadeloupe, French West Indies; Mexico; and Bar Harbor, ME, are slated to open later this year.

Conclusion: The first resort product to be designed exclusively to appeal to middle-market families vacationing on a budget. Unlimited audience and potential. Probability strong that SunSpree will become the breakthrough product of the '90s.

facilities and amenities." Corporate intent was clear, Mike noted, as he looked once again at the franchise brochure (Exhibits 8.21 and 8.22). "But, is it clear to the customer?"

At that point Bryan Langton, CEO of Holiday Inn Worldwide, walked into his office. "What are you in such deep thought about, Mike?" asked Langton.

"I'm still working on the proper positioning of our six products," Leven replied. "We've got a lot of growth coming in five of them," said Langton, "and positioning is going to be critical to that growth. You know this business, Mike, make it work."

Case Nine

Bon Ami Restaurant

Robert C. Lewis

"Something is wrong, Phil," said Joe Smith, the manager of Bon Ami Restaurant,

> It just doesn't make sense. Our customers tell us they love us. In fact, we hear nothing but compliments. Read the comments in the guest book that people sign on the way out; they indicate nothing but praise. Newspaper reviews have also been excellent. One writer in Baltimore has stated that we are one of the best restaurants in the state. Yet business is going nowhere but down. Slowly, to be sure, but surely. Customer counts are down. And worse, we're losing from $20,000 to $25,000 a month.

"Okay, Joe," replied Phil Jones, the backer and principal owner of Bon Ami,

> I'm well aware of the figures, and it's my pocket the money is coming out of. We've gone over the costs item by item, and they're certainly not out of line compared with national operating figures. Our food cost stays constant at around 31 percent and our beverage cost at 19 percent. What's killing us of course is our labor cost at 35 percent. But we can't cut labor unless we reduce the service level we're trying to provide. And that would defeat our whole purpose of being here. Clearly we have to find a way to do more volume.

"Well, we've certainly advertised enough," replied Smith.

> Just look at the figures of what we've spent. I'm beginning to think there just aren't enough people in this meat-and-potatoes town who

This case was written by Robert C. Lewis, University of Guelph, Ontario. All rights reserved. Names and locations have been disguised.

appreciate good food. Maybe we'll have to change our concept. But how do we know? And how do we know what to change it to? And how do we know if it will work? Do we really know why people come or don't come here? If they don't come here, where do they go? After all, there's only one other French restaurant in the area that competes with us, and they can't all go there. Maybe we're just not meeting the demands of the market. I think we had better learn something about the market before we go off half-cocked again. I suggest we do a market research study. What do you think?

HISTORY OF BON AMI

Bon Ami Restaurant had been open just two years. It had been well planned and well executed, and almost no expense had been spared. Almost everyone would agree that it was an elegant restaurant. The owners were especially proud of the elegant bathrooms with their gold fixtures.

Jones was the principal owner of Bon Ami, while Smith and his wife were minor partners and managers of the restaurant. Jones was in his sixties and essentially retired from business. He had accumulated a small fortune as one of the original McDonald's franchisees. After selling his franchise back to McDonald's, he had decided he would like to own a truly different type of restaurant for more upscale tastes, but hadn't wanted to be involved in active management. His search for an active and managing partner had eventually led him to Smith and his wife.

Smith was 36 years old. He was the graduate of a four-year university hotel program. After college, Joe had worked for awhile for Radisson Hotels in food and beverage. He had subsequently gone to work for T.G.I. Friday's restaurants and opened three of their new units. Along the way he had obtained substantial cooking experience as well as management know-how. At the age of 27 he had decided he wanted to operate his own restaurant.

The Smiths' first attempt at their own operation had been a restaurant on the Maryland coast that they had leased on a year-to-year basis. The realistic operating season, however, was only four months. They had ended the first season $50,000 in debt. Two years later they had paid off the debt and were making a profit. Three years later the Smiths had felt they had outgrown the location. They had been looking for an expansion location in Baltimore when they heard of Jones's search for a partner. The partners shared a common dream—to establish a top-class French restaurant.

Jones had lived in this same Delaware community all his life and had many friends there. When he had decided to open an upscale restaurant he had conducted his own survey among his friends. This had told him that what people in the area wanted was a French restaurant. Money was no obstacle and Jones was willing to spend what it took. On the other hand, he was not inclined to build an ego monument either. A man of humble origin, he had never had a financial failure and he was determined that his new restaurant would also be profitable.

THE RESTAURANT

Under construction, the new restaurant grew from an original 3,500 square feet to about 7,000 square feet with two dining rooms that seated a total of 135 people. There was also a sizable space for kitchen, office, and storage, and room in the basement for later conversion to small banquet rooms. A nationally known food-and-wine consultant had been retained at a sizable fee to advise on the name, the menu, the layout, the style, the decor, and the promotion of the restaurant. A continental chef with an excellent reputation had been hired.

Upon entering Bon Ami, the patron first passed through a massive double door under an eye-catching kiosk roof. The only external identification of the restaurant was a highly polished brass plate with the name "Bon Ami" on it. Immediately inside was a wide entrance hall with a maitre d's desk at the end. In back of this desk were floor-to-ceiling wine racks. To the right was a room seating 40, with banquettes along the front of the building. Behind the banquettes and in the center of the wall, there was a small cut-glass window to the outside. Across the room was an elegant polished rosewood bar with eight stools.

On the other side of the entranceway was a dining room seating 95 persons on two levels. The front of the room was again banquettes, but there was no window to the outside. Both rooms were furnished with French provincial tables, chairs, and other decor. Joe Smith was quoted in an interview as saying, "We designed the restaurant to be like a French chateau, with one dining room for casual meals and another room for formal dining." The formal room to the left had linen tablecloths; the informal room had no tablecloths or placemats. Both rooms had fine crystal, silver and china, and fresh flowers on every table.

The restaurant property itself was part of a small strip shopping center, built and owned by Jones, in Newport, the wealthiest suburb of Wilmington, Delaware. On one end of the strip and next to Bon Ami was a bank. On the other end was an inexpensive but quality family restaurant, and a branch of an upscale area department store. In between were small exclusive shops. Bon Ami was indistinguishable from its neighbors in this strip except for the front brick façade in place of windows, the kiosk, and the brass nameplate. It was not readily recognizable as a restaurant. In fact, some had said that it looked more like a funeral parlor.

THE AREA

Newport had one of the highest per capita incomes in the state. It was about five miles from the center of Wilmington and was a bedroom community for a blend of corporate executives and small business owners.

The lifestyle, however, was very conservative. The remainder of the greater Wilmington area (population about 150,000) was a changing scene, but one that clung to tradition. Almost on the Maryland state line, eight miles to the southwest, was the well-to-do community of Newark, many residents of which commuted to Baltimore, 50 miles away, as well as to Wilmington. Other areas of Wilmington were more middle-class, and some were strictly working-class. Across the Delaware River, about six miles from Newport, were a number of other communities in Salem County, New Jersey. Many of the residents of this area worked in the Wilmington area. Exhibit 9.1 shows a map of the area.

According to *Restaurant Business'* Restaurant Growth Index (RGI), eating and drinking sales in the Wilmington area were $249 million, but the population was somewhat less likely than the national average to eat out. The RGI index of 106 (where 100 means that supply exactly equals demand) indicated that the market growth potential for the area was slightly higher than for the average American city.

Exhibit 9.1

Map of the Wilmington Area

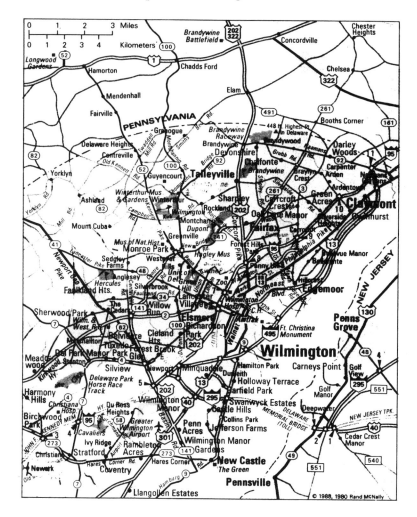

THE DEVELOPMENT

When Bon Ami first opened, it did no advertising. This was because the consultant had said her name was so famous that people would come from the publicity alone. When very few came in the first two months, the partners decided that they had better do something. According to Smith, a rumor started soon after opening that Bon Ami was so elegant that dinner cost $100 per person. Actually, meals with beverage averaged just under $45 per person at dinner.

Creative advertising was commenced with a decidedly French flavor. For example, when a brunch was introduced on Sunday, it was advertised as "Le Bon Brunch." Buffets were called Le Bon Buffet. The restaurant was described as "Bon Elegant" versus "Bon Stuffy" to dispel the $100 check rumor. Area newspapers were the primary media used. Brunch checks came to average $18.00 per person.

Business at Bon Ami picked up after advertising began. Average dinner covers reached 60 per night, partly due to an average of 125 on Saturdays. Bon Ami opened for luncheon with menu items priced from $4.95 to $10.95, and business was excellent almost from the start. Check averages at luncheon eventually grew to $18.00 per person.

Other changes took place as time progressed. Management discovered that the local definition of French food was Caesar salad, quiche, crêpes, and so forth—not nouvelle or classical cuisine. Adaptations were made without sacrificing the integrity of the food. A prime-rib buffet was introduced on Sundays. An eight-item early-bird dinner menu for those who arrived before 6:30 P.M., with all entrees priced at $14.95, was added to meet the demands of customers who wanted lower-priced meals. Originally the management had planned to serve this menu in the casual (bar) dining room, but they found that status-conscious customers didn't want to sit in the "discount" room. Early-bird check averages were constant at around $15.00 per person; business was brisk at this time and eventually became 60 percent of the total dinner covers during the week, with a $22.50 check average. Exhibit 9.2 shows various menus of the restaurant.

The menu was accompanied by an excellent wine list starting at $24.50 per bottle for Muscadet, Alsace riesling, Entre deux Mers, Rose d'Anjou, white Zinfandel, and a Côtes du Ventoux from the Rhône Valley. For around $30.00, diners could obtain Vouvray, Macon, California Chenin Blanc, Sauvignon Blanc, Fumé Blanc, and Gewürtztraminer; Tavel rosé; or a red Graves, Médoc, or Beaujolais Villages. Other listings ranged from California Chardonnay, Pouilly Fuissé, Grand Cru Chablis, Santenay, and Chateau Talbot for $35 to $45.00, to Chateau Latour 1982 at $225.00. No half bottles were offered.

As business developed at Bon Ami, a number of customers became regulars. Others never returned or did so only on special occasions. Business stabilized for a short period at about $105,000 per month. About 10 percent of this was from off-premise catering, 11 percent was liquor sales, and 13 percent was wine sales. The casual or bar dining room was seldom used, either for meals or for drinking.

After 12 months, business began to slip. Some tie-in direct-mail coupon campaigns were initiated with little effect. Two-for-one dinners were very popular for a six-week period with those who "seemed to come out of the woods" but did not fit Bon Ami's clientele image. Business resumed its slide when these dinners were discontinued. Customer comments continued to be good, but customer counts fell at both lunch and dinner. Management tried various new approaches, but none seemed to have any more than initial impact, if that. Revenue dropped to an average of $90,000 a month, including 10 percent from outside catering, with about two-thirds of this at dinner and one-third at lunch and Sunday brunch.

CONCLUSION

"Well Joe," said Phil Jones in response to the question about doing a research study,

> we are a one-of-a-kind restaurant in this area, that is for sure. All of our competition is lower-priced, less formal, and more casual, and none of them have food or service that reaches our level. This certainly defines for us a unique niche in the marketplace. We have made some accommodations to the meat-and-potatoes crowd by taking the tuxedos off our waiters and by introducing buffets, brunch, early-bird specials, and so forth. We have a loyal clientele; we just don't have enough of it. Comments on our food and service continue to be excellent. Yet, obviously, business is slipping and we are losing money, so we must be doing something wrong. I'm not opposed to change and I'm not opposed to a research study. But I am opposed to throwing good money after bad. What is this study going to tell us? What do we expect to learn? The tabletop study conducted by our advertising agency a few weeks ago [Exhibit 9.3] told us that we're doing everything right and nothing about what we should change. As a result, the agency thinks we have

to put even more emphasis on our advertising on the quality of our food and our French ambience. We've thought this all along. How is this new study going to be any different?

"Because," Smith said, "this time we'll do it scientifically. We can't afford to sit here and do nothing, that's for sure. Let's at least get a proposal." The proposal is given in Appendix 9A, the research design in Appendix 9B, and the findings of the research in Appendix 9C.

Exhibit 9.2

Bon Ami Menus

Our Philosophy

We pride ourselves on being a restaurant dedicated to quality. Certainly, by today's standards, any experienced traveler knows our offerings are more than affordable. Bon Ami is for those who appreciate the finer things in life. It is a restaurant built upon attention to detail. With rare exceptions, we make everything on premise. Many of our items are now available for you to take home. Our palmier cookies have been served at a wide variety of functions, from recitals in Baltimore to a meeting with the Governor at the State House. The legend of our rolls has been covered numerous times by the Baltimore papers. Our pride continues. . . . Our fresh herbs are cultivated in our own greenhouse.

Christine's soups are now available by the quart, and we now do regular off-premise catering.

For those of you who are looking for that "special" place for your next private party, consider Bon Ami. We do have certain size restrictions. However, our specialties include executive and business breakfasts, cocktail receptions, luncheons, and small dinner parties.

Thank you for welcoming us into this community. We are proud to be here.

Your Hosts

Active Members of: *National Restaurant Association*
Chaine de Rotisseurs
Les Amis d' Escoffier
Maryland Restaurant Association
Greater Baltimore Ch. of Commerce
American Culinary Federation, Inc.

Exhibit 9.2 *(continued)*

LUNCHEON MENU

SIDE DISHES

Onion Soup	4.95
Bon Ami Salad	3.95
Soup of the Day	5.75

ENTREES
All hot entrees include a Bon Ami salad

Jumbo Shrimp and Orange Salad	12.95
Chicken Livers Madeira with Spaetzle	10.95
Fluffy Omelettes with Sauteed Potatoes	9.95
An Assortment of French Terrines, Pates, and Gallantines served with a glass of wine	12.75
Charcoal Broiled Norwegian Salmon with Summer Vegetables	13.95
Fresh Maine Shrimp and Pasta Salad with Avocados	12.75
Oysters and Scallops on Spinach Fettucine with Pernod Cream Sauce	14.95
A Ragout of Tender Braised Meats with a Bouquet of Vegetables in a Savory Sauce	10.95
Baked Stuffed Sole with Nantua Sauce	12.75
Chicken and Mushroom Crepe	12.75
The Boss's Lunch (low in sodium, cholesterol & calories)	Price varies
Caesar Salad with Croissant	11.95

SUNDAY BRUNCH

BUFFET $21.95

Enjoy a complimentary Bloody Mary, Glass of Champagne, or Orange Juice, and sample our Award Winning Cuisine.

In April, our Chefs received numerous awards from the American Culinary Federation at the Baltimore Restaurant Show, including our Executive Chef, Christine Buchholz, who won a Gold Medal. Each week Bon Ami Chefs will demonstrate these skills in the food items we present on our Sunday Buffet.

The presentation will offer a variety of hot and cold foods, with many items changing each week. Our Buffet will be committed to the quality and artistry we have been recognized for both regionally and nationally.

Exhibit 9.2 *(continued)*

BRUNCH à la CARTE

Entrees include complimentary Baker's Basket, coffee, tea, or milk

Sauteed Chicken Livers with Spaetzle	12.95
Grilled Fresh Norwegian Salmon (compound butter)	16.95
The Classic—Eggs Benedict	15.45
French Style Herb Omelette with Hash Browns	11.95

EARLY BIRD MENU

AMERICAN FARE WITH A FRENCH FLAIR!
$19.50

Appetizers

A Slice of Country Terrine	5.50
Mushroom Caps—Seafood Stuffing and Gruyere Cheese	5.95
Shrimp Cocktail	7.45
Pasta Primavera	6.95

Entrees

Grilled Cod Steaks—Basted with a savory sauce. Served with
   vegetables of the day and Bliss Potatoes

Prime Rib with Watercress and Potato Puree and Braised Carrots
   and Leeks   LIMITED AVAILABILITY

American Cassoulet—Great Northern Beans with Pork Tenderloin,
   Grilled Duck, and Sausage

Baked Stuffed Shrimp

Creole Fried Chicken—Accompanied by Potato Gratin and Green
   Beans

Seafood Kabob—Skewered Grilled Scallops, Shrimp, Halibut, and
   Salmon

California Veal Birds—Medallions of Stuffed Veal with Herbs, Olives,
   and Cornichons

Baked Stuffed Sole with Nantua Sauce

Deep Fried Cape Scallops—Served with Creole Tartar Sauce and
   Cole Slaw

*All entrees are only $19.50 and include a choice of soup of the day
or Bon Ami Salad and Freshly Baked Rolls!*

*This Menu is available 5:00–6:30 Monday through Saturday
3:00–6:30 Sunday*

Exhibit 9.2 *(continued)*

Early dining guests are requested to arrive before 6:30 p.m. to receive the special pricing.

DINNER MENU

APPETIZERS

Fried Stuffed Mushroom Caps with Watercress Sauce	6.75
Wellfleet Oysters Wrapped in Canadian Bacon, Broiled and Served with Hollandaise Sauce	10.95
Escargots, Raisins, and Hazelnuts in a Nest of Filo Dough	9.95
Shrimp and Maine Crab in an Orange Thyme Cream	12.95
Scotch Smoked Salmon with Golden Caviar and Lemon-Pepper Vodka	9.75
Assortment of French Terrines, Patés, and Gallantines	8.75
Soups—Several Selections Available	4.50–6.75

Fresh herbs from our garden is another reason why Bon Ami is the untypical French restaurant.

ENTREES

Each evening our chefs have several signature items available. They represent Classic French, Nouvelle, and American Cuisines.
Bon Appetit!

Charcoal Grilled Norwegian Salmon	22.95
Chicken in Clementine Sauce on a Crispy Noodle Pillow with Snow Peas and Almonds	19.95
Duck Breast Grilled Rare, Native Corn Soufflé, Fresh Raspberries	24.75
Veal and Lobster in Champagne Sauce	27.95
Shrimp and Scallop de Jonghe, baked with Fines Herbes, Shallots, and Sherry	21.75
Veal Medallions Sauteed with Melon, Mushrooms, and Capers	25.95
Veal Oscar—Plume Veal with Chunks of Lobster and Shrimp in a Bearnaise Sauce, Fresh Broccoli	27.75
Charcoal Grilled Pork Tenderloin with Sweet Potato Fettuccini, Cranberry-Nut Compote	19.95
Braised Bay Scallops and Oysters on Spinach Pasta Sauced with a light Pernod Cream	21.95

Exhibit 9.2 *(continued)*

Fusilli (Curly Pasta) with Prosciutto, Leeks, and an Asiago Cream Sauce	*16.95*
Skillet Steak Diane—Medallions of Tenderloin with a Classic Sauce of Cognac, Dijon Mustard, and Demi-Glaze	*22.75*

Exhibit 9.3

Tabletop Questionnaire

Questionnaire

We'd like to make Bon Ami even better for you and your guests. If you'd be good enough to answer the questions below, we'd appreciate it very much. It's totally confidential of course.

About Bon Ami

Did you consider your meal __excellent __good __fair __poor

Do you find the service __excellent __good __fair __poor

Do you dine here __once a week __once a month __less frequent __first time

Compared to other fine restaurants, do you think our prices are: __too high __just right __lower than most

Your favorite entree at Bon Ami is: _____

About You

Where you reside (town, zip) _____

Occupation _____

Approximate household income: __less than $25,000 __$25,000–$50,000 __over $50,000

Favorite type of restaurant: __French __American __Italian __Mexican __Other

Dine out: ____times per week

Business meals per week: ____

Are they primarily __lunch __dinner

Merci!   You can drop this card in the convenient box near the door or mail it to us.

Exhibit 9.3 *(continued)*

Tabletop Questionnaire Results

Survey conducted 11/23 to 12/31; 836 covers, 292 returned.

Considered meal: excellent, 176; good, 97; fair, 17; poor, 2

Considered service: excellent, 235; good, 55; fair, 3; poor, 0

Dine here: once a week, 15; once a month, 53; less frequently, 111; first time, 106

Think prices are: too high, 61; just right, 195; lower than most, 20

Household income: <$25,000, 9; $25,000–$50,000, 69; >$50,000, 138

Favorite type of restaurant: French, 168; American, 42; Italian, 57; Mexican, 10; Chinese, 13; German, 1

Number of times dine out per week: total, 456; business, 390; lunch, 211; dinner, 119

Favorite entrees at Bon Ami: veal, 29; lamb, 28; duck, 15; fish, 13; seafood, 9; chicken, 8; veal and lobster, 7; steak, 7; sole, 6; schrod, 4

Occupation: businessman, 32; doctor, 17; executive, 14; teacher or self-employed, 12 each; vice president or retired, 7 each; administrator, attorney, accountant, or consultant, 5 each; psychologist, sales rep, insurance, advertising, or waiter, 4 each; secretary, district manager, professor, investor, marketing, or real estate, 3 each; engineer, psychotherapist, homemaker, entrepreneur, nurse, stockbroker, artist, public relations, salesman, contractor, designer, florist, or restaurant manager, 2 each; retail manager, lawn service, manufacturer, union rep, computer analyst, economist, barber, tennis pro, fashion designer, dentist, machine operator, book dealer, or auto dealer, 1 each

Specific Comments

"Excellent service—will definitely return."

"First time ever I didn't get change from gift certificate. Will use credit for my last time at Bon Ami. Pure parsimoniousness."

"Waitress very nice. Too much hovering and speediness by waiters."

"For every entree in a French restaurant there should be an intermezzo course and place plates used."

"Heat your coffee [2]," "warm your bread."

"L'Escargot's prices are lower."

Exhibit 9.3 *(continued)*

"Only wrinkled tablecloths were less than excellent."

"Portions too small [4]."

"Suggest less chocolate on dessert menu."

"Veal Oscar not up to expectation, chocolate mousse too small."

"Keep early bird special!"

"Mousse in the cake not good, all else superb."

"Carla great waitress [3]."

"Quality was superb [5]!"

"Yellow pages advertising deceiving as far as attire and atmosphere."

"Have dined here many times and always found excellent but disappointed in early-bird special."

"Prices too high for liquor [2]."

"An elegant restaurant must offer the courtesy to take guests' coats and bring them upon leaving."

"Needs fresh flowers. Too noisy."

"Enjoyed the evening, will return."

"Miss the country room menu."

"People should be well dressed in main dining room."

"Enjoyed our first experience, look forward to returning."

"Choice of menu is excellent."

"Enjoy early diners' specials."

"Charles is the greatest [3]!"

"Reinstate Caesar salad and croissants at lunch."

"More veal dishes for dinner."

"Croissants disappointing, cold and overdone."

"Roast of lamb should be carved at table."

Tabletop Questionnaire Summary

The purpose of this questionnaire was to ascertain certain demographic and lifestyle characteristics of Bon Ami's customer base, as well as to develop a benchmark for customer satisfaction, dining habits, etc.

Customer satisfaction levels at Bon Ami are very high in terms of food, service, and price. It appears that no substantive changes are indicated. The

Exhibit 9.3 *(continued)*

high "just right" answer to the pricing question, however, deserves some notice in that customers ordinarily feel that most restaurant prices are too high. Combined with the high household income scores, Bon Ami should not be reluctant to inch its prices higher. People tend to equate quality with price—prices that are too low (or even "just right") may be perceived as indicating a lower quality.

In analyzing the residence information provided by respondents, it is readily apparent that the bulk of Bon Ami's business comes from the Wilmington area. However, given that Bon Ami has been in this market for two years, and has been a fairly steady advertiser, it must be assumed that awareness is as high as can be expected in the Wilmington market, based on dollar expenditures to date. In other words, Bon Ami's message has reached nearly as many people as affordable within budgetary constraints.

The resultant traffic levels are the product of this awareness level. Therefore, raising the traffic level will require raising the awareness level within the Wilmington market. This will in part be accomplished via word of mouth. However, it can be assumed that lower advertising levels will result in lower traffic levels and conversely. Only by experimenting with increased ad levels will it be known whether there is a wider market in Wilmington.

It is possible that increased ad levels may not draw the increase in traffic necessary to offset the additional expenditure. In other words, it is possible that Bon Ami has already drawn as much as it can from Wilmington.

This assumption is somewhat supported by the high percentage of out-of-state customers. According to the figures, there were 46 percent as many out-of-staters as there were Wilmington residents, 41 percent as many as there were Wilmington area residents. Bon Ami, in other words, has a strong pulling power from the demographically and psychographically different markets of nearby Maryland. This may indicate a strength that Bon Ami has not tapped—a potential reservoir of business that is more accustomed to and receptive to the Bon Ami dining experience.

The occupational information offers some support to this hypothesis. From the figures derived in the study, occupations were categorized into three major groupings: businesspeople (129), professionals (53), and others (19).

The business/professional marketplace, while widely varied and diverse, represents a major strength to Bon Ami. These data strongly suggest that future marketing plans be aimed at maximizing Bon Ami's impact upon this market. Interestingly, the northern Maryland region represents a strong bastion of business and professional people, certainly much stronger than does the Wilmington market.

Exhibit 9.3 *(continued)*

In general, these people tend to be more mobile, more adventuresome, and more discriminating in their choices of food, eating, and entertainment.

With its strong out-of-town pulling power and an apparent softness in its hometown markets, it may behoove Bon Ami to consider making a strong push for attracting this more affluent and receptive out-of-town customer. Considering the truly unique nature of the establishment, this suggests that Bon Ami make a conscious decision to become a regional restaurant rather than a local one. It must be understood, however, that such a decision would require a substantial advertising and public relations effort at first.

APPENDIX 9A   BON AMI RESEARCH PROPOSAL

Purpose of the Research

To determine what kind of restaurant Bon Ami should be in the marketplace in terms of market demand.

Research Problem

What are the needs and wants of the market, and how can they be fulfilled?

Subproblem   How are they currently being fulfilled?

Specific Objectives

1. To learn present eating-out habits of the market, and why.
2. To learn present awareness and perceptions of users and nonusers of Bon Ami.
3. To learn what the marketplace would like to see and would utilize in a new restaurant concept.
4. To project demand of the marketplace for an upscale restaurant concept.

Definitions

Population or marketplace shall mean those persons in Newport or immediate surrounding areas who are potential customers for an upscale restaurant in the suburb of Newport.

Sample frame shall mean a random selection of 5,000 households from the population presumed to have incomes of $30,000 a year or more.

Sample shall mean a random selection from the sample frame of 150 adult members of the sample frame, randomly chosen by sex, who have a per-person check average of $25.00 or higher when dining out for dinner in an upscale restaurant, and who dine out for dinner in an upscale restaurant at least once a month.

What the Research Will Tell Us

Upon completion, the research findings will be projected to the population (as defined above) in the following terms:

1. frequency of dining out by days of the week
2. restaurants patronized and why
3. average per-person check at these restaurants
4. reasons for going out to dinner
5. reasons for choosing an upscale restaurant
6. aided and unaided awareness of Bon Ami
7. dining frequency at Bon Ami
8. impressions and perceptions of Bon Ami
9. overall rating of and intentions to patronize Bon Ami
10. characteristics of those who "like/don't like" Bon Ami
11. perceived need for a new upscale restaurant concept in the Newport area, what it should be, and intentions to patronize it if it existed

Answers to the above will provide management with the information to make decisions consistent with the research purpose. It should be cautioned, however, that there is no such thing as perfect information, and good management judgment is always necessary in interpreting research findings. Statistically, the sample size of 150 provides a 95 percent confidence level that the findings are representative of the population, plus or minus 8 percent.

Method

A list of 5,000 residents with projected household incomes of $30,000 or higher will be purchased from a list supplier. Since these lists are drawn from census-block data and income is projected onto other relevant data, the lists will not be 100% accurate. Screening will be used to select those persons with dining-out eating habits as previously specified. To avoid response problems, income levels will be verified on completion of the questioning. Sufficient names will be randomly drawn to meet required completion rate.

Phone calls will be made to heads of household in the evening and on weekends by a professional research survey firm.

Analysis of frequencies, cross-tabulations, and multivariate procedures will be done by computer.

A written report, including the findings, analysis, discussion of findings, recommendations, and all computer runs, will be submitted within 60 days of confirmation of agreement.

Two follow-up meetings of whatever length to explain and discuss the findings and their implementation are included in the consultation fee.

Limitations of the Research

The research is restricted as follows:

- to evening meals in the upscale dining genre
- to the population of households as previously specified
- to persons from zip-code areas 71001, 71028, 71036, 71089, 71095, 71106, 71108, 76071, 76078, 76082, which are the areas jointly identified as the major potential market for Bon Ami.

These restrictions are for the purpose of limiting the sample size and related costs of the research, and because the sample frame is presumed to represent the major immediate market base for Bon Ami. Inferences beyond this market base should be made with caution.

To obtain the necessary statistical reliability on questions regarding Bon Ami, it is necessary that the sample contain at least 65 respondents who have eaten at Bon Ami. If this number is not obtained in the initial sample, additional calls will be made at additional cost until 65 are obtained.

APPENDIX 9B　THE RESEARCH DESIGN

The survey population was determined to be that of households in areas of, and surrounding Wilmington, with household incomes of $30,000 per year or greater. These areas were presumed to represent the major immediate market base for Bon Ami and to contain those persons most likely to have heard of, or been to, Bon Ami.

Exact data on income by individual household are not available. It is possible, however, to project income based on data that are available, such as house and car ownership. By means of a complex formula, mailing-list firms and others project income levels by household. Edith Roman Associates, Inc. of New York projected 24,493 households with incomes over $35,000 a year in the designated areas. The breakdown by zip code is shown in Exhibit 9B.1.

From this listing, 5,000 names, addresses, and telephone numbers were randomly selected and served as the survey sample frame; then 2,000 names were randomly selected from the sample frame for the survey sample. Exhibit 9B.1 shows the zip-code percentages of the sample frame and the final sample, which indicates that a representative sample of the areas was obtained.

A sample size of 150 was statistically adequate to obtain a 95 percent confidence level that findings would be representative of the population, plus or minus 8 percent. An additional 26 persons were surveyed, however, in order to increase the sample of respondents who had heard of and/or been to Bon Ami. The additional 26 calls were selected from the immediate Newport area and slightly bias the sample for Newport, Minquadele, and Forest Glen.

Exhibit 9B.1 also shows the completion rate of the phone survey. For comparison purposes, the *Sales and Marketing Management* "1994 Survey of Buying Power" indicates the following:

	Households	Effective Buying	Income > $35K
New Castle County	161.2K	24.4%	39.3K
Newark Township	13.5K	48.8%	6.6K

Questions were limited to dinner experiences only. Two screening questions were used at the beginning of the interview. The first of these

Exhibit 9B.1
Sample Frame and Completions

A. Sample Frame

Zip	Town	Households > $35K	Sample Frame (%)	Sample (%) n = 150	n = 176
71001	Salem County	1,826	7.5	6.8	5.7
71028	Minquadele	2,136	8.7	8.2	14.2
71036	Elsmere	818	3.3	3.4	2.8
71089	Salem County	2,226	9.1	8.9	7.4
71095	Forest Glen	2,876	11.7	11.6	13.1
71106	Newport	4,242	17.3	18.5	18.8
71108	Wilmington	1,098	4.5	2.9	2.8
76071	Coventry	1,484	6.1	7.5	6.3
76078	New Castle	1,670	6.8	5.5	5.7
76082	Newark	6,117	25.0	26.7	23.3
Totals		24,493	100.0	100.0	100.0

B. Completion Rate

No answers	580	Callbacks	183
Busys	169	Refusals	230
Disconnects	50	Not eligibles	184
Terminates	17	Completions	176
Not availables	497	Wrong addresses	21

eliminated all persons who did not eat dinner out in an upscale restaurant in the area at least once a month. The second screening question eliminated those who did not spend at least $25.00 per person, excluding tax and tip, when eating dinner at an upscale restaurant. Special care was taken to ascertain that the respondent understood what was meant by an "upscale" restaurant.

Phone calls were made weekday evenings and Saturday mornings over a three-week period by a professional research survey firm in Wilmington, Delaware. Heads of households were randomly chosen between sexes.

Analysis was done by computer using the SPSS (Statistical Package for the Social Sciences) software program.

Respondent Profiles

A total of 176 surveys were completed. On a proportional basis, this represents a possible error rate of plus or minus 7.4 percent at the 95 percent confidence level. For individual questions, typical error rates at the same confidence level are as follows:

	Plus-or-Minus Proportions (%)
Heard of Bon Ami	7.2
Been to Bon Ami	9.2

	Plus-or-Minus the Mean (Averages)
On importance characteristics	4.4
Ratings of Bon Ami	6.0
Only those who have been there	7.6
Those who have heard but not been	9.5

Error rates are interpreted as the potential error in projecting to the true population. For example, if it is projected that 67 percent of 12,500 target households in the survey area have heard of Bon Ami, we can say with 95 percent confidence that the true number who have heard of Bon Ami is somewhere between 7,475 and 9,275 (7.2 percent plus or minus the proportion).

Respondent profiles are shown in Exhibit 9B.2.

Population Projections

There are two ways to project the relevant population as the potential market for Bon Ami.

The initial premise of the research was that potential Bon Ami customers would come from households with annual incomes of $30,000 or higher. It was later decided, and supported by the research, that more pertinent screening measures are frequency of eating out (at least once a

Exhibit 9B.2
Respondent Profiles

1. *Sex*	Female	52.8%
	Male	47.2%
2. *Age*	Under 30	13.8%
	31–40	24.1%
	41–50	26.4%
	51–60	24.1%
	60 up	11.5%
3. *Marital status*	Married	78%
4. *Income*	Under 30	18.7%
	30–35	14.8%
	35–50	27.7%
	50 up	38.8%
5. *People in party* (average)	2	43.0%
	3 or 4	44.3%
	5 or more	12.8%
6. *Spend per person* (average)	$25–$24	40.3%
	$25–$34	27.8%
	$35 up	31.8%
7. *Heard of Bon Ami*		67.4%
8. *Been to Bon Ami*		31.8%
9. *Been to Bon Ami* (if heard of it)		46.7%

month) and average expenditure per person (at least $25.00). In truth, it appears that a combination of income, eating-out habits, and expenditure is the most realistic basis for projection.

Nineteen percent of those responding to the survey income question were found to have incomes under $30,000. However, no significant differences were found on expenditure and other measures between those with incomes under $30,000 and those with incomes between $30,000 and $35,000. These two groups were lumped together for analysis among the respondents as those with incomes under $35,000, between $35,000 and $50,000, and over $50,000. Here again, few significant differences were found. In fact, in some instances, those with incomes under $35,000 were more similar to those with incomes over $50,000. Each group must thus be considered as part of the target population.

It is reasonable to assume, then, that the two criteria of eating out at least once a month and spending at least $25.00 per person are more critical in determining the potential market, given a minimum income base.

Zip Code Areas Surveyed Approximately 25,000 households are projected to have annual incomes greater than $35,000 in the areas surveyed. Even allowing for those whose incomes are lower, as described above, we can reasonably assume these households to be the potential market in these areas. Approximately 50% of those reached were eliminated by the screening questions. This leaves a potential market of 12,500 households or 25,000 persons. It is reasonable to assume that those wrongfully included in the first 50 percent will be balanced by those wrongfully included in the second 50 percent. The figure 25,000 will be used by projections in the findings and conclusions to follow. This will, hereafter, be called the *zip projection.*

Greater Wilmington Areas The greater Wilmington area, defined to include all of New Castle County and the New Jersey border towns, is estimated to include 50,000 households with effective buying incomes of $35,000 or greater. Effective buying income is defined as spendable income after income taxes, state and federal. Thus, actual income for those households is considerably higher and will exclude a portion of the potential market for Bon Ami. Given, however, that this is the best figure available and assuming that the nether regions of the county offer less potential because of distance and alternative choice, we can again reasonably assume a balancing out and project from the research that 50,000 persons form an immediate potential market for Bon Ami, eliminating the 50 percent who do not eat out once a month and/or spend $25 per person. This will, hereafter, be called *area projection.* It is cautioned, however, that the additional 25,000 households were not randomly sampled and could differ in unknown ways. Thus, less accuracy is assumed, and confidence levels and error rates can be applied only to the survey population of 25,000 households.

Other Geographic Areas Customers and potential customers of Bon Ami exist in geographic regions other than those defined. This is clear, at minimum, from addresses in the guest registration book. There is no truly accurate way to measure the potential of this market other than an actual survey of customers in-house. Thus, these people are not included in the projections to follow. They are, in effect, the frosting on the cake and can be best estimated by management. The Greater Wilmington area, as defined, clearly constitutes the base market for Bon Ami.

Market Share It is difficult, if not impossible, to estimate what Bon Ami's fair share of the market should be. The research shows clearly that it competes with many restaurants not in the same class. Some 50 restaurants that the respondents patronize were mentioned in all. Using this as a base, an equal fair share would be 2 percent. We believe this to be a conservative figure for what Bon Ami should do but, for the sake of argument, have used 2 percent as the fair share of the zip projection and 1½ percent as the fair share of the area projection, to illustrate potential.

APPENDIX 9C   RESEARCH FINDINGS

Present Eating-Out Habits and Demand Projections

1. Weekly Habits and Projections   Weekly habits of the respondents and projections to the market are shown in Exhibit 9C.1.

The figures in Exhibit 9C.1 indicate that Bon Ami should be able to meet its objectives if it captures its fair share from the area alone. The problem, however, is in the distribution. If we assume, per month, 17 weekdays, five Fridays, and four each of Saturdays and Sundays, Bon Ami's fair share from the area looks more like the following:

$$
\begin{aligned}
17 \text{ Mon–Thurs @35} &= 600 \text{ customers} \\
5 \text{ Fridays @168} &= 840 \text{ customers} \\
4 \text{ Saturdays @225} &= 900 \text{ customers} \\
4 \text{ Sundays @ 60} &= 240 \text{ customers} \\
2580/30 &= \ \ 86 \text{ customers per night (average)}
\end{aligned}
$$

The opportunity is to meet the restaurant's capacity on Friday and Saturday and capture more than market share on Sunday through Thursday. This indicates the need to do more distant business on the weekend and more local business during the week.

Exhibit 9C.1
Eating-Out Habits and Projections (numbers rounded)

Days	% Who Eat Out	Times/Month	Zip Projection (per month)	Area Projection (per month)
Mon–Thurs	40	2	20,000	40,000
Friday	67	1.64	28,000	56,000
Saturday	73	1.67	30,000	60,000
Sunday	23	1.38	8,000	16,000
Monthly	100	3.46	86,000	172,000

Monthly fair share for Bon Ami:

	@ 2%:	1,720	@1½%:	2,580
Daily average		57		86

It is obvious that there is not a surplus of customers to go around, but an adequate market does appear to exist. Obtaining it and distributing it beneficially is the task at hand. Again, customers from out of the area are the frosting on the cake.

2. Preferred Restaurants The most frequently mentioned restaurants as those particularly liked in the area are shown below. It should be noted that of all restaurants mentioned, approximately 25 others outside of the area were included, particularly in Maryland and particularly by Newark respondents. These are customers that need to be pulled back to the area. The percentages (rounded) of respondents are given in parentheses.

1.	The Laurel	(19%)
2.	Rendezvous	(16)
3.	Colonial Hilton, Pine Woods	(12)
4.	Hofbrauhaus	(12)
5.	Vagabond	(11)
6.	Bon Ami, The Fort, Woodstown Tavern	(10)
7.	Monte Carlo	(9)
8.	Federal Hill, Captain Bob	(8)
9.	E. Newark Inn	(7)
10.	L'Escargot	(6)

Preferences, of course, are dependent upon both awareness and knowledge. Exhibit 9C.2 breaks down the restaurant preferences by those who have heard and not heard of Bon Ami and, for those who have heard of it, those who have been and not been there.

It is a well-known fact in the restaurant industry that restaurant choice is occasion-specific, that is, the restaurant a customer prefers for one occasion is not necessarily the one preferred for another occasion. Exhibit 9C.3 lists restaurants chosen as "the one I would go to for dinner tonight" for specific occasions. The total sample and those who have been and not been to Bon Ami are shown in percentage of respondents.

3. Influence of Advertising The influence of advertising to try a new restaurant is shown in Exhibit 9C.4.

Exhibit 9C.2

Heard/Not Heard and Been/Not Been Preferences

Heard	Not Heard	Not Been	Been
1. Rendezvous (20%)	1. Laurel (22%)	1. Hilton (19%)	1. Bon Ami (34%)
2. Bon Ami (17%)	Captain Bob	Rendezvous	2. Rendezvous (21%)
Laurel	2. Pine Woods (16%)	Woodstown	Hofbrau
Hofbrau	3. E. Newark (13%)	2. Laurel (17%)	3. Fort (18%)
3. Hilton (15%)	4. Passport (9%)	3. Federal (15%)	Vagabond
Woodstown	5. Hilton (7%)	4. Hofbrau (13%)	4. Laurel (16%)
4. Vagabond (13%)	Fort	M. Carlo	5. M. Carlo (11%)
Federal	Rendezvous	5. La Differance (11%)	Willow Glen
5. Fort (12%)	Ivanhoe	6. Vagabond (9%)	Woodstown
M. Carlo		Pine Woods	Pine Woods
		Federal	Hilton
		(Bon Ami—0)	

Note: Percentages apply to all restaurants listed in each specific ranking.

244

4. Bar/Lounge Patronage   Bar/lounge patronage by choice before dinner
was given as follows:

	Percent
Seldom	70
Sometimes	17
Usually	4
Almost always	9

5. Breakdowns by Average Expenditure   Exhibit 9C.5 shows significant differences in behavior by expense groups. Footnotes tell the significance.

A discriminant analysis was run with the expenditure categories as
the dependent variable. The purpose of this analysis was twofold:

a. Unlike the previous analyses, it is interactive, that is, the variables
   interact with each other rather than in a unilateral fashion. For
   example, price may be important as well as elegance but, interac-
   tively, price may be relatively unimportant if elegance is the desired
   feature. This type of analysis tells us how things work in combination.

b. Discriminant analysis tells us what is uniquely more important to
   different groups; that is, it tells us which variables discriminate
   between groups.

The groups in this analysis are those of expenditure: (1) $25 to $34;
(2) $35 to $44; (3) $45 and up. The discriminating variables are the
importance factors when selecting a restaurant plus a number of others,
most of which were eliminated in the early stages of the analysis.

The results show that the groups are significantly different, especially
groups 1 and 3, in the following manners:

a. Group 1 ($25–$34) is discriminated from the other groups by
   age: younger people spend more when they go to an upscale restaurant, while older people spend less. Also, this group especially
   considers friendly employees to be important.

Exhibit 9C.3

Preferred Restaurants for Specific Occasions (percentages rounded)

Total Sample	Heard/Not Been	Been

A. For Fine Food and Service

Total Sample	Heard/Not Been	Been
1. Laurel (8%)	1. Laurel (9%)	1. Bon Ami (19%)
2. Bon Ami (6%)	La Differance	2. E. Newark (7%)
3. Rendezvous (5%)	2. Hilton (7%)	Hofbrau
E. Newark	Hofbrau	Fort
Pine Woods	M. Carlo	3. Federal (5%)
4. Hilton (4%)	3. Lakeside (4%)	Rendezvous
Hofbrau	Woodstown	Woodstown
M. Carlo	Rendezvous	Monte Carlo
5. L'Escargot (4%)	Federal	
	Harold's	
	(Bon Ami—0)	

B. For a Quiet Business Dinner

Total Sample	Heard/Not Been	Been
1. Laurel (12%)	1. Laurel (10%)	1. Bon Ami (18%)
2. Bon Ami (7%)	Rendezvous	2. Vagabond (13%)
3. Woodstown (6%)	2. Hilton (7%)	3. Woodstown (10%)
4. Vagabond (5%)	Federal	4. C. Club (8%)
5. Harold's (4%)	Woodstown	Ciro's
Federal	Willow	Laurel
Rendezvous	(Bon Ami—2%)	5. 5 others (5% each)

C. For a Special Occasion

Total Sample	Heard/Not Been	Been
1. Hilton (11%)	1. Hilton (10%)	1. Bon Ami (29%)
2. Bon Ami (9%)	Federal	2. Hilton (12%)
3. Pine Woods (7%)	2. L'Escargot (8%)	3. Michael's (7%)
4. E. Newark (6%)	Pine Woods	Ciro's
5. Federal (5%)	Woodstown	Pine Woods
6. Laurel (4%)	3. Vagabond (6%)	4. C. Club (5%)
Woodstown	4. Rendezvous (4%)	Federal
7. L'Escargot (4%)	E. Newark	Willow
Vagabond	Canton	
	(Bon Ami—2%)	

Exhibit 9C.3 *(continued)*

Total Sample	Heard/Not Been	Been
	D. For French Cuisine	
1. Bon Ami (26%)	1. L'Escargot (32%)	1. Bon Ami (61%)
2. Don't eat French Food (21%)	2. Don't eat French (24%)	2. Don't know any (9%)
		3. Michaels (7%)
3. Don't know any (13%)	3. Don't know any (13%)	4. Red Lion (5%)
4. L'Escargot (12%)		L'Escargot
5. Chez Robert (4%)	4. Bon Ami (11%)	
	E. For Best Food at Best Price	
1. Laurel (8%)	1. Laurel (9%)	1. Laurel (13%)
2. M. Carlo (6%)	2. Vagabond (7%)	2. Rendezvous (8%)
3. Rendezvous (4%)	M. Carlo	M. Carlo
Captain Bob	Fort	3. E. Newark (5%)
4. Fort (3%)	3. Ivanhoe (4%)	Woodstown
Vagabond	(Bon Ami—0)	Federal
(Bon Ami—1%)		(Bon Ami—3%)
	F. For Good Food in Relaxed Atmosphere	
1. Laurel (9%)	1. Laurel (9%)	1. Hilton (13%)
2. Hilton (7%)	2. Hofbrau (7%)	2. Bon Ami (10%)
3. Rendezvous (4%)	Rendezvous	Rendezvous
4. Hofbrau	Hilton	3. Federal (8%)
5. E. Newark (4%)	3. Woodstown (4%)	4. Tomato's (5%)
Cico's	L'Escargot	Pine Woods
6. Bon Ami (3%)	Willow Glen	Laurel
4 others (3% each)	Ciro's	Woodstown
	Vagabond	Ciro's
	(Bon Ami—0)	Hofbrau
		Vagabond

Note: Percentages apply to all restaurants listed in each specific ranking.

Exhibit 9C.4

Media Influences

Type	Not Influential (%)	Somewhat Influential (%)	Very Influential (%)
Newspaper	34	43	23
Radio	57	33	10
TV	53	35	12
Word of mouth	0	9	91

    b. Groups 2 ($35–$44) is discriminated from the other groups by factors they consider important: beef on the menu, table appointments, and a good wine list.

    c. Group 3 ($45 and up) is discriminated from the other groups by higher income and by the importance of a comfortable bar or lounge.

Note that these interpretations do not mean that these factors are the most important to the groups. They mean, instead, that these are the factors that make them different from the other groups.

6. Breakdown by Income   Breakdown by income is shown in Exhibit 9C.6.

Discriminant analysis by income shows that group 3 (>$50,000) is significantly different from groups 2 ($35,000–$50,000) and 1 (<$35,000).

    a. Group 3 (>$50,000) is discriminated from the other groups by importance of the factors, in selecting a restaurant, of table appointments, quiet atmosphere, by the fact that they spend less and, to some extent, by the desire for light meals and lower-priced alternatives.

    b. Group 2 ($35,000–$50,000) is discriminated by the importance of good, not necessarily fast, service.

    c. Group 1 (<$35,000) is discriminated by the desire for food that is not too expensive, more space, and more beef on the menu.

7. Age Breakdown   Exhibit 9C.7 shows the eating-out and preference breakdown by age category.

Exhibit 9C.5
Expenditure Breakdown

Average Expenditure	$25–$34	$35–$44	$45 up
Total sample	40%	28%	32%
Average times eat out per month*	3.35	3.16	3.22
Income levels**: <$35K	43%	28%	29%
$35K–$50K	37%	37%	26%
>$50K	32%	25%	43%
Frequency of eating on Saturday†	.85	.98	1.32
Age††: under 30	33%	25%	42%
31–50	36%	28%	35%
50 up	48%	29%	23%

Restaurants liked	1. Laurel (23%)
	2. Pine Woods (20%)
	3. Vagabond (17%)
	4. Woodstown (15%)
	   Fort
	   Rendezvous
	5. Hilton (13%)
	6. Captain Bob (10%)
	   (Bon Ami—8%)
		1. Laurel (21%)
		2. Rendezvous (18%)
		3. Hilton (11%)
		   Woodstown
		   Hofbrau
		   E. Newark
		   M. Carlo
		4. Bon Ami (8%)
		   3 others (8% each)
			1. Hofbrau (16%)
			2. Bon Ami (14%)
			   L'Escargot
			   Rendezvous
			3. E. Newark (12%)
			   M. Carlo
			   Laurel
			   Hilton

* No significant difference.
** People with higher incomes are slightly likely to spend more (p < .05).
† People who eat out on Saturday are more likely to spend more (p < .05).
†† Younger people are likely to spend more (p < .05).
Note: Percentages in "Restaurants liked" rows apply to all restaurants listed in each specific ranking.

Exhibit 9C.6
Breakdown of Restaurants Liked

Income	<$35K	$35K–$50K	>$50K
Total sample	33%	28%	39%
Average times eat out per month*	3.38	2.89	3.92
Restaurants liked	1. Rendezvous (20%)	1. Laurel (24%)	1. Rendezvous (20%)
	2. Laurel (17%)	2. C. Clubs (17%)	2. Hofbrau (18%)
	Pine Woods	3. Fort (16%)	3. Bon Ami (16%)
	3. Vagabond (13%)	Woodstown	Woodstown
	4. Captain Bob (11%)	Captain Bob	4. Laurel (14%)
	5. M. Carlo (9%)	4. Bon Ami (11%)	5. Vagabond (12%)
	6. E. Newark (7%)	M. Carlo	Willow Glen
	Hofbrau	Hofbrau	6. C. Club (10%)
	Bridgehead	Federal	Fort
	(Bon Ami—4%)		M. Carlo
Been to Bon Ami (of those who have heard of it)	33%	36%	58%

* Those with incomes >$50 or <$35 eat out more often (p < .05).

Note: Percentages in "Restaurants liked" rows apply to all restaurants listed in each ranking.

Exhibit 9C.7

Age Breakdown of Restaurants Liked

	Age		
	>30	*30–50*	*>50*
Total sample	14%	50%	36%
Average times eat out per month*	3.7	3.33	3.56

Restaurants liked	1. M. Carlo (15%)
	   Rendezvous
	   Hilton
	   Captain Bob
	2. E. Newark (10%)
	3. Numerous (5%)
	   (Bon Ami—0)
		1. Rendezvous (18%)
		2. Hofbrau (16%)
		3. Fort (14%)
		   Laurel
		4. Woodstown (13%)
		5. Bon Ami (12%)
		   Pine Woods
			1. Laurel (35%)
			2. Hilton (16%)
			   Vagabond
			   Pine Woods
			3. Bon Ami (12%)
			   Rendezvous
			   Federal

Been to Bon Ami (of those who have heard of it)	42%	50%	43%

* Not significant.

Note: Percentages in "Restaurants liked" rows apply to all restaurants listed in each specific ranking.

Discriminant analysis by age shows that group 1 (under 30) is significantly discriminated from group 2 (30–50) and group 3 (over 50):

a. Group 1 (under 30) is discriminated by the importance of a casual atmosphere, beef on the menu, a comfortable bar and lounge, and fine food and service.

b. Group 2 (30–50) is discriminated best by the need for a good wine list.

c. Group 3 (over 50) is not well discriminated by any features.

8. Area Preferences   For ease of handling and obtaining meaningful figures, the 10 zip-code areas have been grouped into four areas. Restaurant preferences are shown in Exhibit 9C.8.

9. Sex Preferences   Sex preferences are shown in Exhibit 9C.9.

10. Why People Go Out to Dinner   Exhibit 9C.10 shows interesting comparisons among age, income, and check-average levels as to why respondents say they go out to dinner at upscale restaurants.

Awareness and Perceptions of Users and Nonusers of Bon Ami

1. Awareness and Frequency   Sixty-seven percent of the respondents have heard of Bon Ami, but only 32 percent have been there for dinner. Only 47 percent of those who have heard of it have been there. Thus, one-third of the potential market needs to be persuaded, and one-third needs to be informed and persuaded. Projecting these figures to the zip population reveals the following, plus or minus the error rate:

Potential Number of Zip Area Customers Who Have:

Never heard of Bon Ami	8,150
Never been to Bon Ami	17,000
Heard of it but not been	8,850
Been to Bon Ami	8,000

Exhibit 9C.11 provides a breakdown of awareness and usage by demo-

Exhibit 9C.8

Area Percentages and Restaurant Preferences

	New Jersey	Newark Area	Newport Area	Around Newport
Total sample ratio:	13%	35%	22%	30%

Restaurants*	1. Rendezvous (23%)
	   M. Carlo
	   Vagabond
	   Hofbrau
	2. Hilton (18%)
	3. Federal (14%)
	   Pine Woods
	   Woods
	   (Bon Ami—5%)
		1. Laurel (34%)
		2. Captain Bob (20%)
		3. E. Newark (18%)
		4. Pine Woods (13%)
		5. Rendezvous (10%)
		   (Bon Ami—3)
			1. Bon Ami (32%)
			2. M. Carlo (19%)
			   Hofbrau
			   Vagabond
			3. Ivanhoe (16%)
			   Rendezvous
			4. Canton (13%)
				1. Woods (24%)
				2. L'Escargot (21%)
				   Rendezvous
				3. Fort (18%)
				4. Hilton (15%)
				5. Pine Woods (12%)
				   Willow Glen
				   Bridgehead
				   Lakeside
				   (Bon Ami—6)

Sample percent that have been to Bon Ami:	22%	15%	66%	32%
Sample percent that eat out frequently per month:	2.83	3.45	4.10	4.96

* Many other restaurants out of the immediate area were mentioned by respondents from the New Jersey and Newark areas.

Note: Percentages in "Restaurants" rows apply to all restaurants listed in each specific ranking.

253

Exhibit 9C.9
Restaurants Liked, by Sex

	Male	Female
Total sample	47.2%	52.8%
Restaurants	1. Laurel (17%)	1. Laurel (21%)
	2. Fort (15%)	2. Rendezvous (20%)
	3. Hofbrau (13%)	3. Hilton (17%)
	4. Rendezvous (11%)	4. Bon Ami (16%)
	M. Carlo	Pine Woods
	5. Federal (8%)	5. Vagabond (13%)
	Pine Woods	6. Woodstown (12%)
	Woodstown	7. Hofbrau (11%)
	Willow Glen	8. M. Carlo (8%)
	Bridgehead	Captain Bob
	Captain Bob	Federal
	Vagabond	
	(Bon Ami—4%)	

Note: Percentages in "Restaurants" rows apply to all restaurants listed in each specific ranking.

graphic categories. It can readily be seen in this exhibit where awareness and persuasion campaigns are needed. These have been marked with an asterisk.

2. Perceptions   Respondents were asked to rate Bon Ami on a 1-to-4 scale on 15 separate characteristics, and on one overall evaluation, as a place they would like to go for dinner, on how well the phrases describe the restaurant. As perceptions can obviously be quite different and of considerable interest depending upon whether responses are based on actual experience or hearsay, the two categories are shown separately in Exhibit 9C.12.

3. Positives and Negatives   Respondents who have heard and/or been to Bon Ami were asked what they liked most and least about it. Exhibit 9C.13 shows the responses by those who have been and not been. Percentages exceed 100 because of multiple responses.

4. Regression Analysis   The factors used to rate Bon Ami (see Exhibit

Exhibit 9C.10

Reasons for Going Out to Dinner

	Total Sample (%)	By Age (%)			By Income (%)			By Amount Spent (%)		
		<30	30–50	>50	<$35	$35–50	>$50	$25–34	$35–44	$45 up
Good food	23	15	19	33	15	24	32	22	23	24
Special occasion	23	30*	21	24	25*	27*	16	26*	28*	16
To relax	20	10	29*	10	10	22*	28*	21*	15	22*
To get out	19	15	19	20	21	14	20	21	21	16
Treat	16	25*	18	10	17*	14	20	10	15	24*
Atmosphere	12	10	8	20	10	11	12	14	8	14
Socialize	12	20	13	8	10	5	16	16	8	12
Waited on	12	5	10	16	13	11	12	17	5	10
Cooking/dishes	10	30	12	6	10	8	14	9	3	18
Children (get away)	8	0	13	4	8	11	6	10	5	8
Change of pace	5	0	4	10	8	0	6	3	10	4
Private conversation	5	0	8	4	6	3	6	5	3	8
Business	3	5	5	0	0	5	6	3	0	6
Total Sample	100	14	50	36	33	28	39	40	28	32

* Significant differences (p < .05).

Exhibit 9C.11

Bon Ami Awareness and Usage by Demographic Categories

	Not Heard (%)	Have Heard of It But Have Not Been (%)	Have Been (%)	Average No. of Times Been	Percent of Those Who Have Heard and Still Not Been (%)
By average expenditure:					
$25–$34	41	35	24	2.8	60
$35–$44	31	43	26	3.3	62
$45 up	22	32	46	3.7	41
By area:					
New Jersey	26*	52*	22	2	71*
Surrounding	9	61*	30	2	67*
Newport	5	26	69	4.7	30
Newark	69	16	15	3.1	53*
By income:					
<$35	53*	31	16	3.5	67
$35–$50	35*	42	23	2.7	64
>$50	17	35	48	3.8	42
By age:					
<30	50	29	21	3.2	58
30–50	32	34	34	3.6	50
>50	26	42	32	3.2	57
Total Sample	33	35	32	3.4	53

	Period	%
By last time eaten at Bon Ami		
	Last month	21.4
	Last 31–60 days	23.2
	Last 61–90 days	10.7
	Last 91–180 days	26.8
	Over 180 days	17.8
Average	Four months ago	
By frequency of eating at Bon Ami in the past 12 months:		
Once		41
Twice		18
Thrice		13
Four times		7
Five times		4
Six times		9
Over six times		8

* Significant differences (p < .05).

Exhibit 9C.12
Perceptions of Bon Ami

	Been There		Hearsay	
	Mean	*S.D.***	*Mean*	*S.D.***
Expensive*	3.34	.64	3.62	.53
Fine food and service	3.38	.75	3.48	.78
French food	3.63	.59	3.60	.73
Good food	3.55	.71	3.38	.83
Worth the price*	3.16	.95	2.45	1.09
Elegant atmosphere	3.52	.79	3.71	.52
Comfortable, relaxed atmosphere	3.50	.81	3.70	.54
Comfortable cocktail lounge	3.30	.98	3.21	.98
Good wine list	3.65	.65	3.62	.50
Intimidating*	1.55	.86	1.97	1.15
Special occasion place only*	2.18	1.12	2.67	1.16
Interesting menu	3.44	.83	3.24	1.02
Friendly	3.36	.82	3.36	.99
Unique	3.27	.84	3.11	1.11
Relaxing	3.38	.73	3.41	.74
Overall rating as a place to go for dinner*	3.26	.96	2.61	1.02

Scale: 1 = very unimportant, to 4 = very important.

* Significant differences between actual and hearsay perceptions (p < .05).

** S.D. = standard deviation. The larger the standard deviation, the more heterogeneous is the response. The expected standard deviation for 95 percent of the population is .75.

9C.12) as well as spending levels, satisfaction with upscale restaurants, marital status, and age and income, were regressed with the overall rating of Bon Ami as a place respondents would like to go.

Regression analysis is a multivariate procedure that weighs the interaction of various predictor variables. This process determines which variables, in combination with all the others, are the most important factors in predicting the dependent variable, in this case the overall rating of Bon Ami. Regression analysis is a much more powerful tool than univariate analysis because we know that consumers make decisions based on "benefit bundles," that is, a combination of factors. For example, one might rate almost everything about a restaurant as desirable but not go there because of its prices.

Regressions with overall ratings of Bon Ami were run for both those who had been there and those who had heard of it but not been there.

A. Regression with Those Who Have Been to Bon Ami The success of a regression analysis is measured by the amount of variance explained in the dependent variable (overall rating), the significance level of the equation, and the explanation of the dependent variable by the predictor variables.

In this case, 72 percent of the variance was explained (which is very high), the significance level is very high, and five factors provide the major explanation (see Exhibit 9C.14). In short, the regression shows that people who have been to Bon Ami and rate it highly, do so because:

1. First, and clearly most powerful, they believe it is worth the price. This factor is 12 times more predictive of their overall rating than the next two factors.
2. Next, and about equally important, are the two beliefs that Bon Ami has fine food and service, and serves good food.
3. The fourth and fifth factors (and also the sixth if we stretch the significance level a little) are negative. These show that people who rate Bon Ami highly do *not* equate it highly with French food, a good wine list, or an interesting menu; in other words, these are not the reasons they prefer it. The converse also holds.

B. Regression with Those Who Have Heard of but Not Been to Bon Ami In this case, only 52 percent, a lesser but still significant amount of the variance, was explained (see Exhibit 9C.15). Three factors provided the significant explanation. People who have heard of, but not been to, Bon Ami and rate it highly, do so because:

1. (Again, the most powerful reason:) They believe it is worth the price. This factor is seven times more important than the next factor.
2. The second factor, again, is the belief in fine food and service.
3. The third factor, again, is negative. Those who rate Bon Ami highly do *not* believe it is unique.
4. Not significant, but worth noting, are the next two factors, which are also negative. These are "expensive" and "special occasion": high

Exhibit 9C.13

What Respondents Like Least about Bon Ami

A. Percentages of Respondents Rating Bon Ami Poor/Fair, Good, and Excellent

	Heard/Not Been, by Ratings (%)				Been, by Ratings (%)			
	Total	P/F*	Good	Excellent	Total	P/F*	Good	Excellent
Like Most:								
Good food	25	5	40	44	53	27	54	62
Good service	11	0	13	33	26	9	15	38
Nice decor	7	5	13	0	11	0	15	14
Good location	11	0	7	11	13	27	15	7
Atmosphere	21	5	33	33	32	9	39	38
Unusual dishes	7	10	7	0	17	0	8	28
Other	16	20	0	33	8	0	23	3
Don't know	27	25	33	22	0	0	0	0
Negative	16	30	7	0	8	37	0	0
Like Least:								
Food poorly prepared	8	15	0	0	8	20	9	0
Poor/slow service	5	10	0	0	16	30	27	0
Rude waiters	5	10	0	0	11	0	27	6
Too expensive	43	30	63	25	35	30	27	44
Portions too small	15	20	6	25	19	30	18	13
Intimate atmosphere	8	5	13	0	11	20	9	6
Other	18	25	6	25	35	30	27	44
Don't know	20	20	19	25	3	10	0	0

* P/F = poor/fair.

B. Percentages of Those Who Have Been: by Age and Income

	Age (%)			Income (%)		
	<30	30–50	>50	<$35K	$35–$50K	>$50K
Like Most:						
Good food	80	53	42	38	67	62
Good service	20	23	32	25	22	28
Nice decor	0	13	11	25	22	7
Good location	0	20	11	13	22	14
Atmosphere	40	27	42	38	0	45
Unusual dishes	0	23	11	50	0	14
Other	20	0	16	13	0	7
Negative	20	7	5	0	11	7
Like Least:						
Food poorly prepared	33	0	14	0	0	17
Poor/slow service	33	10	29	0	13	28
Rude waiters	33	0	21	0	13	6
Too expensive	67	29	36	50	25	37
Portions too small	33	24	7	33	38	6
Intimate atmosphere	0	14	7	33	0	6
Other	33	43	21	33	13	33
Don't know	0	5	0	0	13	0

Exhibit 9C.14
Regression of Overall Rating for Those Who Have Been There

$R^2 = .72$	Adjusted $R^2 = .65$	Significance = <.0001	
	Significance	β	β^2
Worth the price	<.0001	.76	.58
Find food and service	.048	.24	.06
Good food	.076	.23	.05
Wine list	.048	−.17	.03
French cuisine	.076	−.17	.03

ratings are associated with beliefs that Bon Ami is *not* expensive and *not* only for special occasions. Again, the converse holds.

5. Discriminant Analysis Discriminant analysis was performed in which the groups were those who have been to Bon Ami and those who have heard of it but not been. The results show that these groups are significantly different, as follows (see Exhibit 9C.16).

a. Those who have been to Bon Ami rate it higher overall, and higher on the attributes of good food, fine food and service, and worth the price.

b. Those who have not been there rate Bon Ami as expensive and intimidating.

Discriminant analysis was also performed on overall ratings (poor/fair, good, and excellent) of those who have been to Bon Ami:

Exhibit 9C.15
Regression of Overall Rating for Those Who Have Not Been There

$R^2 = .52$	Adjusted $R^2 = .48$	Significance = <.0001	
	Significance	β	β^2
Worth the price	<.0001	.65	.42
Fine food and service	.026	.24	.06
Unique	.021	−.22	.05
Expensive	.205	−.14	.02
Special occasion	.480	−.08	.004

Exhibit 9C.16

Perceptual Map of Attributes Discriminating Those Who Rate Bon Ami

1st function: eigenvalue = 1.82   chi square significance = <.0001
94% of variance explained

Total variance explained by two functions: 90%

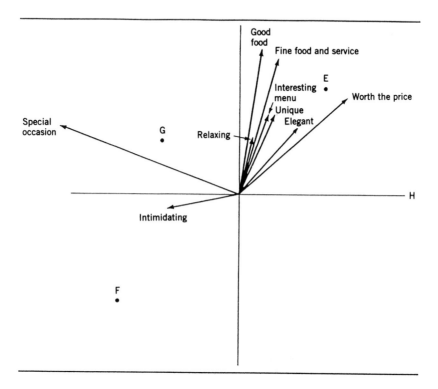

a. Those who rate Bon Ami excellent, rate it highly on good food, fine food and service and worth the price. To a lesser degree, these people rate Bon Ami as unique, having an interesting menu, being relaxing, and having an elegant atmosphere.

b. Those who rate Bon Ami as good, rate it highly for special occasions.

c. Those who rate Bon Ami poor/fair, consider it intimidating.

The discriminant analysis confirms the findings of the regression analysis.

Choosing an Upscale Restaurant

1. Importance Factors   Respondents rated, on a scale of 1 to 4 (1 = very unimportant, 2 = somewhat unimportant, 3 = somewhat important, 4 = very important), the importance of 20 different attributes in choosing an upscale restaurant for dinner. Exhibit 9C.17 shows the mean ratings and standard deviations of these attributes.

Exhibit 9C.18 shows the means of the same attributes by various categories, but only those where a significant difference exists. Where the mean of a group is higher in Exhibit 9C.18, it is interpreted to be significantly more important to that group than to the opposing group or groups. For example, ethnic foods are significantly more important to females than to males. .

Exhibit 9C.17
Ratings of Attribute Importance

	Mean	*S.D.*
Very fine food and service	3.46	.74
Beef and steak on the menu	2.84	1.08
Seafood and fish on the menu	3.38	.86
Ethnic foods (e.g., Italian, French)	2.61	.90
Unusual items on the menu	2.37	.91
Good food but not too expensive	3.18	.79
Comfortable, relaxed atmosphere	3.77	.51
Elegant atmosphere and service	2.82	.90
Casual atmosphere	2.96	.75
Social atmosphere	2.52	.98
Good service, not necessarily fast	3.49	.73
Employee friendliness	3.66	.64
Within a 30-minute drive	2.71	1.01
Type of people who go there	2.22	1.06
Comfortable bar or lounge	2.20	1.02
Good wine list	2.40	1.07
Tablecloths and accessories	2.98	.88
Quiet atmosphere	3.36	.75
Light meals, lower-priced alternatives	2.33	.94
Tables spaced comfortably apart	3.68	.68

Exhibit 9C.18

Mean Ratings of Attribute Importance with Significant Differences ($p < .05$) between Groups

	Sex		Marital		Income			Spend			Been		Age		
	M	F	S	M	<35K	$35–50	>50	$25–34	$35–44	$45 up	No	Yes	<30	30–50	>50
Ethnic foods (e.g., Italian, French)	2.45	2.75													
Good food, not too expensive			3.38	3.12	3.43	3.02	3.02	3.31	3.15	3.04	3.25	3.00			
Light meals, lower price alternatives	2.05	2.56									2.46	2.16			
Tables comfortably apart	3.56	3.78			3.82	3.70	3.57								
Beef and steak on menu					3.08	2.86	2.55	2.96	2.93	2.61	2.92	2.42	3.61	2.62	2.50
Elegant atmosphere and service											2.77	3.06			
Employee friendliness.											3.74	3.46			
Comfortable bar or lounge								1.93	2.42	2.35					
Tablecloths and table accessories					2.69	2.91	3.36				2.92	3.32	2.57	3.01	3.12
Quiet atmosphere					3.18	3.40	3.54				3.18	3.58	2.91	3.41	3.45
Casual atmosphere								3.12	2.83	2.89					

Scale: 1 = very unimportant to 4 = very important.

265

2. Why Respondents Like Certain Restaurants   Respondents were asked why they like the particular restaurants they mentioned. Exhibit 9C.19 shows the reasons they gave, and the percentages of respondents who gave them, for the total sample as well as by category.

3. Regression Analysis   Regression analysis was used to try to predict the overall rating of Bon Ami by importance factors. The results showed that people who had heard of Bon Ami, but not been there, rated Bon Ami highly when French food was important to them in choosing a restaurant. For those who had been to Bon Ami, the most important factor in predicting the overall rating was a negative one. The overall rating was most influenced by the negative importance of a comfortable bar and lounge.

These two regressions are not greatly revealing, as only a small part of the variance is explained in each case. However, the simple regression models do reveal two important insights: (1) those who have not been to Bon Ami, and especially like French food, think of Bon Ami as French and rate it highly for that reason; (2) those who have been to Bon Ami, and consider a bar or lounge unimportant in an upscale restaurant, rate Bon Ami higher.

What the Marketplace Would Like to See in a Restaurant

1. Present Satisfaction with Existing Restaurants   On a scale of 1 to 3 (very satisfied to unsatisfied), respondents had a mean of 1.65 in terms of present dissatisfaction with upscale restaurants within 30 minutes of their home. Thirteen percent are unsatisfied, 39 percent are somewhat satisfied, and a full 48 percent claim to be very satisfied. Contrarily, however, only 25 percent feel no need for a new upscale restaurant in the area, 51 percent feel some need, and 24 percent feel a great need. The mean need on a scale of 1 to 3 is 1.9, significantly higher than the level of dissatisfaction.

For those who have not been to Bon Ami, the mean on the scale of need for a new upscale restaurant is very close to the total sample, 1.95. For those who have been to Bon Ami, it is slightly higher, 2.09—that is, those who have been to Bon Ami feel a slightly greater need. The difference, however, is not statistically significant and could occur by

Exhibit 9C.19

Why Respondents Like Restaurants They Favor (%)

Reason	Total Sample	Sex		Spend			Bon Ami Rating			Age			Income		
		F	M	$25–$34	$35–$44	$45 up	P/F	G	E	<30	31–50	>50	<$35K	$35K–$50K	>$50K
Good food	81	86	76	74	85	88	92	81	84	85	85	74	79	84	84
Good service	52	49	56	53	51	52	65	58	32	45	48	62	56	53	48
Atmosphere	25	30	21	30	21	24	19	23	42	25	27	24	27	16	28
Prices	9	6	13	13	10	4	4	4	7	10	8	12	13	8	8
Quiet atmosphere	7	8	7	12	5	4	8	8	3	10	6	8	8	8	8
Comfortable, relaxing	6	9	3	3	10	6	4	4	7	0	6	8	4	5	8
Menu selection	5	5	6	2	8	8	0	12	3	0	5	8	8	5	4
Fish, seafood	5	5	4	7	8	0	0	0	0	0	6	4	4	5	4
Location	4	1	7	2	10	2	4	12	0	5	3	6	4	5	4
Uniqueness	3	3	4	3	3	4	4	0	10	0	4	4	0	3	6
Bar/wine list	3	1	6	3	3	4	0	8	3	5	1	6	2	8	2
Portion size	3	4	3	0	3	8	0	4	3	10	4	0	0	3	8
Elegant atmosphere	3	4	1	0	3	6	4	0	3	0	3	4	2	3	4
Salad bar	3	5	0	5	3	0	4	0	0	0	4	2	2	0	6
Cleanliness	2	1	2	0	5	2	0	0	3	0	1	4	0	3	4
Friendly service	2	3	1	3	0	2	4	0	0	10	1	0	6	0	0
Spacious seating	1	1	1	0	3	2	4	0	0	5	1	0	2	0	2
Ethnic foods	1	0	3	3	0	0	0	4	3	0	1	2	0	0	2

chance. There is also no significant difference between those who have heard and those who have not heard of Bon Ami.

No significant differences were found in the need for a new upscale restaurant by income, by average check size, by whether they have heard of Bon Ami, or by whether they had been to Bon Ami. The same is true of respondents' satisfaction with upscale restaurants. Overall, the population seems generally satisfied with their present choice alternatives (87 percent), and most (76 percent) do not see a real need for a new upscale concept. Any perceived need or dissatisfaction that exists seems to come demographically from the under-50 age groups, and geographically from Newport's surrounding areas, the Newark area, and especially Newport itself. Thus, the important factors in choosing a restaurant for these groups warrant particular attention.

An interesting comparison is of favored restaurants among those who see no need, some need, or great need for a new upscale restaurant in the area (see Exhibit 9C.20).

Persons at different need levels did not differ significantly from each other in the reasons why they particularly liked these restaurants.

Exhibit 9C.20
Favored Restaurants by Perceived Need for New Upscale Restaurant

Feel No Need	*Feel Some Need*	*Feel Great Need*
1. Pine Woods (21%)	1. Rendezvous (22%)	1. Hofbrau (22%)
2. Laurel (18%)	2. Laurel (21%)	2. C. Club (17%) Laurel
3. Captain Bob (15%)	3. Pine Woods (14%)	3. Fort (14%)
Woodstown	4. Bon Ami (13%)	Hilton
Rendezvous	5. Fort (10%)	4. M. Carlo (11%)
Hilton	Federal	Woodstown
4. L'Escargot (12%)	E. Newark	Bon Ami
Hofbrau	M. Carlo	Canton
(Bon Ami—3%)	6. Hilton (8%)	5. Harold's (8%)
	Ivanhoe	Red Lion
		Vagabond

*Frequency of Eating Out per Month**

2.46	4.00	3.56

* Significantly different (p < .05).
Note: Percentages apply to all restaurants listed in each specific ranking.

Exhibit 9C.21 shows favored restaurants by level of satisfaction with existing restaurants.

The reasons people go out to dinner were cross-tabulated with satisfaction and perceived need. The only finding of singificance to management is that 80 percent of those who go out for business perceive a great need for a new restaurant.

Where are these discontents? Exhibit 9C.22 provides some clues.

Although relatively satisfied with their present choice of upscale restaurants, 92 percent of the respondents indicated they would patronize a new restaurant at least once a month. The mean, in fact, is 1.81 times per month. This, of course, does not offer a solid basis for decision because there are numerous obvious variables that could affect such intent. It does, however, indicate a readiness to try, also a natural phenomenon, but more, a willingness to use. This indication, in fact, may say more than the figures on present satisfaction and perceived need.

2. Factors Important to Those Who Feel the Need for a New Restaurant Concept The importance factors in choosing a restaurant were cross-

Exhibit 9C.21

Favored Restaurants by Level of Satisfaction with Existing Restaurants

Unsatisfied	Somewhat Satisfied	Very Satisfied
1. Bon Ami (21%)	1. Rendezvous (17%)	1. Laurel (25%)
2. Hilton (16%)	2. Laurel (14%)	2. Pine Woods (19%)
Laurel	3. Hilton (9%) C. Clubs	Vagabond
Hofbrau	Federal	3. Rendezvous (18%)
Captain Bob	Woodstown	4. Fort (16%)
3. Fort (10%)	Willow Glen	5. Hofbrau (15%)
	Captain Bob	6. Hilton (13%)
	M. Carlo	Woodstown
	E. Newark	M. Carlo
	(Bon Ami–7%)	7. Bon Ami (10%)
		Federal

Frequency of Eating Out per Month *

3.84	3.48	3.37

* Not significantly different.

Note: Percentages apply to all restaurants listed in each specific ranking.

Exhibit 9C.22
Satisfaction and Perceived Need by Groupings

	Satisfaction (%)			Need (%)		
	Not	Some	Very	None	Some	Great
Area:						
New Jersey	17	35	48	55	36	9
Surrounding	13	33	53	30	43	27
Newport	8	36	56	6	56	38
Newark	15	46	39	21	59	20
Age:						
Under 30	9	57	35	13	65	22
31–50	14	41	45	19	48	33
51 up	14	30	56	41	48	11
Income:						
Under $35,000	12	51	37	24	54	22
$35,000–$50,000	14	29	57	30	48	23
$50,000 up	13	43	45	17	53	30
Sex:						
Male	16	35	49	27	49	24
Female	11	42	47	24	53	24
Spend:						
$15–$19	14	31	55	29	46	25
$20–$24	20	35	46	27	51	22
$25 up	7	52	41	20	57	24
Overall rating of Bon Ami:						
Poor/fair	17	37	45	21	48	31
Good	7	33	60	26	44	30
Excellent	8	36	56	21	56	24

tabulated with the level of satisfaction and perceived need for a new restaurant. The following findings are significant.

a. People who tend to be more satisfied:
   • consider fine food and service less important
   • consider beef on the menu more important
   • consider tables spaced comfortably apart important

b. People who perceive a need for a new restaurant:
- consider beef on the menu less important
- consider a good wine list important
- consider tables spaced comfortably apart unimportant

Regression and discriminant analysis were also used to measure the interactive effect of the importance factors on satisfaction and on perceived need. The regression results are not significant for either case.

In the discriminant analysis for satisfaction levels, the unsatisfied group is significantly discriminated from the other two groups by the importance of a social atmosphere and the type of people who go to a restaurant. In other words, this group is looking for a more clubby, fun place.

The somewhat satisfied respondents are discriminated by the importance of unusual items on the menu and the fact that they spend more. The very satisfied group places more importance on beef on the menu, ethnic foods are less important to them, and they stress employee friendliness.

Discriminant analysis in the need categories discriminated those who perceive great need for a restaurant from the others by the importance of fine food, service, and a good wine list. Those who perceive no need for a new restaurant place special importance on a comfortable, relaxed atmosphere, good food that is not too expensive, and tables spaced comfortably apart.

3. *What Respondents Would Like to See in a New Restaurant* Two specific questions were asked of respondents as to wants, along with open-ended questions. The specific questions asked if they liked the idea of a wine bar, or of being able to eat a lighter supper in the bar or lounge. Frequency responses showed the following:

	Response	*Percent*
Wine bar	Yes	56
	No	44
Light supper	Yes	50
	No	50

Exhibit 9C.23

What Respondents Want in a New Restaurant Concept (%)

	Total Sample	Need for New Restaurant			Been to Bon Ami		Spend			Age			Income		
		No	Some	Yes	No	Yes	$25–$34	$35–$44	$45 up	<30	30–50	>50	<$35K	$50K	>$50K
Good food	39	50	31	41	28	50	31	39	47	45	38	38	42	42	38
Good, friendly service	24	36	23	16	39	61	24	8	35	20	19	33	29	9	27
Nonred meat	3	4	4	0	9	0	0	6	4	5	1	5	8	0	0
Reasonable prices	11	14	14	5	9	16	11	11	12	10	12	12	8	18	10
Atmosphere	11	11	10	11	4	7	5	11	16	15	10	10	15	6	13
Good menu variety	16	11	20	14	17	11	16	8	22	40	13	12	13	18	21
Elegant atmosphere	11	11	13	8	9	14	11	14	8	10	13	7	10	12	8
Relaxed atmosphere	9	0	9	19	7	16	9	6	12	5	16	0	8	9	13
Spacious seating	6	7	6	5	4	7	6	8	4	5	6	5	4	6	6
Seafood	10	4	11	14	13	5	9	14	8	10	9	12	8	9	13
Ethnic food, not Italian	11	7	11	14	11	9	15	6	10	15	10	7	10	6	15
Italian food	4	0	4	5	2	2	7	3	0	0	4	5	6	0	4
Entertainment	4	0	4	5	2	2	2	11	0	5	4	2	6	6	0

No significant differences were found on these factors related to satisfaction or perceived need of a new restaurant except by age. People under 50 clearly like the idea of a wine bar. People under 30 are far more prone to being willing to get a lighter meal in the bar or lounge.

Responses to the open-ended question of what people would like to see in a new restaurant concept are shown in Exhibit 9C.23 for the entire sample and by subcategories.

Part IV
Functional Strategies

Case Ten

Sheraton Tara Weekends

John Wolper and Robert C. Lewis

Richard Chambers, Vice President of Marketing for the Tara Hotel chain, had given careful thought to the proposed agenda for the upcoming general managers' meeting to discuss weekend packages at "nontraditional properties." The meeting had been planned following corporate research that revealed pertinent facts regarding the weekend customer. Chambers saw a need to develop a more appropriate and competitive weekend package plan other than the one presently offered at Tara's more "traditional" properties.

Since the purchase of some Dunfey-owned and -franchised hotels, the need had grown for a more cohesive and uniform image for these properties that would better represent Tara Hotel Company. Tara Hotel Company was the largest franchisee of the Sheraton Corporation in the New England area. They were positioned in the marketplace as upscale properties, catering to higher-rated groups and corporate travelers. The physical hotel product was above that of normal Sheraton standards.

Most of the former Dunfey properties were Sheraton franchise hotels, as were the original Tara hotels, but they had had no capital improvements for the past three years. It was planned to renovate and upgrade each facility to make it consistent with the present image of the original Tara properties. In the meanwhile, these hotels were more innlike than hotellike and presented some serious marketing problems.

One particular problem of the new acquisitions was the sale of the Merry Weekend package throughout the company. This package had been developed for the traditional Tara properties and had proven to be very

This case was written by John Wolper, Mercyhurst College, Pennsylvania, and Robert C. Lewis, University of Guelph, Ontario. All rights reserved.

successful. It sold for $79.00 to $89.00 for two, per night, depending on the property, and is described in Exhibit 10.1. Exhibit 10.2 contains the welcoming letter for Merry Weekenders when they checked into the hotel.

It was suspected that loss of established Merry Weekend customers was beginning to take place within the company due to dissatisfaction with the product offering of the nontraditional properties. Merry Weekend customers were known to be loyal customers who went from property to property to enjoy their Merry Weekends. When they went to the new properties expecting the same facilities, they found that the same product

Exhibit 10.1
Brochure Description of the Merry Weekend Package

The Tara Merry Weekend

What royal memories are made of.

Your everyday routine is demanding. It's important to take a little time to get away.

Relax. We have the solution. A Tara Merry Weekend. It's a great way to get away and live like royalty for 3 days and 2 nights at one of 12 exciting locations.

Choose a castle, country or resort setting. From the romantic, rocky coast of Maine or the idyllic countryside of New Hampshire to the white-duned beaches on Cape Cod, or cosmopolitan ambience of Boston and beyond.

Your Tara Merry Weekend for two includes a sumptuous Saturday breakfast, complimentary fresh fruit basket, use of pool and health club facilities,* and a lavish Sunday brunch.

Join us for a Tara Merry Weekend and be treated like royalty. For reservations call the Tara Hotel of your choice.

*Additional charge for golf, tennis and racquetball. No indoor pool at Lexington.

A thoughtful treat for your favorite couple.

Tara Merry Weekend gift certificates are also available. Simply call the Tara Hotel of your choice for complete information.

Exhibit 10.2

Welcoming Letter for Merry Weekenders

Sheraton Tara Hotel FRAMINGHAM, MASSACHUSETTS 01701 • Tel. 617/879-7200

Welcome Merry Weekender,

This weekend your royal presence is requested to feast and romp royally
while enjoying.....gourmet dining, lively entertainment, the Health Club
and our Continental Pub. Remember our weekend continues on Sunday night.
Check at the Front Desk or call Extension 2647 for details.

For your convenience, we offer some information and a schedule of our
facilities that we hope you will use and enjoy. All facilities are located on the Lobby Level.

To begin your weekend in a relaxed manner, try a selection from our Room
Service Menu, which offers a wide variety of food and beverage. Call
Extension 2513 to place your order.

Our Health Club, complete with indoor/outdoor pools, exercise room, whirlpool, sauna and steam rooms, as well as a racquetball court, is open on
Friday, Saturday and Sunday from 8:00 a.m. to 10:00 p.m. Due to limited
space we ask that you change in your room. Towels are available at the
pool. Call our Health Club for information at Extension 2188.

The Jester's Court Cafe serves some of your all-time favorite American
entrees, as well as some delicious International specialties. The Jester's
Court Cafe is open Friday and Saturday from 6:30 a.m. to 11:30 p.m. and on
Sunday from 7:00 a.m. to 11:30 a.m. Reservations are accepted for Lunch
and Dinner at Extension 2313.

The Upper Crust Restaurant has become one of the best known restaurants
in the area, so by all means give it a try. Favorites from our Menu include Chateaubriand Bouquetiere, Filet of Lemon Sole Oscar, Veal Cutlet
Saute Cordon Bleu, Roast Rack of Lamb Dijonnaise, Fresh Rainbow Trout
Veronique.....too many more to mention. Our Specialty of the House consists
of a crock of clam chowder, a bountiful platter of clams casino, schrod,
fried scallops and baked stuffed shrimp. Leave room for dessert - our
house specialty - the Tara Chocolate Cup, consisting of a cup of fine semi-
sweet chocolate, a scoop of Haagen Dazs coffee ice cream, Kahlua, whipped
cream and a cherry --- sinfully delicious!! Dine with us on Friday from
5:00 p.m. to 10:30 p.m., Saturday from 5:00 p.m. to 11:00 p.m. and on
Sunday from 3:30 p.m. to 10:00 p.m. On Sunday the Upper Crust offers our
fabulous Buffet Brunch from 9:30 a.m. to 2:00 p.m. Reservations are
accepted on Friday for 5:00, 6:00 and 7:00 p.m. and on Saturday for 5:00
and 6:00 p.m. only. Call our Dining Room Manager at Extension 2413 after
4:30 p.m.

Exhibit 10.2 *(continued)*

After dinner you will want to enjoy our Knaughty Knight Club with show entertainment on Friday from 9:00 p.m. to 2:00 a.m. and Saturday from 8:00 p.m. to 1:00 a.m. A $2.00 per person Entertainment Charge will be added to the checks of all guests who are in the Knaughty Knight Club from 9:00 p.m. on. Call our Knaughty Knight Club Hostess after 5:00 p.m. at Extension 2213 for information.

If you are in the mood for something a bit more quiet and casual, ZJ's Pub and Game Room may be your style. Watch the seasonal sport events and relax while having a drink or a snack. ZJ's is open Friday 11:00 a.m. to 2:00 a.m., Saturday from 11:00 a.m. to 1:00 a.m. and Sunday from Noon to 1:00 a.m. Dial Extension 2300 for information.

Please advise the Dining Room Manager or Hostess that you are a registered guest by showing your room key. You will then be placed on the Preferred Seating List.

Located in our Lobby, the Gift Shop is open daily from 7:00 a.m. to 11:00 p.m. and offers a wide variety of gifts, sundries, magazines and newspapers as well as our Avis Rent-a-Car service. Call Extension 2400 for information.

Hotel rates do not include gratuities. May we suggest a $1.00 per day gratuity for your maid service.

The entire Staff is ready to make this weekend merry for you.

Have a great time and return again soon!

Sincerely,

John Van Londen
General Manager

---

wasn't there. In fact, Tara reservationists were reporting irate phone calls after customers had been to the new properties.

This problem had occurred before when the Danvers property was purchased from Radisson Hotels International. At that time, three Tara hotels had the castle motif, and there were a known 20,000 Merry Weekend customers. Advertisements and direct mail were aimed at these customers to lure them to the Danvers property before it was renovated. Many tried the property, taking business away from the other Taras. This also resulted in considerable dissatisfaction. Tara customers now had seven traditional Tara properties from which to choose, in addition to the five nontraditional properties (see Exhibit 10.3), but the known Merry Weekend customer base had increased to only 23,000. Thus, the increase in hotels had not brought a proportionate increase in Merry Weekend customers.

Exhibit 10.3

Locations and Designations of Flatley Hotels

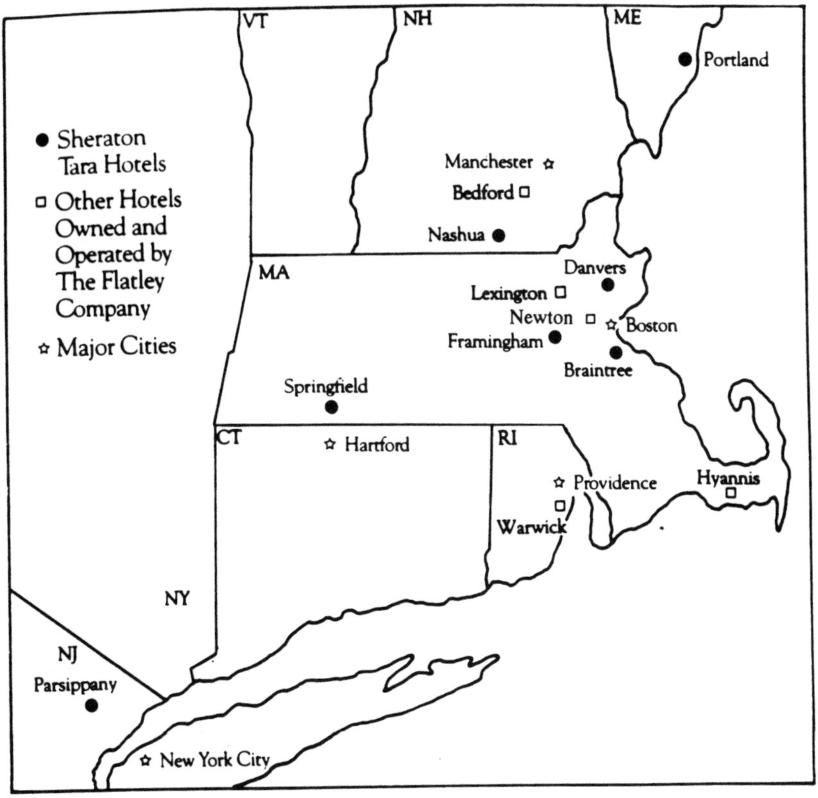

BACKGROUND

Tara Hotel Company was owned by The Flatley Hotel Company of Braintree, Massachusetts, a diversified construction company with diversified real estate holdings. After constructing four traditional Tara hotels, built with an Irish castle motif, the Flatley Company purchased six other properties from Dunfey Hotels along with the one from Radisson Hotels in Danvers, and constructed one contemporary atrium lobby hotel (Springfield). Descriptions of all the properties are given in Exhibit 10.4.

Exhibit 10.4

Descriptions of Tara Properties

Braintree, MA

The Sheraton Tara Hotel, Exit 6 off Route 93 (Route 128), Braintree, MA 617-848-0600. Just 12 miles south of downtown Boston, the 400-room Sheraton Tara in Braintree is a short drive from cultural, historical, and recreational attractions including the Museum of Fine Arts, The Aquarium and the Boston Garden, home of the Boston Celtics. Free shuttle to public transportation. Dine in the casual Jesters Court Cafe, the elegant Upper Crust Restaurant and the lively Tipperary Pub. The Laurels offers live, easy-listening entertainment. Complete health and fitness center with indoor and outdoor pools, and racquetball.

Danvers, MA

The Sheraton Tara Hotel at Ferncroft Village, Routes 95 and I, Topsfield exit to Ferncroft Village, Danvers, MA, 617-777-2500. The 375-room Sheraton Tara, located 15 miles north of Boston on the scenic North Shore of Massachusetts, is only a short drive to "The Witch City" of Salem, and scenic Gloucester, Rockport and Marblehead. Dine in the casual Jesters Court Cafe, the elegant Upper Crust Restaurant, the lively Tipperary Pub and for live, easy-listening entertainment, The Laurels. Enjoy an 18-hole, Robert Trent Jones-designed golf course, outdoor tennis, indoor and outdoor swimming pools, and complete health & fitness center.

Framingham, MA

The Sheraton Tara Hotel, at Massachusetts Turnpike Exit 12 to Route 9 west, Framingham, MA 617-879-7200. Only 20 miles west of Boston, the Sheraton Tara Hotel offers 375 guest rooms and easy access to all of Boston sites and recreational activities. Old Sturbridge Village, a recreation of a New England town of the early 1800's, is minutes away. For dining, enjoy the casual Jesters Court Cafe, the elegant Upper Crust Restaurant, the lively Tipperary Pub and live, easy-listening entertainment in The Laurels. Complete health and fitness center with indoor and outdoor pools and racquetball.

Springfield, MA

Tara Hotel, Route 91 at State Street Exit, Springfield, MA. This 300-room deluxe hotel is centrally located to New York, Boston, Hartford and Worcester in the Berkshire Mountains. The Tara in Springfield is close to Symphony Hall, Stage West Theater, museums, the Springfield Civic Center and the Basketball Hall of Fame. Dine in the elegant Upper Crust Restaurant and the casual Jesters Court Cafe. Enjoy live entertainment in the Tipperary Pub. Complete health & fitness center, indoor pool and racquetball courts.

South Portland, ME

The Sheraton Tara Hotel, Maine Turnpike, Exit 7 to Maine Mall Road, South Portland, ME, 207-775-6161. Across from the Maine Mall this 220-room hotel is just minutes from Portland's Old Port and Cape Elizabeth's famous lighthouses, and 15 miles to Old Orchard Beach. Kennebunkport, Boothbay Harbor and Wiscasset are within an hour's drive. Dining and entertainment include The Season's Restaurant and Lounge and in-room movies. Recreational facilities include an indoor pool and saunas.

Bedford (Manchester), NH

The Sheraton Tara Wayfarer, Bedford Interchange, I-293, Bedford, NH, 603-622-3766. Situated by a mill stream with a pond and waterfalls, this 200-room hotel is just minutes from Manchester and the Mall of New Hampshire, yet also within an hour of the White Mountains, Lake Winnipesaukee, the seacoast, and Boston. For dining and entertainment, you'll find the Upper Crust and The Laurels; and for recreation, both indoor and outdoor swimming pools.

Exhibit 10.4 *(continued)*

Cape Cod, MA

Tara Dunfey Hotel, Route 132 to Exit 6, North Street to West End Circle, Hyannis, MA, 617-775-7775. This 250-room resort hotel is located in the heart of scenic Cape Cod, famous for its sandy beaches, quaint villages and historic attractions. For dining and entertainment, visit the Silver Shell Restaurant and Tingles Lounge. Recreational amenities include indoor and outdoor pools, a Roman Bath, outdoor tennis, an 18-hole golf course and a health spa.

Lexington, MA

The Sheraton Tara Hotel, Marrett Road at Route 95, Exit 45B, Lexington, MA 617-862-8700. Located in the heart of historic Lexington near Minuteman National Park, the 115-room Sheraton Tara is only 15 miles west of Boston and a 40-minute drive to Cape Ann, Rockport, and Gloucester. Dining and entertainment include the Upper Crust Restaurant and The Laurels, as well as an outdoor pool.

Newton, MA

Howard Johnson's Hotel, Washington Street over the Massachusetts Turnpike at Exit 17, Newton, MA 617-969-3010. This 275-room hotel is just six miles west of downtown Boston. It is located near the cultural and historical attractions in Boston and Cambridge and is in close proximity to Harvard, Boston College, MIT and other colleges. Public transportation to Boston is available directly from the hotel. Indoor pool, saunas, a game room and HBO.

Nashua, NH

The Sheraton Tara Hotel, Tara Boulevard, Exit 1 off of Route 3, Nashua, NH 603-888-9970. The 350-room Sheraton Tara Hotel is located just over the Massachusetts border in southern New Hampshire. Close to cultural, historical and recreational attractions including Arts and Science Center, Fort Constitution and Benson's Wild Animal Park. Less than half an hour from Boston. Dine in the Upper Crust Restaurant and Z.J.'s Pub, enjoy live, easy-listening entertainment in The Laurels. Outdoor tennis and complete health and fitness center with indoor and outdoor swimming pools and racquetball.

Parsippany, NJ

Tara Hotel, intersection of Routes 287 and 80, Parsippany, NJ, 201-515-2000. This 400-room hotel is only 25 miles west of New York City and is located in historic Morris County, offering a wealth of local attractions including the Morris Museum, the Edison National Historic Site and Liberty State Park. Dine in the casual Jesters Court Cafe, the elegant Upper Crust Restaurant, or the lively Tipperary Pub. Enjoy The Laurels, for live, easy-listening entertainment. Complete health & fitness center with indoor and outdoor pools and racquetball.

Warwick, RI

The Sheraton Tara Airport Hotel, Route 1 at I-95, T.F. Green Airport Exit, Warwick, RI 401-738-4000. Located just minutes from Providence and Narragansett Bay and only 30 minutes from Newport's historic mansions. The 125-room hotel is near the Cliff Walk, Ocean Drive and one hour from Mystic Seaport and Fall River/New Bedford area. For your recreational and entertainment pleasure, there is HBO, an indoor pool and saunas.

Since opening the first Sheraton Tara, the Tara Hotels division had developed a reputation for excellent physical products. The Sheraton Tara group of hotels offered its guests the finest in comfort with first-class guest rooms, restaurants and coffee shops, ballrooms, meeting rooms, recreational facilities, indoor and outdoor swimming pools, saunas, steam baths, exercise rooms, and a PGA golf course, but not at all properties, as shown in Exhibit 10.5. Each hotel was designed with the business traveler in mind. In addition to the appropriate facilities, the nationwide Sheraton reservation line provided a strong system for confirming rooms to travelers outside New England.

CUSTOMER RESEARCH

Richard Warhola, Director of Market Research for the Tara Hotels group, had conducted a customer survey to learn the likes and dislikes of some of the Merry Weekend customers. The study was designed to determine customer satisfaction of Merry Weekend packages, to identify the most appealing promotional benefits, to assess competitors' package usage, and to develop a Merry Weekend customer profile. The study was conducted at the Nashua and Framingham properties. The survey questions, responses, and a summary of the findings can be found in Appendix 10A.

After completion of the survey, Chambers gathered data for the previous four months and for the same months of the previous year, just prior to the general managers' meeting, in an attempt to draw some conclusions from company sales information on the Merry Weekend packages. A comparison of the sales in the six traditional Tara hotels plus Hyannis (which was a semiresort with Tara standards), versus the other five purchased properties, was revealed in this analysis (Exhibit 10.6).

Chambers distinguished between Tara and non-Tara hotels based on the current facilities offered at each property. The key difference between the two hotel groups was the offering of full or limited service. Merry Weekend customers didn't care whether the hotel looked like a castle; they wanted the health club, the Upper Crust and Jester's Court restaurants, and other full-service amenities of the traditional Taras. Descriptions of typical outlets at these hotels are given in Exhibit 10.7.

Chambers also evaluated the strengths and weaknesses of the chain. Among the strengths he found were:

- the excellent location of all properties
- the excellent services offered
- the extensive marketing research being conducted
- the competitive prices in the traditional Tara hotels
- the positive image of the Tara properties
- the good facilities provided in Tara properties
- the repeat customers, especially those with established brand loyalty to Tara hotels

Among the weaknesses Chambers found were:

- the prices of the non-Taras being perhaps too high with respect to the facilities they offered
- the poor facilities and small room sizes of the non-Taras
- the confused image of the non-Taras because they were recently purchased from Dunfey
- the lack of customer awareness of ownership of non-Tara properties
- the transition period while non-Taras upgraded to Tara levels with inconvenience and disservice to guests
- losing customers of the Tara hotels after they had patronized the non-Tara hotels
- offering Merry Weekenders seven traditional Taras instead of four

Chambers saw the opportunities for Tara Hotel Company to be:

- building on the existing reputation of the Tara image
- maintaining existing repeat customers
- identifying new markets through research
- capturing markets through price value in the non-Taras

Chambers also saw threats in other hotels that offered very competitive value packages, in the loss of Merry Weekend package customers within

Exhibit 10.5
Tara Hotels Inventory

Location	Rooms	Dining and Entertainment	Swimming Pool		Racquetball	Tennis	Golf	Saunas	Health Center
			Indoor	Outdoor					
Nashua, NH	350	Restaurant, pub & lounge	X	X	X	X		X	X
Braintree, MA	400	2 restaurants, pub & lounge	X	X	X			X	X
Framingham, MA	375	2 restaurants, pub & lounge	X	X	X			X	X
Danvers, MA	367	2 restaurants & lounge	X	X	X	X	X	X	X
Springfield, MA	300	2 restaurants & lounge	X		X			X	X
Parsippany, NJ	400	2 restaurants, pub & lounge	X	X	X			X	X
Hyannis, MA	224	Restaurant & lounge	X	X		X	X	X	X
Bedford, NH	200	Restaurant & lounge	X	X					X
Lexington, MA	115	Restaurant, pub & lounge		X					
S. Portland, ME	220	Restaurant & lounge	X					X	
Newton, MA	261	Restaurant & lounge	X					X	
Warwick, RI	125	Restaurant & lounge	X					X	

the Tara system because of disappointment at non-Taras, and in offering existing customers more products from which to choose.

The company used its current base of names and addresses from the traditional Tara properties to help promote the Merry Weekend packages at the new traditional Taras and at the non-Tara hotels. Some of these customers, after buying the package at a non-Tara, never came back to either a non-Tara or a Tara.

Without a distinction of services and facilities, Merry Weekend promotions continued to market the packages to known past customers. Little research, or even thought, had been given to the promotion of these packages and their consequences at the newly added properties.

GENERAL MANAGERS' MEETING

The meeting began promptly at 1:30 P.M. and was conducted by Chambers. Key corporate staff and general managers from the traditional and non-Tara properties were in attendance. The agenda read as follows:

1. overview of the situation
2. identification of problem
3. analysis of competitive offerings
4. product development
5. marketing of product—advertising and direct mail

Each general manager and his director of sales spent 30 minutes discussing their situation. They identified the loss of their customers to new traditional Tara properties as well as customer dissatisfaction with the nontraditional Tara product. Two additional hours were spent analyzing competitive offerings and discussing the product, customers, and prices.

In addition to the survey results reported and discussed at the meeting, the roundtable discussion about the customers who came to non-Tara properties indicated that a majority of these weekend guests loved to receive free in-room gifts, enjoyed shopping but liked to stay in the hotel for other activities (in fact, would sit in the lobby for hours feeling that the more time they spent in the hotel the more they received their money's

Exhibit 10.6

Summary Results of Merry Weekend Packages

Tara Hotels Merry Merry Weekend Analysis (No. of Rooms)

Hotel	Nov.		Dec.		Jan.		Feb.		Totals	
	LP	PY	LP	PY	LP	PY	LP	PY	LP	PY
"Taras":										
Nashua	984	850	316	300	1,067	1,008	934	1,629	3,301	3,787
Braintree	708	410	280	260	395	576	881	1,065	2,264	2,311
Framingham	991	850	314	289	817	911	1,087	1,092	3,209	3,142
Danvers	198	150	73	70	228	200	405	350	904	770
Springfield	24	0	13	0	42	0	156	0	235	0
Parsippany	175	0	76	0	189	0	399	0	839	0
Hyannis	230	36	86	92	414	427	438	503	1,168	1,058
Total	3,310	2,296	1,158	1,011	3,152	3,122	4,300	4,639	11,920	11,068

"Non-Taras":

Bedford	146	34	45	42	84	137	98	273	373	486
Lexington	37	44	32	329	16	16	38	57	123	446
S. Portland	359	250	103	67	154	11	327	333	943	661
Newton	21	26	3	3	15	10	24	39	63	78
Warwick	0	0	0	0	0	0	0	0	0	0
Total	563	354	183	441	269	174	487	702	1,502	1,671
Grand Total									13,422	12,739
% Tara									88.8%	86.9%
% Non-Tara									11.2%	13.1%

Inventory
% Tara 72.3% (2416 rooms)
% Non-Tara 27.7% (921 rooms)

Total 3337 rooms

Note: LP = latest period; PY = previous year.

289

Exhibit 10.7
Descriptions of Tara Outlets

worth), liked coupons for discounts in the restaurants and lounges, liked to have their picture taken with the Beefeater doorman (see Exhibit 10.8), and arrived by automobile. Most non-Tara managers suspected that most of their weekend customers belonged in the blue-collar category.

Chambers wanted to have a new package ready for sale throughout the Tara system by May 30 to ensure customer awareness and to support

Exhibit 10.8
Merry Weekend Brochure Cover

Now You Can Enjoy Your Tara Merry Weekend at Even More Castles.

Tara Hotels is pleased to announce the addition of seven new properties. In Newton, Lexington and Hyannis, MA; Warwick, RI; Bedford, NH; South Portland, ME; and Parsippany, NJ. And coming soon to Springfield, MA.

Sheraton Tara Hotel
  Braintree, MA 617-848-0600
Sheraton Tara Hotel
  Danvers, MA 617-777-2500
Sheraton Tara Hotel
  Framingham, MA 617-879-7200
Sheraton Tara Hotel
  Lexington, MA 617-862-8700
Sheraton Tara Hotel
  Springfield, MA 413-781-1010
Sheraton Tara Hotel
  South Portland, ME 207-775-6161
Sheraton Tara Wayfarer Hotel
  Bedford, NH 603-622-3766
Sheraton Tara Hotel
  Nashua, NH 603-888-9970
Sheraton Tara Airport Hotel
  Warwick, RI 401-738-4000
Tara Newton – A Howard Johnson's Hotel
  Newton, MA 1-800-654-2000 or 617-969-3010
Tara Dunfey Hyannis Hotel
  Hyannis, MA 1-800-THE TARA or 617-775-7775
Tara Hotel
  Parsippany, NJ 201-515-2000

For Sheraton reservations: 1-800-325-3535

Tara Hotels
THE FLATLEY COMPANY

any opportunity for a strong presale market for the upcoming summer season. Buy time, Chambers thought at the time, was averaging about two weeks out. Later he learned, however, that it was more like four to five weeks.

A basic problem discussed was that the Merry Weekend package was not working well at non-Taras because they had fewer facilities to offer the customers. Competition was also a major topic of discussion, centering around key competitors, especially the large-chain-affiliated hotels. These hotels recognized the contribution to revenues of weekend packages in their overall sales strategy. Like the Sheraton Tara properties, they were highly dependent on business travelers, and occupancies plunged on weekends. These hotels courted the markets aggressively through advertising and very attractive prices. Some examples are given in Exhibit 10.9.

Chambers also wanted to use weekend packages to lure new customers, not just bring back or hold on to the old Merry Weekend customers who didn't want the unrenovated product. To accomplish this, Chambers felt a need to attract some different customers such as those who had once utilized the Dunfey "minivacation" concept of weekend packages.

Those at the meeting recognized that the company had to respond quickly and effectively if it was going to meet the competitive challenge. Management recognized the difficulties of competing in each hotel's respective market because of the varied degrees and methods of competition. If the non-Tara hotels were to remain competitive, they would have to compensate somehow for their physical failings.

The meeting came to a close with optimistic enthusiasm regarding the new strategies that were to be put in place.

Exhibit 10.9
Competitive Weekend Packages

Stouffers, Bedford Glen

Four different weekend packages called "Breakations":*

1. $59, one night, double, Friday or Saturday
2. $79, one night, double, Friday or Saturday, champagne on arrival, continental breakfast
3. $139, two nights, double, Friday and Saturday, champagne on arrival, continental breakfast on Saturday
4. $169, two nights, double, Friday and Saturday, champagne on arrival, continental breakfast on Saturday, brunch on Sunday

* All packages based on availability.

Days Inn (Burlington) and Appleton Inn

No package. $65 rate for Friday or Saturday.

Exhibit 10.9 *(continued)*

Marriott, Newton

- Escape #1—$169/$179 double, welcome champagne, dinner for two, breakfast or brunch or room service—one night
- Escape #2—$219 double, Friday/Saturday, dinner both nights, comp newspaper
- $65—supersaver (room only)
- $69 ($89, 4/room) bed and breakfast

Marriott, Burlington

- Escape #1—$125, double, one night, two breakfasts, two dinners
- Escape #2—$149, double, two nights, two breakfasts, two dinners
- $65—supersaver, room only
- $69—($79, 4/room) bed and breakfast

APPENDIX 10A   MERRY WEEKENDER CUSTOMER SURVEY RESULTS

Purpose of Research

- Determine customer satisfaction toward weekend package.
- Identify most appealing benefits of weekend packages.
- Assess competitor package usage.
- Develop Merry Weekend customer profile.

Methodology

Surveys distributed to all Merry Weekend customers on two weekends at the following properties:

- Nashua only on November 13–15
- Nashua and Framingham on November 20–22

In total, 129 surveys were completed of the 273 distributed for a respectable response of 47 percent. The breakdown according to property and weekend is:

	Surveys Returned	*Surveys Distributed*	*Response Rate (%)*
Nashua, Nov. 13–15	45	104	43
Nashua, Nov. 20–22	58	95	61
Framingham, Nov. 20–22	26	74	35
Totals	129	273	47

Two properties with the most Merry Weekend business were selected. In April, a mail survey will be conducted with all Merry Weekend customers from January of last year through March of this year. This later study will be representative of all Merry Weekend customers for all properties.

The present study developed from discussion concerning the January promotion to all Merry Weekend customers; specifically, we wanted to know if a third night free with a Merry Weekend package was an appealing benefit. This opportunity to survey customers allowed the capturing of additional information for directional purposes and also is the foundation for the mail survey to be conducted in April.

Therefore, since this study does not represent all Merry Weekend customers, the results are directional only and should not be generalized to all Merry Weekend customers. However, the results in Exhibit 10A are very useful and give us a good idea and direction to follow.

Analysis of Results

Of the 129 survey respondents, 52 percent were on their first Merry Weekend. The 62 repeating Merry Weekend customers, on the average, had 2.6 Merry Weekend trips in the past two years.

Characteristics of Repeating Customers

- A large majority of Merry Weekend customers (73 percent) have never extended their weekend trip to a third night.

- Three of every four (77 percent) repeating Merry Weekend customers had only one dinner in the hotel. Of the 62 repeat Merry Weekend customers, the breakdown in groups eating dinner in the hotel is as follows:

Friday night only	25%
Saturday night only	52
Both Friday and Saturday	23
Total	100%

- Overall, repeating Merry Weekend customers were very satisfied with the weekend package. The most satisfying aspect of the package was the Sunday brunch. The percentages of repeating customers who rated aspects of the Merry Weekend package as very good or excellent are as follows:

Cocktail party	76%
Fruit basket	68
Saturday breakfast	81

(Text continues on p. 300.)

Exhibit 10A

Merry Weekender Customer Survey Questions and Results

1. How often have you used this Merry Weekend package in the last *two* years (including this weekend)?

First time today	52%
Two	9
Three	23
Four	7
Five	5
Six	1
Seven to nine	3
Total	100% (base = 129)

2. In the last two years, how often have you extended your Merry Weekend stay from two nights (Friday and Saturday) to three nights (Friday, Saturday, and Sunday)?

Never	73%
Once	10
Twice	10
Three times	7
Total	100% (base = 60)

3. During your Merry Weekend stays, how often do you eat dinner in the hotel's restaurant?

Friday night only	25%
Saturday night only	52
Both Friday and Saturday	23
Total	100% (base = 60)

4. Please rate the following characteristics of the Merry Weekend packages, with 5 being excellent and 1 being poor.

	Very Good or Excellent (%)	*Average Rating*
Cocktail party	76	4.1
Fruit basket	68	4.0

Exhibit 10.A *(continued)*

Saturday breakfast	81	4.1
Sunday brunch	100	4.4
Value overall (base = 60)	79	4.1

5. Which one factor was most important to you when selecting this Merry Weekend package?

Location	41%
Price	23
Repeating	10
Friends	6
Other	9
Restaurant	4
Pool	4
Spa	3
Total	100% (base = 129)

6. How did you become aware of Merry Weekend packages?

Repeat customer	29%
Referral	26
Newspaper ads	13
Gift certificate	12
Called hotel directly	12
Friends	4
Other	4
	100% (base = 129)

7. Have you purchased any other weekend packages offered by a hotel other than Tara Hotels?

Yes	32%
No	68
	100% (base = 127)

8. Who were these packages offered by?

Marriott	37%
Sheraton	17

Exhibit 10.A *(continued)*

Hilton	17
Holiday Inn	12
Hyatt	10
Westin	5
Omni	2
Other	4
	100% (base = 41)

9. Below is a list of benefits hotels have used in weekend packages. On a scale of 1 to 5, with 5 being very appealing, how appealing are these benefits to you?

	Percent Appealing or Very Appealing		
	First Time MW Customers	Repeating MW Customers	All MW Customers
Free dinner for 2 in hotel's restaurant	96	89	93
Free tickets to local theater, museum	38	33	34
Free third night MW stay	42	59	50
Free use of pool and health spa	67	64	65
Free in-room movies	73	68	71
Free brunch	96	94	95

MW = Merry Weekend

	Average Rating		
	First Time MW Customers	Repeating MW Customers	All MW Customers
Free dinner for 2 in hotel's restaurant	4.7	4.7	4.7
Free tickets to local theater, museum	3.1	2.8	3.0
Free third night MW stay	3.3	3.6	3.4
Free use of pool and health spa	4.0	4.0	4.0
Free in-room movies	4.1	3.9	4.0
Free brunch	4.8	4.8	4.8

Exhibit 10.A *(continued)*

10. What one addition would you like to see to the Merry Weekend Package?

	Addition	Willing to Pay More (% yes)
Dinner for two	43%	68%
Free third night	6	83
Lounge entertainment	5	100
Later check-out	4	25
Free HBO	4	0
Theater tickets	4	75
Better service	2	100
Golf	2	100
Champagne on arrival	2	50
AM coffee in lobby	2	50
Single mentions	26	

Selected Single Mentions: Coed steam room, more activities, whirlpool for two, children's play area, all-night room service, refrigerator in room, free massage (base = 95).

Customer Profile

11. In the last year, how often did your work require you to travel, including overnight stays in hotels?

Number of Overnights	Percent	
0	57	
1	6	
2	12	
3	4	
4	2	
5–9	11	
10+	8	
Total	100	(base = 115)

Average = 2.4 nights

Exhibit 10.A *(continued)*

12. What is your age?

Under 30	16%
30 to 39	26
40 to 49	41 (avg. age = 41)
50 to 59	12
60 to 69	5
	100% (base = 127)

13. What is your income?

Under $35,000	17%
$35,000 to 49,999	41 (median income = $47,682)
$50,000 to 69,999	27
$70,000 or more	15
Total	100% (base = 123)

Sunday brunch	100
Value overall	79

Awareness and Satisfaction   Respondents were asked to indicate how they became aware of the Merry Weekend package. Almost one in three customers (29 percent) indicated their awareness came from being repeat customers.

• An important finding is that one in every four customers (26 percent) indicated that they were "referred" to the package by someone else.

This demonstrates the power of "positive word of mouth" advertising, but we must remember that the opposite is true as well—customers do not purchase the package because of hearing about bad experiences, which are usually customer oriented.

• Location and price are the two most cited factors for choosing a Merry Weekend package.

Competitive Weekend Package Usage   Only one in every three (32 percent) Merry Weekend customers have purchased competitive packages in the last year.

- Of those customers purchasing competitive packages, Marriott's weekend package was cited as being purchased the most often, followed by those offered by Sheraton and Hilton.
- Customers are purchasing these competitive packages for the same reasons that they purchased a Merry Weekend package: price and location.

Promotional Benefits   In determining benefits that customers desire to receive in a weekend package, the following question was asked:

"Below is a list of benefits hotels have used in weekend packages. On a scale of 1 to 5 with 5 being very appealing, how appealing are these benefits to you?"

Customers indicated that the free brunch was the most appealing benefit. The order of appeal for the six benefits is:

1. Free brunch
2. Free dinner for two in hotel's restaurant
3. Free in-house movies
4. Free use of the health spa and pool
5. Free third night on weekend package stay
6. Free tickets to local theater and museums

Suggested Benefits for Merry Weekend Package   Customers were asked to name what one addition they would be willing to see in the Merry Weekend package, and whether they would be willing to pay a little extra for the package if this amenity was added.

- Dinner for two was cited by 43 percent of the respondents as the one addition they would like to see to the package. It is important to note that 68 percent of these respondents would be willing to pay more for the weekend package to get dinner for two. Dinner for two was the most widely suggested benefit by a wide margin.

- The next most appealing benefit—a "distant" second—was a free third night with the weekend package stay.

Customer Profile   The Merry Weekend customer seems to be an infrequent traveler. In fact, only 43 percent of the respondents stayed in a hotel overnight in the past year for business. Even more, the average number of nights in a hotel for business for the last year is only 2.4 nights.

- The average age of a Merry Weekend customer is 41 years.
- The median household income for Merry Weekend customers is $47,682.

Therefore the average MW customer is an infrequent traveler, who is a middle-class, middle-aged consumer living within driving distance of our hotels.

Conclusion

The customer profile of the Merry Weekend customer is not surprising, as this was very close to our educated guess. The percentage of first-time Merry Weekend customers (52%) strongly suggests that there is new business to be captured. Additionally, the 32 percent of the customers who have used competitors' weekend packages suggests that "brand loyalty" can be established either by adding amenities to the package or by simply reminding the customer of our package through direct mail or other forms of advertising.

"Third night free" is an attractive benefit—one in every two customers indicated this benefit to be "appealing" or "very appealing," although this benefit did not appear as appealing as other benefits. One problem with assessing the response to this benefit is the phrasing of a "third night free," without biasing the question for a positive response. The other benefits rated were already being offered, while a third night free was a new idea for a package.

With 77 percent of the customers already having one dinner meal in the hotel, the suggestion of having dinner for two included in the package (even with a higher Merry Weekend price per day) would "cut into" the food and beverage revenue. Since only 23 percent have both dinner meals at the hotel, our objective should be to increase this percentage.

Case Eleven

Royale Suites

Ronald Stiff

"It's a great day for sitting outside eating crabs." Bill Abbott and his New Property Planning Team were enjoying a lunch break on a sunny July day. After lunch they would return to developing a marketing plan for the new Royale Suites Baltimore hotel. The 12-story, 325-room hotel, opening in 18 months, was located within three blocks of the financial district and Inner Harbor tourist sites. Although only a few rooms would have an Inner Harbor view, they expected to capitalize on the already successful Royale Suites concept. "We've only got two days to bring our plan together before we present it to Corporate Marketing. Where do we stand now?"

THE ALL-SUITES CONCEPT

Although all-suite hotels had been around for a number of years, it wasn't until the late 1980s that the concept really burgeoned. This continued into the 1990s, when all-suite hotels substantially outperformed their single-room counterparts in occupancies and room rates (see Exhibit 11.1).

In the first seven months of 1995, for example, the all-suite average room rate in the United States was $89.30 compared with $66.69 for the entire industry; occupancy was 75 percent compared with the industry's 66 percent, according to Smith Travel Research of Hendersonville, Tennessee. This had led to a proliferation of all-suite hotels at all levels.

All-suite hotels run the range from ultra-deluxe (L'Ermitage) to full-service (Doubletree, Embassy, Royale), to extended-stay (Residence Inn),

This case was written by Ronald Stiff, University of Baltimore. Used by permission. All rights reserved. The case contains disguised data and names.

Exhibit 11.1

Trends among All-Suite Hotels. [From Smith Travel Research, Hendersonville, Tenn.]

Year	Occupancy			Average Room Rate			Room Supply			Room Demand			Room Revenue		
	Current Year (%)	Prior Year (%)	% Change	Current Year ($)	Prior Year ($)	% Change	Current Year (millions)	Prior Year (millions)	% Change	Current Year (millions)	Prior Year (millions)	% Change	Current Year ($ billions)	Prior Year ($ billions)	% Change
1990	67.0	68.7	-2.5	77.55	74.80	3.7	57.6	51.8	11.2	38.6	35.6	8.5	3.0	2.7	12.5
1991	67.1	67.0	0.1	76.61	77.55	-1.2	62.6	57.6	8.6	42.0	38.6	8.8	3.2	3.0	7.5
1992	69.9	67.1	4.2	76.81	76.61	0.3	64.7	62.6	3.5	45.3	42.0	7.8	3.5	3.2	8.0
1993	72.1	69.9	3.1	80.89	76.81	5.3	65.7	64.7	1.6	47.4	45.3	4.7	3.8	3.5	10.2
1994	73.8	72.1	2.4	84.43	80.89	4.4	66.5	65.7	1.2	49.1	47.4	3.6	4.1	3.8	8.1
1995*	75.0	74.9	0.1	89.30	85.16	4.9	39.2	38.5	1.7	29.4	28.9	1.8	2.6	2.5	6.8

* Through July.

to budget (Comfort Inn). Generally, all-suite hotels' combined square footage per unit is about 20 to 25 percent larger than its single-room counterpart. Some offer full kitchens, some kitchenettes, and some only basics such as coffeemakers. For business travelers, all-suite hotels offer functional work areas; for families, they offer convertible couches or pull-down beds; for weekend couples they offer relaxation space. The full-service all-suite hotels offer restaurants and lounges, and many include free breakfast and a happy hour. All-suite hotels have higher construction costs per unit.

ROYALE SUITES

Royale Suites was one of the early entries into the all-suite hotel segment. Recognizing the increasing demand by businesspeople to conduct small meetings in their hotel rooms and families' desires for larger and more private hotel rooms, Royale Suites opened their first property in the early 1980s. Additional units were opened in most of the largest cities in the United States. Baltimore was one of the few prime locations remaining to Royale Suites. Royale Suites Real Estate staff had been fortunate to locate and acquire an outstanding site.

The typical Royale Suites property was 8 to 12 stories high and included 225 to 350 two-room suites. A typical floor plan is shown in Exhibit 11.2. There was almost no variation in this plan from suite to suite except that some suites had twin beds. Kitchen facilities were not

Exhibit 11.2
Typical Royale Suites Layout of One Unit

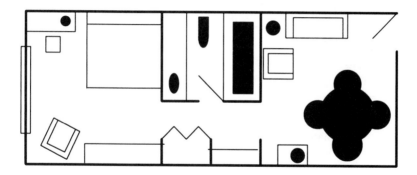

included, since they were believed to be of little interest to businesspeople and created significant additional equipment and cleaning costs.

Interior decorations were adapted to specific markets, and local, classical themes were encouraged. The Baltimore Royale Suites would have two meeting rooms seating 60 persons in each. They could be combined into a larger room seating 100 and used for meals.

The New Property Planning Team

Royale Suites used a New Property Planning Team to plan the opening of each new property. This team consisted of planning managers for each of the major departments in the hotel (Exhibit 11.3). Often those on the planning team continued on as the operating managers for the site.

The team in Baltimore was headquartered in a building overlooking the Inner Harbor, a tourist and upscale business area, near the hotel site. It was charged with developing the marketing plan for the hotel opening and the first year of service.

COMPETITION

About 12 percent of all downtown hotel rooms were suites. These were either in local hotels or included as part of the room inventory of national

Exhibit 11.3
New Property Planning Team in Baltimore

```
                    ┌─────────────────┐
                    │ General Manager │
                    │   Bill Abbott   │
                    └─────────────────┘
         ┌──────────────┬────┴─────┬──────────────┐
   ┌──────────┐   ┌──────────┐ ┌──────────┐ ┌──────────┐
   │  Rooms   │   │          │ │ Food and │ │          │
   │Jim Grover│   │          │ │ Beverage │ │          │
   └──────────┘   │          │ │Diane Brown│ └──────────┘
          ┌──────────┐   ┌──────────┐  ┌──────────┐
          │Marketing │   │Accounting│  │  Minor   │
          │ Ann Young│   │Steve Carr│  │Departments│
          └──────────┘   └──────────┘  └──────────┘
```

chains (Exhibit 11.4). As a result, suites in Baltimore had received little promotion either locally or nationally. This was a relatively untapped product in the downtown market area.

Serving as mainly upscale rooms within nonsuite hotels, suites were generally priced higher than standard rooms in these hotels. Although the specific occupancy rates for suites was not known, the planning team estimated that Inner Harbor hotel occupancy rates averaged 60 percent over the past two years.

Ann Young, Marketing, noted that reservations were made in several ways:

- *Pure Transient* Tourist or business travelers who either dropped in or made reservations direct to the Baltimore site. This group paid the rack rate (published rate charge), Young believed. This group

Exhibit 11.4

Inner Harbor Competitor Published Rates for Previous Year

Hotel	No. of Rooms	Low Rate (Single)	High Rate (Double)	No. of Suites	Low Rate	High Rate
Omni Inner Harbor	688	$ 95	$155	16	250	1,000
Renaissance Harborplace	622	180	230	42	275	875
Marriott Inner Harbor	513	159	199	12	200	450
Hyatt Regency Baltimore	487	160	250	26	275	485
Lord Baltimore Radisson	412	77	119	28	225	225
Holiday Inn Inner Harbor	374	109	139	3	225	225
Sheraton Inner Harbor	319	145	185	20	325	1,300
Days Inn Inner Harbor	242	60	90	8	95	115
Harbor Court	178	195	275	25	255	410
Comfort Inn	120	48	64	2	99	99
Ramada Inn	90	74	95			
Brookshire Suites				90	145	205
Tremont Suites				60	115	170
Tremont Plaza Suites				228	99	179
Total	4,045			560		
Average	368	118	164	43	199	441

Note: Weekend and corporate published rates are often lower. Depending on the season, published (rack) rates may be heavily discounted, especially for groups. Suite rates are usually the same, single or double.

also included those who made reservations through Royale Suites' national toll-free number.

- *Government* Government employees on a relatively low per diem.
- *Bus Tours* Contracts with travel agents for tour groups at negotiated rates.
- *Corporate Groups* Corporation and association meetings. These consisted of very small groups that could meet in the suites and larger groups that attended meetings in the Convention Center or in other hotels.
- *Airlines* Contracts with airlines as a part of a vacation plan and also with flight crews.
- *Weekend Packages* Two-night weekend plans including some special services to make them attractive.

A national customer survey was available to the planning team that suggested parity among major all-suite hotels (Exhibit 11.5). However, these data did not break down quality perceptions for specific market

Exhibit 11.5
Relative Quality Evaluations

Overall Satisfaction	*Residence Inn (%)*	*Embassy Suites (%)*	*Royale Suites (%)*
Very satisfied	42	40	38
Satisfied	53	56	57
Dissatisfied	5	4	5
Specific Attributes	*Ratings**		
Staff	4.1	3.2	4.5
Food	N/A	2.9	3.3
Room Quality:			
Cleanliness	4.2	3.8	4.1
Size	4.8	4.7	4.6
Bed comfort	2.9	3.1	2.9
Climate	3.1	2.8	3.2
Noise	3.3	3.4	3.1
Amenities	2.8	3.1	2.8
Sample size	209	243	256

* 5 = comparatively satisfied, 1 = comparatively dissatisfied.

segments. It was not clear which attributes were most important to these segments and how the chains compared in the minds of these segments.

A second survey provided some overall insights into service attributes that were important to all hotel consumers and consumer's beliefs in a hotel's performance on these attributes (Exhibit 11.6). Young felt that this might provide some guidance in positioning Royale Suites.

THE MARKETING MIX

Product

The physical product was fixed by corporate architectural and planning standards as adapted to the specific Baltimore site. There were a number of possible services that could be offered.

Exhibit 11.6

Hotel Service Attributes: Importance and Perceived Performance (Including Managers and Executives Only). [From Opinion Research Corporation's Executive Travel Tracking Services, 1990.]

Hotel Service Attribute	Importance to Customer (%)*	Consumer Belief of Actual Performance (%)*
Billing accuracy	91	83
Efficient check-in	80	55
Reliable message and wakeup service	79	76
Cares about the consumer	77	54
Competitive room rates	72	52
Reasonable charge for in-room phone	72	37
Express checkouts	68	63
Attractive and generously sized rooms	59	55
Fast breakfast service	54	48
Well-lighted and ample workspace	48	51
Availability of no-smoking rooms	47	49
Quality frequent-traveler program	41	34
Multiple dining and lounge facilities	36	54
Late-evening room service	24	38

* Percentage who answer 8, 9, or 10 on a 1-to-10 scale

Although most Royale Suites offered free breakfasts and happy hours, this was no longer a standard corporate policy or included in corporate advertising. Diane Brown estimated the cost of breakfast to average $4.00 per occupied room and a happy hour at $1.00 per occupied room.

Brown favored these services:

> Although happy hours and breakfasts have become pretty standard throughout the all-suite industry, this is not yet the standard in Baltimore. If we introduce this as a standard feature, we can be a pace-setter here and avoid playing catch-up if others introduce these later.

Ann Young replied,

> It's a great marketing feature; however, will it lead to us charging noncompetitive room rates? Our consumers are sensitive about prices, and there are plenty of alternatives for breakfast and booze downtown. I'm also concerned about our restaurant—its services may be very important to our customers.

Restaurant

Royale Suites had a flexible policy on restaurants. Throughout the chain they were both owned and leased. Brown stated,

> We have built a reputation for having restaurants with a little local flair. We don't just "cookie-cut" our food services; they are adapted to each site either by opening our own facility or leasing our space to a local restaurant with a good reputation.

She felt that the contribution to profits would be about the same whether owning or leasing the restaurant, and the primary concern had to be to design food services that enhanced the image of the Baltimore Royale Suites with its customers. Brown also believed that although hotel restaurants traditionally were mainly used by guests, careful design and positioning had increased their potential to attract customers from outside the hotel.

Prices

Steve Carr, Accounting, commented,

We pay 1½ percent of room revenues into the corporate computer system. This would seem to be a lot just to book rooms; however, it provides us an opportunity. As you know, we can implement a yield management pricing system using the corporate computer. [See Appendix 11A for a description of yield management.] The information system permits us to do much more than we could last year. We can develop a set of pricing rules and update them in just a minute or two. If we make all our advance, group, and transient booking through corporate's computer, we can fully implement a yield management pricing program.

Let me give you some background on this. When we opened our first units, we stressed a single-price policy nationwide. This made a lot of sense to the consumer and it made a lot of sense to us. However, as competition got tougher, we all learned that each city is a unique, local market with different costs and competition. Market pricing became a necessity. This made accountants into marketers and marketers into accountants—probably a good idea. Our computer has turned us into an airline in a pricing sense. If we are clever enough, every room will be booked and profits would be maximized. Of course, every room might have a different price. We have to start somewhere, so let's develop a fairly simple set of pricing rules. I have used a rooms department (housekeeping and front desk) cost of $30 per occupied suite, which is our system-wide average.

To simplify this, let's develop rules that give us average prices and occupancy rates for Monday to Thursday, Friday, Saturday, and Sunday. These can be used in our pro forma. We can make use of competitor's prices (Exhibit 11.4) and some of our company historic prices and occupancy rates (Exhibit 11.7), although there is more all-suite competition in these cities. Let me propose a starting point. There are 52 Sundays, with 16,900 rooms available. Perhaps 25 percent of these will be sold at rack rate. How do we price and sell the remaining rooms?

Advertising, Sales, and Public Relations

Corporate headquarters assessed each Royale Suites 2 percent of room revenues for national advertising. This was used to position Royale Suites,

Exhibit 11.7

Average Occupancy and Room Rates for Royale Suites, Previous Year: Selected Sites

		Average Occupancy Rates					
		August		*September*		*Annual*	
City	*Annual Average Room Rate* ($)*	*Mon.–Thurs. (%)*	*Fri.–Sun. (%)*	*Mon.–Thurs. (%)*	*Fri.–Sun. (%)*	*Mon.–Thurs. (%)*	*Fri.–Sun. (%)*
Chicago	115.00	56.1	51.1	63.4	61.7	62.3	56.8
Dallas	120.00	55.5	57.4	63.2	58.7	60.2	58.1
Denver	120.00	61.5	57.4	67.8	59.2	63.5	58.8
Detroit	120.00	68.4	61.5	70.2	60.2	69.3	61.4
New Orleans	120.00	68.4	56.4	71.4	62.4	70.4	58.8
Phoenix	115.00	68.4	47.7	73.2	51.4	71.2	49.2
San Francisco	125.00	75.2	76.0	80.2	73.5	78.2	75.5
Average		64.8	58.2	69.9	61.0	67.9	59.8
Weekly average—7 sites			62.9		67.4		65.6
Weekly average—all sites			61.5		64.7		63.7

* Room rate increases of 5 percent or higher per year are expected.

provide information about its features and locations, and promote the toll-free reservations number. Media included national TV, consumer and business magazines, airline in-flight magazines, and travel trade publications.

Each Royale Suites location was responsible for any national or local advertising featuring its specific property. Media rates for magazines and newspapers under consideration are given in Exhibit 11.8. Ann Young addressed her concerns about advertising:

> We have to develop a plan that creates a favorable awareness in the minds of our target market segments. An opening kick-off is a must, and then we must sustain interest and expand awareness through the rest of the year. Our budget is limited, so we should be very creative

Exhibit 11.8
Media Rates and Circulation

Magazine—Edition	Rate* ($)	Circulation	CPM** ($)
Time—National	120,130	4,339,029	27.69
Time—Eastern	63,290	1,457,910	43.41
Time—National Business	73,500	1,679,998	43.75
Newsweek—National	100,980	3,180,011	31.75
Newsweek—Eastern	39,278	951,000	41.30
Newsweek—National Business	42,460	753,043	56.38
New Yorker	32,275	622,123	51.88
Business Week—National	56,700	889,535	63.74
Business Week—Northeast	21,210	199,316	106.41
Business Week—Mid-Atlantic	14,380	131,813	109.09
Fortune—National	40,900	668,972	61.14
Fortune—Northeast	19,360	160,135	120.90
Fortune—Mid-Atlantic	11,500	85,175	135.02
Forbes	45,550	743,533	61.26
Baltimore Magazine	4,760	55,442	85.86
Wall Street Journal—National	99,384	1,835,713	51.14 B&W
Wall Street Journal—Eastern	43,956	757,483	58.03 B&W
Baltimore Sun—Morning	11,241	238,533	47.13 B&W

* Except as noted, rates are for color, full-page ads with one insertion.
** CPM = cost per 1,000 circulation.

with our public relations for the opening. It's important that we're noticed among all the other attractions here.

I'm also concerned about our sales effort. Salary and expenses will average $50,000 per salesperson. This includes a car and quite a bit of travel. We should be able to trade some travel with the airlines. However, we must be much more specific about our target market segments before we allocate our budget between advertising and salespersons. Are we a business hotel, or are we aggressively going after other segments? Help me to define the targets and I'll define the promotional plan.

FINANCIAL ANALYSIS AND FINAL MARKETING PLAN

Using the corporate format, Carr had produced a first cut at an income statement based on these initial ideas of the market situation and marketing mix (Exhibit 11.9). He estimated food and beverage revenues at about 60 percent of room revenue. "The bottom line just isn't good enough. Most other units are averaging over 10 percent profits as a percent of revenues, and several are at 15 percent."

Abbott concurred.

I know we've done a lot of work on this project, and now we have to concentrate and focus our efforts on a specific marketing plan that provides a realistic, reasonable return to Royale Suites. This is a good location and I know we can build a top performer. Let's see how we can improve this.

Exhibit 11.9

Pro forma Income Statement for New Royale Suites Hotel

Summary

Average daily rate =	$113.59	←Calculated
Pretax income =	$750,454	←Calculated
Percent of revenues =	5.1%	←Calculated
Occupancy rate =	62.58%	←Calculated
Number of rooms	325	

Note		Mon.–Thurs.	Fri.	Sat.	Sun.	Average
1	Average daily rate	$120.00	$105.00	$105.00	$105.00	$113.59
2	Occupancy rate (estimated)	66.0%	58.0%	58.0%	58.0%	62.58%
	Days	209	52	52	52	365
	Variable costs:					
	Rooms department	$30.00	per room per day			
3	Breakfast	$4.00	per room per day			
4	Happy hour	$1.00	per room per day			
	Advertising charge	2.0%	of room revenues			
	Computer charge	1.5%	of room revenues			

Revenues	% of Revenue	Annual Total ($)	Comment
Rooms	57.4	8,435,108	
Food @ 40% of rooms revenue	25.4	3,740,043	
Beverages @ 20% of rooms revenue	11.5	1,687,022	
Other @ 10% of rooms revenue	5.7	843,511	Telephone, gifts, newspapers, etc.
Total revenue	100.0	$14,705,684	

Exhibit 11.9 (*continued*)

Expenses	% of Revenue	Annual Total ($)
Rooms, variable costs:		
Rooms department	15.1	2,227,066
Advertising charge	1.2	168,702
Computer charge	0.9	126,527
Food and beverage/other:		
Fixed costs/payroll @ 45%	16.6	2,442,179
Variable costs @ 28%	10.3	1,519,578
Breakfast and/or happy hour	2.5	371,178
Undistributed expenses:		
Administration	10.2	1,500,000
5 Marketing	5.4	800,000
Operations/maint.	10.2	1,500,000
Other—telephone, property tax, etc.	8.8	1,300,000
Depreciation	13.6	2,000,000
Total	94.9	$13,955,230
Income before taxes	5.1	$750,454

Note: Those rows numbered 1 through 5 on the left can be revised.

1 and 2   Average daily rates and occupancy rates are weighted average of all available rates.

3 and 4   Breakfast and happy hour costs must include all expected costs. These rows can also be used to include any other variable costs in your marketing plan. Specify these to the right of your cost.

5   Includes all advertising and sales force costs. This row can also be used to include any other fixed costs in your marketing plan. Specify these to the right of the cost.

Price elasticity: Management estimates that as rates change by $1.00, occupancy moves in the opposite direction in percentage points as follows: Monday through Thursday (.50%), Friday (1%), Saturday or Sunday (1.25%). Price elasticities will change if services offered are either increased nor decreased.

APPENDIX 11A   YIELD MANAGEMENT PRICING

Airline deregulation, coupled with large computer reservations systems, encouraged the development of the first computerized yield management systems. The principle of yield management is recognition of the price sensitivities of specific market segments. Ideally, as many full-fare seats as possible are sold, and then unfilled seats are sold at decreasingly lower prices until the load factor approaches 100 percent and profits are maximized. Competition ensures that full fares will seldom be achieved for 100 percent of capacity. Therefore, a block of lower-fare seats can be made available for advance purchase. Seat inventory is monitored to expand or reduce this block of seats before the advance reservations deadline or to open them again closer to flight time. This requires computers to manage the seat as a perishable commodity. Some large airlines make over 30,000 fare changes daily.

The yield management system must have specific rules to match prices to the demands of different segments. These can include services provided, time of day for the flight, day of week, length of stay, time in advance the ticket is purchased, and other factors. Penalties are often required to minimize high-price segments' use of low-price tickets. These are generally advance payment and loss of all or part of the fare when canceling.

Airlines, like many services, have low variable costs. Any seat priced above variable costs contributes to fixed costs or profits. Empty seats are lost contribution. Low variable costs permit significant added contribution even from deeply discounted seats. Frequent-flyer awards only cost an airline the variable cost of the seat provided the awards do not displace a paying fare. Thus, travel restrictions are placed on free seat awards.

Yield management pricing has been adopted by communications companies, banks, car rental companies, hotels, and other service firms.

Hotel Room Yield Management

Walter Relihan describes yield management applied to hotel rooms.[1] Hotel guests can be grouped into a wide variety of market segments. At the

[1] Walter J. Relihan, "The Yield-Management Approach to Hotel-Room Pricing," *Cornell Hotel and Restaurant Administration Quarterly* (May 1989), pp. 40–45.

Exhibit 11A

Revenues and Occupancy

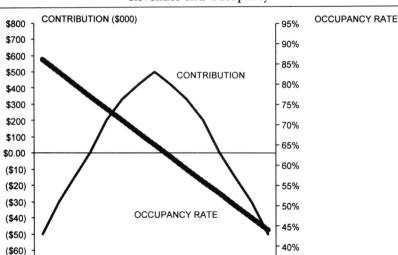

most general level, business and leisure segments must be served. The leisure segment tends to plan ahead, booking earlier than the business segment, and is more price-sensitive. Business consumers often are unable to book ahead and are more concerned with the availability of a room than its price. The hotel must accurately forecast demand to maximize the contribution produced by these segments. The basis for this is accurate reservations history information.

Reservations history can provide the occupancy rate as a function of the average room rate for the total property and for specific market segments. An example of occupancy rate as a function of average room rate is given in Exhibit 11A. Occupancy rates and average room rates can be entered into an income statement to estimate the expected total contribution as shown in the graph. In this example, contribution is maximized at an average room rate of $120 with an expected occupancy rate of 65 percent. Breakeven occurs at any rate between $100 and $140; however, profits are very sensitive to room rates at this hotel and decline rapidly at rates other than $120. Lower rates produce low unit-contribution margins, and higher rates drive away too many consumers.

Case Twelve

Anfi del Mar, S.A.

Madhur Mehta and Erich A. Joachimsthaler

Sitting in his office in Arguineguin, in the south of Gran Canaria (in the Canary Islands, off the western coast of Africa), Erik Sørensen, the Danish-born Managing Director of Anfi Beach Marketing and Sales, Ltd., was gazing out at the beautiful turquoise waters of the cool Atlantic ocean, where a school of bonito made the surface sparkle. This is where he met with the case author about the project he had been involved with over the past 18 months. He had just finalized all arrangements with the bank syndicate involved in the financing, and now his mind was occupied with the challenges before him to make this venture a true success. Sales at Anfi del Mar, a new time-share concept, would commence in October. From then on, success would depend on the marketing and sales program he had designed over the past year and a half. He was happy to have the case author visit Anfi del Mar thinking that he could take this opportunity to one more time go over his marketing and sales program point by point. "Perfect," he thought, "if an outside marketing expert approves of the program, I will have a better chance of getting it passed in the management meeting next month."

BACKGROUND

Erik Sørensen

After having received his bachelor's degree from the University of Tennessee and an M.B.A. from the University of Hawaii, Erik Sørensen embarked

This case is from the Investigation Division of IESE (Barcelona). It was prepared by Madhur Mehta, M.B.A., under the supervision of Professor Erich A. Joachimsthaler, September 1992, with thanks to Terry Nelidov, M.B.A., for his many suggestions. Revised July 1993. Reproduced by John Wiley & Sons with permission. Copyright 1992 IESE, University of Navarra. Total or partial reproduction is prohibited without written authorization from IESE. Certain information in the case has been disguised.

on an international career in Europe. He worked for Wrangler Europe for six years, in Austria, Sweden, Germany, and Belgium, first as Finance Director and later as Director of Business Development. Sørensen commented, "After this success in my international career I wanted to take a sabbatical year off and then make myself professionally independent." In 1983, Sørensen accepted a job offer as the Project Planning Manager at La Santa Sport, a time-share resort, on Lanzarote, one of the Canary Islands. A year later, he founded a marketing company, with two Belgian entrepreneurs, to market time-share resorts—or, as he preferred to call it, "vacation ownership." He managed the company for five years and then negotiated a buyout of his shares by his partners. Sørensen continued, "I then devoted almost a year to an in-depth study of customer services and the psychology of selling, marketing, and customer service. Then, when I was ready to look for the next project to which to devote my energies and to put my knowledge into practice, I was head-hunted by the Anfi Group."

Sørensen had also attended the Executive Finance Program of Harvard Business School and would be attending the Owners Presidents Managers Program at Harvard Business School.

Time-sharing in Europe

The concept of time-sharing began in Europe in the 1960s when a Swiss-based company began offering its shares for sale. The proceeds were used to buy holiday properties throughout Europe. The shares gave the holders right to use the holiday properties on a regular basis. At approximately the same time a French hotelier in the Alps started what had become the most common form of time-share—the sale of a right to use a certain amount of fixed weeks of accommodation for holiday purposes. After adapting the marketing and sales methods to the U.S. market, time-sharing was born in Florida, the state which still had the highest annual time-share sales. The U.S. economy's difficulties in the 1970s fueled time-share sales growth as property developers flooded to this new concept to sell their unsold holiday apartments.

Time-share sales in Europe did not take off until 1984, when American time-share developers and marketers arrived (in particular, on Spain's Costa del Sol) in search of Florida-like conditions and opportunities to repeat the success time-sharing had had back home.

Time-sharing consisted of the owner paying a capital sum to own one or more weeks of residence in a holiday property or resort for a fixed number of years (typically 30 years) or in perpetuity, depending on local laws. Ownership was reflected in a person's right to use a fixed week/s during the year. In addition to the purchase price, the time-share buyer paid an annual maintenance fee and/or local charges. He arranged his own transportation to the resort. Nevertheless, some of the leading time-share developers and marketers also provided transportation from the buyer's home to the resort.

The time-share industry attracted the attention of many prestigious firms in the real estate, hospitality, and tourism sectors. Walt Disney World Corporation, Fairfield Communities, Marriott Hotels, Wimpeys, Hilton International, and Barratts International all offered some form of time-share holiday accommodation, among many others.

Time-share owners in the early 1970s did not like going back to the same place to vacation each year. In response, time-share exchange organizations were founded. There were two main organizations—Resort Condominiums International (RCI)[1] and Interval International (II) which offered their clients as many as 3,000 different holiday destinations. The objective of having exchange organizations was that owners of a time-share could take their holiday at a different resort at a different time of the year, by exchanging the weeks they owned. The weeks of the year were divided into red, white, and blue, depending on the high/low seasons, red being the high season. Most resorts were affiliated with one of these organizations and a time-share buyer was automatically enrolled as a member of the exchange company, normally for a period of three years. A flat fee of about U.S.$107[2] was charged by the exchange organization to the owner for administering the exchange. Annual membership was $130.[3]

---

[1] See case "RCI Europe Ltd: Service Quality and Its Measurement," by Brian Hare, Erich A. Joachimsthaler, and Luis Mª. Huete, 1992 (IESE Case Library no. 0-593-023; M 905 E, 1992).

[2] Throughout this case, $ refers to U.S. dollars. Also, DM = deutsche mark and pta = peseta.

[3] Source: RCI Europe. Often, resorts offered to pay the first three years of membership.

According to an independent study conducted by the American consulting firm Ragatz Associates, in 1990 the worldwide sales of time-sharing weeks were $3 billion and the cumulative sales worldwide were in excess of $23 billion. Europe represented about 25 percent of worldwide sales of time-sharing. It was the fastest growing and most important geographic area. Exhibit 12.1 gives information on the size and growth of the European time-share industry.

Canary Islands

The archipelago formed by the Canary Islands lies approximately 100 kilometers off the northwest coast of Morocco, about 1,000 kilometers southwest of the Spanish peninsula. The islands consisted of two provinces: the Las Palmas province, which is made up of Gran Canaria, Lanzarote, Fuerteventura, Graciosa, Alegranza, Montana Clara, Roque del Este, and Lobos; and the Province of Santa Cruz de Tenerife, which includes Tenerife, Gomera, La Palma, and Hierro. The Islands are largely dependent on tourism, which at the time accounted for approximately 70 percent of the economy, followed by industry, agriculture, and construction, each with 10 percent. Even after Spain's accession to the European Community (EC) the Islands retained their status in regard to agriculture and tax laws. They avoided being drawn into the Common Agricultural Policy and retained the distinct advantage for tourists and residents alike of liberal tax laws and duty-free import regulations. In the near future, one of the most important political issues would be the Islands' relationship with the EC, since that would largely determine the area's future prospects. The tourism industry had grown steadily at a compound rate of 7.8 percent, from 1986 to 1991 (see Exhibit 12.2).

Gran Canaria   Gran Canaria, with 1,500 square kilometers, was the third largest of the Canary Islands. The capital of Gran Canaria was Las Palmas, situated in the north of the island. The northern part of the island was substantially above sea level. Most of the cloudy and rainy weather coming in from the north was blocked by the high terrain, leaving the south with clear and sunny weather all year around.

Most of the tourist activity was located in and around Playa del Ingles on the south side of the island, where many developments had sprung

Exhibit 12.1

Size of the European Time-Share Industry. [From RCI/Hapimag/HPB.]

Country/Region	Where Time-share Owners Live				Where They Own Their Time-share			Number of Time-share Developments		
	1987	1990	1991	% Change (1987–1991)	1987	1990	% Change (1987–1990)	1987	1990	% Change (1987–1990)
UK/Ireland	120,000	220,000	266,000	122	35,000	50,000	43	60	85	42
France	50,000	60,000	66,500	33	45,000	55,000	22	50	84	68
Italy	30,000	40,000	48,000	60	30,000	40,000	33	60	75	25
Germany	40,000	70,000	94,000	135	20,000	30,000	50	50	87	74
Scandinavia	20,000	40,000	45,200	126	15,000	20,000	33	30	45	50
Iberia*	3,000	18,000	37,400	1,147	107,000	200,000	87	110	213	94
Benelux	3,000	9,000	13,700	357	—	—	—	—	2	—
Other	1,000	3,000	13,700	1,270	5,000	15,000	200	15	53	253
Total	267,000	460,000	584,500	119	257,000	410,000	60	375	644	72

* Approximately 18,000 in Spain in 1991.

Note: The two major European "holiday points systems"—the Swiss-based Hapimag with 75,000 shareholders, and the U.K.-based Holiday Property Bond (HPB) with 12,500 bondholders—are included in estimates. Although they try to disassociate themselves from conventional time-sharing due to concerns about time-sharing's image in some countries, both companies are in fact promoting the concept of paying in advance for future holidays.

Exhibit 12.2

Tourist Flows to the Canary Islands and Gran Canaria (in Thousands)

	Foreign Visitor Arrivals to the Canary Islands*			Foreign Visitor Arrivals to Gran Canaria*		
	1986	1991	% Change	1986	1991	% Change
Germany	1,004	1,590	58.4	467	657	40.7
Denmark	144	93	−35.4	78	49	−37.2
Finland	147	252	71.4	86	93	8.1
United Kingdom	1,120	1,571	40.3	240	299	24.6
Holland	147	370	151.7	107	181	69.2
Italy	93	141	51.6	18	39	116.7
Norway	197	99	−49.7	118	47	−60.7
Sweden	333	251	−24.6	137	151	10.2
Switzerland	92	145	57.6	65	77	18.5
Belgium	77	145	88.3	N/A	N/A	N/A
Austria	N/A	N/A	N/A	25	48	92.0
France	46	134	191.3			
Other	94	295	213.8	128	140	9.4
Total	3,494	5,086	45.6	1,469	1,771	20.6
Compound annual growth			7.8%			3.8%

* Not included in these figures are Spanish mainland residents. Those who visited the Canary Islands in 1991 were 1,021,617; those who visited Gran Canaria in 1991 were 105,000.

up. There were a number of hotels, apartments, and rental houses available for the vacationer. Many hotels were tied up with tour operators offering week-long vacations that included the flight, lodging, and boarding. Exhibit 12.3 gives information on some packages offered by tour operators and their fares. Most of the tourists to Gran Canaria were from Germany and the United Kingdom. However, the typical tourist to Gran Canaria normally bought one of the many budget or economy holiday offers. Due to Gran Canaria's predictable and warm climate and its extensive and early development as a tourist destination, the island had become a synonym for mass tourism for people seeking sun and beach variety at a lower price point in southern Europe. Last-minute holidays, which were used by travel agencies to unload unsold holiday tours during the last week of departure, were very popular.

Exhibit 12.3
Tour Operator Prices to Gran Canaria

Dates	From Spain		From Germany	
	With Breakfast ($)*	*With Dinner ($)**	*With Breakfast ($)*	*With Dinner ($)*
5/1–6/14	634	815	968	1,087
7/1–7/15	709	899	1,017	1,136
7/16–7/31	719	912	1,245	1,364
8/1–8/15	743	939	1,245	1,364
8/16–8/29	719	912	1,245	1,364
8/30–9/15	719	912	1,197	1,316

* All prices are for one week's stay, per person, double occupancy at a five-star hotel in the south of Gran Canaria. Prices include the charter flight to and from Gran Canaria and transfer to the hotel. The prices are taken from magazines published by tour operators and available through travel agencies at the time of the case.

At the time of writing the case, there were 15 time-share developments with a total of 1,033 apartment units in Gran Canaria (Exhibit 12.4). Of the 15 resorts, none were Gold Crown resorts, which was the highest of the three levels of quality used by RCI to segment time-share resorts. The top-ranked resort achieved the rating of "international distinction" which was the middle category of quality European resorts.

ANFI BEACH CLUB

The idea for the Anfi Beach Club, the first time-share resort of Anfi del Mar, principally had come from Bjorn Lyng, a Norwegian industrialist, now settled in Gran Canaria, who had seen the mountainous site and envisioned it excavated to make room for a luxury resort, a private beach, an artificial island, and a private marina. Lyng considered this project the apex of his career. In 1986 the Anfi del Mar Group was formed with the objective to "build a luxury resort that is different from most other resorts on the Canary Islands." The project was started by Lyng together with Norwegian and local investors.

Juan Antonio Fernandez, the Director of Finance of Anfi Holding and a graduate of IESE, Barcelona, said, "I have been with Anfi for six years

Exhibit 12.4

Time-Share Developments on Gran Canaria in Decreasing Order of Quality

Rank	Name of Resort/Development	Location	Number of Units	Pricing per Week* (U.S. $)	Maintenance per Week (U.S. $)
1	Club Excelsior	Playa del Ingles	44	10,120	166
				13,248	
				16,192	
2	Tisaya Golf	Campo de Golf	5	12,512	166
3	Cala Blanca	Mogan	93	11,040	232
4	Bahia Blanca	Mogan	113	9,200	232
5	Portonovo Beach Club	Puerto Rico	12	Sold out—no resales	
6	Club Vista Verde	Maspalomas	16	8,280	230
7	Club Vista Flov	Maspalomas	84	8,280	180
8	Club Vista Serena	Maspalomas	48	8,280	180
9	Puerto Calma	Puerto Rico	120	11,244	204
10	Puerto Azul	Puerto Rico	180	9,200	166
11	Tindaya	Puerto Rico	12	Sold out—no resales	
12	Aptos Aloe	Playa del Ingles	100	8,096	123
13	Club Primavera	Playa del Ingles	16	Sold out—no resales	166
14	Mariposa del Sol		40	8,832	156
15	Club Monsenor	Mogan	150	7,667	256
		Total	1,033		

* Price per week refers to an average red week, based on overall judgments by Anfi management.

now and finally we will realize sales this year. For a project this size it takes patience to wait until construction has finished and start to receive income so that debt can be paid back." According to the company the total construction cost would amount to $22.9 million. Sales and marketing were expected to amount to 40.7 percent of the total projected costs of $49.1 million (see Exhibit 12.5). The loan repayment would begin in January of 1994.

The site, acquired in 1986, was located on the south coast of Gran Canaria, between the two established tourist developments of Maspalomas and Puerto Rico, near the small town of Patalavaca.

From an initial 100,000 square meters the site was enlarged through land reclamation to a total area of almost 200,000 square meters. The site was the last on Gran Canaria to get a permit to build within 100 meters of the coastline. On the west side a large breakwater next to a 250-meter-wide beach had been constructed, and on the east side the existing breakwater had been extended, resulting in a large and well-protected bay. Although all beach areas by law were accessible to the public, the beach seemed an integral part of Anfi.

The area surrounding the site had already been developed. To the east of the site were two quality developments, the Montemarina and Aquamarina, which were freehold (individually owned) apartments. Adjacent to them was the Steigenberger La Canaria, a five-star resort hotel. One could go to the town of Arguineguin following the coastline from the Steigenberger hotel, where there were various apartment and resort complexes. To the west of Anfi no developments were visible except one low-grade development located on the adjacent side of the hill.

The distance from the Las Palmas airport to the site was approximately 50 kilometers and was best navigated via the GC1 motorway, which led

Exhibit 12.5
Budgetary Projections in July 1992 (in U.S.$ million)

Expenses	Up to 1992	1993	1994	1995	Total
Construction	6.4	11.5	5.0	0	22.9
Sales and marketing	1.7	6.3	12.0	0	20.0
Financing	1.6	3.1	1.5	0	6.2
Loan repayment	0	0	18.0	4.0	22.0

* Numbers have been disguised.

to Maspalomas. The motorway from Maspalomas to Arguineguin was currently under construction and was expected to be finished soon.

The site consisted of four plots to be developed as a five-star luxury hotel, apartments to be sold on time-share or freehold, a four-star hotel, and a commercial area.

The time-share developments were planned for construction on the eastern side, next to the Aquamarina apartments. One hundred fifty apartments would be constructed in the first phase and sold on a time-share basis. The second phase would also have 150 apartments constructed to be sold on time-share or as freehold apartments. Gran Anfi, the five-star hotel, would have 550 beds and was to be situated to the west. Two four-star hotels, Centro Anfi and Monte Anfi, were to be constructed in the center of the development and would have a total of 1,540 beds.

All of the apartments would face the sea. In the front of the apartments was a manmade island to be used for a restaurant and recreational areas. Palm trees would be planted all around to give a "tropical effect." The swimming pool, on the main land, would be 1,000 square meters and include a jacuzzi, a sunken bar, slides, tunnels, and air mattresses "carved" into the landscaping for sun bathing. The surrounding greenery would lend a true tropical-vacation feeling.

Target Markets

The sale of the apartments would be through the company where Erik Sørensen was Managing Director—Anfi Beach Marketing and Sales, Ltd., a wholly owned subsidiary of Anfi Holdings. When asked about the markets and the type of buyer that Anfi would be targeting, Sørensen replied that the effort would be focused primarily on the German, British, and Spanish markets and secondarily on the Scandinavian markets. The focus of Anfi's marketing activities would be the buyer over 45 years of age, of an income bracket in the top 30 percent of the population, well educated, and oriented toward a quality lifestyle. "We are thinking of people belonging to the middle/upper-middle classes of society. The upper class has other options for taking vacations, and below the middle class are people who we do not want at our resort. The common denominator among future time-share owners at Anfi is that they share the same value system: to have, to be, and to indulge," said Sørensen. In defining Anfi's target market, Sørensen was referring to the well-known Everyday Life Research and segmentation typology of European consumers from SINUS, a Heidelberg-based research firm that had tracked consumer values and lifestyles across Europe since 1979, resulting in Eurosegments that combined status and value into classes. Exhibit 12.6 provides the Everyday Life Research profile for the United Kingdom.

Exhibit 12.7 provides some key country statistics on the primary country markets. The exhibit shows that these three countries alone accounted for 175.1 million or 53.1 percent of the total of 330 million Europeans. It also shows the vast differences that exist among the three country markets; the United Kingdom and Spain, for example, each had an inflation rate more than double that of Germany.

With regard to the secondary target market (the Scandinavian countries), the only information available at the time was their relative sizes in terms of population: Denmark, 5.13 million; Sweden, 8.44 million; Finland, 4.95 million; and Norway, 4.2 million. The primary markets, however, were further identified.

Germany Said Tonny Nielsen, Country Manager for Germany, with three years of experience in time-sharing.

> German customers are very demanding. If you say something will be there, it has to be there. They spend the most money as a nation on travel. Most of the time when they buy holidays, they buy package tours with fixed meals, etc. In Germany there is a law which says that if a German tourist was not happy with the package tour he went on, he can get his money back. It is easier to sell a time-share resort located in Germany as they will drive their cars down to the resort and back. There is no problem with getting cheap flights, changeover days, etc. But we are on an island, and people have to get down here by plane. You need to be able to adjust so that you can make sure there are flights when you need to check in and out.

In 1990, Germans spent DM 48 billion traveling abroad, 20 percent of which was spent in Spain, Italy, and Austria.

The German market had a late start in time-sharing, mainly because the first sales and marketing directors who brought the time-sharing idea to Europe were English-speaking and therefore naturally directed their

Exhibit 12.6
Everyday Life Profile of the United Kingdom

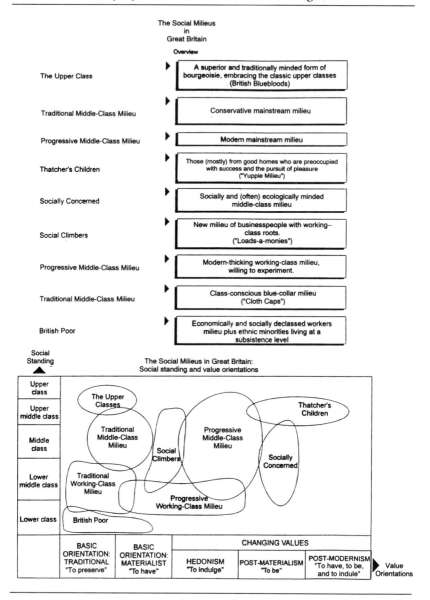

Exhibit 12.7
Comparative Country Statistics*

	Germany (DM)	United Kingdom (U.K. £)	Spain (ptas)
GDP (billions, 1991)	2,615.0	495.6	54,780.2
Savings rate (% of GDP)**	23.9	17.2	22.0
Cost-of-living index (New York = 100)***	86.1	99.7	101.1
Annual inflation (%)	2.9	7.3	6.6
Population (in millions, mid-1990)	78.8	57.4	38.9
Interest rate†	11.0	10.3	13.0
Households (in millions, 1990)††	33.4	21.0	14.4

* All statistics are taken from *Country Reports 1992–1993,* Economist Intelligence Unit, unless otherwise mentioned. For Germany, GNP (not GDP) is shown.
** *Source:* National Accounts 1988, OECD.
*** *Source:* International monitor on recent changes in taxation and living costs, 1989 PE Inbucon, International Salary Research, Surrey, U.K.
† Prime leading rate, July 1992.
††*Source:* Statistiches Bundesamt, Wiesbaden, 1992; OECD; World Bank reports.

first efforts to the English-speaking market. Consequently, only when the U.K. market started reaching maturity did other customer groups become more attractive. The German time-share buyer tended to be older, with 89.6 percent of them married, and 26.4 percent self-employed. This contrasts with a self-employment rate of 6.1 percent for the German population at large (see Exhibit 12.8).

United Kingdom　　The United Kingdom was the most mature market for time-sharing. It was estimated that there were around 266,000 time-share-owner families in the United Kingdom in 1991.

Furthermore, almost two-thirds said that their time-share holiday experience was better or very much better than their nontime-share holiday. The ones who were less satisfied were mainly younger, low-income families or retired persons, who considered time-sharing as an investment and who could not see a positive price/benefit ratio. Most owners in the United Kingdom were professional employees, employers, or managers in small firms (see Exhibit 12.8).

Exhibit 12.8

Demographics of the Time-Share Owner. ["General Population" statistics from: World Bank Reports; OECD Reports; Country Reports 1992–1993, Economist Intelligence Unit.]

	German		British		Spanish	
	Time-share Owner	General Population	Time-share Owner	General Population	Time-share Owner	General Population
Age (years)	44.5	38.8	48.4	49.2	39.4	45.1*
Marital status (%):						
Married	89.6	49.0	89.0	N/A	78.0	46.4
Single/Other	10.4	51.0	11.0	N/A	22.0	53.6
Profession (%):						
Self-employed	26.4	6.1	6.0	11.6	N/A	8.0
Employed	59.3	49.0	77.0	80.3	N/A	25.4
Ownership of residence (%)	63.3	43.5**	N/A	N/A	86.0	58.0
Percentage of households in top 30% income bracket		9.7		9.5		11.5

* Weighted average of population over the age of 20.
** Of nontime-share owners.

Spain Not many families in Spain owned a time-share, and almost none on Gran Canaria. The initial promoters concentrated on the U.K. market, and it was not until as recently as 1989 that the Spanish market started to develop. As in the case of Germany, the industry attributed this imbalance not only to the cultural and linguistic problems of the first American and British promoters selling time-shares in Spain, but also to inadequate legal and fiscal structures for doing business with contract-conscious Spanish nationals. Now that the Spanish government was developing norms for the industry, this imbalance should lessen. The current profile of Spanish time-share buyers showed that they were more likely to be married (78 percent) compared with the general population (46.4 percent). They were even more likely to own rather than rent their current residence (86 percent). Exhibit 12.8 provides further demographic information on the Spanish time-share buyer.

Other Characteristics In addition to the demographic and socioeconomic differences among the time-share owners in Anfi target countries, research showed some remarkable similarities and differences as to how time-sharing by Germans, British, and Spaniards was bought. Exhibit 12.9 shows that the time-share purchase is motivated primarily by the exchange opportunity, followed by the motivation to save on future vacations, and the insurance of good accommodations. Most time-share purchases were joint husband/wife decisions. The majority of time-share owners had bought their weeks on the same day of the sales presentation with relatively little prior search for information or evaluation of alternative offers. Only 19.7 percent of the German, 22.0 percent of the British, and 23.1 percent of the Spanish owners had visited another resort prior to purchasing.

When asked if they would purchase time-shares again, 46.6 percent of the Germans, 67.0 percent of the British, and 74.0 percent of the Spaniards answered that there was a very good chance that they would do so.

Brian Hare, an independent and prominent consultant on the tourism and time-share market, commented on these research results:

> Time-share is not for everyone. Time-share is one of several alternative ways of taking holidays, and as such this form of vacationing competes with other alternatives for a holiday maker's pocket money. These alterna-

Exhibit 12.9

Results from Marketing Research in the Time-Share Industry*

	Germany (%)	U.K. (%)	Spain (%)
Motivations for Purchasing a Time-share			
Exchange opportunity	84.8	55.1	85.7
Save on future vacations	52.7	39.3	34.9
Insurance of good accommodation	49.7	50.8	23.8
Resale and investment potential	33.2	33.0	23.8
Ownership at reasonable price	24.0	23.0	29.3
Liked the recreation facilities	11.6	20.6	7.9
Other People Involved in the Decision			
None	19.0	N/A	17.4
Spouse	74.9	N/A	64.5
Family	2.3	N/A	6.6
Friends	1.3	N/A	11.6
Purchase Occasion			
From on-site salesperson	58.1	84.8	78.2
From off-site salesperson	40.3	11.8	18.5
Resale from previous owner	1.4	0.0	0.0
Other	0.2	3.3	4.4
Purchase same day of presentation	42.3	N/A	37.5
A few days after sales presentation	38.1	N/A	31.7
A few weeks after sales presentation	N/A	N/A	21.7
No information search prior to purchase	N/A	N/A	77.0
Visit to resort prior to purchase	61.1	72.0	70.0
Visit to other resort prior to purchase	19.7	22.0	23.1
Time-share Information Sources			
Approached at the resort	38.4	45.8	44.5
Friends or relatives	27.5	10.4	15.1
Direct mail from resort	12.7	21.8	N/A
Newspaper or magazine ads	8.5	12.1	N/A
Newspaper or magazine article	4.8	7.8	15.1
Booth in shopping area	5.7	N/A	N/A
Radio/TV	0.8	0.4	0.8

Exhibit 12.9 *(continued)*

	Germany (%)	U.K. (%)	Spain (%)
Phone call from resort	1.2	N/A	N/A
Other	0.4	N/A	22.7
Repeat Purchase			
Very good chance—positively yes	46.6	67.0	74.0
Some chance—good chance	24.9	12.0	15.9
No chance—little chance	28.5	21.0	10.1

* Based on research involving over 6,000 owners conducted by Alza Ltd. in 1990 and 1991, Ernst & Young in 1990, and Ragatz Associates in 1987.

tive ways of taking holidays include independent vacations, which range from the complete self-catering type (e.g., apartment rentals), to full-service hotel lodging, to second-home vacations—as well as package-tour vacations, since they are commonly purchased at a travel agency. Time-share thus competes for a holiday maker's "share of suitcase." My experience shows that the choice of time-share vacation over the others is very much a function of a family's stage in the family life cycle, as well as the family's country of origin. In research, we have found that nationalities differ when asked which of these alternatives they view as their way of taking vacation. For example, 18 percent of the Germans view time-share as their most preferred alternative for vacation, compared to 15 percent of the Spaniards, and 9 percent of the British, who would opt for the time-share alternative.

Exhibit 12.10 provides an evaluation of the alternative accommodation offerings (including hotels and second homes, that is, purchasing an apartment or a holiday home on a freehold basis) to visitors in Gran Canaria with respect to service, as well as resort amenities. The evaluation also includes the service offer of the Anfi Beach Club (once fully constructed) to facilitate comparison.

MARKETING

Marketing in the time-share industry almost always implies a lead generation to produce a steady flow of prospects to attend a sales presentation.

Exhibit 12.10

Comparison of Quality Establishments on Gran Canaria

	Establishment Name			
	Montemarina Apartments	*Steigenberger La Canaria*	*Cala Blanca*	*Anfi Beach Club*
Type	High-quality apartments	5-star hotel	Apartments/Penthouse	Apartments/Penthouse
Accommodation	Apartments on ownership	Rooms on rent	Time-share	Time-share
Total # units	199 rooms	220 rooms	93	150
Prices (average)	$160,000 to $200,000	$1,000/week/person*	$11,040/week	$12,895/week
Annual dues	$2,700	N/A	$232/week owned	$257/week owned
Unit size in square meters (m²)	66 to 200 m²	40 to 103 m²	N/A	73 to 171 m²
Possible length of stay	Permanent	Daily	Weekly	Weekly
Services				
Restaurants/Bars	X	X	X	X
Discotheque	<3 km	<3 km	<1 km	<3 km
Grocery Store/Supermarket	X	<500 m	X	X
Other shops	X	X	0	X

Laundry	X	X	X	X
Child-care facility	0	X	X	X
Fax	X	X	0	X
Conference facilities	0	X	0	0
Parking	X	X	X	X
Linen/towels change	Can be rented	X	3 times/week	3 times/week
Cleaning	Can be rented	Daily	Daily	Daily
Room service	0	X	0	0
Travel services	Air/car/excursions	Air/car/excursions	Air/car/excursions	Air/car/excursions
Power and electricity	At cost	No extra charge	Included in maintenance	Included in maintenance
*Outdoor Facilities***				
Golf course	0	0	<28 km	<15 km
Outdoor pool	X	X	X	X
Tennis	X (1 court)	X (2 courts)	X (paddle tennis— 1 court)	X (6 courts)
Water sports	<500 m	0	<5 km	X
Fishing	<500 m	<500 m	<5 km	X
Beach	<500 m	X	<1 km	X
Marina	0	0	0	X

X = on-site; 0 = not available; m = meters; km = kilometers.

* European plan (no meals included).

** Not all facilities listed

337

Anfi planned to use essentially three programs: off-site marketing, on-site marketing as well as other direct-marketing programs. Off-site marketing involved the placement of advertisements in credit card magazines that would lead to minivacations at the Anfi Beach Club. On-site marketing involved various OPC (Off Premise Canvasser) programs with the objective of inviting prospective buyers to a sales presentation on the grounds of Anfi. Exhibit 12.11 provides an overview of the different programs.

With regard to the usage of minivacations, Sørensen said: "Düsseldorf is the major charter airport in Germany and caters to areas around it that are within a one-hour driving distance. These areas have a total population of around 16 million." The idea was to get the customer down on a spontaneous unplanned vacation for a weekend. A flight would cost the customer around DM820 ($497)[4] from Düsseldorf, Germany. Anfi was also trying to negotiate wholesale prices through RCI Germany and Suntours Reisen (a travel agency in Düsseldorf). Once the potential customers arrived in Gran Canaria, they would be lodged in surrounding resorts. Anfi was negotiating a favorable deal with the Steigenberger La Canaria Hotel until Anfi had sufficient capacity of its own. As part of the offer, the customer would be asked to take a tour of Anfi. They would be taken to the site on one of the days they were there for a sales presentation.

Apart from these were the OPCs, who would be canvassing for clients at street corners, shopping centers, hotels, beaches, and places of tourist interest. Around 25 OPCs would be actively canvassing to bring in clients. They were to be supervised by the Marketing Manager, Mark Robinson, who had three years' experience in time-sharing and in his previous job worked with John MacDonald, the Sales Director. There were plans to entice clients to come to the sales presentation by giving gifts such as walkman radios, sunglasses, suntan kits, baseball caps, and clock radios, among others. OPC training on the sales script and courteousness normally lasted one to two days. OPCs were paid through commission[5] on how many qualified clients (ups)[6] they brought in. MacDonald was thinking

---

[4] The cost of an Iberia flight from Barcelona or Madrid to Gran Canaria was about $650 in the summer of 1992. Cost of a flight from the United Kingdom varied from $184 to $460.

[5] OPCs would be paid about $110 per client brought in.

[6] A qualified "up" is a person who is willing to go to a sales presentation. This person must be between the ages of 25 and 65 years and, if married or living together, must be accompanied by the spouse or partner. A person who is single is known as a "one-legged" and does not qualify for the sales presentation.

Exhibit 12.11
Marketing Techniques

Off-site Marketing

Credit card magazines	Advertisements are to be placed in the American Express and Diners Club magazines. The advertisements contain a return postcard that invites interested readers for a minivacation at the Anfi Beach Club. Research has shown that a credit card advertisement is four times more likely to be read than a normal ad.
Minivacations	The minivacation at the Anfi Beach Club will be arranged at the interested credit cardholder's home country. Within a few days of the receipt of the return postcard, an employee of Anfi will call to arrange a weekend visit to Gran Canaria.

On-site Marketing

Flowers	Well-dressed OPCs will hand out flowers to people in up-market restaurants, with an invitation attached to the stem of the flower to visit Anfi for a sales presentation, and the opportunity to see a new way of vacationing in Gran Canaria.
Beach	The beach in front of the Anfi site will have various water sports that will attract clients from surrounding hotels. These prospects will be approached when on the beach for a presentation at Anfi.
Photo	Clients are photographed in restaurants and invited to Anfi to pick up their pictures the next day, and at the same time to attend an Anfi sales presentation

Other Direct-Marketing Programs

Las Palmas	Juan Francisco Hernández, a native of Gran Canaria with years of experience in real estate, in charge of this program said, "A resident of Gran Canaria has sun, sea, and sand, all through the year. For me to sell the time-share program to residents here is going to be a challenge. The USP [unique selling proposition] is certainly the opportunity to exchange holidays." He plans to invite a select group of people to Anfi over the weekend, with a one-night free stay in La Canaria. They will go through the sales presentation the next day.

Exhibit 12.11 *(continued)*

Deep Sea Fishing	Bjorn Lyng's yacht *Charlotte* (a princess 450) will be used to invite a select group of clients for a day of deep-sea fishing, after which they will be taken on-site for a sales presentation.
Pegasus	The *Pegasus* is a schooner owned by Wolfgang von Schwarzenfeld, who has lived in Gran Canaria for many years. He runs day trips on his schooner for tourists. Through the years he has collected a database of 18,000 addresses of people who have (to some extent repeatedly) come to Gran Canaria and made day trips with him. Anfi plans to market through the database that von Schwarzenfeld has developed, in addition to distributing printed invitations for sales presentations to the clients on his fishing trips.
Rent a Car	Clients will be offered a one-day free rental if they visit Anfi for a sales presentation. The car rental agency will advise tourists who rent a car that they can have one day's rental fee waived if they agree to participate in a sales presentation about a new holiday concept.

of qualifying clients by "A" client and "B" client and basing the commission for OPCs accordingly.

OPCs in Tenerife, another of the Canary Islands, had a bad image, as some of them had forcefully brought in clients, continuously and repeatedly soliciting people who at first were uninterested. Furthermore, the large number of resorts in Tenerife increased the possibility of a tourist being solicited by OPCs very frequently throughout the day. This created an image of OPCs as being rough handlers and a disturbance to the tourists who were peacefully enjoying their vacation. Due to this fact, the promoters of Anfi were reluctant to have OPCs in their resort. Sørensen was aware of the problems OPCs had created in other resort areas. A report by the U.K. Director General of Fair Trading had been previously published. This report was prepared because the Office of Fair Trading[7] had received several letters of complaint from British tourists taking holidays in Spain.

[7] Office of Fair Trading, "A Report of the Director General of Fair Trading" (London, 1990).

Two such complaints follow:

> We think we were stopped around 100 times in three weeks. There were always two working together, either on a scooter, in a car or on foot. They ran across main roads to us, stopped us in our cars in the middle of main roads. The people on the street said they received between £40–£50 for every couple they sent, as long as they spent 35 minutes in the complex. They all said you only needed to stay for about 30–45 minutes, but when you reached the complex, they said you would have to be prepared to stay for one to one-and-a-half hours, but a lot of times it was at least two hours. [Mrs. F]

> Being stopped was bad enough, but they would not take no for an answer. They pleaded with you, promised you free champagne, lunches, taxis there and back, anything just to get you to go and visit their time-share development. They admitted quite freely that they were not interested in whether you bought or not. They got their commission as long as you attended. [Mr. H]

Sørensen added the following:

> I know it is difficult to run an OPC operation well. Most resorts with heavy emphasis on OPCs have also fairly high cancellation rates. This reduces net profits after all costs and taxes have been accounted for. Actually, costs of running OPCs will be increasing further as we go into the second year. There is a problem in finding qualified OPCs, not to mention the problems we have with them once they work for us. But there are no alternatives in the short run. Until offsite works, at least one more year will go by. Until then, we need a strong OPC program. We will dress all OPCs in Anfi del Mar uniforms, and we will train them so that they will not be a nuisance to the tourists and so that the solicitations will be done in a courteous manner. Bjorn's white-and-gold-plated Rolls Royce will be used to help the Anfi OPC activities, in order to position the Anfi Beach Club at the top end of the market, where it belongs. I believe this will have strong symbolic value.

ANFI SALES TEAM

"We will have a range of nationalities working in our sales organization," said John MacDonald, the Sales Director for Anfi. Under him would be the line managers responsible for each nationality. They would be English,

Dutch, Scandinavian, Spanish, and German. Each would be responsible for a line of salespeople of the same nationality who would be selling to prospective clients in their mother tongue. In July 1992, there were six salespeople; this was expected to grow to 30 when the 150 time-share apartments went up for sale in October 1992. The sales organization chart is shown in Exhibit 12.12.

The Sales Presentation

Imagine meeting a couple of complete strangers, and after two and a half hours you ask them to buy a product that costs about $12,000 and expect them to say yes.

Exhibit 12.12
Organizational Chart: Anfi Beach Marketing & Sales, Ltd.

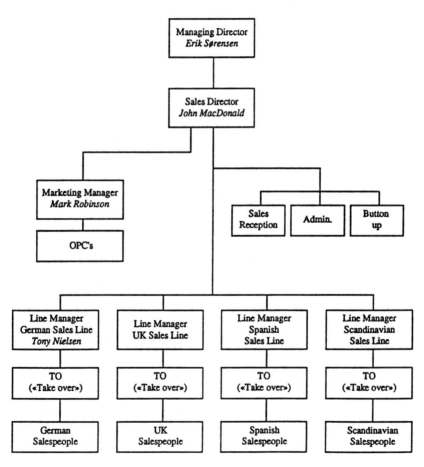

MacDonald, who had four-and-a-half years' experience time-sharing, commented.

> In order to do a good selling job, we need to make the right impact when the client comes in to see the resort. It is very rare that we have a "be-back customer" (those who come back to buy later). Thus, the objective is to try and close the deal at the end of the sales presentation. The client comes into the resort with the OPC and is introduced to the receptionist, who then qualifies the client to make sure they are in a position to buy. Then the salesperson takes them over to the sales area.[8]

Sørensen said that at this point in time the salesperson told the couple that he (the salesperson) would ask them (the couple) at the end of the presentation to purchase the product, and this is known as "breaking the pact," as the couple will have told themselves in their minds that they are not going to buy and the salesperson tries to break this pact by saying so. There are four phases in the sales presentation: warm up, discovery, presentation, and closing.

Said MacDonald, "We have a different warm-up area and closing area, as we call it, as the last thing you want is someone having the concept getting explained to them, hearing someone else who is buying, saying yes or no, or getting prices, as you do not want that until the very end."

The Process The first phase, the warm-up phase, is when the client is made to relax. Until the client feels that he can sympathize with and relate to the salesperson, the warm up is not complete. Soon thereafter, in the discovery phase, the salesperson tries to make the client talk about himself, about his likes, dislikes, and interests, by asking open-ended questions, trying to find out information about the client. MacDonald continued, "The next stage is explaining the concept and how time-sharing works, since some people have confused ideas about time-sharing." Using the information gathered in the discovery phase, the product is presented in such a manner as to help the client see the values of the product and how they will help meet his personal

---

[8] Salespersons were paid on a commission basis, approximately 11 percent of the amount of the sale.

goals. The presentation follows: the couple find themselves walking into the video room where they watch a videocassette on RCI and the exchange program. This lasts about 10 minutes, after which, MacDonald continued, "The couple is taken around the resort first and then the apartment, and really building the excitement and the emotion during that time, that is when we want to have the impact. This is so important as we have only got about five or 10 minutes doing this." Soon thereafter, they are taken to the closing area.

In the closing area the clients' misunderstandings are flushed out, by the client asking questions and receiving empathetic, clear, and concise answers from the salesperson. "We explain the financial logic to them as compared to going on package holidays and try to get the commitment from them," said MacDonald. "At this point of time, we bring in the TO[9] [person who Takes Over to close the deal], who negotiates the prices.[10] Then it's a matter of getting them to say yes and closing the deal." A kind of excitement is created in this area to give special feeling. Champagne bottles are opened when someone buys. There is a certain buzz floating around. "When someone else buys, the client knows that another week has gone, and he may feel that if he waits too long, he might not get his apartment."

MacDonald continued.

> Once the client has said yes, the couple signs the contract with the Button-Up manager (also known as the Completions Manager, paid on salary basis), who tries to make sure that the salesperson has done his job, that the couple is happy with what they have bought, that they understand the concept, and that they have not been lied to or misled in any way. That is the final part, and the couple signs to that effect. We invite them to the barbecue on the site, give them their gifts, and then they go home, and we hope that they will come back to the site for the barbecue when they are on the island, to sort out any more queries they may have and meet with others like them who have bought time-share too.

[9] Paid on commission basis.

[10] The industry calculates a closing percentage to determine the performance of salespersons and TOs. The closing percentage is calculated as the number of sales divided by the number of tours taken. Ten percent is taken by the industry to be the average net closing percentage, and on average a salesperson sells 1.7 weeks to a couple.

After Sales Service

"The time-share buyer buys a dream and a few days later, when back in his home, may think 'Oh my God! What commitment have I made?'" said MacDonald. "That's why the follow-up is so important." Anfi would give, as a gift to new time-share owners, a day trip on the private yacht *Pegasus.* This was to serve as a buyer's remorse instrument, to reinforce the buying decision through the quality of this day trip out to view the Anfi site from the sparkling waters of the Mediterranean. MacDonald continued, "When the time-share buyer gets back home, the salesperson sends him a postcard and calls him regularly to continue the relationship. We send flowers and a video of the resort, as we do not want them to cancel their purchase after a few weeks."[11]

Sales Projections

Anfi would start selling on October 1, 1992, with four apartments completed. Sixteen apartments would be finished by February 1993, 50 by May, and the remaining apartments were planned to be finished in batches of 50 by May and July of 1994. By mid-1994, Anfi would have 150 apartments on a time-share. The prices for the apartments were not yet finalized but Exhibit 12.13 presents estimates. The average price would be around $12,895 per week.

By December 1994, Anfi expected to have sold 6,240 weeks of the available 7,500, as shown in Exhibit 12.14.

MANAGEMENT TEAM MEETING, JULY 1992

Sørensen's final remarks in the presentation of his marketing and sales program were:

> We have a superb product. We know how to build complex resorts. We know that the target group is out there. We know how to communicate with them. Each of the markets presents us with a different marketing challenge, but between them there is a total market of over 150

[11] The law on the rescission period is 14 days for local buyers and 28 days for foreign buyers.

Exhibit 12.13
Apartment Prices and Weeks

Weeks budgeted for sale	Super Red*	Red	White	Total
One-bedroom apartment	1,133	2,078	1,511	4,722
Two-bedroom apartment (type 1)	40	74	54	168
Two-bedroom apartment (type 2)	182	334	244	760
Studios	40	74	54	168
Penthouse	101	186	135	422
Pricing per unit/week ($)	Super Red*	Red	White	Average
One-bedroom apartment	13,752	11,460	9,168	11,277
Two-bedroom apartment (type 1)	19,253	16,044	12,835	15,777
Two-bedroom apartment (type 2)	21,453	17,878	14,302	17,586
Studios	12,123	10,237	8,190	10,028
Penthouse	27,504	22,920	18,336	22,550

* School holidays.

million consumers, and in each country there are a number of families who are waiting for our product. There seems to be every opportunity for success.

"O.K., O.K.," remarked Bjorn Lyng:

This sounds to me all fine and good. I have put a lot of money into this project. I also believe that you have done an outstanding job with the

Exhibit 12.14
Sales Projections

Month/Year	12/92	04/93	12/93	12/94
Apartments finished	4	16	50	150
Weeks available*	200	800	2,500	7,500
Expected cumulative weeks sold	80	400	2,040	6,240

* The apartments would remain closed for repair and maintenance two weeks of the year.

design of the marketing activities. But I cannot help myself wondering whether there are enough people interested in visiting Anfi del Mar. I calculate that we need to show about 30,000 couples this resort, and, if 10 percent buy, we will achieve the sales objectives by December of 1994. I have lived a long time on this island, and there are not that many people visiting of the kind I want to have in the resort. We don't want to have just anyone buy at Anfi. This has to be the most exclusive vacation club in Gran Canaria.

"You're right, Bjorn," replied Sørensen.

That's why I have begun to plan for our off-site marketing activities. We will not accept just anyone or anybody. This will be a vacation club for some very fine people.

I think that the bulk of couples who visit Anfi del Mar will be generated through on-site marketing activities. My experience in other resorts tells me that off-site marketing will never generate a significant and steady flow of tours, unless you run massive operations in each country, which are extremely costly.

"Besides they take a long time to be set up," added MacDonald. During this discussion about the generation of tour flows, Finance Director Fernandez became increasingly nervous. He interjected,

Frankly, from my point of view, I don't care very much for the steady flow of tours. I only care about one flow and that is cash flow. It seems illogical to turn someone away because he does not seem to "fit" into the club. As long as the couple's pockets are deep enough, I would say we take the money. In fact, as always we need to finance our marketing and sales activities from the cash we take in. In the time-share business, you make money on the last 20 percent of your inventory, so goes the saying. If we think today that there is a potential shortfall in the number of tours, I would suggest that we substantially increase the price per interval week. This would do good for the cash flow. It seems to me that we can always reduce the price later on if it doesn't work out.

"I agree with you," said Mr. Lyng. "People of class don't look at the prices that much. They are buying something they like, despite the price."

"No, no, no! My salespeople will not be able to justify an increased price," said MacDonald firmly. "Remember that we explain to every potential buyer the financial logic during the closing phase of the tour. It would be hard to justify the value of a time-share purchase relative to other ways of coming down to Gran Canaria and taking vacation here."

The meeting was adjourned without agreement on specifics. Sørensen promised to study the question of increasing the price levels. He would spend the next several months analyzing and rethinking his marketing-and-sales program with respect to the key issues that came up during the meeting: Will the current marketing program generate a sufficient flow of tours in the defined target market for Anfi del Mar to achieve its sellout projection? Assuming only on-site marketing activities, will there be a sufficient number of tours, per month and per week? Given that off-site marketing activities will be added, can potential and interested buyers be invited to visit Anfi del Mar at a reasonable cost? As he walked down the hall to his office, he wondered about his own words: "There seems to be every opportunity for success."

Case Thirteen

Eagle Crest Country Club

D. Michael Fields and Allen D. Schaefer

As Tom Ridell walked up to the ninth green on an unusually warm January afternoon, he glanced over to the bulldozers in the distance defining the fairways of what would soon be the back nine. He was looking forward to the coming season, when he could offer public golfers in the Springfield, Missouri area a new 18-hole course. Tom considered the amount of play the front nine had recorded in its first year and concluded that the course was the area's best-kept secret. With the additional investment in the physical facilities that he was making, he knew he would soon have to make sure the secret got out or he would have no chance of achieving his objective of retiring his $168,000 debt by the end of the third year. For the moment, however, he turned his attention to a 20-foot birdie putt.

COURSE HISTORY

Eagle Crest Country Club was located in Republic, a small town of 6,200 that was located immediately to the south of Springfield, Missouri, a city of 140,000. As one Republic car dealer prominently advertised on the Springfield media, "Republic is one minute south of Springfield at 360 miles per hour!" The course, which was located on a farm road three miles from the major highway (U.S. 60) that went through Republic, was approximately 25 minutes from downtown Springfield (see Exhibit 13.1).

This case was written by D. Michael Fields and Allen D. Schaefer, Southwest Missouri State University. Used by permission. Copyright © 1993 by the *Case Research Journal*, D. Michael Fields, and Allen D. Schaefer.

Exhibit 13.1

Locations of Eagle Crest Golf Club and Nine Competitive Facilities

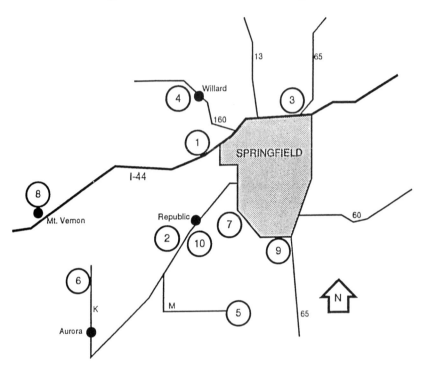

```
 1. Deer Lake Golf Course
 2. Eagle Crest Golf Club
 3. Grandview Municipal Golf Course
 4. Greene Hills Country Club
 5. Hidden Valley Golf Course
 6. Honey Creek Golf Course
 7. Horton Smith Municipal Golf Course
 8. Mt. Vernon Municipal Golf Course
 9. Siler's Shady Grove Golf Course
10. Tri-Way Golf Club
```

The course had evolved as a solution to a land-use decision for acreage that Ridell had acquired. "As a developer, my initial plan was to develop an exclusive residential area with its own private landing strip," noted Tom. However, a subsequent study indicated that the only area acceptable for a runway would not support one that was the length that Tom considered necessary. "That forced me to explore other options. Being a lifelong golfer, I felt that this area needed another public course. The subsequent report prepared by the National Golf Federation (NGF) seemed to justify that," explained Ridell.

The initial nine holes had been completed just prior to the first season. Those nine measured 3,460 yards and featured two holes with sand traps and some for which a water hazard came into play. However, the attractiveness of the layout was hampered by the lack of trees to help differentiate one hole from another. "We have heard comments to the effect that the course is like playing golf in a big field," admitted Ridell, "and if we don't keep the fairways well cut, then the holes do seem to run together." To better define the course, 100 trees had been planted on the front nine. However, they were all very young and would take several years to mature.

"We were very fortunate and were able to reduce construction costs. Because of the high quality of the topsoil on the land, which retains moisture so well, we did not have to establish an underground watering system for the fairways. We do anticipate adding it at some point in the future, but at least it was an expense that we could defer," explained Ridell. This and other savings—such as using existing structures on the property and trading other properties for necessary work—meant that Ridell had been able to construct the front nine with little debt. The recent debt had been taken on to complete the back nine.

The course was designed as a public course. That is, anyone who paid the green fee could play the course without having a membership to the club. "We never considered developing a membership-only course," explained Ridell. "We will have memberships, and that is a revenue source that we wish to expand, but the majority of our players will be golfers who will pay only daily fees," he continued.

In southwest Missouri the 240-day golf season stretches from mid-March until mid-November. However, it was not unusual for 320 or more days per year to be considered acceptable for golf. "It's been my experience that roughly 90 percent of your annual play occurs during the usual playing season," said Ridell. The course had recorded 4,680 rounds of golf in its first year. (See Exhibit 13.2 for projected revenue and information.)

"A nine-hole course operates at a disadvantage," explained Ridell. "The average golfer wants to play 18 holes, and if you've only got a nine-hole course, then golfers are forced to play each hole twice as opposed to playing 18 different holes. The back nine will take care of that." He

Exhibit 13.2
Actual and Projected Revenue and Expense Data for Eagle Crest

	First Year Actual	*Second Year Projected*
	Revenue	
Memberships	None	Equivalent of 10 full-year memberships at $500 each; each member would average 65 18-hole rounds per year.
Green fees	10% of players played only nine holes	Same
Carts	5% of players rented pull carts $1 each	Pull-cart rate to remain constant; 25% of players to rent motorized carts, 90% of these would be rented by two players who would share cost.
Food	$3 average per player	With liquor license, expected average of $5 per player.
Pro shop	None	$2 per player
	Expenses	
Salary	$16,800	$16,800
Property taxes	$5,120 ($400,000 valuation)	$8,960 ($700,000 valuation)
Cost of goods sold (food)	35%	33% with liquor license
Pro shop	None	Cost of goods sold, 60%
Advertising	$1,800 total	$400 per month
Depreciation	Building, $3,000 Equipment, $5,000 Furniture and fixtures, $500 Other, $200	Same, plus $3,000 power golf carts
Course maintenance	$2,000 per month	Labor, $37,500 Chemicals and seed, $5,400 Utilities, $2,400 Repair on fixed assets, $1,000

continued: "Also, the back nine will have more personality. The terrain is more hilly, there are more trees, each hole will have a sand trap, and a lake we have constructed will come into play on four separate holes."

Most nine-hole courses were located in rural areas. Demand and competition were the factors that most often dictated course size. The trade-off for the additional nine holes was the obvious increased construction and maintenance costs.

Scott Puryear, a local sports columnist, profiled Eagle Crest in his column. In that column he noted, "If you'll enter a round at Eagle Crest with an open mind, what you'll find is a course still in the growing stages, as the sometimes shaggy greens and a couple of rugged tee boxes will suggest." The tone of the piece was generally favorable, as Puryear felt that course maturity would take care of most of the problems, and he wrote that the course was "challenging and interesting to play." He also noted that the course had not had time to develop a following among the local golfing public.

A sample of area golfers indicated that only 5 percent were aware of Eagle Crest and approximately 1 percent had actually played the course. "We're seriously underutilized," noted Ridell, "and I guess that's great for the golfers we serve because they do not have to wait." He continued: "But we have got to reach more golfers because right now 80 percent of our business is from repeat golfers." At least a portion of the golfers that Tom hoped to reach were students at one of Springfield's numerous institutions of higher learning. Enrollment at these schools was over 22,500.

Ridell had spent $21,000 to purchase a fleet of 10 motorized golf carts for rental in the second year. Because of the flatness of the front nine, Ridell anticipated that 18 percent of the golfers would rent carts. With the completion of the more hilly back nine, Ridell projected that the percentage renting these carts would increase to 25 percent. Each of these gasoline-powered carts could service up to two 18-hole rounds per day.

One of the difficulties associated with determining the degree of success (that is, profitability) of the course—both for the present and the future—was Ridell's present bookkeeping system. The golf club had not been set up as a separate business; both the revenue and the expenses had been included with those of Ridell's surveying and developing business.

As a result, for the first year the determination of revenue and expenses for Eagle Crest could only be estimated. Tom had taken some action to insure that in the future the financial information for the golf club would be segregated so that its true profitability could be determined.

THE COMPETITION

There were nine courses within a 30-minute drive of Eagle Crest that the public could play (see Exhibit 13.1). Deer Lake, Siler's, Grandview, and Horton Smith were all located in Springfield. Grandview and Horton Smith were municipally owned. Those, plus Tri-Way (in Republic), Honey Creek (in Aurora), Hidden Valley (in Boaz), Greene Hills (in Willard), and Mount Vernon Municipal Course, comprised the competition (see Exhibit 13.3 for a comparative analysis). Tri-Way, Honey Creek, Mount Vernon were nine-hole courses; the others had eighteen holes.

Several of the competitors were committed to making significant improvements to their courses. Some had already made changes. A recent article, "Golf in the Ozarks," appearing in the local newspaper highlighted the following improvements.

- Grandview: Reconstructed three greens and built new tee boxes (the area from which a golfer takes the first shot) on two holes.
- Horton Smith: Rebuilt two tee boxes, moved and improved their driving range, and are considering adding a "Cayman Course" (a smaller-sized golf course for the younger player).
- Tri-Way: Rebuilt two new tee boxes and are planning to rebuild another.
- Siler's: Adding more cart trails, one sand trap, and wooden tee markers on each hole.
- Greene Hills: Enlarged four greens and have plans to improve several sand traps in the spring.
- Hidden Valley: Improved several water hazards, constructed a new tee box, and resodded several tee boxes.

Exhibit 13.3

Comparative Course Analysis: First Year

Course	Fee Weekday/Weekend ($)		Cart Fees/Person ($)		Percentage Using Carts	Estimated Annual Rounds	Annual Maintenance	Playing Distance (Yards)	Members	Amenities
	9 Holes	18 Holes	9 Holes	18 Holes						
Deer Lake	6.00/7.00	11.00/13.00	8.50	17.00	N/A	35,000	$350,000*	7,001	N/A	A,B,D,E,H
Eagle Crest	6.00/6.00	10.00/10.00	9.00	16.00	18	4,680	$24,000	3,410 7,000		A,D,F,I
Grandview	4.25/5.00	7.00/8.00**	9.00	16.00	17	62,000	$190,000†	6,102	248	B,D,F
Greene Hills	—	10.00/12.00	—	16.00	80††	22,500	$75,000†	6,199	330	A,B,C,D,F,G,H
Hidden Valley	9.00/9.00	12.00/12.00	8.00	16.00	50	32,000	$90,000†	6,963	100	D,F,G
Honey Creek	6.00/7.00	6.00/7.00	7.00	14.00	15	23,500	$85,000†	3,180	450	A,B,C,D,F
Horton Smith	4.00/4.00	6.50/7.50**	8.00	14.00	13	53,000	$145,000	5,687	248	B,D,F
Mount Vernon	3.50/4.00	6.00/7.50	7.00	13.00	10	16,000	$54,500	2,986	136	D,F
Siler's	5.00/5.00	8.00/10.00	8.50	17.00	35	32,000	N/A	5,320	30	D,F
Tri-Way	9.00/11.00	9.00/11.00	—	—	95††	10,000	$30,000	3,269	113	A,B,D

* First-year estimate.

** Special senior citizens and junior rates.

† Estimated.

†† Members have personal carts stored at the course.

Amenities: A = clubhouse, B = driving range, C = locker rooms, D = pro shop, E = restaurant, F = snack bar, G = swimming pool, H = tennis courts, I = health equipment.

355

THE NATIONAL GOLF FEDERATION STUDY

The Springfield Park Board had commissioned a feasibility study by the NGF to help determine whether it should pursue building an additional municipally owned course in the greater Springfield area. The proposed course was projected to be a "high-quality" course for the public golfer. The report had been completed two years before. Based in part on its findings, the board moved forward and the city prepared a bond issue that would ultimately be totally retired from revenues from the course, but the voters soundly defeated the bond issue. The park board had made no apparent additional efforts to construct the course. The NGF study, although dated, was a matter of public record, and Ridell was able to secure a copy for his use.

The NGF report cited certain "course selection" characteristics, which had first been noted in an earlier NGF research document entitled "Golf Consumer Profile." Among these were:

- On the average, golfers travel about 10 miles one way to play at a golf course (translating into a 17-minute trip to the average golfer's most-often-played course).
- Average golfers report a willingness to travel 30 miles (41 minutes) for an occasional round of golf.

The report also cited the following statistics (from the NGF's *Golf Participation in the United States*):

- Missouri had a 7.8 percent participation rate.
- Almost 74 percent of golfers were public golfers.
- The average number of rounds played annually by a public golfer was 12.8.

As part of its study, the NGF had considered three sites for the proposed course. One of the three was within five miles of Eagle Crest, and therefore much of the analysis of this site was directly applicable to Eagle Crest. Exhibit 13.4 gives a participation analysis for this site, and Exhibit 13.5 relates participation information to household income.

Exhibit 13.4

Market Area Population and Participation for Public Golfers. [From National Golf Federation Study, September 1989.]

Age	Percent of Population*	Percent Playing Golf**	Average No. of Public Rounds/Golfer**
5–11	10.46	2.1	5.8
12–17	8.97	10.8	10.8
18–24	13.51	17.0	8.7
25–34	18.05	17.1	9.0
35–44	15.12	15.9	12.5
45–54	10.59	13.6	14.6
55–64	8.94	13.2	21.7
65–74	7.87	9.4	21.6
75+	6.49	1.3	6.1

* The 1989 population over 4 was 251,724; the estimated 1994 population over age 4 was 270,844.
** Participation percentages and average round projections were based on NGF estimates for the west/north-central region of the United States.

Exhibit 13.5

Market Area Income Distribution and Potential Golfer Population Participation. [From National Golf Federation Study, September 1989.]

Household Income ($)	Household Population	Percent Playing Golf*	Average No. of Public Rounds/Golfer*
0–9,999	56,671	3.5	6.5
10,000–14,999	28,335	6.8	14.6
15,000–24,999	54,464	10.3	11.6
25,000–34,999	42,984	12.8	10.7
35,000–49,999	44,029	18.5	15.5
50,000–74,999	23,926	21.2	11.9
75,000+	10,818	20.0	7.6

* Participation percentages and average round projections were based on NGF estimates for the west/north-central region of the United States.

The NGF study included consultants' analyses of the area's courses. Selected excerpts from these observations for Eagle Crest and its nine competitors are given below.

Deer Lake The course . . . utilizes four sets of tees for a variety of lengths and appears to be a good layout to challenge all levels of golfers. The course will have double row irrigation to provide good water coverage. . . . The course will also feature a lighted driving range.

Eagle Crest According to local sources, the course was previously a hayfield and minimal amounts of money are being spent to develop the property. . . . This course is not expected to have much impact on the local golf market based upon the quality of construction.

Grandview The course is maintained fairly well, even with the amount of play it receives. There is a sufficient amount of tree cover that comes into play as well as greenside bunkers. There are no fairway bunkers on the course and a minimal amount of water. . . .

Greene Hills The layout appears to be relatively interesting and slightly hilly on a parcel with moderate to semiheavy tree cover. There is little use of water hazards and no fairway bunkers. There are a moderate number of greenside bunkers on the course. The bent grass greens appear to be in good shape, but the majority of the maintenance effort appears to be average.

Hidden Valley Several of the holes are next to the James River and there are other lakes and streams on the property that come into play. The layout appears to be interesting with large amounts of tree cover. The greens [look] to be in good shape, but other parts of the course [need] improvement in the quality of maintenance.

Honey Creek The facility is quite hilly and provides a good layout. While there are not many sand traps, there is a large amount of tree cover and some water hazards. The course appeared to be maintained in good shape and the greens were exceptionally nice.

Horton Smith This . . . facility stays extremely busy throughout the year. Due to its relatively short length, it is popular with senior citizens and junior players. . . . The level of maintenance on the course would be perceived as fair. This is partially due to the irrigation system covering only greens and tees. There are virtually no hazards on the course with the exception of tree cover, which comes into play.

Mt. Vernon This . . . facility appears to be a relatively interesting layout. The course has ample tree cover, a fair number of sand traps, but minimal water hazards. The property is somewhat hilly, which helps the layout of the course. The facility was maintained in a fair manner.

Siler's The . . . course is quite hilly with a relatively short layout. Water hazards are found only on two holes and there is limited tree cover. Additionally, very few bunkers are utilized on the course. The maintenance on the facility appears to be just fair.

Tri-Way The facility is an interesting layout, with water coming into play on three holes. There are a fair number of greenside bunkers, but no fairway traps. The course is maintained in an average manner with fair greens. . . . Approximately 80 percent of the annual rounds are played by the members of the course.

In addition, the consultants, in consideration of 18-hole courses, concluded that Horton Smith, Grandview, and Siler's were relatively comparable. They also felt that the upper-end public golfers in the area were served by Hidden Valley, Greene Hills, and Deer Lake.

THE MEDIA

The Springfield market provided Tom Ridell with what could be considered a traditional array of options to allocate the promotional dollars for Eagle Crest. Among the media options were circulated print media, radio, television, outdoor advertising, and direct mail.

Circulated Print Media

Springfield was served by one daily newspaper (*Springfield News-Leader*), a biweekly business publication (*Springfield Business Journal*), a weekly shopper (*Pennypower*), a monthly magazine (*Springfield Magazine*), and the *Republic Monitor,* a weekly newspaper. Circulation and advertising rate data are included in Exhibits 13.6 and 13.7, respectively.

Springfield News-Leader The *Springfield News-Leader* claimed to reach daily 36 percent of the city's 18 to 24 year olds, 42 percent of people 25

Exhibit 13.6

Black-and-White Open Advertising Rates for Springfield Publications ($)

Publication	1	3/4	2/3	1/2	1/3	1/4	1/6	1/8	1/12	1/16
					Fraction of Page					
Pennypower	700	N/A	N/A	395	N/A	212	N/A	125	N/A	65
Springfield Business Journal	756	681	N/A	526	N/A	373	N/A	198	N/A	N/A
Springfield Magazine	800	N/A	575	530	380	N/A	275	N/A	175	N/A
Springfield News-Leader (daily)	3,418	N/A	N/A	1,987	1,658	1,328	986	644	482	320
Republic Monitor	280	N/A	N/A	142	N/A	71	N/A	35	N/A	17

Exhibit 13.7
Readership of Springfield Area Publications

Publication	Circulation	Readers Per Copy
News-Leader	60,000	2.1
Springfield Business Journal	5,000	7.0
Springfield Magazine	10,000	18.3
Pennypower	135,000	2.0
Republic Monitor	2,500	2.2

to 34, 52 percent of people 35 to 49, 64 percent of people 50 to 64, and 67 percent of people over 65 years of age. Percentages of readership were 13 percent for ages 18 to 24, 17 percent for ages 25 to 34, 28 percent for ages 35 to 49, 20 percent for ages 50 to 64, and 22 percent for ages 65+. Individuals with household incomes greater than $35,000 comprised 36 percent of the *News-Leader*'s subscribers.

Springfield Business Journal   Males accounted for 67 percent of the readership, and 43 percent of the readers were between the ages of 35 and 49. Average household annual income for the *Business Journal* exceeded $40,000.

Pennypower   *Pennypower,* a local shopper, claimed to have a 98 percent penetration rate in Springfield and surrounding counties. However, it was widely believed that the shopper's readership consisted primarily of lower-income consumers.

Springfield Magazine   *Springfield Magazine* claimed that 75 percent of subscribers held college or university degrees, 60 percent earned more than $40,000 per year, and 94 percent were professionals, managers, and/or owners of their own businesses.

Republic Monitor   The *Republic Monitor* was subscribed to by 90 percent of Republic's households.

Radio

A number of radio stations served the Springfield market. Exhibit 13.8 shows the demographic reach of those stations as well as the cost of a 30-second spot on each.

Television

Local television offered a potentially high reach of the Springfield population. Rates varied by program, but local television in the Springfield area usually cost around $30 per 1 percent of population reached (rating point). A 30-second spot during the area's top-rated local evening news broadcast cost approximately $450.

Local cable television offered a relatively new medium for reaching the Springfield market, one that featured a 52 percent penetration of households. Time could be purchased during specific programs on specific stations for approximately $25 per 30-second spot. Rates were lower when the station and program were not specified and when the advertiser agreed to purchase time in bulk. For example, advertisers agreeing to purchase 50 spots per month were charged $16 per 30-second spot when commercials were rotated across a variety of cable stations at varying times.

Outdoor Advertising

Outdoor advertising in the Springfield market was available through Pioneer Outdoor. The company claimed that 20 billboards strategically placed throughout the metropolitan area would allow an advertiser to reach 88 percent of the adult population daily. The cost of the 20 billboards was $5,000 monthly. Thus, $2,500 and $1,500 monthly would secure enough billboards to reach half or a quarter of the adult population daily, respectively. Single billboards at a specific site could be purchased as available, for a cost of $1,300 per month for a two-month minimum. Each two additional months in the contract reduced the cost by roughly 10 percent, down to a minimum of $675 per month.

Direct Mail

Direct-mail advertising was another avenue open to Eagle Crest. Val-Pak coupons offered an inexpensive direct-mail option for local businesses. Val-

Exhibit 13.8

Estimated Market Shares for Springfield Radio Stations

Station	Cost of 30 sec. spot ($)	Men					Women				
		18–24	25–34	35–44	45–54	55–64	18–24	25–34	35–44	45–54	55–64
KADI	15	2	4	3	4	—	19	4	4	—	—
KGBX	50	4	8	16	18	—	15	12	20	15	—
KGMY	30	4	23	7	8	—	9	9	10	17	7
KKHT	25	14	7	5	7	—	18	17	16	3	5
KLTQ	9	5	6	8	7	—	3	9	6	—	—
KTTS-AM	43	3	4	7	11	18	—	4	5	7	—
KTTS-FM	66	23	6	9	12	33	3	16	24	36	24
KTXR	17	—	8	9	10	21	—	5	6	19	43
KWTO	32	—	1	2	5	18	—	—	5	—	17
KXUS	49	45	33	13	18	—	33	24	3	3	3
KHOZ	12	—	—	—	—	10	—	—	—	—	—

Pak divided the Springfield market into 10 areas, each with a population of 10,000. Retailers could reach any number of those areas through Val-Pak, at a cost ranging from 3 to 5 cents per person reached, depending upon the number of areas selected. The cost included postage, printing, production, artwork, copywriting, and layout.

THE DECISION

Ridell's objective was to be able to retire the entire debt associated with the course in two year's time. The loan had been structured as a two-year, 10 percent, simple-interest loan. That is, at the end of the two-year period, Ridell would have to pay a total of $184,800 to eliminate the debt. It was obvious that he would need to increase the play on his course from the present level of less than 20 rounds a day. He hoped for the course to be able to average 100 rounds per day within two years. Ridell had established an upper limit of $4,800 for promotional expenses for the year to help move Eagle Crest in this direction. Although Ridell was very comfortable with the course's present pricing structure, he had promised himself to keep an open mind on pricing. Ridell was aware that the quality of his marketing plan would play a big role in determining the ultimate level of success that Eagle Crest would achieve.

Case Fourteen

The Biltmore Inn

Peter Keizer and Robert C. Lewis

Craig White, General Manager of the Biltmore Inn, was pondering the decision of whether to flag the independent hotel with a franchise brand name. Approached by a big player in the branding game, Days Inns–Canada, he had to decide if the Days brand offered what the Biltmore needed to increase occupancy. White knew that to provide an acceptable quality level to the target market, money had to be spent on renovations. The owners, however, were adverse to spending more without results. Without a commitment to spend, White was ready to leave and let the owners fend for themselves.

White had been considering numerous franchise brands but felt the Days Inn product offered the best match, if any of them did (see Exhibit 14.1). A Hotel and Food Administration graduate from the University of Guelph, Ontario, with extensive industry experience, White had gathered the necessary information on which to base his decision and to chart the path of the Biltmore's future: to brand with Days Inn, to brand with another chain, or not to brand at all.

BACKGROUND

The Biltmore Inn was situated in Guelph, Ontario, located in Canada's Technology Triangle, on one of four main access routes into the city. The city of 88,000 offered a solid and growing economic base, a highly reputed university, a vibrant downtown, and a lifestyle that fostered a strong sense

(Text continues on p. 374.)

This case was written by Peter Keizer and Robert C. Lewis, University of Guelph, Ontario. All rights reserved. All amounts are in Canadian dollars unless otherwise stated. One Canadian dollar equaled about U.S.$.715 at the time of the case.

Exhibit 14.1

Franchise Lodging Listings

Franchise	History, Plans	Franchise Costs	Services
Best Western			
Best Western Best Western International, Inc. P.O. Box 10203 6201 N. 24th Parkway Phoenix, Ariz. 85064-0203 (602) 957-4200 fax (602) 957-5575 VP Membership Development & Quality Assurance: Brian Murcott	-established 1946 in Long Beach, Calif. -122 units in Canada, 3,309 foreign -plans to add 140 North American properties in '95 in central provinces	-initial fee US$32,000 based on 100 rooms -advertising fee varies according to size and reservations delivered	-advertising/marketing -architectural design -corporate communications -design -insurance -purchasing -quality control -reservations system -staff training -supplies -technical services -worldwide sales office
Budget Host International			
Budget Host Budget Host International P.O. Box 14341 Arlington, Tex. 76094 (817) 861-6088 fax (817) 861-6089 President: Ray Sawyer	-established 1976 in Fort Worth, Tex. -2 units in Canada, 172 foreign -referral chain of independently owned and operated inns -new units planned in '95 for U.S. and Canada	-initial franchise fee US$3,500 -royalty fee US$350/unit/year, includes advertising fee -reservations system fee estimated US$20/unit/year	-advertising/marketing -directory/reservations system -purchasing -supplies

Choice Hotels Canada, Inc.

Clarion (Inns, Hotels and Resorts) Quality (Inns, Hotels and Quality by Journey's End) Comfort (Inns, Hotels and Suites and Comfort by Journey's End) Sleep Inns, Econo Lodge, Friendship Inns, Rodeway (Suites and Inns)

Choice Hotels Canada Inc.
5090 Explorer Dr.
6th Floor
Mississauga, Ont.
L4W 4T9
(905) 602-2222
fax (905) 602-6200
VP Franchise Development:
Jim Baldassari

-established in 1939
-175 units in Canada, 3,300 foreign
-estimated sales in Canada $215 million
-plans for 300 Canadian units over the next 5 years

-initial franchise fee varies from $25,000 to $75,000
-royalty fee 3% to 5% of gross room revenue
-advertising fee 1.3% of gross room revenue

-advertising/marketing
-management
-purchasing
-site location
-staff training
-supplies

Exhibit 14.1 (*continued*)

Franchise	History, Plans	Franchise Costs	Services
		Days Inns–Canada	
Days Inn Realstar Hotel Services Corp. 2 St. Clair Ave. W. Suite 700 Toronto, Ont. M4V 1L5 (416) 966-3297 fax (416) 923-5424 Director of Development and Franchise Sales: Dennis Ricci	-40 units in Canada -estimated 1994 sales $35 million	-initial franchise fee $350/room -royalty fee 5% -advertising/marketing fee 1.5% -reservations fee 2.3%	-advertising/marketing -design -purchasing -supplies -training
		First Canada Inns	
First Canada Inns First Can Hotels Inc. 1 First Canada Ct. Kingston, Ont. K7K 6W2 (613) 541-1111 fax (613) 549-5735 President: William J. Swan	-established 1987 in Kingston -12 units in Canada	-initial fee $15,000, over 50 rooms; additional $100/room -royalty fee 3% of sales -reservation fee 1% of gross sales	-advertising/marketing -development and design -group tour manual -purchasing -quality assurance audits -reservations system -sales support -training

Holiday Inn

Holiday Inn
Holiday Inn Worldwide
970 Dixon Rd., Suite 242
Toronto, Ont. M9W 1S9
(416) 674-4393
fax (416) 675-9779
Director, Franchise Sales: Doug Gamble

-established 1952 in Memphis, Tenn.
-60 units in Canada
-20 new units planned in Canada in '95

-minimum initial fee US$500/ room, or US$40,000, whichever is greater
-royalty fee 5% of room revenue
-advertising/marketing fee 1.5%
-reservation system fee 1% of room sales, plus US$6.12/ room/month

-advertising/marketing
-architectural assistance
-central purchasing
-central reservations
-inspection system
-management
-site location
-supplies
-training
-worldwide sales

Holiday Inn Express

Holiday Inn Express
Holiday Inn Worldwide
970 Dixon Rd., Suite 242
Toronto, Ont. M9W 1S9
(416) 674-4393
fax (416) 675-9779
Director, Franchise Sales: Doug Gamble

-established 1990
-16 units in Canada

-minimum initial fee US$500/ room, or US$35,000, whichever is greater
-royalty fee 5% of room revenue
-advertising/marketing fee 2%
-reservation system fee 1% of room sales, plus US$6.12/ room/month

-advertising/marketing
-architectural assistance
-central purchasing
-central reservations
-inspection system
-management
-site location
-supplies
-training
-worldwide sales

369

Exhibit 14.1 (*continued*)

Franchise	History, Plans	Franchise Costs	Services
Howard Johnson			
Howard Johnson Hotels and Restaurants Accommodex Franchise Management 940 The East Mall Etobicoke, Ont. M9B 6J7 (416) 620-4656 fax (416) 620-1697 President: Stephen H. Phillips	-35 locations in Canada, 575 foreign -plans to open 40 additional units by 1999	-initial fee $300/room -royalty fee 5% -advertising fee 1.5% -reservations fee 2.5%	-advertising/marketing -architectural assistance -central reservations system -purchasing -site location -staff training -supplies
Knights Inn			
Knights Inn, Knights Court Knights Lodging, Inc. 26650 Emery Pkwy. Cleveland, Ohio 44128 (216) 464-5055 fax (216) 464-2210 Director, Franchise Services: D.R. Benford	-established 1991 in Cleveland, Ohio -2 units in Canada, 185 foreign -continued growth in the U.S. and Canada -estimated sales revenue $149.6 million	-initial franchise fee $15,000 -royalty fee 4% -advertising fee 2% -reservation fee 2%	-advertising/marketing -management -purchasing -staff training -supplies

Ramada Franchise Canada, Ltd.

Ramada
Ramada Franchise Canada, Ltd.
89 Chestnut St.
Suite 2700
Toronto, Ont. M5G 1R1
(416) 971-6700
fax (416) 971-8015
Executive VP: Warren Adamson

-established 1969
-26 units in Canada, 800 foreign
-8-12 hotels planned for '95, planned growth in Canada to 70 locations by '99

-initial fee up to $35,000
-royalty fee 3% of room sales
-advertising fee 4% of room sales, includes reservation services, all national advertising and sales support services

-advertising/marketing
-central reservations
-purchasing
-quality assurance audits
-site location
-staff training
-worldwide directory

Super 8 Motel

Super 8 Motels Inc.
CF Hospitality Inc.
1298 Exmouth St.
Sarnia, Ont. N7S 1W6
(519) 337-5302
fax (519) 337-0543
VP, Planning and Development: Aldo Rotondi

-30 properties in Canada, 1,168 foreign
-aggressive growth in Atlantic Canada and Quebec planned for '95

-initial fee US$20,000
-royalty fee 5%
-advertising fee 2%

-advertising/marketing
-lease negotiation
-management
-purchasing
-site selection
-staff training
-supplies

Exhibit 14.1 (continued)

Franchise	History, Plans	Franchise Costs	Services
	Travelodge		
Travelodge Hotels and Resorts Ltd. Royco Hotels #5, 5940 Macleod Trail S. Calgary, Alta. T2H 2G4 (403) 259-9800 fax (403) 255-6981 Sr. Vice President: Greg Plank	-established 1935 in California -48 units in Canada, 420 foreign units -plans 30 new units in '95 in Canada, 20 new units by '98 -estimated sales in Canada $69.6 million	-initial fee negotiable -royalty fee 4% -advertising fee 2% -central reservation fee 2%	-advertising/marketing -architectural design -central reservation -lease negotiation -management -purchasing -site locations -staff training -supplies/purchasing
	Venture		
Venture Inns Venture Inns Inc. 925 Dixon Rd. Etobicoke, Ont. M9W 1J8 (416) 674-2222 fax (416) 798-0368 Senior Vice President and COO: Leon V. Manning	-established 1983 -11 units in Canada, 10 corporate owned -plans 6 new units in '95 -estimated sales $25 million	-initial fee $20,000 minimum -royalty fee 1.5% of gross room revenue, paid monthly -advertising fee 1% of gross room revenue	-advertising/marketing -architectural design -lease negotiation -purchasing/supplies -site location -staff training -staff/management

Les Auberges Wandlyn Inns

Wandlyn
Wandlyn Inns Ltd.
58 Prospect St. W.
Fredericton, N.B. E3B 5P8
(506) 452-0550
fax (506) 452-8894
President: Gary Llewellyn

-established 1956 in Fredericton
-18 in Canada, 2 foreign, 6 corporate owned
-continued expansion in eastern Canada, and northeast U.S. as opportunties occur

-initial fee $10,000
-royalty fee and advertising fee negotiable

-advertising/marketing
-architectural design
-lease negotiation
-management
-purchasing
-reservation system
-site selection
-staff training
-supplies

Note: All dollar amounts are Canadian unless indicated as US$.

373

of community. The Biltmore was a benefactor of the community's economic base and the university.

The Biltmore Inn consisted of fifty rooms of varying sizes plus one suite connection in a motel-style format and main building (see Exhibit 14.2). The main building contained guest rooms, the front desk, an administrative office, a boardroom, a licensed restaurant, and a banquet

Exhibit 14.2

Biltmore Inn's Property Layout. [From the Biltmore Inn.]

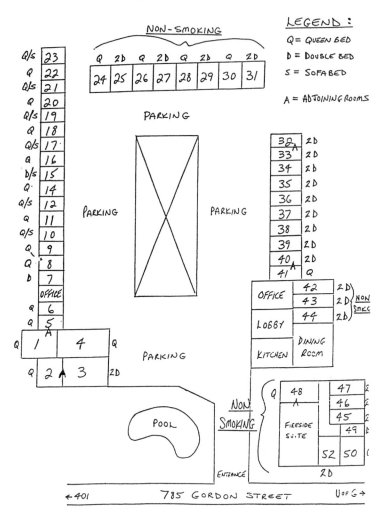

room. An outdoor pool was located across the parking lot from the main building.

White had assumed the position of General Manager at the Biltmore Inn the year before, and had overseen extensive renovations to make the property more appealing to its guests. Prior to his arrival, the Biltmore had not been maintained to industry standards for several years. In fact, it had a negative image, largely due to former guests complaining to local associates and families. The owner had let the hotel operate until it was "to the point where you could not legitimately sell a hotel room," according to White. Low occupancy levels and high capital costs contributed to a dismal financial situation. Depressed occupancy and profits left two options: "give it back to the bank" or "sink significant money back into it, renovate, and bring it back up."

An investor had been found with significant capital that he was willing to invest in the renovation of the Biltmore. His condition for investing had been the hiring of an experienced hotel manager. After extensive analysis, the owners had been convinced that the Biltmore could be a viable moneymaker, once significant renovations had been completed and proper management established by White. White had accepted the job on the condition that the owners would proceed with the renovations, which they had discontinued when the poor returns did not improve. Obtaining a commitment to spend and a hands-off attitude from the owners, White had put his experience to work.

Over four months, $400,000 had been invested in updates to the Biltmore. Funds were limited, so White had concentrated on aesthetic features and cosmetic changes, such as new bedspreads, drapes, and carpets. Televisions had been replaced earlier, along with some beds. The property and structure had also received a new sidewalk, roof, and plumbing, as well as new windows, doors, and locks on all the rooms.

White was pleased with the results of this effort, but thought more investment was needed. He felt the majority of room furniture to be unacceptable. The tired furnishings made selling the hotel as "newly renovated" a little misleading. He estimated that an additional $100,000 was needed to finish all the rooms and bring the hotel up to an acceptable quality level, but he was not sure where he was going to get the money. It was at this point that he decided to consider a franchise brand.

THE TARGET MARKETS

The Biltmore's target markets consisted of university-related, government, commercial, and transient business. The Biltmore room rates at the time are shown in Exhibit 14.3.

The University of Guelph provided the majority of the guests for the Inn. A five-minute walk from the center of campus made the Biltmore a convenient resting place for visiting professors and conference delegates, whether they were attending a week-long conference or presenting a one-day seminar. The University also used the boardroom for regular meetings and union negotiations. The Biltmore had always been able to rely on this market, but government cutbacks in education funding could result in a decrease in seminars and conferences offered, thereby affecting the market potential of this segment.

Federal and provincial government officials were also Biltmore guests. Known for its leading position in agricultural research, the University Research Park was home to federal and provincial testing facilities. In addition, the federal government planned to move its agriculture offices to the research park in the near future. Although the regular government employees at the research park were residents of Guelph, a large number of government and private employees from other areas visited the park and thus were potential hotel guests. Government cutbacks had reduced

Exhibit 14.3
Biltmore Inn's Latest Room Rates (Canadian $)

	Single	*Double*	*Each Additional Person*
Regular	59.00	66.00	7.00
Corporate and government:			
Daily	53.00	59.00	7.00
Weekly	336.00	385.00	
Monthly	1,200.00	1,500.00	
Weekly:			
5 day (no Friday or Saturday)	225.00	260.00	
5 day (Friday or Saturday)	250.00	285.00	
7 day	336.00	385.00	
Monthly	1,200.00	1,500.00	

employee expense accounts, which could enable the Biltmore to attract those who needed to trade down in price.

White wanted to increase the commercial business. Attracting corporate business back to the Biltmore, after losing the majority of it over the past several years, was his most difficult task. To date, the majority of this market at the Biltmore Inn had been returning guests. Mr. White also wanted to attract more first-time guests.

Other significant markets included university and minor-league sports teams, and parents visiting university students. Transient pleasure business was largely spring and summer holiday travelers touring southern Ontario, visiting local family and friends, or attending a wedding or festival.

Occupancy

Under White's management, occupancy had steadily increased. He had reversed the downward trend of previous years, when guests would not return because of poorly maintained rooms, tired furnishings, and under-trained staff. Locals previously would not book associates and families at the Biltmore because of its negative image.

The largest portion of revenue was generated from May to September, with November through March experiencing lower occupancy. The most significant share of business was done on Friday and Saturday; weekdays were slow except during the summer conference season.

After a four-year decline, occupancy in White's first year (1993) was up 8 percent, and revenue was up $100,000 over the previous year. Exhibit 14.4 shows the five-year figures. A target of 60 percent occupancy had been set for 1994.

Exhibit 14.4
Occupancy Rates and Room Revenue Levels, 1989–1993 (Canadian $)

Year	Occupancy (%)	Room Revenue	Operating Profit (Rooms Only)
1989	59	620,292	151,265
1990	52	508,318	(165,797)
1991	42	415,628	(172,397)
1992	43	409,679	(108,238)
1993	51	509,294	(71,256)

As White saw these results,

We have begun the renewal process, but competitive forces demand that we take it to the finish. Our aim is to keep the clients we do have and force new potential clients to consider our renovated property as a consistent affordable alternative, like it once was. While owners expect the most from the least, we must continue our improvements if we are ever to approach profitability. The trend is positive with last year's results. Obviously, a fair chunk of the improvement can be attributed to the fact that you would *want* to stay here now.

COMPETITION

The Biltmore Inn was in competition with three Guelph properties: Holiday Inn, Comfort Inn, and College Inn. The three hotels represented 321 rooms. The Holiday Inn and the Comfort Inn were internationally branded hotels with reservation systems, while the College Inn was managed by a small Canadian company called Atlific Hotels and Resorts. In the summer, another competitor, the University of Guelph, offered 150 rooms in student residences and a large banquet and convention operation for conference delegates. Exhibit 14.5 shows details of the competition.

The Holiday Inn, the College Inn, and the Biltmore were located close to the university, a major access route, and business parks. The Holiday Inn and the College Inn were positioned to attract the midmarket guest. The Comfort Inn was on the north edge of the city and competed for the budget-level transient and commercial traveler. All three of these properties had been recently refurbished and were in good condition. Only two were nationally branded but Atlific was well known in the area as a good operator.

BRANDING IN THE CANADIAN HOTEL INDUSTRY

The Canadian lodging industry was changing as the United States' leading hotel franchisors entered the branding game. Canada provided the "big guys" from the south with a whole new market. The presence of U.S.

Exhibit 14.5

Competition Details

Holiday Inn	
Room rates:	Single—$89.00 Suite—$105.00
Number of rooms:	137
Room mix:	Standard, VIP, and honeymoon suites
Food and beverage:	Courtyard Restaurant, Lounge
Facilities:	Indoor garden and recreation area featuring swimming pool, sauna, whirlpool, and putting green
Meeting facilities:	Various for up to 400 people

College Inn	
Room rates:	Single—$80.00 Suite—$165.00
Number of rooms:	104
Room mix:	Standard and suites
Food and beverage:	Gordon Restaurant, Library, Lounge
Facilities:	Indoor swimming pool
Meeting facilities:	Conference and breakout rooms for up to 600

Comfort Inn	
Room rates:	Single—$55.00 Double—$60.00
Number of rooms:	80
Room mix:	Standard rooms
Food and beverage:	None
Facilities:	None
Meeting facilities:	None

brand names was increasing at a rapid pace. Compared with the United States, where 80 percent of the lodging industry was branded, 80 percent of Canada's industry was still independent. The branding trend in Canada, however, had impetus for three major reasons: profit, lending requirements, and consistency.

Current-day hoteliers had to get a little business from a lot of people. Independents did not have the resources to compete in this environment. Branding gave them a recognizable name and the benefits of a large organization including awareness, an international reservation system, and instant drive-by identity, which was especially important for small, unknown properties.

Most independent hoteliers needed to approach outside lenders in order to expand and renovate their properties. These lenders were exceedingly wary while the industry was experiencing low occupancy rates. Lenders, wanting to insure a return on their investment and to minimize the risk, were insisting that independents brand with larger organizations. They believed that a larger organization's name would get more people through the door, and produce a more favorable return on investment—if the property was run efficiently.

Customers were demanding quality for their dollars. In the hotel industry, this meant providing consistently high-quality accommodations compatible with the price range. A brand name told customers what level of quality they should receive; that is, it represented consistency. Independents converting to brands were obligated by their contracts to adopt the standards of the franchisor and to deliver a consistent experience to their guests. This did not mean, however, that there were not inconsistencies among properties. Some franchisees were more dutiful about their obligations; some franchisors were more strict in enforcing compliance.

DAYS INN

Days Inn had a long and profitable history in the United States. It also had worldwide agreements. Realstar Hotels Services Corporation, owner of the successful Delta Hotel and Resorts Company, held the Canadian rights to the Days Inn franchise.[1] The Canadian Days Inn division had focused its sights on being one of the key players in the branding game. To achieve growth, it was dedicated to signing independents it could help. This did not mean it was not discretionary. The potential had to exist to be tapped. Days Inns–Canada had grown from five hotels in 1989 to 40 in 1994 (see Exhibit 14.6).

Days Inns–Canada found potential franchisees by two methods: strategically and opportunistically. Strategic development accounted for 20 to 30 percent of new franchises. This involved searching for a property after deciding on a particular market area. The next step was to contact a

---

[1] The Canadian division retained the Days Inn name on its properties, but used the name Days Inns–Canada as a corporation.

Exhibit 14.6

Growth of Days Inns–Canada. [From Days Inn franchise package.]

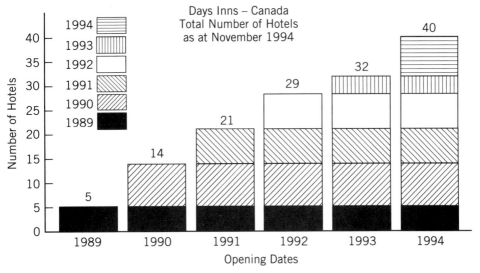

potential franchise property by letter to pique any interest the owners might have in branding. If there was interest and market potential, development personnel would visit the property for a visual inspection and to see if Days Inns–Canada could help the independent. For example, if a hotelier was looking to increase corporate executive traveler business, Days Inns–Canada could not help because that was not its target market. Days Inns' management did not believe in franchising a property just for expansion; a poor performer would not improve or enhance the Days Inn image.

Opportunistic development occurred when a hotelier inquired about branding with Days Inns–Canada. The same process was followed. Most new branding, in fact 70 to 80 percent of development, was opportunistic.

If a property appeared desirable, Days Inns–Canada operations personnel inspected it. Property inspections involved checking all common areas and rooms to see what, if any, improvements needed to be undertaken for it to meet Days Inn specifications. The report formulated was called a "punch list." Irwin Prince, Director of Franchise Services for Realstar, called it "a shopping list to bring the property up to standards at a significant capital investment. It is the cost to enter the game."

Depending on the variance in room styles, the inspection team might inspect over 50 percent of the rooms. If the physical layout and fixtures were identical in each room, the inspection was shorter than if a property had many room styles and fixtures. Upon signing, the punch list became an appendix to the franchise agreement. The new franchise had to fulfill the requirements of the punch list; the time period varied depending on the content of the list.

Days Inns' Demands

Days Inns–Canada wanted to franchise a property in Guelph when it approached the Biltmore Inn. After contacting Craig White, who had been considering franchising, development personnel visited the property, followed by an inspection team. The Days Inns–Canada inspection team formulated a punch list that contained an extensive list of changes that it wanted made.

Days Inns–Canada would give the Biltmore six to nine months in which to replace the furniture in 20 rooms. The furniture in these rooms had not been replaced during the earlier renovations, and therefore did not meet Days Inns–Canada's quality standards. Exhibit 14.7 is a copy of the Biltmore Inn's punch list, which White felt was comparable with his $100,000 estimate. Upon completion of the punch list, the Biltmore would become a Days Inn franchise if it could cover the fees. The standard fee terms are shown in Exhibit 14.8, but had been negotiable in the past.

Days Inns–Canada expected all its franchisees to maintain a level of consistency. "Consistency keeps the consumer happy," Dennis Ricci, Director of Development for Days Inns–Canada, explained. "If you give them something less, you disappoint them this time. If you give them something more this time, you disappoint them the next time."

To regulate consistency, Days Inns–Canada inspectors arrived for an unannounced property inspection three times a year. Quality Assurance Department inspections helped assure that each Days Inns–Canada property consistently met the high standards for cleanliness, service, and appropriateness in accommodations.

Inspections were customer-oriented and very comprehensive. Service evaluations, inspection of grounds, recreational facilities, building exteriors, public facilities, and a sampling of guest rooms were included. For example, the area behind the toilet was checked for dust. Inspections were intended to identify, correct, and prevent any deficiencies. Days Inns–Canada believed the relationship was not adversarial, but a positive method of improving a franchisee's rating: "A better educated franchise will perform better."

Days Inns–Canada Support

Days Inns–Canada offered franchisees a reservation system, national marketing, a franchise directory listing of the property and its facilities, drive-by identity, training, an approved supplier list, and association representation. Dennis Ricci, who had previously been franchise developer for Holiday Inn in Canada, told White that reflagging as a Days Inn would increase sales 15 percent to 25 percent in the first year alone.

The reservation system allowed the independent to get a little business from a lot of people. Exhibit 14.9 summarizes key statistics of the system. Days Inns–Canada catered to a diversified target market. Commercial travelers such as salespersons, technical representatives, and entrepreneurs were a large proportion of the market. During the summer months, the system provided the franchisee with families on vacations, seniors, and groups. The reservation system and brand recognition helped to capture these travelers.

National marketing efforts of Days Inns–Canada included advertising and promotion. National advertising and promotions created awareness of the product (see Exhibit 14.10). Awareness created demand and resulted in people booking rooms at a Days Inn. Days Inns–Canada encouraged regional alliances to minimize advertising and promotion costs within the region. Promotional materials included everything from business cards for the General Manager to Days Inn amenities for the guest rooms.

Each franchise was listed in a national and a worldwide directory. The national directory contained a bilingual listing of the amenities offered, facilities, location, and proximity to local points of interest. Exhibit 14.11 shows a sample page. The worldwide directory also contained a listing of addresses and phone numbers and the Days Inns–Canada quality rating (see Exhibit 14.12). These directories gave the properties exposure around the world—something difficult, if not impossible, to gain as an independent.

Exhibit 14.7
Biltmore Inn Punch List. [From the Biltmore Inn.]

DAYS INNS–CANADA
PUNCH LIST SUMMARY
BILTMORE INN
GUELPH, ONTARIO

TOTAL ROOMS: 50
SINGLE: 2
QUEENS: 18
DOUBLE/DOUBLES: 22
QUEEN WITH P-OUT: 8

Property Condition Summary:

Property consists of an interior corridor, two-story section housing the lobby and restaurant, and a single loaded motel wing. Buildings are solid brick construction.

ITEMS TO BE COMPLETED PRIOR TO
ENTERING THE DAYS INN SYSTEM

EXTERIOR:

1. Signage
   a) Provide DAYS INN exterior signage. Signage must meet Company standards and be purchased through an approved vendor. **No DAYS System signage may be installed without written approval from the Franchise Services Department.**
   b) Deidentify existing property location.
2. Parking lot:
   a) Construct a dumpster enclosure to conceal from the guests' view.

PUBLIC AREAS

1. Lobby:
   a) Professionally steam-clean all upholstered furniture.
   b) Refinish and/or replace furniture on upper patio above lobby.
2. Public restrooms:
   a) Replace stained ceiling tiles in both restrooms.
   b) Replace torn wall vinyl in men's restroom.

Exhibit 14.7 *(continued)*

c) Professionally clean all grouting in both restrooms.

d) Repair vanity trim in ladies' restroom.

3. Vending Area: Attach veneer covering to plywood box under ice machine, or remove box completely.

4. Corridors: Provide additional directional signage to rooms on exterior and interior.

5. Meeting Rooms: Professionally steam-clean carpet in room #51. Existing carpet is acceptable providing it scores a "B" or higher on future Quality Assurance inspections. Should the grade fall below "B" condition, then carpet must be replaced according to specifications.

GUESTROOMS AND BATHS:

1. Install 1-inch full-function mortise or mechanical card-type inn room entrance door locks with deadbolt capabilities meeting Days Inn–America (DIA) standards. Separate deadbolt-and-latch combinations are acceptable providing both locks meet DIA specifications. Recommend installing magnetic card-type entrance door locks (mandatory effective June 1). Local and provincial codes should be checked prior to any lock installation.

2. Install mortise twist-type deadbolts on all connecting doors.

3. Renovate guestrooms to include the following:

   a) DIA requires 100% nylon cut-pile carpet in all guestrooms. Existing carpet is substandard; however, it is acceptable providing it scores a "B" or higher on future Quality Assurance inspections. Should the grade fall below "B" condition, then carpet must be replaced according to specifications.

   b) Painted walls are acceptable; however, should they fall below a "B" score in a Quality Assurance Inspection, property must install vinyl wall coverings, minimun 14 oz. required.

   c) Ensure that all rooms have the required lamp package: one bed lamp per bed required on headboard wall, one wall lamp in credenza area, and one floor lamp in the leisure area. Eliminate all swag lamps.

   d) Replace all stained and worn pull-out couches and all occasional chairs.

   e) Remove all domestic-type ceiling lights in two-story building.

   f) Professionally clean all floor tile grouting in all bathrooms.

   g) Replace marble-style arborite top vanities (e.g., room #50).

MISCELLANEOUS:

Install reservations system equipment. May be purchased or leased.

Exhibit 14.7 *(continued)*

BRAND STANDARDS:

Must comply with Brand Standards, including but not limited to: employee uniform package, amenities, logo'd supplies, and all signage/graphics. Logo'd amenities and supplies must not be placed in rooms prior to company approval.

ITEMS TO BE COMPLETED WITHIN SIX MONTHS OF OPENING

GUESTROOMS AND BATHS:

1. Install wing wall to enclose closet area from guest view.
2. Replace domestic-type vanity lights with fluorescent.
3. Replace all "cane" and "Cherrywood"-style casegoods (approximately 10 rooms of each), to include: credenzas, headboards, nightstands, wall mirrors, writing tables or desk and desk chairs.

ITEMS TO BE COMPLETED WITHIN NINE MONTHS OF OPENING

EXTERIOR:

1. Parking Lot: Restripe parking lot.
2. Pool: <u>Item to be completed prior to spring reopening:</u> Provide new pool furniture per company standards (minimum four tables with umbrella and 16 chairs).

HANDWRITTEN OR UNAUTHORIZED REVISIONS TO THIS PUNCH LIST ARE NOT VALID AND WILL NOT BE CONSIDERED DURING FUTURE EVALUATIONS. ANY AND ALL REVISIONS TO THIS PUNCH LIST MUST BE MADE AND APPROVED BY THE QUALITY ASSURANCE DEPARTMENT.

This punch list has been prepared on the basis of a random sample inspection of the property on the date specified. The owner is responsible for improvement of areas not inspected to meet Days Inn System Standards. All repairs, replacements and improvements must meet standards published in the Days Inn System Planning and Design Standards Manual.

The punch list will be subject to revision by Days Inn if the condition of the inspected property changes materially or the License Agreement to which this is attached is executed more than 90 days after the date of the punch list. Also, if the property does not enter the system within 180 days after the punch list date, the punch list may be invalidated or revised at the discretion of the

Exhibit 14.7 *(continued)*

Quality Assurance Department; this punch list becomes subject to revision six months from the date above.

Prepared By: Debbie Murree
PUNCH LIST WAS REVISED NOVEMBER 11. ALL OTHER COPIES ARE INVALID.

DIA Approval: _____   Date: _____

CANADA\ONTGUELP.DI

The Days Inns' head office provided ongoing training for all Days Inns–Canada franchise staff. Training sessions were free of charge to the franchisee; the owner only had to pay the transportation and lodging costs. Days Inns–Canada believed in developing customer service in a proactive manner. For example, front-desk personnel in a region would meet in May to discuss how to effectively handle any potential problem in the upcoming busy summer season.

Days Inns–Canada also provided an approved supplier list to each franchise. The head office made agreements with suppliers but received no title. Franchises were able to purchase quality supplies at a lower cost because of these arrangements. They were encouraged to report to the head office on how suppliers were performing. If necessary, the head office would review any supplier.

Days Inns–Canada and its franchisees were members of major industry associations (see Exhibit 14.13). Membership in these associations gave Days Inns–Canada and its franchisees representation and input on associations that played important roles in industry decisions.

THE FRANCHISE RELATIONSHIP

Craig White had been concerned about the quality of accommodation the Biltmore was providing to the guest. He knew more renovations and a developed marketing plan were needed to increase occupancy.

Exhibit 14.8
Fees for Days Inns–Canada

DAYS INN FEES*

START UP FEES

Application Fee (non-refundable)	$1,000 (credited towards initial fee)
Initial Fee	$350 per room with a $35,000 minimum
Other	
Reservation Entry Fee	$100 per room or $10,000 whichever is less
Reservation Software	$1,800 for Days Inn Reservation Software
Reservation Hardware	$2,500 for Reservation Terminal System

ON-GOING MONTHLY FEES

Royalty Fee	5.0% of gross room revenues
Advertising/Marketing Fee	1.5% of gross room revenues
Reservation Fee	2.3% of gross room revenues
Reservation System Support	
Travel Agent Commission	10% of gross room revenue at confirmed room rate for each reservation
Airline Reservation Charges	US$4.00 per gross room reservation

OTHER

Training	No tuition fees for most courses and workshops. Travel, food, lodging and out of pocket expenses are paid by the franchisee.
Franchise Conference	Usually C$400-600 plus travel expenses.

* Summary of the typical franchisee fees as of June 1, 1994 and is subject to change. The cost of a franchisee's initial investment, such as construction/renovation costs and supplies, is additional.

Exhibit 14.9
Days Inn Key Reservation Statistics (1993).
[From Days Inn franchise package.]

Days Inn–Chainwide

1. 10,360,000 reservation calls (1992—9,600,000).

2. 43 percent conversion (calls to reservations) (1992—40.1 percent).

3. 2.4 room nights per booking.

4. 10,692,689 room nights booked through the reservation system.

5. 35 to 38 percent of total room nights came from the reservation system.

Days Inns–Canada

6. 49 percent of achieved room nights at a Canadian downtown property came from the reservation system.

7. 22 percent of total Canadian chainwide room nights achieved in 1992 came from the reservation system.

To renovate, he needed capital resources. The owners were hesitant, and the bank wanted to see improved operating numbers. Without increased occupancy, the Biltmore would lose money in the near future. White needed a solution that would please the owners, the bank, and the guests.

Approached by Days Inns–Canada, White considered the advantages and disadvantages of branding. He felt that, although the Biltmore could be successful on its own, with the appropriate renovations a relationship with Days Inns–Canada provided a number of extra benefits.

Days Inns would insure that the quality of accommodations remained consistent with their standards. If the Biltmore did not meet the standards, it would lose points and, ultimately, its franchise if it continued to be negligent. White felt this pressure would commit the owners to the renovations.

The Biltmore wanted to increase its commercial, family, and senior business. Days Inns–Canada would provide these markets through its commercial incentive program and reservation system. The simple recognition of the Days Inn name would allow the Biltmore to attract more transient guests.

The Biltmore did not have the capital to develop and implement an extensive marketing plan. A Days Inn franchise would provide the exposure

Exhibit 14.10

National Advertising and Promotions. [From Days Inn franchise package.]

RESULTS-ORIENTED ADVERTISING

Days Inn® continues the tradition of innovative advertising with a comprehensive integrated advertising and promotions program which utilizes Willard Scott from the "NBC Today Show" and the world famous Flintstones from Hanna-Barbera. Playing to our strength with families, this outstanding marketing duo will catapult Days Inn into the travel plans of millions of traveling families and establish Days Inn as "the chain" for family travel.

MEDIA

TELEVISION The TV advertising combines animation and live action in an audience-grabbing series of commercials that drives home the Days Inn distribution and value message as never before. Days Inn - the only place to find Flintstone Family Fun.

RADIO The familiar voices of Willard and Fred combined with the unmistakable Flintstones theme song make for memorable radio spots. Our strong commitment to radio will impact the all-important drive market.

PRINT Willard, Fred and the Flintstone family are the keystone of our national newspaper, AAA Tour Book and Rand McNally Road Atlas print media campaign. Pre-approved formats for local ads are also available.

WORLDWIDE SALES SUPPORT

Sales specialists work on your behalf across the country and around the world to generate roomnights for each Days Inn facility. These experienced professionals work with travel agents, tour and motorcoach operators, associations, government departments and corporations to achieve our number one goal - driving incremental business to Days Inn properties.

A GUEST-FRIENDLY DIRECTORY

More than four million Days Inn worldwide directories are distributed to traveling consumers. Directories are a powerful and highly recognizable advertising media for Days Inn. Now more than ever, travelers have a new information standard on which to base their buying decisions.

Exhibit 14.10 *(continued)*

DAYS INN

FREQUENT STAY™ CLUB

YOUR 10ᵗʰ NIGHT IS FREE*!

WE APPRECIATE YOUR LOYALTY

The Days Inn Frequent Stay Club was created specially for travellers on the road. As a club member, you are entitled to exclusive benefits at any Days Inn location in Canada. Plus, your tenth night is free*. Simply present your Frequent Stay™ Club card upon check-out from any Days Inn in Canada, and you will receive one stamp for each night's stay at the Frequent Stay Club preferred rate. **It is our way of saying "thank you for your loyalty to Days Inn".**

FREQUENT STAY™ CLUB BENEFITS

✓ Frequent Stay Club corporate rate
✓ Free local phone calls
✓ Complimentary coffee and newspaper
✓ Free upgrade to the best available room
✓ Free incoming faxes
✓ Spouses stay free
✓ Preferred rates from participating Budget Rent a Car locations
✓ Cheque cashing privileges up to $50 with a valid American Express Card
✓ Exclusive reservation number

PLUS

Your 10th night is free*

MEMBERSHIP IS FREE

To join simply fill out the attached card and use it at any Days Inn in Canada. Call today for reservations.

1-800-TEN-DAYS

Printed in Canada / Imprimé au Canada
TM ® Used under licence from American Express Company. Copyright © Amex Bank of Canada 1994
© 1993 Days Inn of America Inc.

The great offer that's been 50 years in the making.

If you're 50 or over, you probably think you've seen it all. But as a member of The September Days Club, you'll see a lot more of the world, and save big time in the process. In fact, you'll save 15%-50% on already low room rates at any of over 1,500 participating Days Inns worldwide. But the savings don't stop there.

Join The September Days Club, and you'll receive discounts on car rentals, meals, local attractions, insurance, travel services and pharmaceuticals. Plus you'll get a free subscription to the award winning September Days Club Magazine, listing discounts at hundreds of Days Inns worldwide. These are just a few of the benefits that make The September Days Club one of the smartest deals around.

---

that the Biltmore needed to attract guests. Two competitors, Holiday Inn and Comfort Inn, were branded. The Days Inns–Canada national marketing program would provide similar exposure.

The Biltmore offered the franchisor a prime location. Situated on a major access route, it provided a convenient location for Days Inns–Canada to have a hotel. It allowed exposure to transients and was easily accessible to others.

Exhibit 14.10 *(continued)*

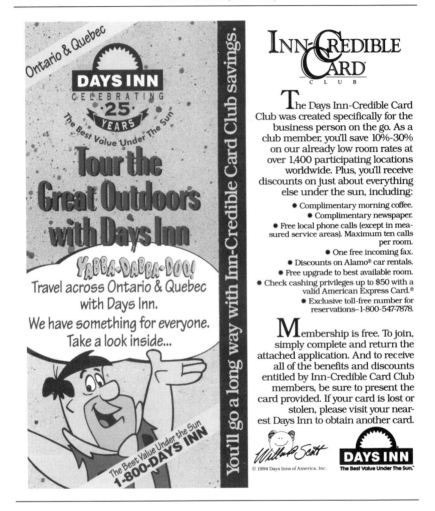

© 1994 Days Inns of America, Inc.

Although it needed renovations, the property had the potential to be successful. Its success would provide increased revenue for the owners and for Days Inns.

THE DECISION

Reviewing all the information, Craig White had to draw on his experience and education to decide what alternative to choose. He outlined three

Exhibit 14.11
National Directory Listing

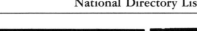

ONTARIO	ONTARIO

6405

CAMBRIDGE - DAYS INN
(519) 622-1070 FAX: (519) 622-1512
Exit 24 South of Hwy 401
650 Hespeler Road, Cambridge, Ontario N1R 6J8

118 Rooms • Restaurant • Meeting Room • Playground • Heated Outdoor Swimming Pool • Non-Smoking Rooms • Fax and Photocopier Services • Cribs and Rollaways Available Upon Request • Plenty of Free Parking • Commercial and Corporate Rates •Toronto International Airport 45 Minutes Away.

5058

CORNWALL - DAYS INN
(613) 937-3535 FAX: (613) 936-0542
From USA, crossover Int'l Bridge, 1 mi N, left at 2nd light, Exit 789
from Hwy 401, 2 mi S, right at 2nd light.
1541 Vincent Massey Drive, Cornwall, Ontario K6J 5K6

60 Rooms •Meeting Facilities •Walking Distance to Major Shopping Centres & Restaurant • Bridge to USA 4.8 km •St Lawrence Parks & Beaches 24.1 km • Rooms Equipped for PC use •Fax Machine available •Ottawa 96.6 km •Montréal 88.5 km •Upper Canada Village 25.7 km •Nearby Golf & Fishing •Civic Complex 8 km • Handicapped Facilities • Non Smoking Rooms available.

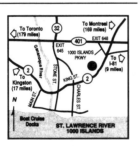

4514

GANANOQUE - DAYS INN
(Heart of the 1000 Islands)
(613) 382-7292 FAX: (613) 382-4387
Hwy 2-1/4 mi. W of Intersection of Hwy 401, Hwy 2, & 1000 Islands Pkwy.
650 King Street E., Gananoque, Ontario K7G 1H3

30 Rooms •Queen Beds •Lobster Trap Seafood Restaurant •Lounge • Bridge to USA 14.5 km •Live Theatre, 1000 Islands Cruises, Zoo 2 km •Fishing •Boat Ramp •Golf •Bike Path Nearby •Fort Henry 15 min. •Ottawa 90 minutes •AAA 3 Diamond • Mini Golf 150m • In-Room Coffee Makers.

1-800-DAYS INN	1-800-DAYS INN

alternatives: resign as General Manager and let the owners manage the inn, continue to fight the owners for capital to complete the renovations, or convince the owners to join a franchise system and find the capital to get approval. White realized that a franchise could help the Biltmore Inn achieve its goals, but he had a few questions. Was the best strategic match between the Biltmore Inn and Days Inns? Would other franchisors insist

Exhibit 14.12
Worldwide Directory

THE DAYS INN SUNBURST QUALITY RATING SYSTEM

Days Inn's Sunburst Rating System is the first rating system published by any hotel chain in the lodging industry. We are proud to assist you in identifying the best values under the sun. We also feel you deserve to be kept informed about the quality of Days Inns.

Just as AAA's "Diamonds" are different from Mobil's "Stars," so too are Days Inn's "Sunbursts." For those of you who don't know, Days Inn's Quality Assurance Department is made up of over 40 well-trained hotel professionals who conduct several inspections per year at every Days Inn.

<u>How We Inspect Hotels</u>

The standard QA inspection begins with an inspector arriving <u>unannounced</u> and checking in to a property just as you do, as a guest. This allows us to experience the service offered to a Days Inn guest. The physical inspection is performed the next day. The day is spent inspecting everything from landscaping to bathroom cleanliness. In total, up to <u>550 individual line items are evaluated at each property</u>. Typically, the property's general manager and executive housekeeper accompany the inspector on the tour of the hotel. This is done so that the property staff can see, first hand, what improvements need to be made. Our goal is to identify a potential problem before you arrive and correct it before it affects your stay.

You will find the Sunbursts in each property listing. There are six different Sunburst ratings with 5 Sunbursts representing the highest scoring locations in the system. One Sunburst means the property meets Days Inn standards.

Those properties with an NR rating did not meet our minimum standards at the time of printing, but are in the process of correcting deficiencies.

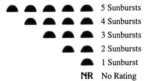

▲ ▲ ▲ ▲ ▲	5 Sunbursts
▲ ▲ ▲ ▲	4 Sunbursts
▲ ▲ ▲	3 Sunbursts
▲ ▲	2 Sunbursts
▲	1 Sunburst
NR	No Rating

Note: Sunburst ratings reflect the quality score only. They do not reflect the amount of amenities offered or the size of the hotel. Please see remainder of hotel's listing to determine hotel's size and amenities offered.

Other important notations designate newly constructed or recently opened properties:

<u>NEW New Construction:</u>

Locations which have been Newly Constructed and have recently opened, but have yet to receive their first unannounced inspection.

<u>TBR To Be Rated:</u>

Locations which have just joined the Days Inn System, but have yet to receive their first unannounced inspection.

3

ONTARIO Continued

Kenora
(807) 468-2003
920 Hwy 17 E, Kenora, ON P9N 1L9
FAX: (807) 468-8551 $53-$75 **Site 1977**

Kingston
(613) 546-3661
33 Benson St, Kingston, ON K7K 5W2
FAX: (613) 544-4126 $66-$85 **Site 4962**

Leamington
(519) 326-8646
Hwy 18 S, Leamington, ON N8H 3V4
FAX: (519) 326-5531 $45-$150 **Site 4444**

Lindsay
(705) 324-3213
Hwy 35 S, RR 4, Lindsay, ON K9V 4R4
FAX: (705) 324-9121 $49-$64 **Site 4921**

London
(519) 681-1240
1100 Wellington Rd S, London, ON N6E 1M2
FAX: (519) 681-0830 $49-$99 **Site 4391**

Niagara Falls
(905) 356-6666
4029 River Rd, Niagara Falls, ON L2E 3E5
FAX: (905) 356-1800 $36-$106 **Site 6621**

Niagara Falls
(905) 374-3333
5943 Victoria Ave, Niagara Falls, ON L2G 3L8
FAX: (905) 374-0669 $49-$249 **Site 6639**

Niagara Falls
(905) 358-3621
7280 Lundy's Ln, Niagara Falls, ON L2G 1W2
FAX: (905) 358-0277 $39-$129 **Site 6293**

Niagara Falls
(905) 357-7377
6361 Buchanan Ave, Niagara Falls, ON L2G 3V9
FAX: (905) 374-6707 $49-$199 **Site 4060**

Niagara Falls
(905) 562-4101
3305 N Service Rd, Vineland Station, ON L0R 2E0
FAX: (905) 562-7781 $39-$150 **Site 4464**

North Bay
(705) 474-4770
255 McIntyre St. West, North Bay, ON P1B 2Y9
FAX: (705) 497-1437 $56-$75 **Site 2393**

Ottawa
(613) 237-9300
123 Metcalfe St, Ottawa, ON K1P 5L9
FAX: (613) 237-2161 $59-$99 **Site 5378**

Sarnia
(519) 383-6767
751 N Christina St, Sarnia, ON N7V 1X5
FAX: (519) 383-8710 $65-$89 **Site 4203**

Sault Ste Marie
(705) 759-8200
320 Bay St, Sault Ste Marie, ON P6A 1X1
FAX: (705) 942-9500 $55-$110 **Site 4398**

Sudbury
(705) 674-7517
TBR
117 Elm Street, Sudbury, ON P3C 1T3
FAX: (705) 688-0369 $59-$79 **Site 6291**

Toronto
(905) 678-1400
6257 Airport Rd, Mississauga, ON L4V 1E4
FAX: (905) 678-9130 $69-$135 **Site 4472**

Toronto
(416) 977-6655
30 Carlton St, Toronto, ON M5B 2E9
FAX: (416) 977-0502 $79-$130 **Site 4095**

Toronto
(905) 238-5480
4635 Tomken Rd, Mississauga, ON L4W 1J9
FAX: (905) 238-1031 $49-$125 **Site 4596**

To identify symbols, see page 5.

11

Exhibit 14.13
Days Inns–Canada Association Memberships.
[From Days Inn franchise package.]

Our company and/or its individuals hold memberships in the following organizations:

Alliance of Canadian Travel Agents

Canadian Franchise Association (preliminary approval)

Canadian Hotel Marketing Sales Executives

Meeting Planners International

Through our franchises and their staff, we are also members of the following organizations:

Association des Propiétaire D'Autobus du Quebec

American Business Association

Business Association of New York

Canadian Society of Association Executives

Hotel Association of Metropolitan Toronto

Metropolitan Toronto Convention & Visitors Association

Mississauga Board of Trade

National Association of Catering Executives

National Association of Senior Travel Planners

Ontario Hotel & Motel Association

Ontario Motorcoach Association

Pennsylvania Business Association

Toronto Airport Directors of Sales

Toronto International Airport Hotel Association

on a greater investment? Would they be even interested? Would White be able to convince the owners to join a franchise and invest more capital in renovations? Was the capital available to do either? Would the advantage of a franchise warrant its cost and eventually repay the capital? Would Days Inns–Canada be flexible with its requirements? Was Days Inns–Canada the best way to go, given the moment?

White had to decide today. Dennis Ricci would be calling tomorrow to see if the Biltmore Inn wanted to do what had to be done to join the growing ranks of Days Inns–Canada hotels.

Case Fifteen

Riu Partner Club

Luis Mª. Huete and Javier de los Santos

The place and time were Palma de Mallorca, November 15, 10 A.M., a conference room at Riu Hotels, S.A.: All who were part of senior management were seated around the table. Order of the day: discussion and ultimate modification or approval of a plan baptized with the name "Riu Partner Club" and presented by Luis Rullán, General Manager of Riu since 1985. The project was risky and had opponents. Much was at stake, for example, the company's focus on the client, which had given such good results up until now. Opinions were far from unanimous, which was becoming the norm in recent meetings:

> "Have you calculated the costs that the new guarantee could mean for us in the not-at-all hypothetical case of a breakdown in the heating or air-conditioning? What sense does it make to give away a 14-day stay to a client if his television doesn't work? This proposal is ridiculous and could end up costing us a lot of money."

> "I don't agree with that. In my opinion it's a question of believing or not believing in our product and of committing ourselves seriously or not to giving our clients what we promise. We can have hotels from '73, with problems, but they have to work. The guarantee has always been a part of our way of thinking; it's our business philosophy: no deceiving our clients, no lying."

This case is from the Investigation Division of IESE (Barcelona). It was prepared by Professor Luis Mª. Huete with the help of Javier de los Santos, M.B.A.; March 1993. Revised, May 1996. Reproduced by John Wiley & Sons with permission. Copyright 1993 IESE, University of Navarra. Total or partial reproduction is prohibited without written authorization from IESE. All amounts in this case are in pesetas unless otherwise noted. One hundred pesetas (100 pta) equals approximately U.S.$.79, Canadian $1.09, FF 4.1, DFL 1.32, SF .95, £0.52, and DM 1.2.

"I think it's fine that our flaws cost us money. Haven't you heard about the cost of no quality? Well, let's face it! For years I've been telling everyone in the company that an unsatisfied client translates into 32,768 lost reservations in five years. It's time we put our money where our mouth is. If you calculate the income from these lost reservations we're talking about 900 million pesetas. If the guarantee keeps me from losing a client, then look at what a good job we're doing."

"I don't like the nature of the guarantee. I think that we're coming up short. With a guarantee, the fewer conditions it has for its use, the better. The guarantee states that it comes into effect only if a problem is not solved in 24 hours. Why don't we get rid of that clause?"

"And what will happen then? There'll be clients with a guarantee and clients without a guarantee. If the air-conditioning breaks down, you can't make a distinction. You're going to have to invite all of them. And all of them, with one of the large hotels full, could mean more than 700 people; 700 people, two weeks free . . . , that's a lot of money!"

"Money won't be the problem. Our people can take care of any problem in 24 hours!"

"Oh, sure! Tell me what our people are going to do, in 24 hours, if the city starts digging near the hotel and the guests who are in the pool are bothered by all the noise and the smell."

"O.K., and if this money has to be paid because of the city? Have you thought about the public relations show we could start? We'd be all over the press!"

"We have to think about the possible reaction of our competitors. Can you imagine them offering a guarantee that was similar to ours? For them it could turn out to be very expensive!"

"Do you really think that the restitution contained in the guarantee has to be a free vacation? Shouldn't we just return the money they paid?"

"But, then why give a guarantee? The channel tells us that the only complaints that they receive from our clients is for overbooking. I don't think this guarantee does anything to fix that. Have you thought about the problem of overbooking that we'll have if our plan is so successful that demand increases by 30 percent? Where do we put them?"

"This year, no, but when we have the guarantee in place, we can raise our prices by 5 percent; the channel won't be able to say anything to us."

"That, on top of everything else! We're already almost 20 percent higher than our competition. While they're reducing prices, you want to raise them? I remind you that in '91 our sales figures fell by 5 percent. More than talking about guarantees, we should be thinking about how to reduce our costs even further and how to buy more hotels that, with the present crisis, are a real bargain."

"I think it's dangerous to think about the guarantee as a lure to attract more clients. The guarantee is useful to us in catching flaws that, with our present system, slip by us."

"I don't understand this obsession with getting clients to come back. It's been our experience for a long time that their demand is proportional to the number of times that they've stayed with us. I'm up to my ears in 'Riunomanos'![1] Yesterday a hotel manager was telling me how, since they're all familiar with the evaluation system, a regular client had told him that he wasn't going to put 'Very Good' so that they'd have to try harder to improve. Working with people like that is bothersome. And if there's something that we all have enough of it's stress. Enough is enough!"

"We're only discussing one of the points in the Riu Partner Club plan. Why don't you all do me a favor and take a good look at the other five points? What do you think? Are they justifiable from an economic point of view? Are they coherent with our values and with our positioning? What effects can the entire plan have on our hotel managers and on our employees? I know that some of you are disappointed with the lack of trustworthiness of some of our employees. They are a key part of our success and are under a lot of pressure from their work. With the 16,000 beds that we have now we cannot limit ourselves to being good providers of service. Now we have to add some know-how to our sales. We have to make it easy for our channel to sell Riu. At the end of this century we have to be a company that is global in reach and of significant size, one that is solid and even more profitable."

COMPANY BACKGROUND

The story of Riu Hotels began in 1953 with the purchase of Hotel San Francisco, on the Palma beachfront in Mallorca. Juan Riu and his son

---

[1] Customers "addicted" to Riu Hotels.

Luis took charge of the hotel, into which they invested the savings they had earned, through much hard work, in South America. They planned to put all of the family's energy into the hotel. Soon, Luis would take over the management of the company.

From the beginning, Juan Riu shunned the business norms of the times. He was the first hotelier to sign on with a tour operator,[2] initiating charter tourism in Spain, and he was a pioneer in energy conservation, installing a single, central heating system in all of his hotels in Palma. He also ignored the criteria of the era, putting extensive gardens and swimming pools in his hotels.

At the end of the 1970s, the strongest tour operators began to focus on purchasing hotels. Juan Riu thought that if the tour operator had ownership in his hotels (or under management), he would tend to fill these hotels first, especially during the off-seasons. Faced with this dilemma, Riu made a drastic decision: he separated the ownership of his hotels from their management, created Riu Hotels as a management entity, and sold 40 percent of the shares of this company to Touristik Union International (TUI).[3]

After 40 years, Riu Hotels was still a family company, with Luis Riu as President, and with a group of professionals managed by Luis Rullán, who was in charge of day-to-day business. In the opinion of outside observers, Rullán's management style was not shared by some of his managers. Exhibit 15.1 gives a brief description of the history of Riu Hotels.

In 1992, Riu Hotels had 34 three- and four-star beach hotels located in eight geographic areas. Two-thirds of these were owned and the rest were leased. There were no management contracts. They did not believe in that way of operating "because we like to get completely involved, without interferences of any kind." They had never considered opening hotels in cities, although they had not lacked offers. According to Rullán:

---

[2] The tour operators bought bookings at wholesale prices and then designed "vacation packages," completing these bookings with airfare and sometimes other amenities. These packages were described in full-color brochures that were distributed to travel agencies, who, as agents of the tour operators, sold the packages to the end users.

[3] TUI was the largest tour operator in Europe, established in Germany through the merger of five regional entities.

Exhibit 15.1
Brief Description of Riu Hotels' Background

1953	Juan Riu and his son Luis bought the Hotel San Francisco on the Palma de Mallorca beachfront.
1955	First charter flight to Mallorca with stopovers in Lyon and Barcelona.
1962	Collaboration between the vacation organizer Dr. Tigges, the airline company LTU, and the hotelier Luis Riu. They agreed to cooperate during the winter season by offering economical vacations and, especially, long-distance stays in Mallorca.
1963	The Riu family began the construction of new hotels, first on the Palma beachfront.
1976	Creation of a management company, Riu Hotels, S.A., in association with the tourist organizer TUI. Profits were invested in the construction of new hotels and in the reform of already existing establishments. The family continued to hold the majority of shares with 51 percent.
1985	The Riu Palmeras opened its doors on the island of Gran Canaria, the first hotel outside of Mallorca.
1988	Opening of the Riu Ventura, a four-star hotel, and the Aparthotel Riu Maxorata on the island of Fuerteventura.
1989	The openings in the Canary Islands were temporarily halted by a special project: the Riu Palace on the island of Gran Canaria. Designed by the artist and architect César Manrique, its location facing the dunes of Maspalomas is breathtaking.
1991	In November the Riu Taino had its grand opening in the Dominican Republic; the first part of a complex 700,000 square meters in size.
	In Lanzarote, Riu Hotels took charge of two four-star establishments. Starting in 1993, these vacation complexes were also to be incorporated into Riu management.
	In Puerto de la Cruz in Tenerife, Riu incorporated three four-star establishments.
1992	In April the Hotel Riu Palace Canela opened its doors, the first of the chain's hotels on the Spanish mainland.
	In the Dominican Republic, near to the Hotel Riu Taino, the Hotel Riu Nalboa also opened, with four stars.

"Not long ago we were offered two hotels in Madrid. We didn't even consider them. The opportunity costs of those hotels are seven times those of a beach hotel. Also, marketing is totally different." It was estimated that in 1992, the investment necessary for each additional bed of a beach hotel fluctuated between 4 and 5 million pesetas.

In the last five years Riu Hotels had doubled its capacity, measured in available beds. It had gone from 2 million hotel stays to 4 million in 1992. Riu Hotels believed that the trend toward long-distance trips would continue to rise. After the successful opening of two hotels in the Dominican Republic,[4] its plans for expansion became focused on the Caribbean and Miami. In the case of the Caribbean it could count on very cheap labor, which would translate into the lowest prices for vacationers, so that the total price for a European to go there—including airfare—was very similar to what he or she would pay for other European destinations. Miami, on the other hand, had the added advantage, according to the company, of representing a destination with the additional attraction of shopping.

RIU HOTELS' PRACTICES

Riu was careful not to put its name on hotels that did not meet the chain's usual standards. It therefore renounced more than 20 million pta in profits by leaving behind, one year earlier, a hotel whose contract was expiring because an agreement with its owner for doing reforms could not be arrived at. Riu Hotels' policy was to not buy hotels that were already operating because they felt that the structure of these hotels would not adapt to their type of management. In recent years, they had not always adhered to this policy. This brought about some problems: during one year, three hotels in Tenerife that had been purchased from Husa Hotels did not appear with the Riu name since their installations, and many aspects of the hotels, especially the attitude of their employees, were considered lacking. At the same time, some

---

[4] During the first year in the Dominican Republic, it was found that 60 percent of clients had previously stayed at other Riu hotels. Half of these were in hotels located on the island of Fuerteventura. These repeat guests were called Riunomanos.

of the hotels in the Canary Islands, purchased by Riu after they were constructed, turned out to be rather strange when compared with the traditional concept of Riu.

The first hotel on the Spanish mainland had opened in 1992 and was in Huelva, a short distance from the Portuguese Algarve. Riu was not content with either the hotel's performance or its management. Part of the difficulties stemmed from the fact that it had not been constructed by Riu Hotels, as was the usual practice.

When Riu opened a new hotel, it sent a large team of veterans from the company to introduce their know-how. This team not only included managers (hotel or section) but also lower-level personnel such as dishwashers. The company felt it was important that all new employees quickly capture Riu's style of doing things. According to Rullán: "It's amazing how much money is saved and the increased quality that is obtained by washing dishes well."

To reduce costs, it was Riu's policy to put hotels together in the same location. This allowed the company to centralize the kitchen, laundry, bakery, administration, finance, personnel, and other functions. The idea, according to Rullán, was to centralize everything that headquarters could do through a hotel manager. Here they were betting on savings in costs, better control of the quality of these activities, and time savings for the hotel managers—time they could dedicate to clients and employees. Thus, in Palma there was a central kitchen that prepared 7,000 meals each day, with consequent savings in labor. Heating was also centralized. The philosophy of putting hotels together, while clearly perceptible in Palma, was less observable in other geographic areas.

Luis Riu took great pains to adapt services (such as activities, schedules, meals, entertainment, and languages) to the culture of his clients. He was also famous for his obsession with "checklists" (lists of questions referring to company rules and regulations) concerning each position, and for the detail with which he followed deviations of costs over budget.

Personnel expenses over income for Riu were 10 points less than for comparable hotels: 35 percent compared with 45 percent. When the Hotel Playa Park was purchased from Thompson Holidays, it had 140 employees; two years later there were 85. The 22 people that it had in the kitchen were reduced to 10 due to the economies of scale with other nearby Riu hotels. Also, as a result of Riu's centralization of technical services and maintenance, the company could do away with the 11 people that the Hotel Playa Park employed in these areas before it was purchased.

For every 100 pta that Riu Hotels took in, 35 went to paying personnel expenses, 15 to food, and 18 to 20 to other costs. The resulting margin, 30 percent, could go as high as 45 percent in the Canary Islands.

Since the beginning of its operations, Riu Hotels' policy had been to not pay dividends. All profits were reinvested into the company. In 1992, the group was valued at close to 25,000 million pta, and it generated considerable profits. TUI earned almost the same amount of money with Riu Hotels as with its own tour operator operations.

Exhibit 15.2 lists the number of establishments and beds by category, Exhibit 15.3 gives income and expenses broken down by hotel category, and Exhibit 15.4 shows the organizational chart for the group and for a typical hotel.

The Riu Family

Luis Riu got started in the hotel business in Venezuela, together with his father, where by working 365 days a year they were able to save 1 million pta, which they brought with them to Spain—money with which they purchased the Hotel San Francisco in 1953. His wife, Pili, was closely involved in the hotel operations from the beginning. Many of the first chambermaids had learned the trade under her guidance. Both were very charismatic people.

Luis and Pili had two children, Luis and Carmen. Luis, who lived in Santo Domingo, was in charge of international operations and was Vice President of the group. Carmen worked in Palma as a consultant in charge of financial issues. The family was respected and appreciated in the company.

Riu Hotels professed to having its own style. This came from the way of thinking and acting exhibited by its founder and his wife. In 1980, this style, practiced since the very beginning, was written up in the form of a declaration of company policy (see Exhibit 15.5).

Exhibit 15.2

Number of Riu Partner Club Establishments and Beds by Category, 1992

Category	Number of Establishments by Category				Number of Beds per Category			
	Two Stars	Three Stars	Four Stars	Total	Two Stars	Three Stars	Four Stars	Total
Mallorca	2*	7	2	11	1,584*	2,429	729	4,742
Gran Canaria	—	4	5	9	—	1,541	2,123	3,664
Fuerteventura	—	—	3	3	—	—	1,371	1,371
Tenerife	—	—	3	3	—	—	1,217	1,217
Lanzarote	—	2	3	5	—	606	1,190	1,796
Olot	—	—	1	1	—	—	60	60
Huelva	—	—	1	1	—	—	704	704
Dominican Republic*	—	—	3	3	—	—	2,257	2,257
Total	2	13	21	36	1,584	4,576	9,651	15,811

* The hotel Riu Palace Caribe was to open in early 1993 with 400 rooms (800 beds). The two-star establishments were to be eliminated by the same time.

Note: Hotel rooms had two beds per room, which was the way most tour packages were sold. Thus, the price per room was the price of two packages. Riu was to have approximately 7,113 rooms in the three- and four-star categories in 1993 and none in the two-star category.

Exhibit 15.3
Average Earnings and Costs per Day per Person
by Category

	*Revenue***	*Costs****
Two stars:		
Room and half pension	2,300	1,800
Extras*	450	135
Three stars:		
Room and half pension	3,400	2,150
Extras*	500	150
Four stars:		
Room and half pension	5,000	3,300
Extras*	1,140	340
Four stars plus (Palace):		
Room and half pension	7,000	4,500
Extras*	1,800	540

* Extras included drinks taken at the bar and certain extras in the dining room, such as natural fruit juices, half lobster, or a bottle of wine.
** Revenues were Riu's. The price that a client might end up paying was 60 or 100 percent higher. This markup included the margins of the channel, the tour operator, and transportation costs.
*** Costs included food, personnel, and general costs associated with the hotel. These did not include the cost of the central offices, amortization, reforms, or the price of leasing the buildings.

THE *SOL Y PLAYA* VACATION INDUSTRY IN SPAIN

In the context of the world market, Spain occupied third place in world earnings for tourism, behind the United States and France, with a 7.8 percent market share. In the European market, it occupied second place, with a 12 percent share, and was the leader in the European market for Mediterranean vacations, with 30 percent. The Spanish strategy had been to sell tourist products for mass market at very competitive prices.

Starting in 1988, a significant decline in the principal indicators of tourist activity in Spain was detected. The average spending per tourist per day was decreasing, due to the concurrence of three factors: a decline in the amount of money being spent on vacations, the fact that vacations different from the *sol y playa* type had higher prices, and a reduction in

Exhibit 15.4

Organization of the Company and of a Typical Hotel

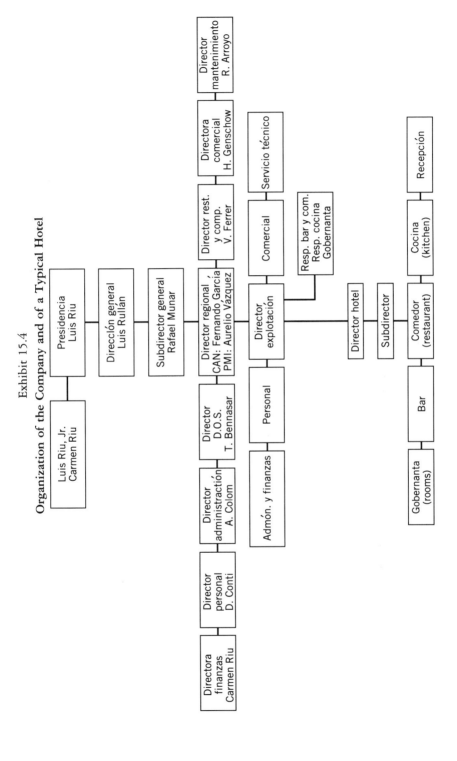

Exhibit 15.5

Basic Principles of Riu Hotels

1. The company must fundamentally pursue its continuity and, to guarantee this, must grow and create wealth. Its growth will be limited only by market expectations and its capacity for expansion.

This wealth belongs first to the company and second to the Capital and Labor that have generated it.

2. The Capital-Labor relationship (equally important forces) must tend toward equilibrium, principally through dialogue and mutual respect.

Achieving the objectives of the company requires the labor and effort of all of its members without exclusivism at the hierarchic level, recognizing and rewarding in an equitable manner the performance of these members.

The company must encourage the professional development of its employees, in a framework of personal development, without interfering in the objectives of the Company.

Managers must be enterprising, capable, dedicated, and self-motivated.

The management team is a group of professionals of different and complementary natures who, with the natural leader at the head, have as their mission the management of the Company.

3. Customer satisfaction is a value in itself. The Company is in debt to its clients 365 days a year and 24 hours a day.

The Company must create and maintain an internal and external image that includes its positive, differential characteristics.

Relationships with Tour Operators and Agencies must tend toward minimizing any antagonism at sales intermediaries of the sale of our product, reaffirming the RIU name.

4. Shareholders are more than mere contributors of Capital, and therefore we continue to search for them among the Riu family, the workers themselves, or those persons who can contribute something nonfinancial that reinforces the activity of the Company.

Shareholders are not simply creditors of a return proportional to their investment and risk, but preferably watch over the security of this investment, prestige, and growing value.

The independence of the current group is a positive value, which we would only renounce in the case of a common consent for the continuity of the Company.

We believe that the Company owes its recognition and consideration to the members of the Riu family in their capacity as promoters without presupposition of a preponderance of family interests over those of the Company.

Exhibit 15.5 *(continued)*

5. The Company, as an entity in the service of the Community, is obligated to contribute to the improvement and greater well-being of this Community.

Both the Public Administration and business organizations are entities that affect us, although with different degrees of intensity, and therefore our collaboration with them will be shaped in each case by the relationship of expected results to total cost (economic and human).

The Unions are a necessary force as a counterpoint to the interests of Capital, and relations with them must be marked by a spirit of dialogue and cooperation as long as their philosophy does not go against the existence of the Company itself.

Indigenous cultures and the ecological infrastructure where they arise are values which must be supported and promoted.

6. We understand Competition to be a dynamic force in the market and a stimulus to our creativity: a basic factor in a free economic system, in which we shall struggle to maintain a growing presence.

---

consumption in the vacation destination due to the high prices of the complementary offer. Also, the average length of stay was shortening, due to the fragmentation of vacation periods. Lastly, the total number of tourists was falling, mostly in the *sol y playa* market, due to the maturity of the market and the appearance of more attractive destinations (such as Greece, Tunisia, Turkey, and Yugoslavia).

The leadership position that Spain maintained in the *sol y playa* market was being threatened by the declining quality of the tourist product (deterioration of the landscape, poor infrastructure, deficient services, and aging hotels) and by increased prices. This was particularly serious in the Balearic Islands. In the Canary Islands the situation was somewhat different. On one hand, the high season occurred during winter, which meant that they could work 12 months out of the year with good prices. On the other hand, the structure of the offer was very different. While in the Balearic Islands 75 percent of beds were in hotels and the rest in apartments, in the Canary Islands the proportion was just the opposite: 75 percent in apartments and 25 percent in hotels.

With excess supply and an appreciable decline in demand, the tendency in the industry was toward price erosion. That, together with strong pressure from tour operators, squeezed profit margins and forced hotels to trim costs and services in order to survive. All of this led to a vicious cycle of attracting tourists with vacation packages with lower levels of profitability that, in consuming only those services included in the combined trip (not the complementary offer), decreased tourism earnings in addition to lowering the level of quality and services being offered.

CLIENTS AND VACATION SALES

Riu had exclusive contracts for its countries with the following tour operators: TUI (Germany), Luxair (Luxembourg), and Sunair (Belgium). In the case of TUI, this exclusivity referred only to Mallorca and not to the Canary Islands. Contracts were for 10 years, with revision clauses for prices based on inflation. These three contracts contributed to 80 percent of rooms sold. The remaining 20 percent were filled by individual agencies and clients who went directly to the reservation centers or to one of the hotels.

Seventy percent of the 320,000 clients who went to Riu hotels each year were German. The next three largest markets by country origin were Holland, Belgium, and Italy, each with 4 percent. Rullán had taken trips to Germany to observe these clients' way of life. "If I want to satisfy them in the two weeks that they spend with me, I have to give them what they don't receive during the rest of the year: personalization."

The German market was comprised of 82 million people. In Germany there were 9,000 travel agencies, 7,000 of which worked with Riu. The majority of these travel agencies were small, independent businesses that sold on commission the packages organized by various tour operators, although important chains of travel agencies were beginning to appear. The number of salespeople in these agencies could fluctuate from three to 15. The turnover for these agencies was very high, since the job was seen as an entry-level position.

A typical travel agency could have a list of up to 3,000 hotels in its brochures. Riu hotels' prices in German travel agencies were 10 to 20 percent more expensive than those of similar hotels of other chains. Riu thought that its product was different and that this justified its higher prices.

A client might spend about 15 minutes in the agency deciding on the hotel for his or her vacation. If the client opted for Riu, the average stay would be 10 days. Other services, mainly transportation, intervened in the process and were coordinated by the tour operator.

According to recent surveys, 50 percent of Riu's clients came on the recommendation of friends, 25 percent through an agency referral, 18 percent through the tour operator's brochure, 4 percent through special brochures, and 3 percent through advertising. Company management believed that 40 percent of its clients would change their tour operator in order to continue going to Riu hotels, should the tour operator change its supplier. This assumption was reinforced by the high rate of Riu's repeat clients (more than 60 percent in winter and over 40 percent in summer).

The value of the peseta against the mark was of the utmost importance to Riu Hotels. The devaluation of the former with respect to the latter had made it possible that, for a German, the cost in marks of a vacation at a Riu hotel had not varied since 1963. In the past, Riu Hotels' higher costs had not resulted in higher prices for its clients, since these costs were absorbed in successive devaluations. From 1988 to 1992 the tendency in the currency markets was different, due to a strengthening of the peseta, putting all Spanish hoteliers in a tight spot.

RIU MANAGEMENT

Luis Rullán had joined the company in 1980 at the age of 25, after finishing the M.B.A. program at IESE, University of Navarra, Barcelona. His first title was Assistant to the General Manager. In 1983 he was promoted to Assistant General Manager (a newly created position, since there was no upper management structure) and in 1985 to General Manager. During his years at Riu Hotels the company had experienced a period of intense growth and had undertaken a serious effort to professionalize management.

Immediately upon arriving, Rullán began to focus on developing a "budget" mentality and an awareness of controlling the economic aspects of the business, developing rules and regulations manuals, and changing the system of compensation for managers:

The first thing that I did when they named me General Manager was to increase salaries. I saw to it that some managers' salaries were doubled or tripled in a few years. I also told them: 'I want you to earn 7 million pesetas. I want you to know that if you only earn 5 million, you're not worth it and I'll have to replace you.' The compensation system that I introduced had a large variable part based on the results in the efficiency variables (extra earnings and cost control), the results of the satisfaction ratings, and abiding by the rules and regulations manual. Also, I gave them qualitative objectives, and whether or not they met them influenced the variable part of their salary.

In order to manage a service company you have to work very hard. If I'm not the first to arrive at the office every day, the rest slack off. If I apply the brakes, there's a traffic jam behind me. I can't stop because it would have a bottleneck effect; the same thing happens with traffic: the car in front puts on his brakes and creates a line of traffic three or four kilometers behind.

I like to tell my managers that they'll be General Managers, not when their business cards say it, but when their employees recognize them as such. The position that you occupy in the organizational chart is defined by the type of problem that comes to you and the person who comes to you to solve it.

I think that one of the things that I have brought to the company has been making executives out of hotel managers, and starting to force this mentality downward: section managers, assistant managers, etc. Managers whom I've had to fire because they didn't tow the line at Riu Hotels are now 'star' managers at other chains. This makes me proud.

The manager of a hotel has to be in constant contact with the public. They're worth nothing to me if they close themselves in their offices to solve accounting or purchasing problems. Their job is to satisfy customers and employees.

I often tell my people: let's see if we can do better what we already do well. It's our motto, the spirit of perfection. Other products don't tempt us.

Rullán had seen to it that suppliers were spoken to very seriously about not offering Riu employees prices for bottle caps. It was common practice in the industry that the suppliers of alcoholic beverages, for example, be given a certain amount of money for the caps that the waiters accumulated. Riu Hotels' argument was that it was the company that paid its workers and that therefore the incentive should be given to the chain, in the form of a discount. Details of this type were common to Rullán's management style.

The Hotel Managers

Riu Hotels had a philosophy that the most important role of hotel managers was to be visible for clients, to make them feel welcome, and to talk to them. According to management: "This personal treatment is what allows us to exceed the expectations of our clients." In addition, it was reasoned, "the company can do everything for its clients, except introduce itself and say to them, 'I'm the hotel manager.' Here the managers are irreplaceable." Luis Rullán wanted to keep his hotel managers from falling into two stereotypes: "Those who plan everything so they don't have to face up to things or those who don't plan and fix things by facing up to them. I want the middle ground: that they plan and face up to things."

Internally, this concept of hotel manager was called host manager. In actuality it was only a general idea that was intended to be made much more explicit. The typical day in the life of a Riu manager is described in Exhibit 15.6.

Riu Hotels had installed an information system that allowed the manager of each hotel to get a list of clients who were staying at the hotel, along with their history of stays at Riu. The information informed the managers of the percentage of repeat clients, the names of the new ones, and the purchasing patterns of those who came back. All of this information was just another excuse for the manager to converse with clients and to surprise them.

The evaluation of hotel managers had three elements. The first measured their management efficiency as far as cost control was concerned. The second was related to the rate of client satisfaction and the third to a series of management elements called "qualitative budgeting." This included goals for training employees, interaction with clients, evaluations of their employees, and so on. To date, a reduction in the rate of employee turnover had never been a qualitative objective.

Exhibit 15.6

Normal Activities of a Hotel Manager at Riu

A typical day for a Riu Hotel Manager began around 7:45 A.M. with the first visit to Reception, to check on the news of the previous night, and then to the kitchen to observe all of the preparation activities for breakfast. "Breakfast is an important moment for the client; in addition to constituting the hotel's 'good morning' to its clients, it's an opportunity for clients to begin the day with optimism and excitement," said the General Manager of the Hotel de Isla Cristina.

Later the manager had breakfast in the dining room (sometimes in the company of a client), where he remained until 9:30 A.M. From there he stopped by Reception once again and then began his first round of the hotel, greeting clients, asking employees for information, observing the cleanliness and tidiness of the rooms, instilling enthusiasm in his colleagues, and lending a hand when necessary. The first round ended around 11:00 A.M., after which he went to his office to review his mail and other correspondence, and where he met with his most direct colleagues, the Section Managers.

At 1:00 P.M. he left his office to visit the pool area and to check on the progress of lunch preparations. This round was another opportunity to talk with guests. He normally had lunch in the company of the Assistant General Manager at 1:45 P.M.

At 3:30 P.M. he went back to his office to send headquarters the information sheet for the previous day, with information on the close of the day related to the cash situation, occupation, business activities, and staff that had been prepared for him by the Assistant General Manager. The central office in Palma preferred that this information be sent in the morning so they could rest from 3:00 to 6:00 P.M.

Having finished this activity, the manager made a short round that included Reception, the pool area, and other common areas; the length of this round could vary, but on occasion he put aside some time, from 5:00 to 6:00 P.M., to rest or attend to some other personal activity.

At 6:00 P.M. the kitchen and dining room activities began in preparation for dinner. This was the time of the two rituals in which the Host Manager participated. The first occurred between 6:45 and 7:00 P.M. It involved the transfer of information from the chef to the kitchen and dining room employees concerning the menu and coordinating and carrying out the activities of these two departments during the dinner.

At 7:00 P.M. the dining room was opened for the first dinner shift and with it began the second ritual in which all dining room and kitchen employees, together with the Manager and Assistant Manager, welcomed guests at the door

Exhibit 15.6 *(continued)*

of the dining room, properly dressed and trained, forming a line, wishing them a nice dinner. The Manager remained, welcoming guests for about 30 minutes, while the kitchen and dining room personnel went on—after about 5 minutes—to finish their tasks. When the first shift had been seated, the Manager went to the kitchen to observe the progress of the hot meals (the most delicate part of the dinner).

Around 8:00 P.M., the Manager went to the bar to talk to the Section Manager and to the guests. Then he made another round by the pool, Reception, and common areas.

At approximately 8:50 P.M., he returned to the dining room to check on the progress of the first shift and to assist in the preparations and reception of the guests in the second shift, a task that could take until 9:20 P.M. At 9:30 P.M. he had dinner.

At 10:30 P.M. he returned to the bar to interact with the guests, and he remained there until 11:00 P.M. Before retiring to his room, he stopped by Reception and his office one last time, in case there were any new developments. Once in his room, he was available for any emergency that could arise during the night.

Choosing personnel was done by taking into account their personality traits and their potential fit in the company's culture. Rullán had once stated: "The best way to interview a candidate is by talking to the candidate's wife or husband."

Employees received a formal evaluation from their bosses once a year. The frequency of these evaluations was greater for section managers (once a month) and for hotel managers (quarterly).

SERVICE AT RIU HOTELS

Riu advertisements in Germany spoke of Riu as "the friendly hotels with service from the heart [Riu Die Freundliche Hotels]." General management put great emphasis on making sure that service was as personalized as possible. Its goal was to combine the best of the Nordics (back-office planning) with the best of the Mediterraneans (the capacity for improvisation and initiative in personal interaction). The fruit of this concern was the recent introduction of the host managers concept and many other amenities that had been conceived years before.

It was normal for Riu employees to know enough German to be able to maintain a conversation with their guests. When a guest came upon any of the hotel's employees, it was almost a rule that the employee address the client with a friendly phrase and a smile. At the reception desk, the client's name was placed near his or her key so that he or she could be called by name when picking it up. It was also customary to call rooms to ask if everything was in its place. In the dining room, the staff was careful to always seat guests in the same place in order to locate them more easily and to be able to refer to them personally. Every day management asked its team for any incidents (for example, fixing a pipe, the irritation of a guest for having run out of good lounge chairs at the pool, a guest's illness, suggestions made to someone in the hotel) that could serve as an excuse for personally contacting clients.

Upon arriving at the hotel, clients were welcomed at a cocktail reception which the section managers (of the Kitchen, Dining Room, Chambermaid, Reception, Bar, Entertainment, and other departments) and the General Manager and Assistant General Manager all attended. At this cocktail party, hotel management formally introduced itself and told clients that, when they had any problem whatsoever, they could address any hotel employee or go to them directly. This welcome was given during the arrival of large groups or any set day of the week when there were important changes in the composition of clients, usually Tuesday or Thursday.

Also, at the end of their stay, it was customary for the manager to board their bus and to thank them, with microphone in hand, for staying at Riu, wishing them a good trip and asking them to come back soon. This initiative came about as the result of a comment from a client who had stated, upon returning to Riu, that he had thought it strange that at the end of his previous stay nobody had said good-bye to him after he had been treated like a friend: "When friends part, they say good-bye to one another."

Male guests at the hotel had to wear long pants and a jacket in order to enter the dining room to have dinner. Employees, especially the manager, watched out for this bit of etiquette during the time that they spent at the door of the dining room welcoming the guests. It was normal for clients to appear at dinner wearing their best clothes and with enviable color on their skin, fruit of the sunbathing they had done that morning. Both things created an atmosphere of distinction among the guests.

Dinner normally consisted of an appetizer that was offered buffet-style and a hot entree with four choices that was served at the table with all of the protocol found at a good restaurant. The hotel made sure that the table at which clients were seated, as well as the shift in which they were served, were always the same. If someone asked for a bottle of wine and did not finish it, he could be sure that the following day, without having to ask for it, a waiter would bring the same bottle to him at his table.

One night a week the company surprised clients with a gala dinner, which included extras like softer lighting, a flower for each woman, a menu with Nordic lobster, crêpes for dessert, and champagne. On these occasions, guests took even greater pains to dress elegantly.

EVALUATION FORMS

At dinner time on a previously unannounced day, all clients received a questionnaire with which they evaluated certain aspects of the quality of the hotel's service. Despite the fact that the questionnaire was very simple (see Exhibit 15.7), while it was being distributed, clients were told of its importance for improving service (other consequences of the survey were not mentioned to avoid restricting the client), and they were reminded of the hotel's category, which was to be taken into consideration so that they would make a proportionate assessment.

The survey was made up of six elements to be evaluated by one of three options: "very good," "good," and "bad." A "very good" was worth two points; a "good," one point; and a "bad," minus one. Each question had a small space for comments, which was rarely filled in. This was a source of frustration for Riu employees, when clients assigned a "bad" rating to some aspect of service without writing in their reasons why.

The hotels explained to their employees that the difference between a "very good" and a "good" rested in the quality of their treatment of the client, in the details of their interaction with him or her, and in human warmth. According to Rullán:

> The difference is personalization, the personal detail, that they see that
> the manager does something directly for them, calling them by name,

Exhibit 15.7
Satisfaction Questionnaire

Hotels

Al objeto de poder mejorar nuestro servicio al cliente, le
agradeceríamos nos diera su opinión sobre los siguientes
servicios, teniendo en cuenta la categoría del Hotel.
Muchas gracias. La Dirección.

Um unseren Dienst am Kunden zu verbessern, bitten wir Sie
freundlichst um Ihre Meinung und die folgenden Fragen
(unter Berücksichtigung der Hotelkategorie) zu beantworten.
Besten Dank - Die Hotelleitung.

För att kunna förbättra var service till kunderna, ber vi eder
svara pa de fragor vi här ställt och filla i rutorna samt
betändande hotellets kategori även ge oss eder uppriktiga asikt.
Vi tack ar för vänlighten - Hotelldirektionen.

In order to improve our service we would like to have your
opinion and answers to the following questions.
(In accordance with the Hotel category).
Thank you - Hotel Management.

A fin de pouvoir améliorer notre service au client, nous
vous prions de bien vouloir donner votre opinion sur les
questions suivantes, tout en considérant la catégorie de l'Hôtel.
Merci bien - La Direction.

Om onze service te verbeteren, verzoeken wij u vriendelijk
volgende vragen, met inachtname hotelcategorie,
te beantwoorden.
Hartelijk dank - de directie.

A fine di migliorare i nostri servizi al cliente, saremo grati
ci desse una sua opinione sui nostri servizi tenendo conto
della categoria dell'albergo.
Molte grazie. La Direzione.

Por favor doble este papel y deposítelo en el buzón

Bitte falten Sie dieses Papier und stecken Sie es in den
dafür bestimmten Kasten

Var vänlig vik detta papper och lägs det i den för detta
ändamät avseda breviadan

Please, fold this paper and put it into the box provided
for this purpose

Veuillez plier ce papier et le deposer dans la boite
installée à ce fin

Dit papier alstublieft dubbelvouwen en in de daarvoor
bestemde bus doen

Per favore pieghei questa lettera e la depositi nella casetta

Exhibit 15.7 *(continued)*

	MUY BIEN SEHR GUT MYCKET BRAA VERY GOOD TRES BIEN ZEER GOED OTTIMO	BIEN GUT BRAA GOOD BIEN GOED BUONO	MAL SCHLECHT DALIG BAD MAL SLECHT MALE

LIMPIEZA HABITACIÓN
ZIMMERREINIGUNG
RENGÖRING AV-RUM
CLEANING ROOM
PROPRETÉE CHAMBRE
REINIGING KAMER
PULIZIA DELLE CAMERA
☐ ☐ ☐

SERVICIO COMEDOR
BEDIENUNG IM SPEISESAAL
BETJÄNINGEN I MATSALEN
DINING-ROOM SERVICE
SALLE A MANGER
SERVICE RESTAURANT
SERVIZIO DELLA SALA DA PRANZO
☐ ☐ ☐

SERVICIO BAR
BEDIENUNG IN DER BAR
BETJÄNINGEN I BAR
BAR SERVICE
SERVICE BAR
SERVIZIO BAR
☐ ☐ ☐

SERVICIO BAR DE PISCINA
BEDIENUNG IN DER POOLBAR
SERVICE-BAR-SVÖMMEBASSIN
SERVICE BAR PISCINE
SERVICE POOLBAR
SERVIZIO BAR-PISCINA
☐ ☐ ☐

COCINA
KUECHE
MATEN
MEALS
CUISINE
KEUKEN
CUCINA
☐ ☐ ☐

RECEPCIÓN
REZEPTION
RECEPTIONEN
RECEPTION
RECEPTIE
RECEZIONE
☐ ☐ ☐

OTROS SERVICIOS
ALLGEMEINE LEISTUNGEN
ANDRA TJÄNSTER
OTHER SERVICES
AUTRES SERVICES
ALGEMENE DIENST
ALTRI SERVIZI
☐ ☐ ☐

SUGERENCIAS PARA MEJORAR EL SERVICIO:
VERBESSERUNGSVORSCHLÄGE:
EDER RAD FOR ATT GÖRA EN FÖRBÄTTRING:
SUGGESTIONS FOR IMPROVEMENTS:
SUGESTIONS POUR AMÉLIORER:
UW SUGGESTIES:
SUGGERIMENTI PER MIGLIORATI I SERVIZI:

commenting upon things with them. The client gives a 'very good' when he is made to feel like a person. This is the client who comes back. We have a hotel with a very high rating. Its manager is a great public relations person. He knows by heart the names of all clients who return, and he loves being with them; he finds them a special meal if they need it or, simply, if they feel like it. The economic cost is very low, and it lifts spirits enormously. Another extremely important challenge is to 'deflate' the 'dynamite guest.' That's the client who starts complaining about everything, and his discontent becomes contagious.

The average rating for the chain was 1.72. General management set different goals for each hotel, depending on the different circumstances. These goals oscillated between 1.6 and 1.8 points. The rating obtained was a factor in the bonuses earned by all employees.

The hotel managers had the choice of not computing some questionnaires. In Rullán's words:

I recognize that there are difficult clients, with problems. That's why I allow hotel managers to mark some questionnaires, so that they are not counted in the satisfaction rating. The funny thing is that, 95 percent of the time, the difficult client puts a very high rating. We have proof that the average results from the marked questionnaires are higher than the ratings of other questionnaires—which is a paradox that, for us, is very important.

Satisfaction Ratings and Central Services

In 1991, Riu Hotels introduced an internal satisfaction index. It consisted of a quarterly survey that was done among hotel managers, in order to judge the services that the central offices were providing them. Thus, a manager had to evaluate the quality offered by Administration, Finance, Technical Services, Laundry, Marketing, and other departments.

From the very beginning there was great opposition on the part of those people who had to be evaluated. Their arguments were of the following sort: "They won't know how to evaluate what we do," "They're just going to make us angry," "Now they'll want everything to be done just for them." After a period of stops and starts, general management decided to put it into practice, first making sure that those being evaluated determined the text of what was going to be asked. The result of the first survey was disappointing—the resulting average was 0.57.[5]

General management had to insist that the surveys were being used only to see how the receivers of central services perceived the weaknesses of these services. The ratings rose quarter after quarter. In September 1992 the rating was 1.50 in Palma and 1.23 in the Canary Islands. (Exhibit 15.8 shows 1992 evaluations of central services for the Riu hotels in Palma and Gran Canaria.) The increase had been achieved through increased personalization in central services' treatment of hotel managers and through some mischievous "vote buying." The discussion at that time was whether the behavior of general management should be included explicitly or not in evaluating hotel managers.

The manager of the Department of Systems and Organization (DSO), Tomeu Bennasar, explained it in this way:

I have to admit that, in the beginning, the idea of measuring internal satisfaction based on our services didn't thrill me. Not because I believed that I wasn't capable of satisfying our users, but because I believed that it would take an enormous effort to qualify something as intangible as the quality of computer services. The first difficulty we faced was finding the right questions to ask users so that they could make evaluations. In our case we opted for three management indicators: (A) treatment they receive from the members of the department, (B) response time for a reported problem, and (C) level of information that is received from the resolution of their problems. The first evaluations were painful. We went through a period of reflection concerning the why of these evaluations. Our conclusion was very simple: we weren't *doing* it poorly, we were *selling* it poorly. Therefore, we computer people realized that, in order to make the quality of our work tangible, we had to develop activities like sales and public relations, which was rather curious.

Our first step was to put together a register of all problems reported, and we challenged ourselves to giving the utmost priority to solving these problems. This forced us to do an in-depth analysis of a situation in order to attack the root of the problem and thus to avoid multiple occurrences of the same type of difficulty. Another important change

---

[5] The rating system was identical to the one for clients. A "very good" counted for two points, a "good" for one point, and a "bad" was minus one.

Exhibit 15.8
Hotels' Evaluations of the Main Office

Department	Sept. 1992	Percent Increase	July 1992	Percent Increase	April 1992
		Hotels in Palma			
Laundry	1.17	32.58	0.88	57.14	0.56
Technical Services	0.97	−10.21	1.08	28.57	0.84
Maid Service	1.86	6.35	1.75	10.06	1.59
Administration	1.84	1.34	1.82	6.43	1.71
Personnel	1.58	−0.65	1.59	35.90	1.17
Organization and Systems	1.89	−0.06	1.89	5.00	1.80
Purchasing	1.45	6.67	1.36	11.48	1.22
Restoration	1.36	−0.06	1.36	25.93	1.08
Marketing	1.41	5.24	1.34	8.94	1.23
Technical consulting fee	1.52	2.52	1.48	8.03	1.37
Gardening	—	—	—	—	—
Final average	1.50	3.42	1.45	15.75	1.26
		Hotels in Gran Canaria			
Laundry	0.98	18.12	0.83	25.76	0.66
Technical Services	0.69	−22.75	0.89	25.35	0.71
Maid Service	1.28	11.41	1.15	−3.36	1.19
Administration	1.55	5.28	1.47	24.58	1.18
Personnel	1.13	3.39	1.09	0.93	1.08
Organization and Systems	1.90	4.49	1.78	15.58	1.54
Purchasing	0.97	−0.40	0.97	−1.02	0.98
Restoration	1.13	6.13	1.06	−3.64	1.10
Marketing	1.38	26.15	1.09	−16.79	1.31
Technical consulting fee	1.06	−26.59	1.45	39.42	1.04
Gardening	1.53	4.17	1.47	10.53	1.33
Final average	1.23	1.98	1.20	9.32	1.10

was to make improvements in notifying the user that the problem had been taken care of. It also occurred to us that, as far as making our work tangible, it was worth contacting the user after one or two days to reconfirm that the solution had been effective. In the case when a situation remained open longer than usual, the user was periodically informed of the reasons that impeded its resolution, as well as the steps that had already been taken.

Based on the register of problems, we can calculate response time and make summaries of these by hotel which, together with the original lists of problems, allow us to respond to the second and third questions.

Once the evaluations are received from the hotel managers, we analyze their opinions, and we begin a round of visits in those cases where the evaluation has surprised us. In 95 percent of cases the managers are unaware of the real problems that their hotel has with our department, as well as the response time that it is receiving. With this type of aggressive action we attempt to make it possible for us to receive a true evaluation of the service that we offer and to avoid as much as possible opinions based on feelings that, in the case of computer services—for lack of understanding—were mostly negative.

The result of managing the satisfaction of internal clients in this way has been a spectacular improvement in quarterly ratings. On the other hand, we have had to put a lot of effort into making evident what I already knew: the quality of the department as a collective of professionals.

Exhibit 15.9 shows the evolution of satisfaction ratings of users of the Department of Systems and Organization from April 1991 to September 1992. The questions A, B, and C correspond to those indicated previously (above) by the manager of the department.

THE RIU PARTNER CLUB PROJECT

Riu was considering introducing the "Partner Club" card for some of the agencies with which it worked. The card would consist of a group of elements with the objective of developing the loyalty of the channel. The agencies that wanted to be a part of the club would have to fill out an application addressed to Riu Hotels. The application could be filled out

Exhibit 15.9
Satisfaction Rating of Users of the Department of Organization and Systems (DOS)

Consolidated Figures from All Areas

	April 1991	July 1991	October 1991	January 1992	April 1992	July 1992	September 1992	January 1993	Average
A	1.39	1.50	1.71	1.93	1.88	1.95	2.00		1.76
B	0.35	1.07	1.53	1.79	1.63	1.76	1.71		1.41
C	0.41	1.00	1.47	1.75	1.44	1.71	1.89		1.38
Average	0.73	1.19	1.57	1.83	1.65	1.81	1.86		1.52

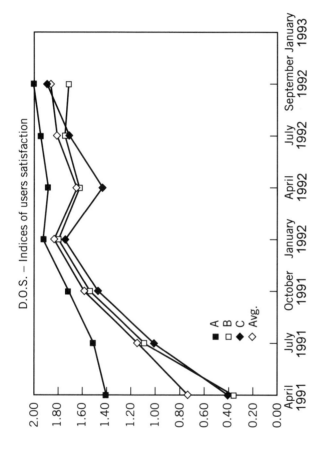

D.O.S. – Indices of users satisfaction

by—and therefore the subject of its associated benefits could be—both the individual seller as well as the particular agency or chain.

The prepared documentation stated: "Make each person a content client and profit from your effort with Riu." It continued: "You are familiar with Riu and our dedication to customer satisfaction. Your degree of professionalism and personal recommendation is what will make us successful in seeing that your clients have comfortable vacations. . . ."

The promotion consisted of six elements. The first was that the hotel would leave a gift in the room for the clients of travel agencies who possessed the card. The cost for Riu was 500 pta, and the company planned to alternate gifts in order to avoid repeats with regular customers. At the request of the agencies it was planned that the text accompanying the gift would say that it was a joint initiative of both the agency and of Riu.

The second element was a system of accumulating points per clients sent to Riu. When a certain number of points was accumulated, Riu offered free trips to its hotels for the agency's employees. The number of points needed to redeem the trip varied according to the destination and season of the year. They had thought about giving incentives during the off-season periods, but in the end it was decided not to do this and instead to allow them, with the exception of Christmas, the freedom to redeem points at any time of the year. Riu Hotels wanted the system of accumulating points to be an excuse for personally contacting the channel salespeople.

The third element was a free fax line (24-hour hotline) by which salespeople could make special requests for their clients: questions like type of meals and desired room number. In the beginning they thought it should not be a fax but a telephone line. In the end it was decided to use a fax to reduce costs and to keep someone from spending half an hour talking about other things.

A fourth element of the "Riu Partner Club" card was an explicit guarantee that the hotel would solve, in less than 24 hours, any problem that a client might have during his or her stay. If Riu did not fulfill its promise, it would invite the client to return for free at another time. Riu offered the guarantee to the channel, who had the option of giving the client a copy of the text of this guarantee.

The company had for years been implicitly offering a guarantee of satisfaction. In October 1992, for example, it had received two complaints, and in each case it offered to return the client's money. One case involved

Exhibit 15.10
Forecasted Cost of the Riu Partner Club Program (pta)

Year	1993	1994	1995
Riu Partner Concept			
Send extracts	3,509,616	5,569,608	7,629,600
Send offerings	548,504	870,452	1,192,400
Confirmation of prizes	72,107	90,133	108,160
Send cards	233,653	186,546	186,546
Client attention (gifts)	28,800,000	36,000,000	43,200,000
Salespeople attention (gifts)	1,860,000	1,485,000	1,485,000
Training visits	60,800,000	76,000,000	91,200,000
Personnel	22,408,325	22,408,325	22,408,325
Marketing Plan			
Presentations at Riu	14,580,000	14,580,000	14,580,000
Presentations in the country	16,630,000	20,725,000	20,725,000
Agency visits	8,617,500	3,247,500	3,247,500
Advertising material	7,728,924	6,530,560	6,530,560
Computer Support			
Relationship central areas	249,865	249,865	249,865
Interface with tour operators	4,096,128	4,096,128	4,096,128
Operator Riu Partner Club	900,000	900,000	900,000
Use of IBM network	357,780	357,780	357,780
Total	171,392,402	193,296,897	218,096,864

a guest in Santo Domingo who complained of having seen a black kitchen worker with sweat on his forehead. The client alleged that the sweat from this kitchen worker's forehead could have fallen in her food and been the cause of a bout of diarrhea that she suffered for several days. The second case was that of another guest who, when she returned home, became ill; she attributed the illness to a virus that she said she contracted because of the hotel's air-conditioning.

During 1992 a pilot test of an explicit guarantee was carried out with a Belgian tour operator. The wording was similar to that presently being discussed for introduction in the German market. After a year of trial, not one single reclamation had been registered.

The fifth element was to offer a 50 percent discount to salespeople in the travel agencies who stayed at a Riu hotel with one relative sharing the same room.

Finally, the company was considering publishing, on a quarterly basis, a small magazine with information about new offers, Riu, and other details, which would accompany the information sent about accumulated points.

The forecasted investment for the Riu Partner Club project was 37 million pta for purchasing information equipment (hardware and software) and marketing equipment (card printer, material design, and other items). The cost of operating the program in its first year of functioning was forecast at more than 170 million pta, with an annual increase greater than 10 percent (see Exhibit 15.10).

Part V
Integrative Case

Case Sixteen

Virgin Atlantic Airways

Pantéa Denoyelle and Jean-Claude Larréché

In June 1994, Virgin Atlantic Airways celebrated the 10th anniversary of its inaugural flight to New York. Richard Branson, the airline's Chairman and Founder, reminisced about its tremendous growth. In 10 short years, he had established Virgin Atlantic as Britain's second largest long-haul airline, with a reputation for quality and innovative product development. Branson turned his thoughts to the challenges that lay ahead.

ORIGINS OF THE VIRGIN GROUP

"Branson, I predict you will either go to prison, or become a millionaire." These were the last words the 17-year-old Branson heard from his headmaster as he left school. Twenty-five years later, Branson ruled over a business empire whose 1993 sales exceeded £1.5 billion. He had started his first entrepreneurial business at the age of 12, selling Christmas trees. Soon after leaving school, he set up *Student,* a national magazine, as "a platform for all shades of opinion, all beliefs and ideas . . . a vehicle for intelligent comment and protest." The magazine, whose editorial staff had an average age of 16, featured interviews by Branson with celebrities and articles on controversial issues.

This case was prepared by Pantéa Denoyelle, Research Associate, under the supervision of Jean-Claude Larréché, Alfred H. Heineken Professor of Marketing at INSEAD. It is intended to be used as a basis for class discussion rather than to illustrate either effective or ineffective handling of an administrative situation. Copyright © 1995 INSEAD, Fontainebleau, France. Used with permission. In June 1994, £1.00 ≈ U.S. $1.50.

In 1970, Branson founded a mail-order record business—called Virgin to emphasize his own commercial innocence. The first Virgin record shop was opened in London's Oxford Street in 1971, soon followed by a recording studio and a label that produced records for performers such as Phil Collins, Genesis, and Boy George. The Venue nightclub opened in 1978. In 1980, Virgin Records began expanding overseas, initially on a licensing basis; it later set up its own subsidiaries. Virgin Vision was created in 1983, followed by Virgin Atlantic Airways and Virgin Cargo in 1984, and Virgin Holidays in 1985.

In November 1986 the Virgin Group, which included the Music, Communication, and Retail divisions, was floated on the London stock exchange. The airline, clubs, and holidays activities remained part of the privately owned Voyager Group Ltd. In its first public year, Virgin Group Plc had profit of £13 million on £250 million turnover—far beyond expectations. Its public status, however, was short-lived: Branson believed he could not be an entrepreneur while chairing a public company. In October 1988 he regained full control by buying back all outstanding shares. The constraints that he had struggled with during the company's public life were replaced by an overwhelming sense of relief and freedom. A partnership with Seibu Saison International, one of Japan's largest retail and travel groups, was equally brief. In 1990, Branson sold 10 percent of the equity of Voyager Travel Holdings, the holding company for Virgin Atlantic, to the Japanese group in return for an injection of £36 million of equity and convertible loan capital—only to buy out his Japanese partner for £45 million in 1991.

In 1992, Branson sold Virgin Music (by then the world's sixth-largest record company) to Thorn EMI for £560 million. By 1994 the Virgin Group consisted of three holding companies: Virgin Retail Group, Virgin Communication, and Virgin Investments which controlled over 100 entities in 12 countries. Exhibit 16.1 summarizes the group's activities.

VIRGIN ATLANTIC AIRWAYS

In 1984, Richard Branson was approached by Randolph Fields, a 31-year-old lawyer who wanted to start a transatlantic airline. Fields' plan was to operate a business class–only B747 service to New York. Richard Branson

Exhibit 16.1

The Virgin Group of Companies. [From Virgin Atlantic.]

Virgin consists of three wholly owned separate holding companies involved in distinct business areas from media and publishing to retail, travel, and leisure. There are over 100 operating companies across the three holding companies in 12 countries worldwide.

Virgin Retail Group	Virgin Communication	Virgin Group	Voyager Investments	
			Voyager Group	Virgin Travel Group
Operates a chain of megastores in the U.K., Continental Europe, Australia, and Pacific selling music, video, and other entertainment products. Operates game stores in the U.K. Wholesale record exports and imports	Publishing of computer entertainment software Management of investments in broadcasting including Music Box. Investments in related publishing and entertainment activities, television post production services Book publishing Virgin Radio, Britain's first national commercial contemporary music station	Investments: joint-ventures Property developments Magnetic media distribution Management and corporate finance services to the Virgin organization	Clubs and hotels Airship and balloon operations Storm model agency	U.K.'s second largest long-haul international airline: Virgin Atlantic Airways Freight handling and packaging Inclusive tour operations: Virgin Holidays
Note: Marui of Japan own 50% of Virgin Megastores Japan; WH Smith own 50% of Virgin Retail U.K.				

433

quickly made up his mind. He announced that the new airline, to be named Virgin Atlantic Airways, would be operational within three months. Needless to say, his decision struck Virgin's senior management as completely insane.

Branson, who knew nothing about the airline business, set out to learn from the downfall of Laker Airways, an airline launched in 1970 by Freddie Laker with six planes and 120 employees. Laker Airways was originally designed as a low-risk business, flying under contract for package-holiday firms; in 1971, however, it introduced a low-budget, no frills service between London and New York. Laker's overconfidence led to several mistakes, including purchasing three DC-10s before the U.S. government had approved his London–New York line, and generally ordering more aircraft than he could afford. He accumulated a £350 million debt while the big transatlantic carriers slashed prices. This eventually led to Laker Airways' demise in 1981.

Branson hired two former Laker executives, Roy Gardner (who later became Virgin Atlantic's co-managing director) and David Tait. Branson decided that his new airline should not be all business class, but combine an economy section with a first-class section at business-class prices. His goal was clear: "To provide all classes of travelers with the highest-quality travel at the lowest cost." Branson also leased a second-hand 747. The contract he negotiated with Boeing had a sell-back option at the end of the first, second, or third year—a clause protecting Virgin against currency fluctuations. Another priority was to recruit air crew. Fortunately, British Airways had recently lowered the optional retirement age for its crew, creating a pool of experienced pilots from which Virgin could draw; this gave it the most experienced crew of any British airline.

Obtaining permission from American regulatory bodies to fly to New York was not easy; authorization to land at Newark was granted only three days before Virgin's first flight was scheduled. Forbidden to advertise in the United States until the approval, Virgin decided to launch a teaser campaign. Skywriters festooned the Manhattan sky with the words "WAIT FOR THE ENGLISH VIRGI . . . ."

Virgin Atlantic's inaugural flight took off from London on June 22, 1984, packed with friends, celebrities, reporters, and Branson wearing a World War I leather flight helmet. Once the plane had taken off, passengers were surprised to see on the video screen the cockpit, where the "crew"—Branson and two famous cricket players—greeted them. Although this was obviously a recording, it was a memorable moment for passengers.

Early Years (1984–1989)

Virgin Atlantic's early years were slightly chaotic. "I love the challenge," Branson said. "I suspect that before I went into the airline business, a lot of people thought I would never be able to make a go of it. It made it even more challenging to prove them wrong." Branson's determination and enthusiasm, as well as the experienced management team he assembled, made up for this initial amateurism.

Virgin Atlantic extended its operations progressively. Its early routes, all from London, were to New York (Newark since 1984 and John F. Kennedy (JFK) Airport since 1988), Miami (1986), Boston (1987), and Orlando (1988). Flights to Tokyo and Los Angeles were added in 1989 and 1990. In 1987, Virgin celebrated its one millionth transatlantic passenger. Until 1991, all Virgin flights left from London's Gatwick Airport, which was much smaller than Heathrow (LHR). Virgin countered this commercial disadvantage with a free limousine service for Upper Class passengers and a Gatwick Upper Class lounge, inaugurated in 1990.

While Branson had always befriended rock stars, he had otherwise kept a low profile. This changed when he launched the airline: "I knew that the only way of competing with British Airways and the others was to get out there and use myself to promote it," he explained. Branson made a point of being accessible to reporters and never missed an opportunity to cause a sensation, wearing a stewardess' uniform or a bikini on board, or letting himself be photographed in his bath. What really caught the public's attention were his Atlantic crossings. In 1986, his *Virgin Atlantic Challenger II* speedboat recorded the fastest time ever across the Atlantic, Branson on board. Even more spectacular was the 1987 crossing of the *Virgin Atlantic Flyer*—the largest hot-air balloon ever flown and the first to cross the Atlantic. Three years later Branson crossed the Pacific in another balloon from Japan to Arctic Canada, a distance of 6,700 miles, breaking all existing records with speeds of up to 245 miles per hour.

Years of Professionalization (1989–1994)

The professionalization of Virgin Atlantic's management began in 1989. Until then Virgin Atlantic had had a flat structure, with 27 people reporting to Branson directly. As the airline expanded, it had outgrown its entrepreneurial ways and needed to become customer-driven.

Branson asked Syd Pennington, a veteran Marks & Spencer retailer, to look into the airline's duty-free business in addition to his other responsibilities at Virgin Megastores. Some time later, Pennington, coming back from a trip, learned that he had been promoted to Co-managing Director of the airline. When Pennington expressed his surprise, Branson explained: "It's easier to find good retail people than good airline people." Pennington saw that Virgin Atlantic lacked controls and procedures, and he devoted himself to professionalizing its management. His objective was to infuse the business with Branson's charisma and energy while also making it effective enough to succeed. Exhibit 16.2 has a five-year summary of

Exhibit 16.2

Financial Results and Labor Force of Virgin Atlantic Airways. [From Virgin Atlantic.]

Financial Year	Turnover (£ millions)	Profit (Loss) Before Tax (£ millions)
1988–1989	106.7	8.4
1989–1990	208.8	8.5
1990–1991	382.9	6.1
1991–1992	356.9	(14.5)
1992–1993	404.7	0.4

Note: The reporting year ended on July 31 until 1990, and on October 31 as of 1991. The 1990–1991 period covered 15 months.

Year	Number of Employees*
1988	440
1989	678
1990	1,104
1991	1,591
1992	1,638
1993	1,627
1994	2,602

* As of December 31 (May 31 for 1994).

Virgin Atlantic's financial performance and labor force. Exhibit 16.3 shows the three-year evolution of passengers carried and market shares.

After years of campaigning, Virgin Atlantic was granted the right to fly out of Heathrow in 1991. Heathrow, Britain's busiest airport, handled 100,000 passengers a day—a total of 40 million in 1990, compared with 1.7 million at Gatwick. Virgin Atlantic was assigned to Heathrow's Terminal 3, where it competed with 30 other airlines serving over 75 destinations on five continents. In Branson's eyes, gaining access to Heathrow was a "historic moment and the culmination of years of struggle." His dream to compete with other long-haul carriers on an equal footing had come true. A new era began for Virgin Atlantic. Flying from Heathrow enabled it to have high load factors all year and to attract more business and full-fare economy passengers. It could also carry more interline flyers and more cargo, since Heathrow was the United Kingdom's main airfreight center. On the morning of the airline's first flight from Heathrow, a Virgin Atlantic "hit squad" encircled the model British Airways Concorde at the airport's entrance and pasted it over with Virgin's logo. Branson, dressed up as a pirate, was photographed in front of the Concorde before security forces could reach the site. A huge party marked the end of the day.

In April 1993, Virgin Atlantic ordered four A340s from Airbus Industries, the European consortium in which British Aerospace had a 20 percent share. The order, worth over £300 million, reflected the airline's commitment to new destinations. "We are proud to buy an aircraft which is in large part British-built, and on which so many jobs in the U.K. depend," said Branson. The A340, the longest-range aircraft in the world,

Exhibit 16.3
Market Shares of Virgin Atlantic Airways (Revenue Passengers).* [From Virgin Atlantic.]

Route	*1993*	*1992*	*1991*
New York (JFK and Newark)	19.6%	17.2%	18%
Florida (Miami and Orlando)	33.2%	30.6%	25.2%
Los Angeles	23.6%	21.8%	25.8%
Tokyo	18.4%	15.5%	16%
Boston	22.2%	20%	15.3%
Total passengers carried	1,459,044	1,244,990	1,063,677

* All flights from Gatwick and Heathrow airports.

accommodated 292 passengers in three cabins, and had key advantages such as low fuel consumption and maintenance costs. When the first A340 was delivered in December, Virgin Atlantic became the first U.K. carrier to fly A340s. Virgin Atlantic also ordered two Boeing 747-400s and took options on two others. It also placed a $19 million order for the most advanced in-flight entertainment system available, featuring 16 channels of video, which it planned to install in all three sections. In keeping with the airline's customization efforts, the new aircraft's cabin was redesigned. Upper-class passengers would find electronically operated 54-inch seats with a 55-degree recline and an on-board bar. There was a rest area for flight and cabin crew.

In June 1993, Virgin Atlantic scheduled a second daily flight from Heathrow to JFK Airport. "We've given travelers a wider choice on their time of travel," said Branson. "The early evening departure is timed to minimize disruption to the working day, a welcome bonus to both busy executives and leisure travelers." In March 1994, Virgin put an end to British Airways and Cathay Pacific's long-standing duopoly on the London–Hong Kong route, launching its own A340 service.

Virgin Atlantic's first Boeing 747-400 was delivered in May 1994. Only days later, Virgin opened its San Francisco line (until then a British Airways–United duopoly). In a press release shown in Exhibit 16.4, Virgin emphasized the continuation of its expansion plans, the renewal of its fleet, and the "better alternative" that it offered customers on both sides of the Atlantic. During the inaugural flight, 150 guests—and some fare-paying flyers who had been warned that it would not be a quiet flight— were entertained with a fashion show and a jazz band. In San Francisco the aircraft stopped near a giant taximeter. The door opened, and Branson appeared, and inserted a huge coin in the taximeter, out of which popped the Virgin Atlantic flag. Airport authorities offered Richard Branson a giant cake decorated with a miniature Golden Gate Bridge. Guests were entertained for a whirlwind five days, which included a tour of the Napa Valley and a visit to Alcatraz Prison, where Branson was jailed in a stunt prepared by his team. Virgin also took advantage of the launch to unveil a recycling and environmental program. A stewardess dressed in green— rather than the usual red Virgin Atlantic uniform—gave passengers infor-mation on the program, which had delivered savings of £500,000 since it had been launched in late 1993.

Exhibit 16.4

Press Release for the Opening of the San Francisco Route

17th May 1994

NEW SAN FRANCISCO ROUTE MARKS CONTINUED EXPANSION FOR VIRGIN ATLANTIC

A new service to San Francisco, its sixth gateway to the US, was launched today (17th May 1994), by Virgin Atlantic Airways, marking another stage in the airline's development as it approaches its tenth anniversary.

The daily Boeing 747 service from London's Heathrow airport follows further route expansion in February 1994 when the airline introduced a daily service to Hong Kong, using two of four recently acquired Airbus A340 aircraft.

Virgin Atlantic Chairman Richard Branson said: "San Francisco was always on our list of the 15 or so great cities of the world that we wanted to fly to, so it's a very proud moment for us finally to be launching this new service today.

"We regularly receive awards for our transatlantic flights, so I hope that this new service will be able to provide consumers on both sides of the Atlantic with a better alternative to the current duopoly which exists on the San Francisco/London route.

"Today's launch is also the culmination of a number of significant developments at Virgin Atlantic, not least of which is our recent acquisition of two new Boeing 747-400s and four Airbus A340s. This comes on the back of our $19 million investment in new 14-channel in-flight entertainment, which, unlike other airlines, we have made available to all of our passengers."

Mr. Branson added that it was the airline's intention to have one of the most modern and passenger-friendly fleets in the world. Virgin's current fleet comprises: eight B747s, three A340s, and an A320 and two BAe 146 Whisper Jets which are jointly operated with franchise partners in Dublin and Athens.

A daily service will depart Heathrow at 11.15, arriving in San Francisco at 14.05 local time. Flights leave San Francisco at 16.45, arriving in the UK the following day at 10.45. For reservations call 0293 747747.

For further information:

James Murray
Virgin Atlantic Airways
Tel: 0293 747373

At the time of Virgin Atlantic's 10th anniversary, its fleet comprised eight B747-200s, a B747-400, and three A340s. The airline awaited delivery of its second B747-400 and fourth A340 and also planned to retire two older B747-200s by the end of 1994. By then, half of its fleet would be brand new. By comparison, the average age of British Airways' fleet was eight years.[1] Branson planned to expand his fleet to 18 planes that would serve 12 or 15 destinations by 1995. Proposed new routes included Washington, D.C., Chicago, Auckland, Singapore, Sydney, and Johannesburg. The London–Johannesburg license, granted in 1992, had been a major victory for Virgin Atlantic: when exploited, it would end a 50-year duopoly enjoyed by British Airways and South African Airways.

All Virgin Atlantic planes were decorated with a Vargas painting of a red-headed, scantily dressed woman holding a scarf. The names of most Virgin aircraft evoked the *Vargas Lady* theme, starting with its first aircraft, *Maiden Voyager* (Exhibit 16.5 lists the aircraft's names). The first A340, inaugurated by the Princess of Wales, was christened *The Lady in Red.*

Exhibit 16.5
Virgin Atlantic Fleet. [From Virgin Atlantic.]

Aircraft	*Type*	*Name*	*Into Service*
G-VIRG	B747-287B	*Maiden Voyager*	1984
G-VGIN	B747-243B	*Scarlet Lady*	1986
G-TKYO	B747-212B	*Maiden Japan*	1989
G-VRGN	B747-212B	*Maid of Honour*	28/08/89
G-VMIA	B747-123	*Spirit of Sir Freddy*	09/05/90
G-VOYG	B747-283B	*Shady Lady*	10/03/90
G-VJFK	B747-238B	*Boston Belle*	06/03/91
G-VLAX	B747-238B	*California Girl*	28/05/91
G-VBUS	A340-311	*The Lady in Red*	16/12/93
G-VAEL	A340-311	*Maiden Toulouse*	01/01/94
G-VSKY	A340-311	*China Girl*	21/03/94
G-VFAB	B747-4Q8	*Lady Penelope*	19/05/94
G-VHOT	B747-4Q8		Delivery 10/94
G-VFLY	A340-311		Delivery 10/94

[1] British Airways' fleet had 240 aircraft, including some 180 Boeings, 7 Concordes, 10 A320s, 15 BAe ATPs, and 7 DC10s.

Virgin Classes

Branson originally proposed to call Virgin's business and economy classes "Upper Class" and "Riff Raff," respectively; in the latter case, however, he bowed to the judgment of his managers, who urged him to desist. Virgin Atlantic strove to offer the highest-quality travel to all classes of passengers at the lowest cost, and to be flexible enough to respond rapidly to their changing needs. For instance, Virgin Atlantic catered to the needs of children and infants with special meals, a children's channel, pioneering safety seats, changing facilities, and baby food.

"Offering a First Class service at less than First Class fares" had become a slogan for Virgin Atlantic. Marketed as a first-class service at business-class prices, Upper Class competed both with other carriers' first class and business class. Since its 1984 launch, this product had won every major travel industry award.

The Economy Class promised the best value for money, targeting price-sensitive leisure travelers who nevertheless sought comfort. It included three meal options, free drinks, seatback video screens, and ice cream during movies on flights from London.

After years of operating only two classes, business and economy, Virgin had introduced its Mid Class in 1992 after realizing that 23 percent of Economy passengers traveled for business. Mid Class was aimed at cost-conscious business travelers who required enough space to work and relax. This full fare economy class offered flyers a level of service usually found only in business class, with separate check-in and cabin, priority meal service, armrest or seat-back TVs, and the latest in audio and video entertainment. Exhibit 16.6 shows Virgin's three sections: Upper Class, Mid Class, and Economy Class.

Virgin's B747 configuration on the Heathrow/JFK route consisted of 50 seats in Upper Class, 38 in Mid Class, and 271 in Economy Class. The typical British Airways B747 configuration on the same route was 18 First Class seats, 70 seats in Club World, and 282 in World Traveller Class.[2]

---

[2] As of April 1994, the Club World and World Traveller—Euro Traveller for flights within Europe—were the names given to British Airways' former Business and Economy Classes, respectively.

Exhibit 16.6
Virgin Atlantic's Three Classes. [From Virgin Atlantic.]

Upper Class

- reclining sleeper seat with 15 inches more leg room than other airlines
- latest seat-arm video/audio entertainment
- unique Clubhouse lounge at Heathrow featuring health spa (includes hair salon, library, music room, games room, study, and brasserie)
- Virgin Arrival Clubhouse with shower, sauna, swimming pool, and gym
- in-flight beauty therapist on most flights
- onboard lounges and stand-up bars
- "Snoozzone" dedicated sleeping section with sleeper seat, duvet, and sleep suit
- complimentary airport transfers including chauffeur-driven limousine or motorcycle to and from airport
- free confirmable Economy ticket for round trip to U.S. or Tokyo

Mid Class

- separate check-in and cabin
- most comfortable economy seat in the world with 38-inch seat pitch (equivalent to many airlines' business class seat)
- complimentary pre-takeoff drinks and amenity kits
- Frequent Flyer program
- priority meal service
- priority baggage reclaim
- armrest/seatback TVs and latest audio/video entertainment

Economy Class

- contoured, space-saving seats, maximizing leg room, seat pitch up to 34 inches
- three-meal option service (including vegetarian) and wide selection of free alcoholic and soft drinks
- seatback TVs and 16 channels of the latest in-flight entertainment
- pillow and blankets
- advance seat selection
- complimentary amenity kit and ice cream (during movies on flights from London)

Service the Virgin Way

Virgin Atlantic wanted to provide the best possible service while remaining original, spontaneous, and informal. Its goal was to turn flying into a unique experience, not to move passengers from one point to another. It saw itself not only in the airline business but also in entertainment and leisure. According to a staff brochure:

> We must be memorable, we are not a bus service. The journeys made by our customers are romantic and exciting, and we should do everything we can to make them feel just that. That way they will talk about the most memorable moments long after they leave the airport.

Virgin Atlantic saw that as it became increasingly successful, it risked also becoming complacent. The challenge was to keep up customers' interest by keeping service at the forefront of activities. Virgin was often distinguished for the quality and consistency of its service (as shown in Exhibit 16.7); it won the *Executive Travel* Airline of the Year award for an unprecedented three consecutive years. Service delivery, in other words "getting it right the first time," was of key importance. The airline was also perceived to excel in the art of service recovery, where it aimed to be proactive, not defensive. It handled complaints from Upper Class passengers within 24 hours and those from Economy Class flyers within a week. If a flight was delayed, passengers received a personalized fax of apology from Branson or a bottle of champagne. Passengers who had complained were occasionally upgraded to Upper Class.

Innovation

Virgin Atlantic's management, who wanted passengers never to feel bored, introduced video entertainment in 1989. They chose the quickest solution: handing out Sony Watchmans onboard. Virgin later pioneered individual video screens for every seat, an idea that competitors quickly imitated. In 1994, Virgin's onboard entertainment offered up to 20 audio channels and 16 video channels including a shopping channel and a game channel. A gambling channel would be introduced at year end. In the summer, a "Stop Smoking Program" video was shown on all flights—Virgin Atlantic's contribution to a controversy over whether smoking should be permitted on aircraft.

Exhibit 16.7
Awards Won by Virgin Atlantic. [From Virgin Atlantic.]

1994

Executive Travel:
  Best Transatlantic Airline
  Best Business Class
  Best In-flight Magazine
Travel Weekly:
  Best Transatlantic Airline

1993

Executive Travel:
  Airline of the Year
  Best Transatlantic Carrier
  Best Business Class
  Best Cabin Staff
  Best Food and Wine
  Best In-flight Entertainment
  Best Airport Lounges
  Best In-flight Magazine
  Best Ground/Check-in Staff
Travel Weekly:
  Best Transatlantic Airline
Travel Trade Gazette:
  Best Transatlantic Airline
TTG Travel Advertising Awards:
  Best Direct Mail Piece

1992

Executive Travel (Awards given for 91/92):
  Airline of the Year
  Best Transatlantic Carrier
  Best Long Haul Carrier
  Best Business Class
  Best In-flight Food
  Best In-flight Entertainment
  Best Ground/Check-in Staff

Business Traveller:
  Best Airline for Business
    Class—Long Haul
Travel Weekly:
  Best Transatlantic Airline
Travel Trade Gazette:
  Best Transatlantic Airline
Courvoisier Book of the Best:
  Best Business Airline
ITV Marketing Awards:
  Brand of the Year—Service
Frontier Magazine:
  Best Airline/Marine Duty Free
BPS Teleperformance:
  U.K. Winner
  Overall European Winner
Meetings and Incentive Travel:
  Best U.K. Base Airline
Ab-Road Magazine:
  Airline "Would most like to fly"
  Best In-flight Catering

1991

Executive Travel:
  (Awards given in 1992)
Business Traveller:
  Best Business Class—Long Haul
Travel Weekly:
  Best Transatlantic Airline
Travel Trade Gazette:
  Best Transatlantic Airline
  Most Attentive Airline Staff

Exhibit 16.7 *(continued)*

Avion World Airline Entertainment Awards:
   Best In-flight Video—Magazine Style
   Best In-flight Audio—Programming
   Best In-flight Audio of an Original Nature
Which Airline?:
   Voted by the Reader as one of the Top Four Airlines in the World (the only British airline among these four)
The Travel Organization:
   Best Long Haul Airline
CondéNast Traveller:
   In the Top Ten World Airlines
Air Cargo News:
   Cargo Airline of the Year

1990

Executive Travel:
   Airline of the Year
   Best Transatlantic Carrier
   Best In-flight Entertainment
Business Traveller:
   Best Business Class—Long Haul
Travel News (now *Travel Weekly*):
   Best Transatlantic Airline
   Special Merit Award to Richard Branson
Travel Trade Gazette:
   Best Transatlantic Airline
   Travel Personality—Richard Branson

Avion World Airline Entertainment Awards:
   Best Overall In-flight Entertainment
   Best Video Programme
   Best In-flight Entertainment Guide
Onboard Services Magazine:
   Outstanding In-flight Entertainment Programme
   Outstanding Entertainment (for Sony Video Walkmans)
The Travel Organization:
   Best Long Haul Airline

1989

Executive Travel:
   Best Transatlantic Airline
   Best Business Class in the World
   Best In-flight Entertainment
Business Traveller:
   Best Business Class—Long Haul
Avion World Airline Entertainment Awards:
   Best Overall In-flight Entertainment
   Best In-flight Audio Entertainment
   Best In-flight Entertainment Guide
Onboard Services Magazine:
   Overall Onboard Service Award (Upper Class)
Avion Which Holiday?:
   Best Transatlantic Airline
Nihon Keizai Shimbun (Japan):
   Best Product in Japan—for Upper Class

Exhibit 16.7 *(continued)*

1988	1986
Executive Travel:	The Marketing Society:
Best Business Class—North	Consumer Services Awards
Atlantic	*What to Buy for Business:*
Business Traveller:	Business Airline of the Year
Best Business Class—Long Haul	
Travel Trade Gazette:	
Best Transatlantic Airline	

The presence of a beauty therapist or a tailor was an occasional treat to passengers. The beautician offered massages and manicures. On some flights to Hong Kong, the tailor faxed passengers' measurements so that suits could be ready on arrival. In 1990, Virgin became the only airline to offer automatic defibrillators on board and to train staff to assist cardiac arrest victims. A three-person Special Facilities unit was set up in 1991 to deal with medical requests. Its brief was extended to handle arrangements for unaccompanied minors or unusual requests such as birthday cakes, champagne for newlyweds, public announcements, or midflight marriage proposals. The unit also informed passengers of flight delays or cancellations, and telephoned clients whose options on tickets had expired without their having confirmed their intention to travel. Another service innovation was motorcycle rides to Heathrow for Upper Class passengers. The chauffeur service used Honda PC800s with heated leather seats. Passengers wore waterproof coveralls and a helmet with a built-in headset for a cellular phone.

In February 1993, Britain's Secretary of State for Transport inaugurated a new Upper Class lounge at Heathrow: the Virgin Clubhouse. The £1 million Clubhouse had an unusual range of facilities: Victorian-style wood-paneled washrooms with showers and a grooming salon offering massages, aromatherapy, and hair cuts; a 5,000-volume library with antique leather armchairs; a game room with the latest computer technology; a music room with a CD library; a study with the most recent office equipment. Many of the furnishings came from Branson's own home: a giant model railway, the *Challenger II* trophy, a three-meter galleon model. A two-ton, five-meter table, made in Vienna from an old vessel, had to be installed with a crane. Upon the opening of the Hong Kong route, a blackjack table was added at which visitors received "Virgin bills" that the dealer exchanged for tokens. There was also a shoe-shine service. Passengers seemed to enjoy the lounge. One remarked in the visitors' book: "If you have to be delayed more than two hours, it could not happen in a more pleasant environment."

Customer Orientation, Virgin-Style

Virgin tried to understand passengers' needs and go beyond their expectations. While it described itself as a "niche airline for those seeking value-for-money travel," its standards and reputation could appeal to a broad spectrum of customers. It managed to serve both sophisticated, demanding executives and easy-going, price-sensitive leisure travelers in the same aircraft. According to Marketing Director Steve Ridgeway, Virgin attracted a broader range of customers than its competitors because it managed this coexistence between passenger groups better. This had enabled the airline to reach high load factors soon after opening new lines, as shown in Exhibit 16.8.

Virgin Atlantic initially had marketed itself as an economical airline for young people who bought Virgin records and shopped at Virgin stores,

Exhibit 16.8

Load Factors of Virgin Atlantic Airways. [From Virgin Atlantic promotional material.]

Year	Load Factors (%)					
	Newark	*Miami*	*Tokyo*	*JFK*	*Los Angeles*	*Boston*
1990–1991	82.0	89.5	65.9	76.9	84.5	83.3
1989–1990	83.3	92.1	68.3	74.2	79.8	
1988–1989	82.8	86.7	52.4			
1987–1988	77.1	85.0				
1986–1987	74.4	76.4				
1985–1986	72.9					
1984–1985	72.0					

Note: Since 1991, this information is no longer made public.

but gradually its target shifted. The danger, which Branson saw clearly, was that people would perceive it as a "cheap and cheerful" airline, a copy of the defunct Laker Airways. Branson knew that his airline's survival depended on high-yield business travelers. After establishing a strong base in leisure traffic, Virgin turned to the corporate segment and strove to establish itself as a sophisticated, business class airline that concentrated on long-haul routes. The idea of fun and entertainment, however, was not abandoned. Upper Class was upgraded, and incentives were added to attract the business traveler. By 1991, 10 percent of the airline's passengers and 35 to 40 percent of its income came from the business segment. Virgin's competitive advantage was reinforced through the combination of the corporate travel buyer's price consciousness and the rising service expectations of travelers. Branson actively wooed business customers by regularly inviting corporate buyers to have lunch at his house and seeking their comments.

As part of Virgin Atlantic's drive to meet customers' standards, on each flight 30 passengers were asked to fill out a questionnaire. Their answers formed the basis of widely distributed quarterly reports. Virgin's senior managers flew regularly, interviewing passengers informally, making critical comments on the delivery of service, and circulating their reports among top management. Branson himself, who welcomed every opportunity to obtain feedback from customers, took time to shake hands and chat with passengers. The preoccupation with service was so strong that staff were often more exacting in their evaluation of each other than the customers were of the staff.

Business executives, unlike younger leisure travelers, did not readily relate to other aspects of the Virgin world: the records, the Megastores, the daredevil chairman. Their good feelings about Virgin stemmed mainly from their positive experiences with the airline. These tough and demanding customers appreciated Virgin's style, service, innovations, and prices. Some were enthusiastic enough to rearrange their schedules in order to fly Virgin Atlantic despite punctuality problems. Aside from complaints about flight delays, their only serious criticism was that Virgin did not serve enough destinations.

Virgin Atlantic's People

Virgin Atlantic attracted quality staff despite the relatively low salaries it paid. In management's eyes, the ideal employee was "informal but caring": young, vibrant, interested, courteous, and willing to go out of his or her way to help customers. Branson explained:

> We aren't interested in having just happy employees. We want employees who feel involved and prepared to express dissatisfaction when necessary. In fact, we think that the constructively dissatisfied employee is an asset we should encourage, and we need an organization that allows us to do this—and that encourages employees to take responsibility, since I don't believe it is enough for us simply to give it.

Branson believed that involving management and staff was the key to superior results: "I want employees in the airline to feel that it is *they* who can make the difference, and influence what passengers get," he said. He wrote to employees regularly to seek their ideas and to ensure that relevant news was communicated to them. His home phone number was given to all staff, who could call him at any time with suggestions or complaints.

Virgin Atlantic's philosophy was to stimulate the individual. Its dynamic business culture encouraged staff to take initiatives and gave them the means to implement them. Staff often provided insights into what customers wanted or needed—sometimes anticipating their expectations better than the customers themselves. Virgin Atlantic had a formal staff suggestion scheme and encouraged innovation from employees, both in project teams and in their daily work. Employees' suggestions were given serious consideration; many were implemented, such as the idea of serving ice cream as a snack, although formal marketing research had never shown the need for such a service.

Branson himself was open to suggestions and innovations. He talked to everyone and was a good listener, inquisitive and curious about all aspects of the business. He spent time with passengers, and visited the lounge without any advance notice. While he personified a hands-on approach to management, he never appeared controlling or threatening. His constant presence was a sign of involvement and a source of motivation for staff, who felt a lot of affection for him. It was not unusual to hear crew discuss his recent decisions or activities, mentioning "Mr. Branson" or "Richard" with admiration and respect.

In the difficult environment of the late 1980s and early 1990s, most airline employees were anxious to keep their jobs. With most operating costs—fuel prices, aircraft prices, insurance, landing and air traffic control fees—beyond management's control, labor costs were the main target of cutbacks. In 1993, the world's top 20 airlines cut 31,600 jobs, or 3.6 percent of their workforce, while the next 80 airlines added nearly 14,000, or 2.4 percent. That same year, Virgin Atlantic maintained its labor force, and was in the process of recruiting at the end of the year. In June 1994, Virgin Atlantic had 2,602 employees and recruited 880 cabin crew members. Opening a single long-haul line required hiring about 400 people.

THE AIRLINE INDUSTRY

Deregulation of the U.S. air transport industry in 1978 had reduced the government's role and removed protective rules, thereby increasing competition among American airlines. A decade later, deregulation hit Europe. The liberalization movement began in an effort to end monopolies and bring down prices. In fact, European carriers had been engaged in moderate competition in transatlantic travel while the domestic scheduled market remained heavily protected through bilateral agreements. European airlines were mostly state-owned, in a regulated market where access was denied to new entrants. In April 1986, the European Court of Justice ruled that the Treaty of Rome's competition rules also applied to air transportation. Deregulation took place in three phases between 1987— when price controls were relaxed and market access was opened—and 1992, when airlines were allowed to set their own prices, subject to some controls.

In this atmosphere of deregulation and falling prices, traffic revenue grew briskly until 1990, when a global recession and the Gulf War plunged airlines into their worst crisis since World War II. The 22-member association of European airlines saw the number of passengers plummet by 7 million in 1991. Traffic recovered in 1992, when the world's 100 largest airlines saw their total revenue, measured in terms of tonnage or passengers, increase by just over 10 percent. However, the airlines recorded a net loss of $8 billion in 1992, after losses of $1.84 billion in 1991 and $2.66 billion in 1990. Some experts believed that the industry would ultimately be dominated by a handful of players, with a larger number of midsize carriers struggling to close the gap. Exhibits 16.9 and 16.10 show financial and passenger load data for some international airlines, while Exhibit 16.11 ranks Europe's top 20 airlines.

VIRGIN ATLANTIC'S COMPETITORS

Virgin's direct competitor was British Airways (BA). Both carriers were fighting each other intensely on the most attractive routes out of London. BA, the number-one British airline, was 15 times the size of second-placed Virgin. Exhibits 16.12 and 16.13 compare Virgin's and British Airways' flights and fares.

British Airways became the state-owned British airline in 1972 as the result of a merger between British European Airways and British Overseas Airways Corporation. In the early 1980s, BA was the clear leader in the highly lucrative and regulated transatlantic route, where operating margins were approximately 15 percent of sales. However, its overall profitability was shaky when Lord King became Chairman in 1981. He transformed BA into a healthy organization and prepared it for its successful privatization in 1987. Since that time, BA has remarkably out-performed its European rivals.

BA traditionally benefited from a strong position at Heathrow, but competition toughened in 1991 when TWA and Pan Am sold their slots to American and United Airlines for $290 million and $445 million, respectively. In the same year, Virgin Atlantic also received slots at Heathrow. These slot attributions so infuriated King that he scrapped its annual £40,000 donation to Britain's ruling Conservative Party. At the time of the Heathrow transfer, BA scheduled 278 flights a week across the Atlantic from London, with 83,000 seats, while American had 168 flights with 35,000 seats, and United had 122 flights with 30,000 seats. Virgin Atlantic had 84 flights with 30,000 seats.

Despite these competitive pressures and the recent airline recession, British Airways remained one of the world's most profitable airlines. The largest carrier of international passengers, serving 150 destinations in 69 countries, it was making continuous progress in terms of cost efficiency, service quality, and marketing. BA recruited marketing experts from consumer-goods companies who implemented a brand approach to the

Exhibit 16.9

Financial Results of Selected International Airlines. ["Much Pain, No Gain," *Airline Business* (September 1993).]

Airline Company	Ranking 1992	Ranking 1991	Sales U.S.$ Million 1992	Sales % Change	Operating Results (U.S.$ million)	Net Results, 1992 (U.S.$ million)	Net Results, 1991 (U.S.$ million)	Net Margin, 1992 (%)	Jet and Turbo Fleet	Total Employees	Productivity, Sales/Employee ($000)*
American	1	1	14,396	11.7	(25.0)	(935.0)	(239.9)	−6.5	672	102,400	140
United	2	2	12,889	10.5	(537.8)	(956.8)	(331.9)	−7.4	536	84,000	153
Delta	3	4	11,639	15.7	(825.5)	(564.8)	(239.6)	−4.9	554	79,157	147
Lufthansa	4	5	11,036	7.1	(198.5)	(250.4)	(257.7)	−2.3	302	63,645	173
Air France	5	3	10,769	−1.1	(285.0)	(617.0)	(12.1)	−5.7	220	63,933	168
British Airways	6	6	9,307	6.5	518.4	297.7	687.3	3.2	241	48,960	190
Swissair	16	16	4,438	7.0	152.8	80.7	57.9	1.8	60	19,025	233
TWA Inc.	18	18	3,634	−0.7	(404.6)	(317.7)	34.6	−8.7	178	29,958	121
Singapore	19	19	3,442	5.4	548.0	518.5	558.3	15.1	57	22,857	150
Qantas	20	20	3,099	2.9	79.1	105.7	34.6	3.4	46	14,936	207
Cathay Pacific	21	21	2,988	11.3	464.0	385.0	378.0	12.9	49	13,240	225
Southwest	34	41	1,685	28.3	182.6	103.5	26.9	6.1	141	11,397	148
Virgin Atlantic	62	62	626	7.3	(22.0)	Not reported	3.8	Not reported	8	2,394	261

* Productivity computed for this exhibit.

Exhibit 16.10

Passenger Load Factors of Selected International Airlines. ["Much Pain, No Gain," *Airline Business* (September 1993).]

Airline Company	1992 Revenue Metric Ton Km (million)				1992 Revenue		1992 Passengers		Passenger Load Factor			
	Passenger	Freight	Total	% Change	Passenger Km (million)	(% Change)	(million)	% Change	1992 (%)	1991 (%)	Year End	1992 Rank
American	14,223	2,176	16,399	19.7	156,786	18.3	86.01	13.3	63.7	61.7	Dec. 92	1
United	13,489	2,522	16,010	12.0	149,166	12.6	67.00	8.1	67.4	66.3	Dec. 92	2
Delta	11,761	1,765	13,525	20.2	129,632	19.6	82.97	11.8	61.3	60.3	Dec. 92	3
Lufthansa	5,882	4,676	10,725	14.4	61,274	17.1	33.70	14.2	65.0	64.0	Dec. 92	4
Air France	5,238	3,970	9,208	5.3	55,504	4.0	32.71	3.4	67.4	66.8	Dec. 92	5
British Airways	7,622	2,691	10,313	13.2	80,473	15.6	28.10	10.5	70.8	70.2	Mar. 93	6
Swissair	1,573	1,063	2,684	9.1	16,221	7.0	8.01	0.4	60.3	61.6	Dec. 92	16
TWA Inc.	4,258	734	4,992	1.4	46,935	1.8	22.54	8.5	64.7	64.7	Dec. 92	18
Singapore Air	3,675	2,412	6,086	14.2	37,861	8.5	8.64	6.3	71.3	73.5	Mar. 93	19
Qantas	2,684	1,220	3,904	4.9	28,836	7.2	4.53	9.4	66.2	66.0	Jun. 92	20
Cathay Pacific	2,695	1,671	4,366	13.3	27,527	12.7	8.36	13.1	73.5	73.6	Dec. 92	21
Southwest Air	2,032	49	2,082	23.4	22,187	22.0	27.84	22.6	64.5	61.1	Dec. 92	34
Virgin Atlantic	984	285	1,269	27.4	9,001	8.7	1.23	5.6	76.1	81.6	Oct. 92	62

453

Exhibit 16.11

Europe's Top 20 Airlines (1993). ["Much Pain, No Gain," *Airline Business* (September 1993).]

Rank	Airline Company	Sales (U.S.$ million)	Global Rank
1	Lufthansa	11,036.5	4
2	Air France Group	10,769.4	5
3	British Airways	9,307.7	6
4	SAS Group	5,908.2	12
5	Alitalia	5,510.7	14
6	KLM Royal Dutch	4,666.3	15
7	Swissair	4,438.5	16
8	Iberia	4,136.7	17
9	LTU/LTU Sud	1,836.1	31
10	Sabena	1,708.3	33
11	Aer Lingus	1,381.0	38
12	Aeroflot	1,172.1	43
13	Finnair	1,132.2	45
14	TAP Air Portugal	1,110.1	47
15	Austrian Airlines	1,003.8	49
16	Britannia Airways	924.0	53
17	Olympic Airways	922.5	54
18	Turkish Airlines	736.5	59
19	Airlines of Britain Holdings	687.7	61
20	Virgin Atlantic	626.5	62

airline's classes. Some of the actions undertaken by BA in the early 1990s included relaunching its European business class Club Europe with £17.5 million and spending £10 million on new lounges (with a traditional British feel), check-in facilities, and ground staff at Heathrow. It was also rumored that BA was preparing to spend nearly £70 million on an advanced in-flight entertainment and information system for its long-haul fleet before the end of 1994.

BA and Virgin had fiercely competed against one another from the onset. One major incident that marked their rivalry was what became known as the "Dirty Tricks Campaign." In 1992, Virgin Atlantic filed a lawsuit against BA, accusing it of entering Virgin's computer system and spreading false rumors. In January 1993, Virgin won its libel suit against BA in London. The wide press coverage caused much embarrassment to BA. Later that year, Virgin filed a $325 million lawsuit in the Federal Court of New York, accusing BA of using its monopoly power to distort competition on North American routes.

In addition to British Airways, Virgin competed with at least one major carrier on each of its destinations. For instance, it was up against United Airlines to Los Angeles, American Airlines to New York, and Cathay Pacific to Hong Kong. Most of its competitors surpassed Virgin many times in terms of turnover, staff, and number of aircraft. Yet Virgin Atlantic was not intimidated by the size of its competitors; it saw its modest size as an advantage that enabled it to react quickly and remain innovative.

VIRGIN ATLANTIC'S MANAGEMENT STRUCTURE

Virgin Atlantic's headquarters were in Crawley, a suburb near Gatwick. The airline had a loose organization combined with a high level of dialogue and involvement, as well as strong controls. As a senior manager explained: "Our business is about independence, entrepreneurial flair, and people having autonomy to make decisions; yet we pay a great deal of attention to overhead and cost levels." Members of the management team, whose structure is shown in Exhibit 16.14, came from other airlines, other industries, or other divisions of the Virgin Group. The three top executives—Co-managing Directors Roy Gardner and Syd Pennington and Finance Director Nigel Primrose—reported directly to Branson.

Gardner had joined Virgin Airways as Technical Director in 1984 after working at Laker Airways and British Caledonian Airways. He was responsible for the technical aspects of operations: quality, supplies, maintenance, and emergency procedures. Pennington oversaw commercial operations, marketing, sales, and flight operations. Primrose, a chartered accountant with 20 years of international experience, had been part of the senior team that set up Air Europe in 1978 and Air UK in 1983 before joining Virgin Atlantic in 1986. He was Virgin Atlantic's company Secretary with responsibility for route feasibility, financial planning, financial accounts, treasury, and legal affairs.

Steve Ridgeway headed the marketing department. After assisting Branson in several projects, including the Transatlantic Boat Challenge, he had joined the airline in 1989 to develop its frequent-traveler program,

Exhibit 16.12

Virgin Atlantic and British Airways: Comparison of Routes. [From "The Guide to Virgin Atlantic Airways," issued May/June 1994; "British Airways Worldwide Timetable," March 27–29, 1994.]

Destination From London to:	Airline	Frequency	Departure–Arrival (Local Times)	Aircraft
New York (JFK)	Virgin Atlantic	Daily (LHR)	14:00–16:40	747
			18:35–20:55	
	British Airways	Daily (LHR)	10:30–09:20	Concorde
			11:00–13:40	747
			14:00–16:40	747
			18:30–21:10	747
			19:00–17:50	Concorde
		Daily (Gat.)	10:40–13:20	D10
New York (Newark)	Virgin Atlantic	Daily (LHR)	16:00–18:40	747
	British Airways	Daily (LHR)	14:45–17:40	747
Boston	Virgin Atlantic	Daily (Gat.)	15:00–17:10	A340
	British Airways	Daily (LHR)	15:45–18:00	747
		Daily (LHR)	09:55–12:30	767
Los Angeles	Virgin Atlantic	Daily (LHR)	12:00–15:10	747
	British Airways	Daily (LHR)	12:15–15:15	747-400
		Daily (LHR)	15:30–18:30	747-400
Miami	Virgin Atlantic	W, F, S, Su (Gat.)	11:15–15:45	747
		Th (Gat.)	11:15–15:45	
	British Airways	Daily (LHR)	11:15–15:40	747
		Daily (LHR)	14:30–18:55	747
Orlando	Virgin Atlantic	Daily (Gat.)	12:30–16:40	747
	British Airways	Tu, W, Su (LHR)	11:15–19:15	747
		M, Th, F, S (Gat.)	11:00–15:10	747

Exhibit 16.12 *(continued)*

San Francisco	Virgin Atlantic	Daily (LHR)	11:15–14:05	747
	British Airways	Daily (LHR)	13:15–16:05	747-400
		Daily (LHR)	10:50–13:40	747
Tokyo	Virgin Atlantic	M, T, Th, F, S, Su (LHR)	13:00–08:55 (next day)	747/ A340
	British Airways	Daily (LHR)	12:55–08:45 (next day)	747-400
		M, T, Th, F, S, Su (LHR)	16:30–12:15 (next day)	747-400
Hong Kong	Virgin Atlantic	Daily	20:30–16:35 (next day)	A340
	British Airways	F	13:55–09:55 (next day)	747-400
		M, T, W, Th, S, Su	14:30–10:30 (next day)	747-400
		Daily	21:30–17:30 (next day)	

becoming head of marketing in 1992. Paul Griffiths, who had 14 years of commercial aviation experience, became Virgin Atlantic's Director of Commercial Operations after spending two years designing and implementing its information management system. Personnel Director Nick Potts, a business studies graduate, had been recruited in 1991 from Warner Music UK, where he was the head of the personnel department.

MARKETING ACTIVITIES

Ridgeway's marketing department covered a variety of activities, as shown in Exhibit 16.15. Some traditional marketing disciplines, such as advertising, promotions, planning, and the Freeway frequent-flyer program, reported to Ruth Blakemore, Head of Marketing. Catering, retail operations

Exhibit 16.13

Virgin Atlantic and British Airways Fares (£)

Route	Virgin Atlantic			British Airways			
	Upper Class*	Mid Class*	Economy 21-Day Apex**	First Class*	Club*	Economy	21-Day Apex†
New York	1,195	473	489	1,935	1,061	620	538
San Francisco	1,627	595	538††	2,179	1,627	920	638
Los Angeles	1,627	604	538	2,179	1,627	920	638
Tokyo	1,806	783	993	2,751	1,806	1,580	993
Hong Kong	979	600	741	3,280	2,075	1,808	741
Boston	1,082	473	439	1,935	1,061	620	538
Miami	1,144	529	498	2,085	1,144	780	598
Orlando	1,144	529	498	2,085	1,144	780	598

* One-way weekend peak-time fares in pounds sterling (£).
** Economy fare for Virgin is "Economy 21-Day Apex" (reservation no later than 21 days prior to departure).
† 21-day Apex round-trip ticket.
†† Between May 17 and June 30, 1994, a special launch fare round-trip ticket was sold at £299.

Exhibit 16.14

Virgin Atlantic Airways Ltd.: Organizational Structure, May 1994. [From Virgin Atlantic.]

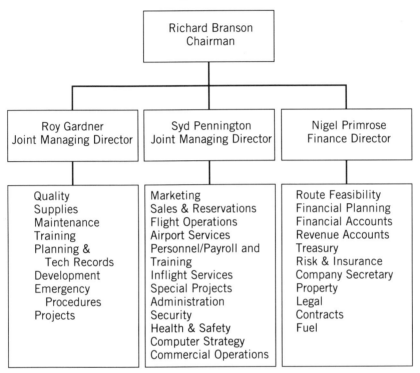

(for example, duty-free sales), product development, and public relations reported directly to Ridgeway.

Virgin Atlantic spent 2 percent of turnover on advertising, well below the 5 to 7 percent industry norm. Virgin's advertising had featured a series of short campaigns handled by various agencies. The winning of a quality award was often a campaign opportunity (as shown in Exhibit 16.16), as was the opening of a new line. On one April Fool's Day, Virgin announced that it had developed a new bubble-free champagne. It also launched ad hoc campaigns in response to competitors' activities (such as Exhibit 16.17). The survey in Exhibit 16.18 shows that Virgin Atlantic enjoyed a strong brand equity, as well as a high level of spontaneous awareness and a good image in the United Kingdom. In order to increase

Exhibit 16.15
Virgin Atlantic: Marketing Department

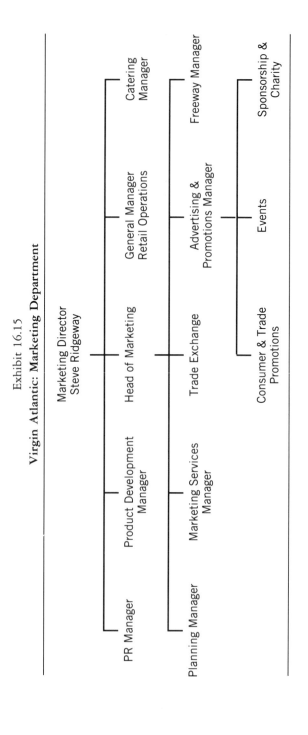

Exhibit 16.16

Virgin Atlantic Advertising

Virgin Atlantic Advertising (1990)

The world's favourite airline?

They must be on a different planet.

It's a brave airline that claims to be the world's favourite.

Now it seems the world has a different idea. For at the 1989 Executive Travel Airline of the Year Awards, Virgin Atlantic have emerged victorious.

Those most demanding and, dare one say, discerning of people, the readers of Executive Travel Magazine voted Virgin Atlantic, Best Transatlantic Carrier.

It's not just over the Atlantic that they hold sway. For Virgin were also named Best Business Class in the World, above airlines they admire such as Singapore and Thai.

A choice that was quickly seconded by Business Traveller Magazine.

It's not hard to see why Virgin's Upper Class commands such respect.

AIRLINE OF THE YEAR AWARDS 1989

VIRGIN ATLANTIC AIRWAYS
EXECUTIVE TRAVEL MAGAZINE

Best Transatlantic Carrier
Best Business Class in the World
World's Best Inflight Entertainment

BUSINESS TRAVELLER MAGAZINE

World's Best Business Class

Passengers enjoy a free chauffeur driven car* to and from the airport plus a free economy standby ticket.†

On the plane there are first class sleeper seats that, miraculously, you can actually sleep in and on-board bars and lounges.

And your own personal Sony Video Walkman with a choice of 100 films.

As you might expect from Virgin, this entertainment is truly award winning. It helped scoop a third major award, Best In-Flight Entertainment.

So the next time you want to travel across the world in style, you know who to favour.

For details call *0800 800 400* or for reservations *0293 551616*, or see your travel agent.

*First 48 seats with our compliments. †Not available on Tokyo route.

LONDON · NEW YORK JFK AND NEWARK · MIAMI · MOSCOW · TOKYO

Exhibit 16.17

Virgin Atlantic Advertising: Response to a British Airways Campaign

The world's favourite airline?
Not in our book.

BEATS THE PANTS OFF BA!
VERY GOOD SERVICE.

JAMES ARMSTRONG
B. S. LIMITED

Excellent.
keep BA on the run!

JEREMY HATTON
NORWICH CRUISE CENTRE

The best service from the best airline in the World!
Absolutely Fabulous - !!

VINCE CRAWLEY
COUNTRY CASUALS LTD

With a deal like this,
who the hell wants to
fly BA anyway!!

BOB BROWN
FILMCO EUROFORM

A previously dedicated and loyal
British Airways customer, now
a dedicated and loyal Virgin
customer!

ROBERT CASSON
PFIZER INC

Best Business Class price
service in the air.

GEOFF TOVEY
SMITHKLINE BEECHAM

Such a refreshing change from BA! Great
entertainment & service! - Looking forward
to another flight!

ANDREW TURNER
REED TRAVEL GROUP

I am your biggest fan -
I promise never to fly
another airline if I can
help it. It is always
a pleasure on Virgin!

KATHY BRADY
BANKERS TRUST

As ever, Virgin
leads the field!

PAUL JACKSON
CARLTON TV

My first time too on Virgin Atlantic and it's
unquestionably better than the equivalent BA.
The service, for example, was first class.

SHERBAN CANTACUZINO
ROYAL FINE ART COMMISSION

Virgin Atlantic's Upper Class costs the same as BA Club Class. And it's not just
the comments in our visitors' book that are better. Hope to see you soon.